Mathematics and the
Medieval Ancestry of Physics

D0168940

Dr George Molland

George Molland

Mathematics and the
Medieval Ancestry of Physics

VARIORUM
1995

Published by VARIORUM
    Ashgate Publishing Limited
    Gower House, Croft Road,
    Aldershot, Hampshire GU11 3HR
    Great Britain

    Ashgate Publishing Company
    Old Post Road,
    Brookfield, Vermont 05036
    USA

ISBN 0-86078-470-3

British Library CIP Data
    Molland, George
    Mathematics and the Medieval Ancestry of Physics.
    (Variorum Collected Studies Series; CS 481)
    I. Title II. Series
    510.9

US Library of Congress CIP Data
    Molland, George
    Mathematics and the Medieval Ancestry of Physics /
    George Molland.   ISBN 0-86078-470-3
    p. cm. — (Collected Studies Series: CS481)
    1. Mathematics, medieval.
    I. Title. II. Series: Collected Studies: CS481.
    QA32.M585 1994   94–38927
    510'.9'02—dc20   CIP

The paper used in this publication meets the minimum requirements of the
    American National Standard for Information Sciences - Permanence
    of Paper for Printed Library Materials, ANSI Z39.48-1984.   ™

Printed by Galliard (Printers) Ltd
    Great Yarmouth, Norfolk, Great Britain

COLLECTED STUDIES SERIES CS481

CONTENTS

This volume contains xii + 336 pages

PUBLISHER'S NOTE

The articles in this volume, as in all others in the Collected Studies Series, have not been given a new, continuous pagination. In order to avoid confusion, and to facilitate their use where these same studies have been referred to elsewhere, the original pagination has been maintained wherever possible.

Each article has been given a Roman number in order of appearance, as listed in the Contents. This number is repeated on each page and quoted in the index entries.

PREFACE

The seventeen studies collected in this volume form a diverse network connected by a variety of (sometimes mutely expressed) leading themes. Item I derives, at a considerable remove, from my doctoral thesis of 1967. The topic was chosen because, although other medieval mathematical, and especially applied mathematical, topics were *prima facie* more exciting, I did not think that they could be adequately comprehended historically without deeper probing into the basics of medieval mathematical consciousness. I therefore decided upon an edition and intensive study of a geometrical textbook written by one of the age's most renowned pure and applied mathematicians, Thomas Bradwardine. Item II looks more closely at an aspect of the work of one of Bradwardine's principal sources, Campanus of Novara, with special reference to how he worked on the mathematical legacy bequeathed to him. Although dealing with pure mathematics, III and IV have a different genesis, arising from a puzzlement concerning the role of construction in Greek geometry. Descartes provided a simple but, as it turned out, distorted answer to my question: hence a large part of the story.

Studies V–X centre on medieval applications of mathematics in other areas of science (including especially natural philosophy), which to my mind provided one of the main motivations for its study. Among these, V pays special attention to Bradwardine's so-called law of motion, and argues that that in the context of the mathematical grammar of its time it was an essentially simple law, as opposed to the often-found view that it employed a logarithmic function, and hence was complicated. Item IX used the appearance in English of a fine textbook on early physics and astronomy as occasion for developing some methodological reflections on the historiography of mathematical science, while X attempts a typology of medieval endeavours to give a mathematical account of the natural world.

Mathematics is less central to XI–XIII than to other studies in the volume. XI arose from a feeling of dissatisfaction that at the time of my early researches in the history of science there seemed to be two Roger Bacons. The older romantic picture of him as either a magician, or a heroic pioneer of experimental science, or both, still persisted, but was regarded askance by most scholarly historians, who preferred to see him in large measure as a typical, and indeed rather unsuccessful and envious, schoolman. My aim was to achieve a more unified picture. Since that time, scholarship has advanced considerably, and Bacon's uniqueness has been more firmly established; my own present researches are still much concerned with him. Item XII arose from an invitation to attend a meeting of the Kölner Mediävistentagung on the general theme of medieval consciousness of tradition and progress. I came to the conclusion that even such an 'advanced' thinker as Nicole Oresme had an ambivalent attitude towards conceptions of scientific progress. Later I essayed a more general approach to the question in an article appearing here as XIII.

The remaining four studies are linked by a concern with what in modern parlance would be called the structure of the continuum, and its relevance to medieval and early modern physics. In XIV this theme enters as one among many, but assumes a more central role in the remaining articles. The genesis of this concern owed much to a sense that in several related writings Stillman Drake had put his finger on something important, but that his interpretation was askew. In XV I try to pinpoint this by a direct comparison between Oresme and Galileo, while in XVI I survey various aspects of medieval approaches to problems of measure. Finally in XVII I consider the tension between holistic and more aggressive mathematical attitudes in a wider range of Oresme's thought. Throughout many of the studies in this volume, there emerges the view that a particularly important feature of the Scientific Revolution was a displacement of the probing attitude of scholasticsm, which aimed principally for a deeper understanding of existing knowledge, by a more thrusting and axiomatic attack, designed for progressing outwards into new fields, and hence, to allude to Galileo, to the conscious and proud creation of *new* sciences.

For permissions and facilitations for republication of these studies I am very grateful to the following: Professor C. Truesdell, Editor, *Archive for History of Exact Sciences* and Springer Verlag (I); Casa Editrice Leo S. Olschki (II); Academic Press Inc. (III); CNRS Editions (IV); Dr J. Browne, Editor, *British Journal for the History of Science* and the Council of the British Society for the History of Science (V); Professor R. Halleux, Secretary General, Division of History of Science, International Union of the History and Philosophy of Science (VI and VII); Librairie Scientifique et Technique Albert Blanchard (VI); Oxford University Press (VIII); Professor R.S. Porter, Editor, *History of Science* (IX); Cambridge University Press (X); Fordham University Press (XI); Dr A. Speer and the Thomas-Institut, Universität zu Köln (XII and XVI); the Johns Hopkins University Press (XIII); Dr R.B. Thomson, Director of Publications, Pontifical Institute

of Mediaeval Studies (XIV); Elsevier Science Ltd (XV); Professor P.
Souffrin and Dr A. Segonds, Directeur Général, Société d'Edition 'Les
Belles Lettres' (XVII).

GEORGE MOLLAND

Aberdeen
September 1994

I

An Examination of Bradwardine's Geometry

I. Introduction

"One might almost say: Bradwardine wanted to write the *Philosophiae naturalis principia mathematica* of his century." So wrote ANNELIESE MAIER[1] in discussing BRADWARDINE's *Tractatus de proportionibus*, which contains his now famous "law of motion". This law may be seen as imposing a rigorous mathematical interpretation on *dicta* which previously had only a vaguely quantitative sense.[2] BRADWARDINE was insisting on "mathematical principles" in a way similar to NEWTON's significant amendment of DESCARTES's title *Principia Philosophiae*,[3] BRADWARDINE's later *magnum opus*, the *De causa Dei*, had characteristics of a *Theologiae Christianae Principia Mathematica*,[4] not only in its attempt to proceed *more geometrico* but in its frequent use of mathematical arguments (particularly concerning questions of infinity), and in its firm assertion of a close connection of mathematics and values.[5] In his *Tractatus de continuo* he made much use of arguments from geometry to uphold the majority view on the composition of the continuum. He can be accused of a *petitio principii*,[6] but this makes all the clearer the depth of his faith in mathematics as *revelatrix omnis veritatis sincere*.[7]

---

[1] A. MAIER, *Die Vorläufer Galileis im 14. Jahrhundert* (2nd edn., Rome, 1966), 86, n. 10.

[2] *Cf.* A.G. MOLLAND, "Ancestors of Physics", *History of Science*, xiv (1976), 54–75, at 67–70.

[3] I.B. COHEN, "Newton in the Light of Recent Scholarship", *Isis*, li (1960), 489–514, at 506–507.

[4] *Cf.* the title of JOHN CRAIG, *Theologiae Christianae Principia Mathematica* (London, 1699).

[5] See *e.g.* THOMAS BRADWARDINE, *De causa Dei, contra Pelagium et de virtute causarum, ad suos Mertonenses*, ed. H. SAVILE (London, 1618), 119–134. On fourteenth-century "mathematical theology" see J.E. MURDOCH, "From Social into Intellectual Factors: An Aspect of the Unitary Character of Late Medieval Learning", *The Cultural Context of Medieval Learning*, ed. J.E. MURDOCH & E.D. SYLLA, Boston Studies in the Philosophy of Science, xxvi (Dordrecht & Boston, 1975), 271–348.

[6] *Cf.* J.E. MURDOCH, "Superposition, Congruence and Continuity in the Middle Ages," *Mélanges Alexandre Koyré*, (Paris, 1964), 416–441, at 439–441.

[7] J.E. MURDOCH, *Geometry and the Continuum in the Fourteenth Century: A Philosophical Analysis of Bradwardine's Tractatus de Continuo*, (Ph.D. thesis, Univ. of Wisconsin, 1957), 401.

If BRADWARDINE were so much influenced by mathematics, we can only get a full insight into his thought if we grasp the particular form and nuances of his mathematical consciousness, for such are not invariant across the ages. An important source for this task is a geometrical text-book written by BRADWAR-DINE, and usually known as the *Geometria speculativa*. A careful analysis of this work may also be of wider relevance. The Middle Ages is not rich in works of theoretical geometry, and many of those extant take the form of commentaries on established authors. BRADWARDINE's treatise is one of the few not in commentary form, and it can give valuable evidence as to medieval geometrical attitudes, both as a representative document, and in its role in shaping the geometrical spirit of its readers. It is particularly helpful in allowing us to see more clearly into the mathematical natural philosophy which is one of the prominent features of the fourteenth century, and which had as one of its most important centres BRADWARDINE's own college of Merton in Oxford.

In this article I examine BRADWARDINE's *Geometria speculativa* with particular attention to what it reveals of medieval geometrical consciousness and the relation of this to other fields of intellectual endeavour. My analysis is based on the new edition of this work presented in my doctoral dissertation.[8] I hope that the text will soon be published; meantime I refer to it by the decimal notation which I used there, and in Section IV of this article I give a synopsis of the work, which may be used to compare my divisions of the work with those in earlier editions. This article also plunders other parts of the dissertation, and among the many scholars who have been generous with their help over the years I must here make special mention of the debt that I owe to my Ph.D. supervisor MICHAEL HOSKIN.

II. The Author

The name "BRADWARDINE" suggests a link with the Herefordshire village of Bredwardine,[9] but the evidence of early chroniclers makes it clear that THOMAS BRADWARDINE was born near the villages of Cowden and Hartfield, close to the Kent-Sussex border.[10] The time is far less definite, and can only be guessed to be

[8] A.G. MOLLAND, *The Geometria speculativa of Thomas Bradwardine: Text with critical discussion* (Ph.D. thesis, Univ. of Cambridge, 1967). The text was established from the following manuscripts: W = Vatican, Pal. lat. 1420, ff. 53r–63r; B = Basle, Öffentliche Bibliothek der Universität, F.IV.30, ff. 58r–96r; K = Krakow, Biblioteka Jagiellońska, 1919, ff. 31r–69r; V = Vatican, Vat. lat. 3102, ff. 85r–111v; T = Toruń, Ksiaznica Miejska im. Kopernika, R.4°.2, pp. 111–153. Although it has several errors T is probably nearest in form to the original exemplar.

[9] In a work first published in 1662 THOMAS FULLER, *The Worthies of England* (London, 1952), 564, asserted, without giving evidence, that the BRADWARDINES were an old Herefordshire family who had migrated to Sussex three generations before THOMAS was born.

[10] *Anglia Sacra*, ed. H. WHARTON (London, 1691), i, 42: "Thomas Bradwardyn, sacrae paginae professor Solempnis, de Parochia de Hartfeld Cicestrensis Dioeceos oriundus ..." *Ibid.*, i, 376: "Per idem tempus Capitulum Cant. M. Thomam Bradewardyn de Condenna Roffensis Dioceseos oriundum ... elegerunt." The first quotation is from a *Vitae Archiepiscoporum Cantuarensis;* WHARTON ascribed it to STEPHEN BIRCHINGTON (d. 1407), but J. TAIT, *Chronica Johannis de Reading et Anonymi Cantuarensis 1346–1367* (Manchester, 1914), 63–68, would only allow that BIRCHINGTON may have written a second continued edition of it.

near the end of the thirteenth century. By 1321 he had become a B.A., and a Fellow of Balliol College, Oxford. Two years later he removed to Merton, where he retained a Fellowship until 1335.[11] It is to this period that must be assigned most of BRADWARDINE's logical, mathematical and natural philosophical works. Among these we have definite evidence that his *Insolubilia* was written while he was a Regent Master in Arts,[12] and this would seem to be a suitable time for his *Geometria speculativa*, an earlier *Arithmetica speculativa*,[13] and possibly an

---

The second quotation is from the *Historia Roffensis* attributed to WILLIAM DE DENE (fl. 1350); cf. C. JOHNSON, *Registrum Hamonis Hethe Diocesis Roffensis A.D. 1319–1352*, Canterbury and York Series, xlviii–xlix (Oxford, 1948), vii. Cowden and Hartfield are only about three miles apart, and so the difference of testimony (probably arising from inter-diocesan or inter-parochial rivalry) may be taken as a sign of veracity. Hartfield has been suggested as the place of origin of the couplet: "Cowden church, crooked steeple,/Lying priest, deceitful people"; see *The Parish Church of St. Mary Magdalene Cowden* (Ramsgate, n.d.), 6.

[11] See A.B. EMDEN, *A Biographical Register of the University of Oxford to A.D. 1500* (Oxford, 1957–59), i, 245.

[12] J.A. WEISHEIPL, *Early Fourteenth Century Physics of the Merton "School" with special reference to Dumbleton and Heytesbury* (D. Phil. thesis, Oxford, 1956), 72–73, citing J. VILLA-AMIL Y CASTRO, *Catalógo de los Manuscritos existentes en la Biblioteca del Noviciado de la Universidad Central* (Madrid, 1878), 37. The text has been edited in M.L. ROURE, "La Problématique des Propositions Insolubles au XIIIe Siècle, suivi de l'Edition des Traités de W. Shyreswood, W. Burleigh et Th. Bradwardine", *Archives d'Histoire Doctrinale et Litteraire du Moyen Age*, xlv (1970), 205–326.

[13] In *Geom. spec.* 1.00 BRADWARDINE makes clear that he has written such a work: "Nos autem in alio tractatu de arismetica expedivimus". The trouble is that four distinct arithmetical works have been ascribed to BRADWARDINE, and it is not plausible to see him as the author of all of them. (1) *Inc.:* "Quantitatum alia continua que magnitudo dictur, alia discreta que multitudo sive numerus appellatur..." An edition of this by PEDRO SANCHEZ CIRVELO was published at Paris in 1495 as *Arithmetica thome brauardini* (title page) or *Arithmetica speculatiua thome brauardini* (colophon). MS Cambridge, Univ. Lib., Ee. III.61, ff. 96v–105v, has an expanded version, and the work is there described as the *Arsmetrica* of SIMON BREDON. (2) *Inc.:* "Numerus est duplex, mathematicus qui dicitur numerus numerans atque naturalis qui dicitur numerus numeratus..." This is ascribed to BRADWARDINE in the version in MS Munich, Clm 24809, ff. 100v–106r, and is substantially identical to the *Arithmetica* published at Venice in 1515 and Mainz in 1538 as the work of JOHANNES DE MURIS. The text has recently been edited by H.L.L. BUSARD, "Die 'Arithmetica speculativa' des Johannes de Muris", *Scientiarum Historia*, xiii (1971), 103–132. Six of the twelve manuscripts that he cites (114–5) ascribe the treatise to JOHANNES DE MURIS and none to BRADWARDINE. (He does not mention the Munich manuscript that we noted above.) (3) *Inc.:* "Eorum que sunt aliud est continuum aliud discretum. Continuum ut arbor, lapis et huiusmodi..." This is ascribed to BRADWARDINE in the version in MS Erfurt, Amplon. F375, ff. 15v–17v, 88v–92v. (4) *Inc.:* "Ovidius qui philosophus fuit atque poeta/Conquearitur quia deseritur possessio leta...." The work is in verse and is found in MS Erfurt, Amplon. Q2, ff. 38r–62v, where it is described as *Theoria numerorum Magistri bragwerdini*. On all this cf. WEISHEIPL, *Early Fourteenth Century Physics* (n.12 above), 73–74; MOLLAND, *The Geometria speculativa* (n. 8 above), 416–419; J.A. WEISHEIPL, "Repertorium Mertonense", *Mediaeval Studies*, xxxi (1969), 174–224, at 178–179; L. THORNDIKE & P. KIBRE, *A Catalogue of Incipits of Medieval Scientific Writings in Latin* (2nd edn., London, 1963), 500, 641, 959, 1023, 1175. Versions (1)–(3) are essentially synopses of BOETHIUS.

elementary work on astronomy.[14] Certainly the *Geometria* seems to precede the *Tractatus de proportionibus* of 1328,[15] and this work in turn precedes the *Tractatus de continuo*. BRADWARDINE's major theological work, the *De causa Dei* appeared in 1344, after he had left Oxford.

In the 1330s BRADWARDINE came under the patronage of RICHARD DE BURY.[16] His first ecclesiastical preferments were obtained in 1333 on their being relinquished by BURY,[17] and two years later the relationship became closer when BRADWARDINE joined the *familia* of BURY, who had now become Bishop of Durham. RICHARD was assiduous in collecting both books and scholars. Besides the benefit of RICHARD's library, BRADWARDINE had the intellectual company of such men as RICHARD FITZRALPH, WALTER BURLEY, JOHN MAUDITH, ROBERT HOLCOT and RICHARD KILLINGTON.[18] In his *Philobiblon* BURY expressed some sadness at how he was deprived of the company of brilliant men by their obtaining well-deserved ecclesiastical promotion.[19] BRADWARDINE may be a case in point, for in 1337 he became Chancellor of St. Paul's Cathedral, and this probably involved him in theological lecturing of a type more abstruse than that found in a normal theological school.[20] Nevertheless an association with BURY remained, and we have glimpses of BRADWARDINE acting as his agent in various matters until almost the time of BURY's death in 1345.[21]

At an uncertain date[22] BRADWARDINE was appointed chaplain to the king,

---

[14] In *Geom. spec.* 4.46 BRADWARDINE says of an elementary conclusion of spheric, "Et hoc multum valet ad notitiam ortus et occasus signorum in Astronomia, sicud alias declaravi." If this is a reference to an astronomical work, it is almost certainly not to the tables mentioned by SAVILE in his edition of *De causa Dei* (n. 5 above), sig. a2v, when he was praising BRADWARDINE's mathematical ability: "Testes sunt tabulae Astronomicae exquisite descriptae aequationum Planetarum, & coniunctionum ac oppositionum luminarium, quas penes me habeo magna cum diligentia manu exartas volumine satis crasso." Dr. J.D. NORTH has kindly informed me that in MS Oxford, Magdalen 182 there are a set of tables referred to on f. 37v as "tabulas de Battecombe alias Bredon sive Bradwardynes vocatas". There is no evidence for BRADWARDINE having a serious interest in mathematical astronomy; SAVILE probably had a case of mistaken identity.

[15] See n. 44 below.

[16] On him see N. DENHOLM-YOUNG, "Richard de Bury (1287–1345)", *Transactions of the Royal Historical Society*, xx₄ (1937), 135–168, reprinted in DENHOLM-YOUNG, *Collected Papers on Mediaeval Subjects* (Oxford, 1946), 1–25, and in *Collected Papers of N. Denholm-Young* (Cardiff, 1969), 1–41.

[17] *Calendar of Entries in the Papal Registers relating to Great Britain and Ireland. Papal Letters* (London, 1893–1955), ii, 395.

[18] WILLIAM DE CHAMBRE, *Continuatio historiae Dunelmensis*, ed. in J. RAINE, *Historiae Dunelmensis Scriptores Tres* (London & Edinburgh, 1839), 128.

[19] RICHARD DE BURY, *Philobiblon. The Text and Translation of E.C. Thomas …* (Oxford, 1960), 86–89.

[20] *Cf.* W.A. PANTIN, *The English Church in the Fourteenth Century* (Cambridge, 1955; repr. Notre Dame, Ind., 1962), 111, and H.A. OBERMAN, *Archbishop Thomas Bradwardine: A Fourteenth Century Augustinian* (Utrecht, 1957), 17.

[21] *The Register of Richard de Kellawe, Lord Palatine and Bishop of Durham ABAC—ABAD* (London, 1873–78), iii, 489–493; *Richard d'Aungerville of Bury. Fragments of his Register and Other Documents*. Publications of the Surtees Society, cxix (Durham, 1910), 56–57.

[22] H.A. OBERMAN & J.A. WEISHEIPL, "The *Sermo Epinicius* ascribed to Thomas

EDWARD III, but until 1346 it is not clear how much attendance at Court this involved. In that year BRADWARDINE accompanied the English forces on the expedition to France that had its climax in the Battle of Crécy. ADAM MURIMUTH quotes a letter from him describing the landing in Normandy and the first skirmishes with the French,[23] and there is also extant a Latin translation of a sermon that he preached after receipt of news of the English victory over the Scots at Neville's Cross.[24] Quite soon after this he approached higher ecclesiastical office. In 1348 he was elected Archbishop of Canterbury, but the Chapter had not obtained a *congé d'élire*, and so the king objected and had the Pope appoint JOHN UFFORD instead. UFFORD was apparently already senile by this time,[25] and soon died of the plague that swept England. This time BRADWARDINE was properly . appointed, and consecrated at Avignon, possibly to the accompaniment of an insulting dumb show.[26] But BRADWARDINE had no chance to prove his qualities in the post, for within weeks of his return to England he too contracted the plague and died on August 26th 1349.

III. Provenance, Sources and Influence

III.1. Authorship

When we turn to the *Geometria speculativa* we must first consider the question of authorship, since this has been disputed. A majority verdict of the manuscript scribes is clearly in BRADWARDINE's favour: if we neglect defective versions, the count is roughly thirteen to two with five abstentions.[27] One of the dissenting voices comes from the Vatican manuscript Ottob. lat. 1389, where the treatise is ascribed to PETER of Dacia; the version was copied in 1414.[28] In 1868 M. CURTZE

Bradwardine (1346)", *Archives d'Historie Doctrinale et Litteraire du Moyen Age*, xxv (1958), 295–329, at 299, say 1339, but they do not give their sources.

[23] *Adae Murimuth Continuatio Chronicarum. Robertus de Avesbury De Gestis Mirabilibus Regis Edwardi Tertii*, ed. E.M. THOMPSON (London, 1889), 201–202.

[24] Edited in OBERMAN & WEISHEIPL, *op. cit.* (n. 22 above).

[25] WILLIAM DE DENE (?), *Historia Roffensis*, in WHARTON, *Anglia Sacra* (n. 10 above), i, 375.

[26] Pseudo-BIRCHINGTON, *Vit. Arch. Cant.* in WHARTON, *Angl. Sac.* (n. 10 above), i, 43; W.F. HOOK, *Lives of the Archbishops of Canterbury* (London, 1860–76), iv, 104; E. BALUZE, *Vitae Paparum Avenionensium*, ed. G. MOLLAT (Paris, 1924–27), ii, 355.

[27] See the enumeration of manuscripts in MOLLAND, *The Geometria speculativa* (n. 8 above), 41–50. There is also apparently a copy or partial copy in MS Catania, Bibliotheche Riunite "Civica e A. Ursino Recupero", Fondo Civico D39, ff. 2–8(?); see P.O. KRISTELLER, *Iter Italicum* (London&Leiden, 1965–67), i, 42. I am grateful to Dr. S. VICTOR for drawing this to my attention.

[28] The work is on ff. 4r–51r. On f. 4r we have, "Incipit summa artis Geometrie valde bona edita a magistro petro de dacia que quidem fuit abstracta a Geometria Euclidis pro maiori parte", and on f. 51r, "Explicit hec brevis Theoria Geometrie valde bona edita a magistro petro de dacia que est multum utilis volenti intelligere que ponuntur in opere sequenti. fuit scripta per me Bartholomeum Juliani presbyterem magistrum in artibus in valentis(?) xxᵃ die junii anno domini millesimo CCCC°X°IIII° Laudetur deus semper, amen." For a description of the codex see J.F. DALY & C.J. ERMATINGER, "Mathematics in the Codices Ottobiani Latini", *Manuscripta*, viii (1964), 3–17, ix (1965), 12–29, at viii, 9–11.

I

118

noted this ascription, but observed that in earlier manuscripts the work was attributed to BRADWARDINE.[29] In 1885 G. ENESTRÖM again drew attention to the manuscript in a query inserted in *Bibliotheca Mathematica*,[30] and this soon drew a response from Prince BALDASSARRE BONCOMPAGNI[31], who pointed out that he had just acquired a manuscript codex including the work, in which it was again ascribed to PETER of Dacia; the date of copying was 1365. This made ENESTRÖM incline to the view that PETER of Dacia was the true author,[32] but CANTOR and CURTZE were firm in rejecting this,[33] and subsequent historians have, I believe rightly, acquiesced in their view. Unfortunately I have been unable to trace BONCOMPAGNI's manuscript beyond the sale catalogue of 1898.[34]

Besides the verdict of the scribes, we may draw positive support for BRADWARDINE's authorship from a comparison of the proportional doctrine in the *Geometria* with that in BRADWARDINE's *Tractatus de proportionibus*.[35] The agreement is very close, often with strong verbal similarities, and as will be made clear later, both works contain an apparently novel development in the doctrine of denominating ratios. If BRADWARDINE were not the author of the *Geometria* it would be tempting to maintain that he was influenced by the work. A further argument may be drawn from considering the *Geometria* in relation to PETER of Dacia. Among the various people of this name, one, PETRUS PHILOMENUS DE DACIA, is renowned as a mathematician, and it is presumably to him that the dissenting manuscripts refer. The established canon of his mathematical works[36] shows that he had an ample interest in astronomy and practical arithmetic, but gives little evidence of a concern with theoretical arithmetic or geometry, whereas the author of the *Geometria* must be credited with both. Moreover, the author of the *Geometria*, although displaying a considerable interest in natural philosophy (like BRADWARDINE, but from the available evidence, unlike PETER), seems to have no

---

[29] M. CURTZE, "Ueber die Handschrift R. 4°.2, Problematum Euclidis explicatio, der Königl. Gymnasialbibliothek zu Thorn", *Zeitschrift für Mathematik und Physik*, xiii (1868), Supplement, 45–104, at 84–85.

[30] *Bibliotheca Mathematica*, 1885, 94.

[31] *Ibid.*, 196. The *explicit* of the *Geometria* is given as, "Explicit tractatus geometrie editus a petro de dacia et scriptus per fratrem marcholinum de coruo provincie sancti antonii peruss. 1365 die quo supra de uariis malis exiens." For another description of the codex see *Catalogo della Biblioteca Boncompagni* (Rome, 1898), i, 185. According to P.O. KRISTELLER, *Latin Manuscript Books before 1600* (3rd edn., New York, 1965), 21, BONCOMPAGNI's collection is now scattered.

[32] G. ENESTRÖM, "Anteckningar om matematikern Petrus de Dacia och hans skrifter", *Öfversigt af Kongl. Vetenskaps-Akademiens Förhandlingar*, 1885, N:o 3, 15–27; 1885, N:o 8, 65–70; 1886, N:o 3, 57–60, at p. 59 of the final part.

[33] M CANTOR, *Vorlesungen über Geschichte der Mathematik* (2nd edn., Leipzig, 1894–1908), ii, 114; *Petri Philomeni de Dacia in Algorismum Vulgarem Johannis de Sacrobosco Commentarius*, ed. M. CURTZE (Copenhagen, 1897), iii–iv.

[34] See n. 31 above.

[35] *Cf.* especially *Geom. spec.*, 3.1–3.3, with THOMAS BRADWARDINE, *Tractatus de proportionibus*, ed. H.L. CROSBY (Madison, 1955), 66–78.

[36] See the list in O. PEDERSEN, "Peder Nattergal og hans astronomiske regneininstrument", *Nordisk Astronomisk Tidsskrift*, 1963, 37–50; *cf.* O. PEDERSEN, "The Life and Work of Peter Nightengale", *Vistas in Astronomy*, ix (1967), 3–10.

more than a passing concern with technical astronomy. All these arguments lead us to conclude with confidence that THOMAS BRADWARDINE and not PETER of Dacia was the author of the *Geometria speculativa* in which we are interested.

Of the extant manuscripts of the *Geometria* two contain abbreviated versions, and several are incomplete. Moreover, as is the case with other medieval textbooks, the manuscripts show numerous trivial variations. But, if we abstract from all this, there are still two distinct traditions. The main difference lies in additional material incorporated in one tradition. An examination of this material strongly suggests that it is collection of glosses and not an integral part of the original text. Some parts aim at clarification and some develop new themes; occasionally the additions seem at variance with the rest of the work. I have therefore concluded that they are not the work of BRADWARDINE, but of someone whom I shall refer to as the "elaborator".[37] But by this designation I do not wish to pre-empt the question of whether they are all the work of one author.

III.2. Origins and Purpose

We must now see what information may be gleaned as to the circumstances of origin of the *Geometria*. The exact nature of mathematical education in the medieval universities is not easy to determine. Certainly it was officially required for the attainment of a Master of Arts degree, but the works of many Schoolmen would suggest that it had not been very effective. Statutes that were probably in force in Oxford before 1350 demanded that those about to incept as Masters should swear that they had heard properly (*competenter*) the [first] six books of EUCLID, the *Arithmetica* of BOETHIUS, *Compotus*, *Algorismus*, and *De spera* (presumably of SACROBOSCO).[38] Times were laid down for how long the hearings should last. In the case of geometry it was five weeks (not counting feast-days) and for the *Arithmetica* three weeks. It appears that students may already have been Bachelors of Arts and perhaps even lecturing on parts of ARISTOTLE's natural philosophy before hearing these lectures. In the early fourteenth century a certain J.T. (?) wrote out a *forma* of "set-books" for inception in Arts, whose mathematical part (though tersely described) corresponds closely to the list that we have just noted. Among the comments appended by the writer is the following:[39]

'Note that I have had from Bokynham [THOMAS BUCKINGHAM of Merton?[40]] twelve days in geometry and the whole text of the second book of geometry and from Westcot nine days in geometry. Also from Bokynham the whole text of the first book of Arithmetic and twelve days of Arithmetic.'

---

[37] Of the manuscripts used in establishing the text (n. 8 above) *W, B* and *T* are unelaborated whereas *K* and *V* are elaborated.

[38] *Statuta Antiqua Universitatis Oxoniensis*, ed. S. GIBSON (Oxford, 1931), 33–34. *Cf.* J.A. WEISHEIPL, "Curriculum of the Faculty of Arts at Oxford in the Fourteenth Century", *Mediaeval Studies*, xxvi (1964), 143–185, at 159–161.

[39] H. RASHDALL, *The Universities of Europe in the Middle Ages*, ed. F.M. POWICKE & A.B. EMDEN (London, 1936), iii, 482: "Memorandum quod habui a Bokynham xii d(ies) in gemetria et totalem literam 2 libri geometrie et a Wescot ix dies in gemetria. Item a Bokynham literam totalem primi libri Arsmetrice et xii dies Arsmetrice."

[40] *Cf.* F.M. POWICKE, *The Medieval Books of Merton College* (Oxford, 1931), 34.

The relation between the days and the texts is unclear. If the days were not devoted to the texts, but to independent expositions of mathematics, then there may have been a place for a work such as BRADWARDINE's *Geometria* to be used, and indeed it could have grown out of such lectures. But this suggestion is weakened by the consideration that J.T. seems to have been mainly interested in noting down how far he had come to meeting the formal requirements for inception, and supernumerary lectures would not have been of interest in that context.

But even if BRADWARDINE's *Geometria* was only loosely related to mathematical lectures, we can see another important function for it, which was highlighted by two fifteenth-century writers. In 1456 FRIDERICUS AMANN noted[41] that it contained "almost all the geometrical demonstrations that the Philosopher [ARISTOTLE] brings forth by way of example in logic and philosophy", and in 1495 PEDRO SANCHEZ CIRVELO described it as "gathering together all the geometrical conclusions that are most needed by students of arts and of the philosophy of Aristotle." The necessity of a mathematical background for interpreting ARISTOTLE had been emphasised with his customary vigour by ROGER BACON,[42] and was indeed evident from the texts themselves. An ill-prepared Master or even worse-prepared Bachelor must have felt a crying need for a hand-book such as BRADWARDINE's *Geometria* in working out his lectures, and, because the work is so well adapted to this need, we may conjecture that it was compiled primarily, although not exclusively, for the purpose. An appropriate time of composition would, as suggested by J.A. WEISHEIPL,[43] have been his time as a Regent Master in Arts in the early 1320s, and internal evidence supports the view that it was written before the *Tractatus de proportionibus* of 1328.[44]

In addition to characterising the relevance of the *Geometria* to ARISTOTLE, FRIDERICUS AMANN gave his opinion of its sources. It was, he said[45], "assembled from the books of Euclid, Campanus, Archimedes, Theodosius, Jordanus, and from the book that is entitled *Ysoperimetrorum*." This list needs some correction. Certainly EUCLID's *Elements* in the version of CAMPANUS of Novara is the principal source,[46] and ARCHIMEDES's *De mensura circuli*[47] and THEODOSIUS's

---

[41] MS Munich, Bayerische Staatsbibliothek, Clm 14908, f. 224r: "Hoc opus geometricum continet fere omnes demonstraciones geometricas quas adducit philosophus gratia exempli vel in loyca vel phylosophia." On FRIDERICUS see E. ZINNER, *Leben und Wirken des Joh. Müller von Königsberg genannt Regiomontanus* (2nd edn., Osnabrück, 1968), 68–70, and D.B. DURAND, *The Vienna-Klosterneuburg Map Corpus of the Fifteenth Century* (Leiden, 1952), 72–76, 326. For CIRVELO's edition see n. 52 below.

[42] See, e.g., R. STEELE, "Roger Bacon as Professor", *Isis*, xx (1933), 53–71, and *The "Opus Majus" of Roger Bacon*, ed. J.H. BRIDGES (Oxford, 1897–1900; repr. Frankfurt, 1964), i, 97–174, *et passim*.

[43] J.A. WEISHEIPL, "Ockham and Some Mertonians", *Mediaeval Studies*, xxx (1968), 163–213, at 191.

[44] *Cf.* MOLLAND, *The Geometria speculativa* (n. 8 above), 350, 358, 363–364.

[45] *Loc.cit.* (n. 41 above): "... et est collectum ex libris euclidis campani archymedii Theodosy Jordani et ex libro qui intitulatur ysoperimetrorum."

[46] This is printed in, among other places, *Preclarissimus liber elementorum Euclidis perspicacissimi in artem Geometrie* (Venice, 1482), and *Euclidis Megarensis ... opera a Campano interprete fidissimo translata ... Lucas Paciolus ... detersit ... emendavit ...* (Venice, 1509).

[47] See Section VI.3 below.

Sphaerica[48] are used in the appropriate places. But there is no sign of any influence from JORDANUS's *De triangulis*, although the *De proportionibus* sometimes ascribed to him may have been used.[49] The principal medieval treatise *De ysoperimetris* was a translation of part of an anonymous introduction to the *Almagest* (possibly by EUTOCIUS) and derived ultimately from the work of ZENODORUS.[50] As we shall see, BRADWARDINE almost certainly did not draw directly upon it. So much for the subtractions. We may add to FRIDERICUS's list arithmetic in the tradition of BOETHIUS's *Arithmetica* (and possibly also his *Musica*), and the ARISTOTELIAN commentary tradition, particularly in the section on *repletio loci*.[51] We must also recognise the pervasive influence of scholastic logical procedures.

III.3. Influence

The major testimony to the influence of the *Geometria* is the number of copies that it generated. Over twenty manuscript versions are extant, and in 1495 it appeared in print in an edition (unsatisfactory for historical purposes) by PEDRO SANCHEZ CIRVELO.[52] Several more early editions followed; all that I have seen are dependent upon CIRVELO's original.[53] CIRVELO also used the work as the basis of the geometrical section of his own *Cursus quattuor mathematicarum artium liberalium*,[54] and large sections of this follow BRADWARDINE word for word. Earlier, in about 1390, WIGANDUS DURNHEIMER had adopted a similar policy in his rather pedantic *Tractatus geometrie date et compilate ... ex dictis Euclidis et Campani super geometriam Brawardini*.[55] These borrowings were acknowledged, but LUCA PACIOLI did not admit that many of the comments that he added to his edition of CAMPANUS's version of EUCLID[56] were lifted verbatim from

[48] This existed in at least two medieval Latin translations, and BRADWARDINE's citations correspond to the version that is ascribed to GERARD of Cremona. See *Theodosius Tripolites Sphaerica*, ed. J.L. HEIBERG, Abhandlungen der Gesellschaft der Wissenschaften zu Göttingen, Philologisch-Historische Klasse, N.F. Bd. xix, 3 (Berlin, 1927), viii–xii; F.J. CARMODY, *Arabic Astronomical and Astrological Sciences in Latin Translation* (Berkeley & Los Angeles, 1956), 22; THORNDIKE & KIBRE, *Catalogue of Incipits* (n. 13 above), 1523. BRADWARDINE makes some use of the work in chapter 4.4.

[49] Ed. in H.L.L. BUSARD, "Die Traktate *De proportionibus* von Jordanus Nemorarius und Campanus", *Centaurus*, xv (1970), 193–227. *Cf. Geom. spec.*, 3.32 and *Tractatus de proportionibus*, ed. CROSBY (n. 35 above), 76.

[50] See Section VII.2 below.

[51] See Section VII.3 below.

[52] At Paris; *Gesamtkatalog der Wiegendrucke* (Leipzig, 1925–   ), no. 5002. On CIRVELO see L. THORNDIKE, *A History of Magic and Experimental Science* (New York, 1923–58), v, 275–278.

[53] Copies of editions at Valencia, 1503 and Paris, 1530 are in the British Museum. Aberdeen University Library has a Paris, 1511 edition. The *National Union Catalogue* lists a Paris edition of 1503 (copy in New York Public Library), and the *Index Aureliensis* one of Paris, 1516 (copy in Augsburg).

[54] Alcalá, 1516. For mention of three other editions see W.A. WALLACE, "The 'Calculatores' in Early Sixteenth-Century Physics", *British Journal for the History of Science*, iv (1968–9), 221–232, at 226, n. 26.

[55] MS Vienna, Nat. Bibl. 5257, ff. 1r–89v; the description is on f. 89v. *Cf.* M. CLAGETT, *Archimedes in the Middle Ages* (vol. i, Madison, 1964; vol. ii, Philadelphia, 1976), i, 143.

[56] See n. 46 above.

BRADWARDINE's *Geometria*. Poetic justice has resulted in his being castigated for the inappropriateness of several of his additions.[57] We should not expect to find many appeals to a text book as authority, but there are at least a couple of medieval citations of this kind.[58] In the sixteenth century JOHN MAJOR criticised part of the work dealing with infinity,[59] and in the seventeenth the Polish mathematician JAN BROZEK took issue with BRADWARDINE's views on star-polygons.[60] All this absolves us from the need to put much reliance on the testimony provided by the rather ill-informed opinion of JUAN LUIS VIVES, who ranked BRADWARDINE with ARCHIMEDES and PTOLEMY among those authors whom the teacher should know, but "whom it is not necessary for those students to study, whose mathematics are only pursued as preparatory to entering on other branches of knowledge."[61] This completely misrepresents the special educational value of the *Geometria*, which was as a propadeutic for other disciplines.

IV. Synopsis of the Geometria [62]

1. Part I

1.00.   *General introduction.* Geometry is posterior to arithmetic. It is divided into theoretical and practical. "The properties of magnitudes that we shall demonstrate are almost all relative." Correlation of ARISTOTELIAN and geometric terminology for the first principles.

1.01.   *Definitions.* Point as the principle of magnitude.
Line, surface and body defined from dimensions.
Logical division of figure (Fig. 1).
Angle — right, obtuse, acute.

1.02.   *Postulates.*
1.021.   "From any point to any point to draw (*ducere*) a straight line." "And this to be the shortest of all those with the same ends (*contermabilium*)."
1.022.   "On any centre and with the occupation of any amount of space, to describe (*designare*) a circle."

---

[57] T.L. HEATH, *The Thirteen Books of Euclid's Elements* (2nd edn., Cambridge, 1926; repr. New York, 1956), i, 99.

[58] In a question on the seven liberal arts in MS London, Brit. Mus., Add. 15692, ff. 23v–25r, the *Geometria* is appealed to for the division of geometry into theoretical and practical ("quia secundum Thomam Bragwardis in primo sue geometrie duplex est geometria scilicet speculativa et practica"—f. 24r). In MS Vatican, Ottob. lat. 1576, ff. 47r–50v there is according to the report of DALY & ERMATINGER, *op.cit.* (n. 28 above) a *Geometria* with, on f. 48v: "Teneo cum Euclide, boetio, archimenide, bravardino atque aliis expertis quod circulus est quadrabilis..." The author is not using his sources well.

[59] H. ELIE, *Le Traité "De L'Infini" de Jean Mair* (Paris, 1937), 146.

[60] JOHANNIS BROSCIUS, *Apologia pro Aristotele et Euclide, contra Petrum Ramum, et alios* (Dantzig, 1652), 16 sqq.

[61] JUAN LUIS VIVES, *Opera* (Basle, 1555), i, 498; F. WATSON, *Vives: On Education. A Translation of the De tradendis disciplinis* (Cambridge, 1913), 207.

[62] The decimal divisons are those of my edition. See Section I above.

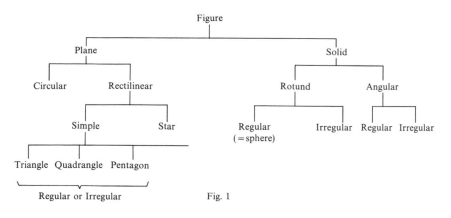

Fig. 1

1.023. "All right angles to be mutually equal."
1.024. "If a straight line fall on two straight lines, and the two interior angles on one side (*ex una parte*) be less than two right angles, for those two lines produced in the same direction (*in eandem partem*) to meet (*coniunctim ire*)."
1.025. "Two straight lines to enclose no surface."

1.03. *Common notions.*
1.031. "Every whole is equal to all its parts taken together, and conversely."
1.032. "Every whole is greater than any of its parts."
1.033. "Those which are equal to one and the same are equal among themselves."
1.034. "Those which are unequal to one and the same are mutually unequal."
1.035. "If equals be added to equals or the same to each (*vel idem commune*), the wholes will be equal."
1.036. "If equals be taken from equals or the same from each, equals will be left."
1.037. "If you add equals to unequals or the same to each of them, the wholes will be unequal."
1.038. "If you take away equals from unequals or the same from each of them, unequals will remain."
1.039. "If some thing be superposed (*supponatur*) to another and applied to it and neither exceed the other, they will be mutually equal."
       How first principles are known.

1.1.   *On lines.*
       Geometry considers properties of lines, surfaces and bodies, but only those of lines for the sake of those of surfaces and bodies.
1.11. "If a straight line stand on a straight line, the two angles on the two sides are either right or equal or two right angles. Whence it is manifest that the whole space which is any plane surface surrounds any point is equal to four right angles."
1.12. "Of any two lines cutting each other the opposite angles are equal."
1.13. "If a third line fall on two parallel lines, then it will make the same kind and size of angles on the one as on the other (*quales quantosque fecerit angulos*

124

super unam tales tantosque faciet super reliquam). From which it follows that each exterior angle is equal to the opposite interior one. Also that any two alternate angles are equal. Also the two interior angles formed on either side are equal to two right angles."

1.14. "An exterior angle of any triangle is equal to the two interior angles opposite to it."

1.15. "Every triangle has three angles equal to two right angles."

1.16. "The angles of any polygonal figure taken together are equal to as many right angles as twice their number less four. From which it follows that each successor in the order of polygonal figures adds two right angles in value over its predecessor."

1.17. "Three regular figures and no other, namely the triangle, the tetragon and the hexagon, fill place."

1.2. *Star-polygons (figurae egredientium angulorum).*
       Assertion of novelty of treatment.

1.21. "Of star-polygons, the pentagon is the first."

1.22. "A star-pentagon has five angles equal to two right angles."

1.23. "Of star-polygons, each successor adds two right angles over its predecessor."

1.24. "In the second order of star-polygons the heptagon is the first."

1.25. "In the infinite remaking (*in infinitum in renovatione*) of figures by the production of sides in the aforesaid way, the first of the subsequent order is always taken from the third of the preceding."

2. Part II

2.0. "In this second part I revert to plane figures considered specially; and I shall speak of triangles, quadrangles and circles, following the order of Euclid; and I shall speak of isoperimetrics, which part Euclid omits." Definition of triangle, and division into equilateral, isoceles and scalene, or into right-angled, obtuse-angled and acute-angled. Definition of right-angled and of equilateral quadrangle. Division of quadrangle; see Fig. 2.

2.1. *On triangles.*
       In the course of the chapter it is pointed out that 2.11–2.13 deal with the triangle in itself. The rest consider the triangle as part of other figures. 2.14–2.17 consider it as part of a circle, and 2.18–2.19 as part of a quadrangle.

2.11. "If one angle of one triangle be equal to one angle of another triangle, and the two sides of the one that contain the equal angle are equal to the two sides of the other that contain the similar angle, the remaining angles will be equal to the remaining angles, and the base equal to the base, and the whole triangle equal to the whole triangle."

2.12. "For every triangle with two equal sides, it is necessary that the angles on the base be equal; and those which are below the base [if the two sides be produced in a straight line]."[63]

---

[63] Bracketed passage added by the elaborator.

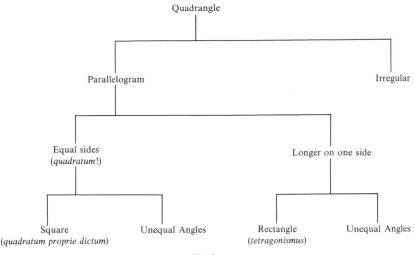

Fig. 2

2.13.   "The longest side of any triangle is opposite the greatest angle, and conversely."

2.14.   "For every triangle set up on the diameter in a semicircle, the angle standing at the circumference will be right."

2.15.   "For every triangle set up on the chord in a segment (*portio*) of a circle, if the segment is greater than a semicircle, the angle at the circumference will be less than right; and if the segment is less than a semicircle, the angle will be more than right. And universally as the segment is greater so the angle is less, and as it is less so the angle is greater."

2.16.   "Every triangle, of which one side is a radius of two circles and the opposite angle is at their section, is equilateral."

2.17.   "Every triangle of which one side is less than the radius of two circles and is terminated at their centres and the opposite angle is at their section, is isoceles. [A triangle] of which the opposite angle is outside the common section is *gradatus* [or scalene, that is][64] of all unequal sides."

2.18.   "The two triangles in a figure of parallel sides, on either side of a diagonal, are equal."

2.19.   "If two triangles be on equal bases and between two parallel lines, they will necessarily be equal."

2.2.   *On quadrangles.*

2.20.   *Descriptio:* "In any parallelogrammic space those parallelograms which the diameter cuts through the middle are said to stand about the same diameter. Of the parallelograms that stand about the same diameter, any one together with the two complements (*supplementa*) is called a gnomon."

---

[64] Bracketed passage added by the elaborator.

126

2.21. "For every parallelogram each diameter divides it through the middle and into equals (*per medium et per equalia*)."

2.22. "Each parallelogram has equal oppositely placed angles."

2.23. "In any parallelogrammic space it is necessary that the complements of the parallelograms that are about the diameter be equal to one another."

2.24. "The square that is described by the side of a right-angled triangle opposite to the right angle multiplied into itself (*in se ducto*) is equal to the two squares that are composed (*conscribuntur*) from the remaining two sides. Whence it is manifest that the square of the diagonal to the square of the side is double."

2.25. "Given (*propositis*) two squares, either equal or unequal, to circumscribe one to the other gnomonically."

2.3. *On circles.*

2.30. Circle does not have logical, but only quantitative, division. Segments (*portiones*) and sectors. Angle of semicircle and of segment. Angle of contingency. Circles touching lines and each other. Concentric and eccentric circles. Panegyric on circle. Ideally it would come before rectilinear figures, but conclusions about the latter are needed for the circle.

2.301. "Circles of which the diameters are equal are themselves also equal."

2.302. "In equal circles, segments are equal which are on one chord or equal [ones]".

2.303. "In unequal circles the same chord cuts off more from the lesser than from the greater."

2.304. "If a straight line touch a circle it is necessary that it touch it only in a point."

2.305. "The diameter of a circle falls perpendicularly on the tangent line, if it passes through the point of contact."

2.306. "The angle of contingency is less than any rectilinear angle, but is divisible *in infinitum*. And as much as it is greater so the circle is less, and as much as the circle is greater so it is less."

2.307. "The angle of a semicircle is greater than every rectilinear acute angle, and less than every right and obtuse angle. Yet it is an angle that may be increased (*augmentalis*) *in infinitum*. Whence it follows that the angle of a semicircle can be less than a rectilinear angle and greater than a [rectilinear] angle, but never equal."

2.308. "The angle of any segment greater than a semicircle is greater than a right angle; of a lesser [segment] it is less than a right angle."

2.309. "Of mutually cutting circles the centres are necessarily diverse."

2.310. It is necessary that mutually touching circles be eccentric.

2.311. "To find the centre of a circle by two cruciform sections."

2.312. "Six radii cutting the whole circumference constitute a regular hexagon inside the circle."

2.313. "Six equal circles touch an equal circle on the outside."

2.4 *On isoperimetrics.*

2.40. *Isoperimetrum* is a name said *ad aliud* not *ad se*.

2.41. "Figures are isoperimetric one to another of which the perimeters are equal."

2.42.   "Of all isoperimetric polygons, that which is of more angles is greater."
2.43.   "On all isoperimetric polygons with the same number of angles, the greater
        is that which is equiangular."
2.44.   "Of all isoperimetric polygons with the same number of sides and equal
        angles, the greater is that which is equilateral."
2.45.   "Of all isoperimetric figures the circle is the greatest. Whence it follows that
        of equal surfaces the circle is contained by the smallest line."

3. Part III

3.1.   Definition and logical division of ratio. See Section VI.2 below.
3.2.   Proportion (*proportionalitas*) is similitude (*similitudo*) of ratios. Ratios are
        similar which have the same denominations. Continuous and discontinuous
        proportion. The six EUCLIDEAN ways of inferring one proportion from
        another.

3.3.   *Rules of ratios.*
        "In this chapter I shall subjoin some rules of ratios in general (*in communi*)."
3.31.   "By as much as some quantity is to another, by so much is the ratio of the
        one to the other denominated."
3.32.   "The ratio of the extremes is composed from the ratios of the means (*ex
        mediorum proportionibus*)."
3.33.   "Ratios are similar or equal of which the denominations are equal."
        Argument that a relation is a thing different from the things related.
3.34.   "Ratios are unequal of which the denominations are unequal. And in
        multiplex [ratios] the denomination and the ratio follow the same order
        (*secundum eundem ordinem se habent denominatio et proportio*), but in
        superparticular ones the inverse."
3.35.   "Quantities are equal which compared to the same quantity have an equal
        ratio." Argument that one infinity not be greater than another.
3.36.   "Quantities of which equimultiples are equal are mutually equal." Argu-
        ment that one infinity be greater than another.

3.4.   *On irrational ratios.*
3.41.   "Any quantity is proportionable to any quantity, but not any is commensur-
        able with any."
3.42.   "Of any two commensurable quantities the ratio of one to the other is as
        [that] of a number to a number. But if their ratio is not as a number to a
        number, they are incommensurable."
3.43.   "The diameter of a square to its side is an irrational ratio. And any diameter
        is asymmetrical (*asymeter*)[65] with its side."
3.44.   "Given two lines that are joined together in a rectilinear fashion (*directe
        coniunctis et linealiter*), if a semicircle be described on the whole line thus
        composed and aggregated from the two, the line that proceeds per-
        pendicularly from the common end of the two lines that are joined together
        to the circumference will be a mean in continuous proportion between the
        given lines."

___

[65] *Cf.* ARISTOTLE, *Anal. Priora*, I.23, 41a27.

3.45. "If there are two quantities commensurable with [another] one, they are also mutually commensurable. If they are not commensurable with each other, they will not be commensurable with another."

3.46. "If there be two commensurable quantities, the whole made out of them will also be commensurable with either."

3.47. "Of any four proportional quantities, if the first be commensurable with the second, the third will also be commensurable with the fourth. But if the first be incommensurable with the second, the third will also be incommensurable with the fourth."

3.5. *On the power of lines.*
"The surface in which some line has power (*in quam potest*) is the square of that line."

3.51. "Equal lines have power in equal surfaces, a double in a quadruple, a triple in a nine-times, a quadruple in a sixteen-times, and generally any multiple of a given line has power in the multiple of the surface of the given line denominated by the square of the number denominating the multiple of the line (*a numero denominante multiplicem linee in se ducto*)."

3.52. "Lines of which one has power in a double [surface] with respect to the other are as diameter and side."

3.53. "If there be three proportional lines, the second is by so much more powerful than the first as is the ratio of the third to the first. From which it is manifest that the line which is a proportional mean (*linea medio loco proportionalis*) between the diameter and the side is incommensurable to either both in length and in power."

3.54. "If there be three lines continually proportional, what arises from the multiplication (*ex ductu*) of the first into the third is equal to the square of the mean."

3.55. "If there be four continually proportional terms, what arises from the multiplication of the least into the fourth is equal to the rectangle which arises from the multiplication of the second into the third."

3.6. *On quadratures.*
To find a square equal in area to a given figure, because a square is of better-known measure.

3.61. "A figure longer on one side [*sc.* a rectangle] is reduced to a square by the finding of the proportional mean (*per medie rei inventionem*) and the multiplication of it into itself."

3.62. "The area of an equilateral or isoceles triangle is equal to the rectangle contained by two lines multiplied into themselves, of which one is half the base and the other divides the base, the angle opposite the base, and the whole triangle in half."

3.63. "The area of a triangle with all sides unequal is equal to half of the rectangle contained under two lines multiplied into themselves of which one is the greatest side of the same triangle and the other proceeds perpendicularly from the greatest angle to the greatest side."

3.64. "It is possible to reduce any polygon to the form of a square by resolution into triangles, and by quadratures of those triangles, and then by gnomonic circumscriptions."

3.65.   "The area of any circle is equal to the rectangle contained by half the circumference and half the diameter."

4. Part IV

4.0   On solids. Body is what has length, breadth and depth. Logical division of body (see Fig. 3). Solid angle. Surfaces bounding solid base and vertex. Lines bounding surfaces; base, perpendicular, hypotenuse.

4.1.   *On lines with respect to solids.*

4.11.   "It is impossible that part of a straight line be in the plane and part in the heights (*in sublimi*)."

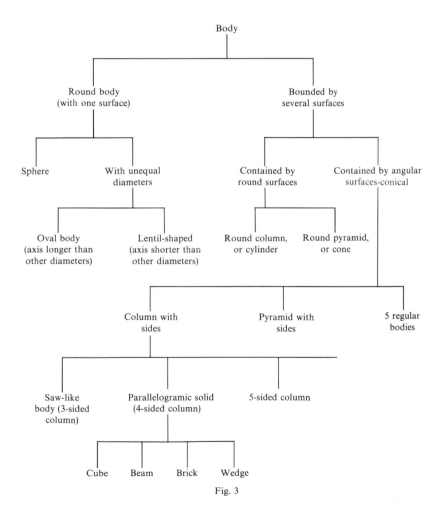

Fig. 3

4.12. "Of all mutually intersecting lines the common section is a point."

4.13. "Every two mutually intersecting straight lines are situated in the same surface."

4.14. "It is possible that one and same line in number be situated in diverse surfaces."

4.15. "If a surface cuts a surface the common section will be a line."

4.2. *On the regular bodies.*

4.21. "If three superficial angles contain a solid angle, then any two of those three angles taken together are greater than the remaining one. From which it is clear that in a pyramid with sides (*in pyramide laterata*) the lateral angles that adjoin the base are greater than the angles of the base."

4.22. "All the lateral angles of any pyramid with sides are worth (*valent*) as much as all the angles of the base and beyond that four right angles precisely."

4.23. "Every solid angle is necessarily less than four right angles."

4.24. "From triangular surfaces it is possible to constitute only three regular bodies."

4.25. "From quadrangular surfaces only one regular body is composed."

4.26. "From pentagonal surfaces only one regular body is composed."

4.27. "Besides the five aforesaid regular bodies it is impossible that there be any other multilateral regular body."

4.3. *On the filling of place.*
Of concern to both mathematicians and natural philosophers. Filling place in solids to be understood analogously with filling place in planes. Definition. Argument of AVERROES, but it is only a persuasion. "I say therefore that according to truth the cube fills place, but according to the opinion of Averroes the cube and the pyramid." Arguments from experience and arithmetic for the cube. Great controversy about the pyramid, for AVERROES holds that twelve pyramids fill place whereas others on the basis of experience maintain that twenty pyramids are needed. No certainty as yet, but AVERROES' arguments are invalid. [The elaborator inclines more definitely than BRADWARDINE to the view that twenty pyramids fill place.]

4.4. *On the sphere.*

4.40. Perfection of sphere. Definitions – in general following THEODOSIUS.

4.41. "If a plane surface touch a sphere, it is necessary that it touch it in only one point. Whence it is all the more manifest that a sphere is touched by a sphere in a point."

4.42. "Twelve equal circumposed spheres touch a single sphere."

4.43. "If on a sphere several circles be designated, that which passes through the centre is greater than all [the others]. Of the remainder, those of which the longitudes from the centre are equal will be equal, and that whose longitude from the centre is greater will be less."

4.44. "There will only be two equal parallel circles on a sphere, but infinite unequal parallel ones. It is necessary that the poles of all parallel circles be the same."

4.45. "It is necessary that the poles of touching circles be different. And the poles of both will be on a single circle passing through the place of contact."

4.46.   "If a circle divides some great circle on a sphere into equal parts, it is necessary that that dividing circle be also among the great circles. If it divides it orthogonally into equal parts, it will be agreed (*conveniet*) that each will pass through the pole of the other."

4.47.   "Every great circle cutting any parallel circles on a sphere and inclined to them divides them all into two unequal portions, except for the great circle parallel to them. And any one of the visible (*apparentium*) portions that are between the great circle among the parallel circles and the manifest pole is greater than a semicircle, but any of them that is between the same great circle and the hidden pole is less than a semicircle. Coalternate portions of parallel equal circles are mutually equal."

4.48.   "When in a sphere two great circles cut each other, if from either of the two points of section for each of them two mutually equal arcs which the point of common section joins be separated out, then it is necessary that the straight lines that join their extremities be equal."

4.49.   "If a great circle on a sphere be inclined to another great circle, and from any quarter of the inclined circle whose beginning is either of the two points of section there be separated out two equal conterminous arcs, then arcs of great circles from the pole of the other [great circle] through the extremities of these two arcs and falling on its [*i.e.* the second great circle's] circumference will cut unequal arcs from that circumference, of which that will be greater which is more remote from their [*i.e.* the first two great circles'] common section."

V. The Objects and Methods of Geometry

V.1. Abstraction and its Problems

The nature and mode of existence of mathematical objects have been a perennial source of philosophical puzzlement. ARISTOTLE, who was the prime authority for medieval discussions of such matters, rejected the PLATONIC belief in a separate realm of mathematical objects, and held instead that the mathematician considered physical objects, but in abstraction from their sensible qualities.[66] In performing constructions the geometer mentally brought to actuality what was only present potentially.[67] Thus both the mental and the physical enter into the analysis of mathematics, and the stage was set for tensions between the freedom of mathematicians' thoughts and the constraints of what the sensible world was taken to be. We have an analogue to the realist-conceptualist tension over the problem of universals. In geometry the realist would concentrate on the external world, while the conceptualist would centre his attention on the mental representations in the *imaginatio*. The realist may have difficulties in adapting his geometry to the physical world, but the conceptualist could not easily find grounding for a mathematical natural science. It is instructive to read BRADWARDINE's *Geometria* with this conflict in mind.

[66] *Cf.* T.L. HEATH, *Mathematics in Aristotle* (Oxford, 1949), 64–67; J. MAYBERRY, "On the Consistency Problem for Set Theory", *British Journal for the Philosophy of Science*, xxviii (1977), 1–34, 137–170, at 20–25.

[67] *Metaph.*, Θ.9, 1051a21–34.

V.2. The Question of Infinite Space

For ARISTOTLE extension was the extension of bodies, and there could be no space without body. Moreover the world was finite, and so there could be no space outside the outermost heaven. On the other hand geometers seemed to operate with an infinite three-dimensional space. How were the two to be reconciled? ARISTOTLE was conscious of the difficulty, and saw it as a prime reason why people believed in the infinite:[68]

> Most of all, a reason which is peculiarly appropriate and presents the difficulty that is felt by everybody — not only number but also mathematical magnitudes and what is outside the heaven are supposed to be infinite because they never give out in our *thought*.

ARISTOTLE made some attempt to separate the mathematical question from the physical, but the principle of plenitude made this solution difficult.

> The size which [a magnitude] can potentially be, it can also actually be. Hence since no sensible magnitude is infinite, it is impossible to exceed every assigned magnitude; for if it were possible there would be something bigger than the heavens.[69]

In order to save mathematics, ARISTOTLE gave the following:[70]

> Our account does not rob the mathematicians of their science, by disproving the actual existence of the infinite in the direction of increase, in the sense of the untraversable. In point of fact they do not need the infinite and do not use it. They postulate only that the finite straight line may be produced as far as they wish. It is possible to have divided in the same ratio as the largest quantity another magnitude of any size you like. Hence, for the purposes of proof, it will make no difference to them to have such an infinite instead, while its existence will be in the sphere of real magnitudes.

This suggestive passage is difficult. For instance, if one can produce a finite straight line as far as one wishes, how far is one allowed to wish? Outside the heaven or not? It seems that the answer should be no, but then as HINTIKKA has pointed out[71] there are difficulties for the EUCLIDEAN postulate of parallels and for the use of constructions in proving theorems. But ARISTOTLE may not have known the postulate of parallels in its EUCLIDEAN form,[72] and perhaps his suggestion of scaling-down in providing proofs could be given a more rigorous form, if it was taken as a postulate that the sum of the angles of a triangle is equal to two right angles.

But, as it happened, geometry was not axiomatised in that way, and so there was a definite tension between the EUCLIDEAN and the ARISTOTELIAN traditions.

---

[68] *Phys.*, III.4, 203b22–24 (Oxford translation).

[69] *Phys.*, III.8, 207b17–21 (Oxford translation). *Cf.* J. HINTIKKA, *Time and Necessity: Studies in Aristotle's Theory of Modality* (Oxford, 1973), 117.

[70] *Phys.*, III.8, 207b27–34 (Oxford translation), but see also *De coelo* I.2, 269a21–24.

[71] HINTIKKA, *op.cit.*, 118–121.

[72] I. TÓTH, "Das Parallelenproblem im Corpus Aristotelicum", *Archive for History of Exact Sciences*, iii (1966–7), 249–422.

PROCLUS spoke of constructions that would obviate the difficulty that there was "no room" in a certain direction,[73] and it seems that HERO of Alexandria was fond of inventing such,[74] although he may have been primarily oriented towards practical problems, where the board (say) was not big enough. Alluding to EUCLID's second postulate ("To produce a finite straight line continuously in a straight line"), SIMPLICIUS said that,[75]

> An opponent may raise an objection on account of the matter (ʿunṣur, materia), saying: I cannot produce a straight line on the surface of the sea, nor can I produce a straight line to infinity since the infinite does not exist.

But he himself held that geometry should be free of such constraints:[76]

> The utility of the first three [postulates] is not to allow the demonstration to be hindered by an incapacity or failing in the matter.

Moreover, SIMPLICIUS (or perhaps his reporter AL-NAYRĪZĪ) associated the reference to infinite production in the EUCLIDEAN definition of parallel lines with the imagination (takhayyul; imaginatio),[77] and thus suggested a conceptualist approach.

The topic was also much discussed in philosophical works, often in commentaries on Text 71 of Book III of the Physics. Here I only give a sample of some medieval views. AVERROES admitted that mathematicians could posit a measure greater than the heavens, but they were not then talking of measure as the bound of a natural body.[78] In the Latin area ALEXANDER NECKHAM had already heard of the problem of constructing an equilateral triangle on the World's diameter, although he thought that ARISTOTLE was a protagonist of an infinite World.[79] ROBERT GROSSESTESTE allowed that the imagination posited an infinite space, but this was not a genuine imagination, for space was nothing other than the three-fold dimensionality of body.[80] HENRY of Ghent blamed the difficulty in understanding that there was nothing outside the heavens (neither plenum nor vacuum) on

---

[73] PROCLUS, In Primum Euclidis Elementorum Librum Commentarii, ed. G. FRIEDLEIN (Leipzig, 1873), 275, 289. PROCLUS, A Commentary on the First Book of Euclid's Elements, tr. G. R. MORROW (Princeton, 1970), has FRIEDLEIN's page numbers in the margins, and I do not cite it separately.

[74] HEATH, Euclid's Elements (n. 57 above), i, 23.

[75] Translation by A.I. SABRA, "Simplicius's Proof of Euclid's Parallel Postulate", Journal of the Warburg and Cortauld Institutes, xxxii (1969), 1–24, at 4, from Codex Leidensis 399, 1. Euclidis Elementa ex interpretatione Al-Hadschdschadschii cum commentariis Al-Narizii, ed. R.O. BESTHORN et al. (Copenhagen, 1893–1932), i, 12–16. Cf. ANARITIUS, In Decem Libros Priores Euclidis Commentarii, ed. M. CURTZE = Euclidis Opera Omnia, ed. J.L. HEIBERG & H. MENGE, Supplementum (Leipzig, 1899), 29–30.

[76] Ibid.

[77] Codex Leidensis…, 10–13; ANARITIUS, 27.

[78] Phys., III, comm. 71, in Opera Aristotelis Stagiritae (Venice, 1560), iv, f. 97v.

[79] ALEXANDER NECKHAM, De naturis rerum Libri Duo. With the Poem of the Same Author, De laudibus divinae sapientiae, ed. T. WRIGHT (London, 1863), 299.

[80] ROBERT GROSSESTESTE, Commentarius in VIII Libros Physicorum Aristotelis, ed. R.C. DALES (Boulder, 1963), 58–59, 147. Cf. A.C. CROMBIE, Robert Grosseteste and the Origins of Experimental Science (2nd imp., Oxford, 1961), 99.

134

excessive reliance on the imaginative faculty.[81] WALTER BURLEY tried to extricate himself from some of the difficulties by a distinction between categorical and hypothetical propositions.[82] All this shows that a genuine problem area was recognised, and I shall propose that this may be used to explain two notable omissions from BRADWARDINE's *Geometria*.

These are the definition of parallel lines and EUCLID's second postulate. In CAMPANUS's version they were given as follows:[83]

> "Equidistant lines are those which are located in the same surface and produced in either direction do not meet, even if they be produced to infinity". "To produce a finite line continuously in a straight line so far as is wished."

Since BRADWARDINE was following CAMPANUS closely in the relevent parts of his work, I think that we may dismiss the hypothesis of carelessness. J.E. MURDOCH[84] noted BRADWARDINE's omission of the production postulate from the *Geometria* when discussing his proof in the *De continuo* of the infinite divisibility of the straight line. MURDOCH saw the trouble as lying in CAMPANUS's introduction of the word *quantumlibet* (so far as is wished), which had no equivalent in the EUCLIDEAN original, and suggested that BRADWARDINE thought that this would lead into a *petitio principii* in his arguments. This is ingenious, but I think too sophisticated in the context of the *Geometria*. Moreover, it is not clear that *quantumlibet* should imply completely indeterminate extendibility rather than extension by a given magnitude, meaning one that already exists in the configuration.[85] A more promising line is presented when we note that the omitted definition and postulate were often cited in discussions of the relation of geometry to a finite world, and that BRADWARDINE himself was explicitly concerned with the problem in later works. We may then argue that the omissions were dictated by a realist view of geometry, and that later the same concern led BRADWARDINE towards an idea of infinite space.

In his *De continuo* BRADWARDINE made a distinction between what was impossible *per se* and what was only *de facto* impossible, which

> by some impediment or other accidental cause could not be according to the course of nature,

---

[81] HENRY of Ghent, *Quodl. II, quest. 9*, in *Quodlibeta Magistri Henrici Goethals a Gandavo* (Paris, 1518), f. 36r. *Cf.* A.G. MOLLAND, "The Geometrical Background to the 'Merton School'", *British Journal for the History of Science*, iv (1968–9), 108–125, at 113.

[82] WALTER BURLEY, *In Physicam Aristotelis Expositio et Quaestiones* (Venice, 1501; repr. Hildesheim, 1972), ff. 85v–86r.

[83] I Def. 22: "Equidistantes linee sunt que in eadem superficie collocate atque in alterutram partem protracte non conueniunt, etiam si in infinitum protrahantur." I, 2nd part of Postulate 1: "Lineam definitam in continuum rectumque quantumlibet protrahere."

[84] MURDOCH, *Geometry and the Continuum* (n. 7 above), 147.

[85] *Cf.* the first definition of the medieval version of EUCLID's *Data* as given in S. ITO, *The Medieval Latin Translation of the Data of Euclid* (Ph.D. thesis, Univ. of Wisconsin, 1963), 61: "Data magnitudine dicuntur et spatia et linee et anguli quibus possumus equalia assignare." Also the ADELARD III version of EUCLID as quoted in M. CLAGETT, "The Medieval Latin Translations from the Arabic of the *Elements* of Euclid, with Special Emphasis on the Versions of Adelard of Bath", *Isis*, xliv (1953), 16–42, at 36: "Data dicunter quibus equalia habitudanter invenire possumus."

and he revealed an awareness that EUCLID's third postulate ("On any centre and occupying any amount (*quantumlibet*) of space to describe a circle") could also be incompatible with a finite world.[86]

> *De facto* no body can be more subtle than fire, nor can a circle be greater than the greatest of the celestial circles, but these things are not impossible *per se*, as is manifest to any intellect ... And Euclid supposes the opposite of the second in the proof of the first conclusion of the first book of his geometry, as is clear enough if someone should wish to set up an equilateral triangle on the diameter of the world.

In the *De causa Dei* the same theme is resumed with a more theological emphasis.[87]

> Because of this infinite strength and power of God and in respect of himself, together with those things touched on above concerning power, I judge to be true what the geometers suppose, that a straight line can be produced continuously in a straight line so far as is wished and a circle can be described on any centre occupying any amount of space, as is clear from the first book of Euclid's *Elements*, and [what] the natural philosophers [suppose] that a medium may be rarefied as much as is wished, and similar things, and universally anything which according to the logicians or any others is said to be possible *per se* and absolutely, namely what does not *per se* formally include a contradiction, although it be not possible by nature, that is by natural power.

In this way the postulates of geometry receive theological justification, but BRADWARDINE's realist view of geometry also led him to take the ontological consequences seriously. This is particularly clear in a passage of the *De causa Dei* to which A. KOYRÉ has drawn attention.[88] As a consequence of the immutability of God, BRADWARDINE maintained that,[89]

---

[86] MURDOCH, *Geometry and the Continuum* (n. 7 above), 464–465: "Aliquod est impossibile per se, quod per se, vel immediate, vel in consequentia bona, contradictionem includit ... Et aliquod est impossibile per actum, sive de facto, et est quod per aliquod impedimentum per aliam causam accidentalem secundum cursum nature esse non potest. Tamen per se non repugnat illud esse. Sicud de facto nullum corpus potest esse subtilius igne, nec aliquis circulus potest esse maior maximo celestium circulorum, illa tamen non sunt impossibilia per se, sicud est omni intellectui manifestum ... Et Euclides supponit oppositum secundi in probatione prime conclusionis primo libro geometrie sue, sicud satis patet si quis voluerit super dyametrum mundi triangulum collocare equelaterum."

[87] BRADWARDINE, *De causa Dei* (n. 5 above), 4: "Secundum hanc autem Dei virtutem et potentiam infinitam, et respectu ipsius iuxta praetacta superius de potentia existimo verum esse, quod Geometrae supponunt lineam rectam posse quantumlibet pertrahi in continuum et directum, et super centrum quodcumque spatium quantumlibet occupando circulum designare, ut patet primo Elementorum Euclidis: et Philosophi naturales medium posse quantumlibet subtiliari et similia: et universaliter omne illud quod apud Logicos, seu quoslibet alios dicitur per se et absolute possibile, quod scilicet per se contradictionem formaliter non includit, licet non sit possibile per naturam, per potentiam scilicet naturalem."

[88] A. KOYRÉ, "Le Vide et l'Espace Infini au XIVe Siècle", *Archives d'Histoire Doctrinale et Litteraire du Moyen Age*, xvii (1949), 45–91, reprinted in A. KOYRÉ, *Etudes d'Histoire de la Pensée Philosophique* (Paris, 1971), 37–92, at 79–92.

[89] BRADWARDINE, *De causa Dei*, 177: "Quod Deus essentialiter et praesentialiter necessario est ubique, nedum in mundo et in eius partibus universis, verumetiam extra mundum in situ seu vacuo imaginario infinito."

God necessarily is essentially and immediately everywhere, not only in the world and all its parts, but also outside the world in the imaginable (*imaginario*) infinite *situs*[90] or vacuum.

God is clearly everywhere in the world. If the *situs* of the world is now A and B is a *situs* outside the world, God could move the world from A to B. He would then be in B, but if he were not in B before, he would have moved, which is absurd. Therefore God is everywhere inside and outside the world, and for Bradwardine this was a sign of infinite perfection.[91] In this we come near to NEWTON's position, in which God by his omnipresence constituted absolute space.[92] In both cases the world was made safe for EUCLIDEAN geometry.

V.3. Geometrical Exactness

We now turn to the problem of geometrical exactness, which since Antiquity had provided a focus for attacks upon the subject. ARISTOTLE raised the issue in *Metaphysics* B.2:[93]

On the other hand astronomy cannot be dealing with perceptible magnitudes nor with this heaven above us. For neither are perceptible lines such lines as the geometer speaks of (for no perceptible thing is straight or round in the way in which he defines 'straight' and 'round'; for a hoop touches a straight edge not at a point, but as Protagoras used to say it did, in his refutation of the geometers), nor are the movements and spiral orbits in the heavens like those of which astronomy treats, nor have geometrical points the same nature as the actual stars.

Elsewhere ARISTOTLE pointed out that the geometer does not speak of his diagram but of what is understood by it.[94] ARISTOTLE rejected the substantial existence of mathematicals, whether separate or in perceptible things (the statue of HERMES is only potentially in the block of marble[95]), but he achieved no satisfactory solution

---

[90] The medieval use of the concept of *situs* demands further study. The term was often used interchangeably with *positio*, despite the obscure distinction that ARISTOTLE tried to draw in *Cat.* 7, 6b11–15. Two traditions are evident. It was an ARISTOTELIAN category (about which ARISTOTLE said little) and referred to the ordering of the parts of an object; paradigm examples of predication in this category were saying that someone was lying or standing or sitting. But in other usages *situs* referred to the position of an object with respect to another or others, and this was probably connected with the description of a point as unity having position or *situs*: see *e.g. De anima* I.4, 409a4–6; *Metaph. Δ*.6, 1016b25–27; ANARITIUS, *op. cit.* (n. 75 above), 1. The concept was often applied in discussions arising from difficulties in the ARISTOTELIAN doctrine of place. For an example see JOHN BURIDAN, *Super octo phisicorum libros Aristotelis*, IV, q. 6 (Paris, 1509; repr. Frankfurt, 1964), f. 72v; *cf.* A. MAIER, *Metaphysische Hintergründe der Spätscholastischen Naturphilosophie* (Rome, 1955), 348–350.

[91] BRADWARDINE, *De causa Dei*, 180.

[92] I. NEWTON, *Mathematical Principles of Natural Philosophy*, tr. A. MOTTE, rev. F. CAJORI (5th edn, Berkeley & Los Angeles, 1962), 761; *Unpublished Scientific Papers of Isaac Newton*, ed. and tr. A.R. HALL & M.B. HALL (Cambridge, 1962), 99–105.

[93] 997b34–998a6 (Oxford translation).

[94] *An. Post.*, I.10, 76b40–77a3; *cf. An.Pr.*, I.41, 49b33–37.

[95] *Metaph.*, B5, 1001b15–25; *Δ*.7, 1017b6–9; *Θ*.6, 1048a31–35.

of his own. If mathematical objects only differ from sensible objects in the mode of conceiving, and if the abstractive process is only a stripping away of sensible qualities, it is hard to see how exactness arises,[96] and there is again room for realist-conceptualist tension. In the seventeenth century this may be exemplified by ISAAC BARROW's attack on BLANCANUS and VOSSIUS for denying the extramental existence of mathematical objects.[97] In BARROW's view they did exist *actu* in outside objects, although not furnished to the senses. And indeed the statue of CAESAR was hidden away in the rude block of marble.

In the Middle Ages one way in which to tackle this and similar difficulties was to distinguish between natural and mathematical bodies, or between what was true *in re* and what was true *secundum imaginationem mathematicorum*. ARISTOTELIAN references to intelligible matter could give some authority for this. But to those with a more realist conception this was not very satisfactory, for it seemed to refuse mathematics any strong purchase on the world. Thus ROGER BACON looked to astronomical and optical phenomena to provide a grounding for geometry.[98]

On account of the irregularity or tortuosity or difformity of corporeal matter in these inferior things the first [postulate of EUCLID] cannot be realised in practice by man, or scarcely and with great difficulty. But it is possible for operative nature, as in the multiplication of virtue and species in the things of the world, as in the diffusion of light and rays, which [diffusion] is made multiplicatively along straight lines in a single body, and also the [rays] perpendicular to the first bodies [*sc.* the elemental spheres] are straight. The geometer therefore considers the possible paths of nature, because it was for the sake of making known the works of nature that geometry was first and essentially constituted, and after that for the sake of human works. For the writers on perspective show us that lines and figures reveal to us the whole operation of nature, its principles and effects. And similarly it is clear by celestial matters, which both natural philosophy and astronomy consider. The geometer therefore does not attend to tortuous sensible matter, but he understands regular nature, as in celestial things, and as nature knows how to

---

[96] *Cf.* O. BECKER, *Mathematische Existenz* (Halle, 1927), 246.

[97] *The Mathematical Works of Isaac Barrow*, ed. W. WHEWELL (Cambridge, 1860), 84–85.

[98] MS Oxford, Bodl., Digby 76, f. 78ar: "Datis diffinitionibus subiunguntur peticiones et prima propter irregularitatem seu tortuositatem vel difformitatem materie corporalis in hiis inferioribus non potest ad opus reduci per hominem aut vix et cum magna difficultate. Possibile tamen est nature operanti ut in multiplicatione virtutis et speciei in rebus mundi, ut in diffusione lucis et radiorum, que multiplicius fit per lineas rectas in corpore uno, et etiam perpendiculares super prima corpora fiunt recta. Geometer igitur considerat vias possibiles nature, quia propter opera nature certificanda constituta est (*ex* in MS) geometria primo et per se, deinde propter opera humana. Auctores enim perspective nobis ostendunt quod linee et figure declarant nobis totam operationem nature, et principia et effectus. Et similiter patet per celestia de quibus naturalis et astronomia communicant. Geometer igitur non curat de materia sensibili tortuosa sed intelligit naturam regularem sicut in celestibus et sicut in hiis inferioribus natura scit invenire in suis operationibus, et vias nature imitatur. Et sic non erit in imaginatione linearum rectarum ut Aristoteles dicit in Posterioribus quod geometer non loquitur de linea sensibili sed de ea que per eam intelligitur."

find it in these inferior things, and he imitates the ways of nature. And so it will not be by the imagination of straight lines as Aristotle says in the *Posterior Analytics* that the geometer does not speak of the sensible line but of that which is understood by it.

BRADWARDINE's faith in the power of mathematics rivalled BACON's, and we should expect him to be uneasy about solving the problem of exactness by dividing between natural bodies and mathematical bodies. But neither does he show any sign of a BACONIAN grounding of mathematics in optics and astronomy. In fact he does not seem concerned by the problem at all. When discussing the five regular solids, BRADWARDINE drew on the elegant EUCLIDEAN proof that there cannot be more than five, but he did not tangle with EUCLID's complicated treatment of their existence. Instead there are hints that this was a matter for empirical verification, and BRADWARDINE repeatedly refers to the making (*fabricatio*) of such bodies.[99] Again, in his chapter on the sphere, he asserted (erroneously) that thirteen equal spheres could be arranged so that one is in the centre and is touched by each of the remaining spheres, while each of these latter, besides touching the central sphere, also touches four of its fellows. For justification he appeals to an experiment with spheres made of wax.[100] He must have recognised the problem of exactness, but he did not regard it as a serious barrier between mathematics and the physical world.

V.4. Construction

From the time of PLATO the role of construction in geometry had caused problems.[101] In the *Republic* SOCRATES was made to complain that the geometers of his day misleadingly spoke as if they were doing something, such as squaring or applying or adding, whereas in fact they were considering eternal and unchangeable objects.[102] Some PLATONISTS evaded the difficulty by saying that the movements were movements of the understanding in which eternal things were regarded as if they came to be.[103] It followed that, strictly speaking, all geometrical propositions were theorems rather than problems. Even if the enunciations seemed to demand that something be done, what was at issue was knowledge not action,

---

[99] "Et ex hiis sequitur via clara ad fabricandum talia corpora" (4.24). "Si igitur tres anguli quadratorum concurrant ad angulum solidum constituendum, tunc in corpore constituto erunt 6 superficies quadrate, sicud in taxillo" (4.25). "Et tunc in isto corpore erunt 12 superficies pentagone, sicud patet in fabricatione talis corporis" (4.26). "Sic ergo in hoc precedenti capitulo investigavimus breviter numerum et dispositiones corporum regularium per evidentiam demonstrationum, et patet nobis via ad fabricandum talia corpora satis clare" (4.27).

[100] "Et sensus hoc indicat, nam, cum fecerimus 13 sperulas equales de cera, videmus quod 12 sic possunt applicari circa tertiam decimam quod quelibet tangit eam inferius, et, cum hoc, quatuor de speris lateralibus ..." (4.42).

[101] On construction in Greek geometry see E. NIEBEL, *Untersuchungen über die Bedeutung der geometrischen Konstruktion in der Antike*, Kantstudien Ergänzungshefte, lxxvi (Cologne, 1959), and A.G. MOLLAND, "Shifting the Foundations: Descartes's Transformation of Ancient Geometry", *Historia Mathematica*, iii (1976), 21–49.

[102] *Republic*, VII.9, 526C–527B.

[103] PROCLUS, *In Primum Euclidis*... (n. 73 above), 77–78.

and there was no real generation among geometrical objects. ARISTOTLE needed a different interpretation. In the process of construction, potentially existing lines *etc.* were brought to actuality by means of the thought of the geometer, which was itself an actuality,[104] but for those with a realist view, this may have seemed uncomfortably subjectivist.

In EUCLID's *Elements* construction plays a central role. The first three postulates lay down conditions for the constructibility (or, in some sense, the existence) of straight lines and circles. Many of the propositions have the form of problems, in which the end result is to be a particular construction. Moreover, for the proofs of most theorems constructions are necessary. PROCLUS said that EUCLID was a PLATONIST,[105] but the austere character of the *Elements* means that no clear indication of his philosophical position emerges from it. The way was open for divergence of interpretation, but not for all the liberties that BRADWARDINE took. One liberty that he did not take was to introduce references to compasses into theoretical geometry. Such a reference had been intruded into the very first proposition of the *Elements* in translations by ADELARD of Bath and HERMANN of Carinthia,[106] and may have originated in the Arabic tradition. It was included in the CAMPANUS version, but BRADWARDINE was more faithful to the division between theoretical and practical geometry that he expounded in his introduction.

BRADWARDINE based his account of the postulates on EUCLID, although, as we have noted, he omitted the production postulate. This raises the question of how he managed to proceed without it. We may also be suspicious of how within five propositions BRADWARDINE has reached the equivalent of the thirty-second proposition of EUCLID. Certainly his general standards of rigour are lower than EUCLID's, but in the early propositions they are not too bad. His path was principally eased by his omission of any proofs of existence for the lines that he used in his constructions. Thus (1.11) he tacitly assumed that, given a straight line and a point on it, we can without further ado speak of the perpendicular to the line at the point. To construct such a perpendicular was the burden of EUCLID I.11. Similarly (1.14), given a straight line and a point not on it, BRADWARDINE immediately demanded that a parallel to the line be drawn (*protrahatur*) through the point. EUCLID's I.31 was the problem of constructing such a parallel. CAMPANUS had explicitly referred to the EUCLIDEAN propositions in the relevant places (I.13, I.32), and so BRADWARDINE's procedure was probably conscious. His principal motivation may have been pedagogical simplicity, but there are other signs of a general uneasiness with constructions.

This may be seen in his treatment of the first proposition of EUCLID ("On a given straight line to set up an equilateral triangle"). This no longer has first place in BRADWARDINE's work, but something like it occurs in 2.16 in the course of a rather unsatisfactory section on triangles in relation to circles:[107]

---

[104] *Metaph.*, *Θ.9*, 1051a21–34.

[105] PROCLUS, *ed. cit.*, 68.

[106] CLAGETT, "The Medieval Latin Translations" (n. 85 above), 31, 36–37, 39; H.L.L. BUSARD, *The Translation of the Elements of Euclid from the Arabic into Latin by Hermann of Carinthia (?)*, reprinted from *Janus* liv (1967) (Leiden, 1968), 12, cf. 13, 18.

[107] "Omnis trianguli cuius unum latus est semidyameter duorum circulorum et angulus oppositus est apud sectionem eorundem est equilaterus."

Every triangle, of which one side is a radius of two circles and the opposite angle is at their section, is equilateral.

This alludes to the construction used in EUCLID I.1, but the formulation is theorematic rather than problematic. Another reference to EUCLID I.1 occurs in BRADWARDINE's Introduction:[108]

Theoretical [geometry] investigates the properties of magnitudes by reason and syllogism, as for instance we conclude that every straight line is fit to be the base of an equilateral triangle, by the definition of a circle and by this premise, that it befalls every straight line to be the radius of two circles.

Once again we have the transposition to the theorematic form. Only two of BRADWARDINE's propositions (2.25, 2.311) are explicitly formulated as problems, and only once in the work does he appeal to a postulate asserting constructibility of a straight line or a circle. This is in 2.306 where BRADWARDINE wishes to show that any rectilinear angle may be divided by a straight line. The sequel is to prove that this does not hold in the case of horn angles, and so we take the citation of the postulate as a desire to make doubly sure what he would normally have regarded as evident enough to pass without remark. BRADWARDINE may not have been very clear about his ontological position in geometry, but we may suggest that he was suspicious of the conceptualist and subjectivist overtones in talk of construction, and avoided it as much as possible.

V.5. Priority and Perfection

Questions of priority and of perfection arose naturally for BRADWARDINE in geometry, and these were not simply a matter of correct deductive order or elegance of demonstration. There was, for instance, the question of geometry's relation to arithmetic. Both ARISTOTLE and BOETHIUS had held that the latter was prior to the former. In the *Posterior analytics* ARISTOTLE explicated the priority in terms of an "additional posit" ($\pi\rho o\sigma\theta\acute{\varepsilon}\sigma\iota\varsigma$, *appositio*): a unit was a substance without position whereas a point was substance having position.[109] Interestingly enough AQUINAS[110] held that ARISTOTLE was here adapting his exposition to the opinion of PLATO whereby the one caused all numbers, and the point, by a succession of motions, caused all continuous quantities. Nevertheless the passage could be adjusted to ARISTOTLE's own opinion in terms of increasing degrees of abstraction. In his comment on the same passage ROBERT GROSSETESTE had introduced an emanationist ring by speaking in terms of the replication of essences to produce numbers and extension, in which indivisibles were in a sense begetting them-

---

[108] "Theorica quidem passiones magnitudinum investigat ratione et syllogismo, quemadmodum concludimus quod omnis recta linea nata est esse basis trianguli equilateri, per diffinitionem circuli et per hoc assumptum, quod omnem lineam rectam contingit esse semidyametrum duorum circulorum" (1.00).

[109] *An. Post.*, I.27, 87a31–37.

[110] THOMAS AQUINAS, *In Post. An.*, lect. 41, in *Opera omnia iussa impensaque Leonis XIII P.M. edita* (Rome, 1882–   ), i, 304–305.

selves.[111] BOETHIUS's account of arithmetic's priority also suggested themes of ontological dependence. Not only had arithmetic provided the exemplar for the Creation of the World, but it was prior to geometry in the way that the genus was prior to the species. If you destroy animal man too perishes, but man may be removed without the abolition of the nature of animal. Moreover, in speaking of man one is implicitly speaking of animal, but not conversely.

> The same is seen to occur in geometry or arithmetic. For if you remove numbers, whence triangle or square (*quadratum*) or whatever is considered in geometry, which are all denominatives of number. But if you remove square and triangle and all geometry be consumed, three and four and the names of other numbers will not perish. Again when I speak of any geometric form, a name of numbers is immediately bound up with it; when I speak of numbers I do not yet name any geometric form.[112]

In the *Geometria* BRADWARDINE does not say much explicitly on this question:[113]

> Geometry is in some way subsequent to arithmetic, for it is of a posterior order, and the properties of numbers play a role in magnitudes. ...

On the other hand his *De continuo* displays an enthusiasm for the BOETHIAN position.[114]

> Mathematics has many parts, of which the first is arithmetic, as is definitively proved in the first book of Boethius's *Arithmetica*, and this is what was said in the prologue of this conclusion, that she is the mother of all mathematics.

Besides these explicit statements, there are other signs that BRADWARDINE's geometry would be well adapted to a quasi-emanationist view of mathematics, and there are even temptations to seek comparisons with GROSSETESTE's cosmogony of light. The dependence on arithmetic would be strengthened if BRADWARDINE did indeed believe that all geometrical ratios were susceptible of numerical denomination.[115] Other signs are in his concern for arranging figures (notably the

---

[111] ROBERT GROSSETESTE, *In Aristotelis Posteriorum Analyticorum Libros* (Venice, 1514; repr. Frankfurt, 1966), f. 22v.

[112] BOETHIUS, *De institutione arithmetica*, I.1, ed. G. FRIEDLEIN (Leipzig, 1867; repr. Frankfurt, 1966), 10–11: "Hoc idem in geometria vel arithmetica videtur incurrere. Si enim numeros tollas, unde triangulum vel quadratum vel quicquid in geometria versatur, quae omnia numerorum denominativa sunt? At vero si quadratum triangulumque sustuleris omnisque geometria consumpta sit, tres et quattuor aliorumque numerorum vocabula non peribunt. Rursus cum aliquam geometricam formam dixero, est illi simul numerorum nomen implicitum; cum numeros dixero, nondum ullam formam geometricam nominavi."

[113] "Geometria assecutiva est arismetrice quodammodo, nam, et posterioris ordinis est, et passiones numerorum in magnitudinibus deserviunt " (1.00).

[114] MURDOCH, *Geometry and the Continuum* (n. 10 above), 401: "Mathematica autem multas habet partes, quarum prima est arismetica, ut primo *Arismetice* Boetii diffinitive probatur; et hoc est quod dicitur in prologo huius conclusionis, quod ipsa est mater totius mathematice."

[115] See Section VI.2 below.

star-polygons[116]) in numerical orders and in his penchant (in contrast to EUCLID-CAMPANUS) for presenting his definitions in a PORPHYRIAN tree. Let us, for instance, look at the early definitions in the first part of the work:[117]

> A point therefore I call the principle of magnitude. Of magnitudes: that which has one dimension is called a line, that which has two a surface, that which has three a body. Body is the most perfect of quantity, because after the third there is not a fourth dimension. I call a figure a magnitude that is bounded linearly or superficially. Therefore every figure is plane or solid. And lines bound plane figures, but surfaces solid ones. Every solid figure is round and without angle, or conical and angular ...

There are precedents for the particular divergences from EUCLID-CAMPANUS. Thus in the geometries ascribed to BOETHIUS the point is the principle of measure (*principium mensurae*),[118] and ANARITIUS reports that SIMPLICIUS and "Herundes" held that the point was the principle of quantity (*principium quantitatis*).[119] BRADWARDINE's references to dimensions are reminiscent of the passage where ARISTOTLE gave a numerological argument for there only being three dimensions.[120] But, as so often with definitions by *genus* and *differentiae*, the whole arrangement may suggest a procession from the point to magnitude and then by successive differentiation to the totality of geometric figures. Number is frequently present to determine the differentiation. An apparent oddity is that the point seems to have the position of the *summum genus*, but this feature enhances the image when we note that PORPHYRY gave as one of the meanings of *genus* the principle of generation, as ROMULUS was *genus* for the Romans.[121]

Although he may appear to speak differently in the *Posterior Analytics*, in *Metaphysics* M ARISTOTLE insists (against ARISTIPPUS and others) that mathematics is concerned with the good and the beautiful.[122] M and N were not included in all medieval versions of the *Metaphysics*,[123] but in his *De causa Dei* BRADWARDINE latched on to this passage to justify mathematical arguments about perfection.[124] In the *Geometria* such arguments are particularly apparent in the case of the circle and the sphere.[125]

---

[116] See Section VII.1 below.

[117] "Punctum igitur voco magnitudinis principium. Magnitudinum: que quidem unam habet dimensionem linea, que vero duas superficies, que vero 3 corpus dicitur. Est autem corpus perfectius omni quantitate, quoniam post tertiam non est quarta dimensio. Figuram voco magnitudinem determinatam linealiter aut superficialiter. Igitur omnis figura est plana aut solida. Et planas quidem terminant linee, solidas vero superficies. Omnis autem figura solida: aut est rotunda et sine angulo; aut conica et angularis" (1.01).

[118] M. FOLKERTS, "*Boethius*" *Geometrie II. Ein mathematisches Lehrbuch des Mittelalters* (Wiesbaden, 1970), 113, 176.

[119] ANARITIUS, *In Decem Libros* (n. 75 above), 1, 3.

[120] *De coelo*, I.1, 268a6–b5.

[121] *Aristoteles Latinus*, ed. L. MINIO-PALUELLO (Bruges & Paris, 1953–   ), I.6–7, p. 6; *cf.* PETER of Spain, *Tractatus*, ed. L.M. de Rijk (Assen, 1972), 17.

[122] *Metaph.*, M3, 1078a31-b5; *cf. An. Post.*, I.7, 75b17–20.

[123] G. LACOMBE, *Aristoteles Latinus*, i (2nd ed., Bruges & Paris, 1957), 61–66.

[124] BRADWARDINE, *De causa Dei* (n. 5 above), 120.

[125] "Sed ut conditiones eius saltem laudabiles commemorem, ipsa figurarum prima et

"[The circle] is the first and most perfect of figures, the simplest and most regular, the most capacious and the most beautiful of figures, and if you wish to add what concerns purely the physicists, it is the most apt for motion."

"Now, after the treatment of regular polygonal bodies, something must briefly be mentioned about the sphere, which is the regular figure *simpliciter* and uniform at the summit of uniformity, mobile and perfect."

In the case of the circle BRADWARDINE includes three conclusions that are explicitly designed to attest to its perfection.[126]

"To find the centre of a circle by two cruciform sections." "Six radii cutting the whole circumference constitute a regular hexagon inside the circle." "Six equal circles touch an equal circle on the outside."

We should probably see a religious allusion in the use of the word *cruciformes* in the first of these propositions, but the main burden was to link the perfection of the circle to the perfection of the number six:[127]

In all these three conclusion Six[128] attests to the perfection of the circle. For in the first we have Six of points which are the extremities of three lines, in the second Six of lines, in the third Six of circles.

The question of perfection also linked itself to the order of treatment. After his panegyric on the circle BRADWARDINE continued:[129]

On that account it seemed to me that the circle should be treated before rectilinear figures, but I found that many things about it could only be shown from conclusions about rectilinear figures. And so it was necessary to invert the order, as Euclid is found to have done.

---

perfectissima, ipsa simplicissima et regularissima, ipsa capacissima et figurarum pulcherrima, et, si velis addere quod pure ad phyisicos pertinet, ipsa est ad motum aptissima" (2.30). "Nunc post tractatum de corporibus regularibus poligoniis tangendum est aliquid breviter de spera, que est figura regularis simpliciter et uniformis in fine uniformitatis, mobilis et perfecta" (4.40).

[126] "Centrum circuli per duas sectiones cruciformes invenire" (2.311). "Sex semidyametri abscindentes totam circumferentiam exagonum regularem infra circulum constituunt" (2.312). "Sex circuli equales circulum equalem extra contingunt" (2.313).

[127] "Et in omnibus istis tribus conclusionibus attestatur senarius perfectionem circuli. Nam in prima habemus senarium punctorum, qui sunt extremitates trium linearum, in secunda senarium linearum, in tertia senarium circulorum" (2.313). MS Milan, Bibl. Ambros., R47 sup., f. 121r has a note entitled, "Qualiter numerus senarius convenit circulis". There is some correspondence to BRADWARDINE's third conclusion, but no reason for supposing influence in either direction.

[128] In translating numerical terms I use capital letters to distinguish the noun forms *binarius, ternarius, quaternarius* ... from the adjectival forms *duo, tres, quattuor* ...

[129] "Propter quod videbatur mihi quod prius de circulo quam de rectilineis esset agendum, sed inveni quod de eo multa ostendi non possunt nisi ex conslusionibus rectilinearum. Ideo necesse fuit preposterare ordinem, quemadmodum Euclides fecisse invenitur" (2.30).

I

144

Earlier PROCLUS had spoken in terms of a movement from the sensible to the intelligible,[130] and ANARITIUS had said that, whereas round figures were more precious (cariores), rectilinear ones were better known. The inverted order accommodated the sphere naturally, for although EUCLID had ended his treatise with the regular solids BRADWARDINE added a (somewhat pedestrian) chapter on the most perfect figure of all.

V.6. Interrelations of Geometrical Objects

Virtually nothing can be asserted of the simple geometrical objects considered in themselves, for if we are given just one straight line, we can only say of it what could be said of any other singly given straight line; and the same applies to circles. Geometrical knowledge comes from considering various elements linked together in a configuration. BRADWARDINE showed a clear consciousness of this when he wrote:[131]

The properties (passiones) that we demonstrate about magnitudes are almost all relative, as equality, inequality, regularity, irregularity, commensurability, incommensurability, same and different.

At this stage BRADWARDINE avoids the ontological issue:

[The question] whether such properties be things distinct from the subjects, about which there are wont to be disputes, belongs to another branch of study (facultatem).[132]

But later he does indicate how an argument could be made for the distinct existence of relations[133] and he seems sympathetic to this realist view.

Another point where there could be nominalist-realist tension was over the distinction between a whole and its parts. Among the arguments that OCKHAM attributed to proponents of the distinct existence of relations was the following:[134]

When the parts composing some whole are separated the parts remain, but the union does not; therefore, the union is something different from the parts.

WALTER BURLEY held that the whole was distinguished from its parts by its unity,[135] whereas JOHN BURIDAN (with appropriate logical qualifications) answered in the affirmative the question,

Whether the whole is its parts.[136]

---

[130] PROCLUS, In Primum Euclidis ... (n. 73 above), 82; ANARITUS, In Decem Libros ... (n. 75 above), 19.

[131] "Passiones quas de magnitudinibus demonstramus sunt pene omnes relative, ut equalitas, inequalitas, regularitas, irregularitas, commensurabilitas, incommensurabilitas, idem et diversum. Utrem autem tales passiones sint res distincte a subiectis, de quo solent fieri altercationes, ad aliam facultatem pertinent" (1.00).

[132] Cf., for instance, WILLIAM of Ockham, Summa logicae, I. 49–54, trans. M. J. LOUX, Ockham's Theory of Terms. Part I of the Summa Logicae (Notre Dame & London, 1974), 158–177.

[133] 3.33. See Section VI.2 below.

[134] Summ.log., I.54, tr. Loux, 177.

[135] BURLEY, In Physicam (n. 82 above), f. 16v.

[136] BURIDAN, Super octo phisicorum libros, I.q. 9, ed.cit. (n. 90 above), ff. 11v–12v.

It is probably in the context of discussions such as these that we should see BRADWARDINE's inclusion of a non-EUCLIDEAN common notion. In addition to the familiar "Every whole is greater than any part of it", (1.032) he has, "Every whole is equal to all its parts taken together, and conversely."[137] (He comments that in both cases the term "whole" is to be taken categorematically rather than syncategorematically: this was to prevent what was asserted of each several part being asserted of the whole.[138]) But we should be careful not to infer from this any commitment on BRADWARDINE's part to wider controversies about the whole and its parts, for the relation he is invoking is equality, which was proper to quantities, whereas identity was appropriate to substances and similarity to qualities.[139] BRADWARDINE's addition of the axiom is not simply window-dressing, for he actually uses it, and refers to it twice in his very first proposition. In both cases the concern was with angles, and it is significant that there had been controversy as to which category these belonged to, whether to quantity or quality or relation.[140] EUCLID had clearly treated them quantitatively, and BRADWARDINE's use of the axiom helps to shore up this view. An objection against their being *quanta* was that,

> When a quantity is doubled it remains a quantity, but when a right angle is doubled it does not remain an angle: therefore an angle is not a quantity.[141]

One of BRADWARDINE's uses of his axiom was to establish that

> the whole space (*spatium*) that in any plane surface surrounds any point is equal to four right angles.

The axiom made more plausible the assertion (found also in CAMPANUS I.13) that a space could be equated with angles.

V.7. Geometrical Argumentation

Like EUCLID, BRADWARDINE divided his first principles into three classes:[142]

> I suppose therefore the principles of demonstration. I call definitions and immediate propositions principles of demonstration, because immediate

---

[137] "Omne totum equum est omnibus suis partibus simul sumptis et econtraria" (1.031). HEATH, *Euclid's Elements* (n. 57 above), i, 232, notes the inclusion of the axiom by CLAVIUS. In his *Liber embadorum* SAVASORDA had, "Omnis vero res suis collectis partibus equalis est"; M. CURTZE, *Urkunden zur Geschichte der Mathematik im Mittelalter und der Renaissance*, Abhandlungen zur Geschichte der Mathematischen Wissenschaften, xii (1902), xiii (1903) (repr. New York & London, 1968), 16.

[138] *Cf.* WALTER BURLEY, *De puritate artis logicae, with a Revised Edition of the Tractatus Brevior*, ed. P. BOEHNER (St. Bonaventure, N.Y., 1955), 256.

[139] *Cat.*, 6, 6a26–35; *Metaph.*, Δ.15, 1021a10–14.

[140] HEATH, *Euclid's Elements* (n. 57 above), i. 177–178; ANARITIUS, *In Decem Libros* (n. 75 above); B. GEYER, "Die mathematischen Schriften des Albertus Magnus", *Angelicum*, xxxv (1958), 159–175.

[141] ANARITIUS, 12; cf. Geyer, *op.cit.*, 174.

[142] "Suppono igitur principia demonstrationis. Voco autem principia demonstrationis diffinitiones et propositiones immediatas, quoniam propositiones immediate non habent se priores ex quibus demonstrentur. Talia enim presupponi habent in qualibet scientia.

propositions do not have [others] prior to them from which they are demonstrated; such have to be presupposed in any science. Of this kind of principle one [sort] is called a dignity or maximal proposition, and to this genus of principles are reduced the immediate propositions that in geometry are called common notions or common conceptions of the mind; the other is what is called by Aristotle a posit. One genus of posit is a complex principle, and is called by Aristotle supposition, and in geometry postulate; the other is only a term (*extremum*) of a proposition and is called by Aristotle and in geometry definition.

The ARISTOTELIAN terminology shows some variation,[143] but BRADWARDINE's reference is almost certainly to *Analytica posteriora* I.2, and probably to the *versio communis* of JAMES of Venice.[144] There a somewhat obscure distinction is made between "dignities" and posits, but BRADWARDINE's general comments do not show how he regarded the division. At the end of his list of postulates he writes:[145]

Propositions or *dicta* of this kind are called suppositions or postulates, because they are supposed and postulated and not proved, for they seem to have sufficient evidence from only the confused conception of terms.

After the common notions we have the following:[146]

These therefore and similar are called first and immediate propositions, because they are known immediately from a confused conception of terms without argument, or if with argument, then argument of this kind is not very perceptible, and so they are taken as if they were first propositions. And on that account Alhazen in the second book of the *Perspectiva*[147] said of the

---

Huiusmodi autem principii: quoddam vocatur dignitas vel maxima propositio, et ad hoc genus principiorum reducuntur propositiones immediate que in geometria dicuntur communes scientie vel communes anime conceptiones; aliud est quod vocatur ab Aristotele positio. Positionis autem: quoddam genus est principium complexum, et vocatur ab Aristotele suppositio, in geometria petitio; aliud est tantum extremum propositionis, et vocatur ab Aristotele et in geometria diffinitio" (1.00).

[143] *Cf. Aristotle's Posterior Analytics*, tr. & ann. J. BARNES (Oxford, 1975), 103.

[144] 72a15–24; *Aristoteles Latinus*, IV.1-4, p. 8.

[145] "Dicuntur igitur huiusmodi propositiones vel dicta suppositiones vel petitiones, quoniam supponunter et petuntur nec probantur. Videntur enim evidentiam habere sufficientem ex solo confuso terminorum conceptu" (1.025).

[146] "Hec ergo et consimiles dicuntur propositiones prime et immediate, quoniam statim ex confuso terminorum conceptu cognoscuntur sine discursu, vel, si cum discursu, huiusmodi tamen discursus non est perceptibilis multum, et ideo tanquam prime admittuntur. Et ideo dixit Alacen in secundo Perspective de hac propositione, omne totum est maius sua parte, quod non comprehenditur solo intellectu, sed prima apprehensio eius est per syllogismum compositum ex intentionibus terminorum, quia, cum intellectus non percipit velocitatem argumentationis que est in ipso insensibili, ideo putatur quod comprehenditur solo intellectu. Et omne quod est istius generis vocatur ab omnibus propositio prima" (1.039).

[147] ALHAZEN, *Perspectiva*, II.13, in *Opticae Thesaurus Alhazeni Arabis Libri Septem*, ed. F. RISNER (Basle, 1572), 32. *Cf.* ROGER BACON, *Communia mathematica*, in *Opera Hactenus inedita Rogeri Baconi*, ed. R. STEELE *et al.* (Oxford, 1905–40), xvi, 69, 124, and BRADWARDINE, *De causa Dei* (n. 5 above), 132–133.

proposition, 'Every whole is greater than its part', that it is not grasped by the intellect alone, but its first apprehension is by a syllogism composed from the intentions of the terms, because, when the intellect does not perceive the speed of the argument that is in its insensible self it is thought that it [the proposition] is grasped by the intellect alone. And everything that is of that genus is called by all a first proposition.

But there was some difference in usage. We have noted how BRADWARDINE did not seem altogether happy with applying the construction postulates. This was not the case with the common notions, which could assume the role that maxims did in scholastic logical discussions. In the introduction to his work BRADWARDINE says that theoretical geometry investigates the properties of magnitudes by *ratio* and syllogism. In a strict sense the work includes few syllogisms, but BRADWARDINE would no doubt hold that other forms of argument could be reduced to syllogistic form. His actual procedure was quite similar to that given in the tracts *De locis* of medieval logical works. For instance, PETER of Spain started his tract on the subject by a discussion of the different meanings of *ratio*.[148] The appropriate sense in this context was a means implying a conclusion (*medium inferens conclusionem*). There is allusion here to the middle term of a syllogism, but this was not the whole story, for PETER's account soon moves on to Topics (*loci*) themselves. A Topic was

the seat of an argument or that from which a suitable argument is drawn for a proposed question,

and an argument was confirmed by a Topic.[149] A Topic was either a topical maxim (*locus maxima*) or a topical difference (*locus differentia maxime*), and a topical maxim was

a proposition to which there is no other prior, that is better known, such as "Every whole is greater than its part", "Of whatever the definition is predicated, so also the defined", "Of whatever the species is predicated, so also the genus".

With this we connect again with the common notions of geometry, which BRADWARDINE had indeed identified with *maximae propositiones*. And their predominant role in the *Geometria* was to serve as inference rules in a sort of metalogical way, just as maxims did in logical writings. With this approach it is not surprising that BRADWARDINE (1.03), like CAMPANUS, says that there are more common notions than the nine that he lists, and in other places he shows a particular interest in other rules of inference. This, comes out clearly in his section on proportion where he discusses how one proportion may be inferred from another.[150]

---

[148] PETER of Spain, *Tractatus* (n. 121 above), 55. On the topical tradition see O. BIRD, "The Tradition of the Logical Topics: Aristotle to Ockham", *Journal of the History of Ideas*, xxiii (1962), 307–323; I. THOMAS, "Maxims in Kilwardby", *Dominican Studies*, vii (1954), 129–146; W. KNEALE & M. KNEALE, *The Development of Logic* (5th imp., Oxford, 1971), 193–194, 216, 221.

[149] PETER of Spain, *Tractatus*, 58–59.

[150] "Contingit autem in eisdem terminis unam proportionalitatem inferri ex alia multis modis, cum fuerint proportionalia disiuncta, et Euclides point 6 modos. Et sunt quasi modi

I

148

It happens that a proportion in the same terms may be inferred from another in many modes, when the proportionals are discontinuous, and Euclid gives six modes. And they are, as it were, modes of arguing, and following this there are, as it were, six species of discontinuous proportion,[151] namely converted (*conversa*), permuted (*permutata*), conjoined (*coniuncta*), disjoined (*disiuncta*), everted (*eversa*), and equalled (*equa*). And the mode of arguing requires at least two proportions, just as a proportion requires two ratios. And one is the antecedent, and the other, which is implied, the consequent. But sometimes the terms themselves are called antecedents and consequents, and that which is prior in any ratio is called the antecedent, but that which is posterior the consequent, and in this way you will take the names in the following descriptions. Converted proportion therefore is when the consequents are made from the antecedents and the antecedents from the consequents in converse order, arguing thus: As A to B so C to D—therefore as D to C so B to A. For here A and C were first antecedents and then consequents, and conversely for B and D....

Such justification as BRADWARDINE gives for these rules is mainly by exemplification. We find similar moves in 3.3 and 3.4, where the propositions often have the form of inference rules and where BRADWARDINE explicitly speaks of *regule*. This veering towards the metalogical fits well with the practice of disputation, where an asserted consequence was often buttressed by one or more rules and subsidiary arguments. If one makes diagrams of scholastic argument forms, one often finds the need to depict some propositions as reinforcing the arrows used to denote the passage from one assertion to another.[152] In geometry it may well have had the effect of relaxing the concentration on the generalised deductive rigour of Greek geometry. We have already seen how BRADWARDINE took some shortcuts in 1.1, and afterwards his standards were laxer. The attitude may have been: let a consequence stand until it is disputed. And often he only exemplified a theorem by means of a special case.

VI. Measure

VI.1. Units; angles

Crudely put measurement is the expression of the size of something in numerical terms. In the case of a flock of sheep or similar collections it is normally

---

quidam arguendi, et secundum hoc sunt quasi sex species proportionalitatis disiuncte, scilicet conversa, permutata, coniuncta, disiuncta, eversa et equa. Et iste modus arguendi requirit ad minus proportionalitates duas, sicud proportionalitas requirit duas proportiones. Estque una antecedens, alia que infertur consequens. Vocantur tamen quandoque ipsi termini antecedentia et consequentia, et qui prior est in proportione qualibet vocatur antecedens, qui vero posterior consequens, et sic accipies hec nomina in descriptionibus sequentibus. Conversa ergo proportionalitas est cum ex antecedentibus fiunt consequentia et ex consequentibus antecedentia ordine econverso, sic arguendo: Sicud A ad B ita C ad D —ergo sicud D ad C ita B ad A" (3.2).

[151] This is an odd way of putting it, but there had been difficulties of expression before; *cf.* HEATH, *Euclid's Elements* (n. 57 above), ii, 134. BRADWARDINE's terminology for the modes is not quite the same as CAMPANUS's.

[152] *Cf.* O. BIRD, "The Re-Discovery of the Topics", *Mind*, lxx (1961), 534–539.

attained by simple counting, and in a discussion of the meanings of "one" ARISTOTLE attempted to assimilate other forms of measure to this.[153]

> "To be one" means "to be indivisible, being essentially a 'this' and capable of being isolated either in place, or in form or thought"; or perhaps "to be whole and indivisible"; but it means especially "to be the first measure of a kind", and most strictly of quantity; for it is from this that it has been extended to the other categories. For measure is that by which quantity is known; and quantity *qua* quantity is known either by a "one" or by a number, and all number is known by a "one". Therefore all quantity *qua* quantity is known by the one, and that by which quantities are primarily known is the one itself; and so the one is the starting-point of number *qua* number. And hence in the other classes too "measure" means that by which each is first known, and the measure of each is a unit – in length, in breadth, in depth, in weight, in speed... In all these, then, the measure and starting-point is something one and indivisible, since even in lines we treat as indivisible the line a foot long. For everywhere we seek as the measure something one and indivisible; and this is that which is simple either in quality or in quantity. Now where it is thought impossible to take away or to add, there the measure is exact (hence that of number is most exact; for we posit the unit as indivisible in every respect); but in all other cases we imitate this sort of measure. For in the case of a furlong or a talent or of anything comparatively large any addition or subtraction might more easily escape our notice than in the case of something smaller; so that the first thing from which, as far as our perception goes, nothing can be subtracted, all men make the measure, whether of liquids or of solids, whether of weight or of size; and they think they know the quantity when they know it by means of this measure.

For various reasons this is not an adequate account of measure in pure geometry, but there is one place where we may see BRADWARDINE as alluding to it. After the postulate, "All right angles to be mutually equal", BRADWARDINE adds the comment,[154]

> For the form of the right angle is posited among indivisibles, and so cannot be varied.

This must not of course be taken to mean that a right angle may not be divided into two smaller angles, but rather that one right angle is no more a right angle than any other right angle.[155] With this type of indivisibility it can play the part of a unit in terms of which other angles are measured.[156] In this case we have a definition of a unit, for:[157]

---

[153] *Metaph.*, I.1, 1052b15–1053a9 (Oxford translation).

[154] "Est enim forma recti posita in indivisibili, et ideo variari non potest" (1.023).

[155] *Cf. Cat.*, 6, 6a 19–26, and THOMAS AQUINAS, *In Phys.*, IV, lect. 7, LEONINE edition (n. 110 above), ii, 167.

[156] *Cf.* E. HOPPE, "Zur Geschichte der Infinatesimalrechnung bis Leibniz und Newton", *Jahresberichte der Deutschen Mathematiker-Vereinigung*, xxxvii (1928), 148–187, at 158.

[157] "Rectus est quem constituit linea recta super rectam perpendiculariter cadens. Est autem linea perpendicularis vel perpendiculariter cadens super aliam que cum ea super quam cadit duos angulos equales constituit" (1.01).

A right [angle] is that which a straight line falling perpendicularly on a straight line constitutes. A perpendicular line or one falling perpendicularly on another is that which, when it falls on the other, constitutes two equal angles.

Such definitions are not usually possible in geometry.

This is highlighted by ARISTOTLE's reference in the passage quoted above to the line a foot long, for how can a foot be geometrically defined? ROBERT GROSSETESTE faced the problem squarely, and came up with the view that a time or a length was properly measured by its number of instants or points.[158] Such was infinite, but for God an infinite number was finite, and he could compare two infinite numbers. It was even possible that one infinite number should have to another the ratio of the diagonal of a square to its side. In the next century HENRY of Harclay spoke similarly, and even allowed a continuum to be composed of indivisibles.[159] In his *De continuo* Bradwardine was to launch a vigorous attack on such views, and in his *Geometria* he showed little sign of flirting with them.[160] In any case, as WILLIAM of Alnwick emphasised, these accounts do not teach us (as opposed to God) how to measure.[161] It is therefore not surprising that BRADWARDINE's approach is in the normal geometrical tradition, and centres on the mutual comparison of given magnitudes as expressed in terms of ratios.

VI.2. Ratios

Ratios between numbers were treated in the arithmetical and musical traditions, but because of the discovery of incommensurability geometry needed a somewhat different approach. In Antiquity the centre point of the geometric theory of ratios was the definition (attributed to EUDOXUS) of being in the same ratio. This definition was not properly understood in the Middle Ages,[162] and, although BRADWARDINE takes the CAMPANUS version of EUCLID as his base he was at pains to link the arithmetical and geometrical theories. He begins the third part of his work by noting that geometry has a wider range of ratios to consider than arithmetic, and moves on to attempt an all-inclusive definition.[163]

Because the intention of "ratio" is extended and is applied to almost all things that are mutually comparable according to greater and less, it can be defined in

[158] ROBERT GROSSESTESTE, *In VIII Libros Physicorum* (n. 80 above), 90–95. *Cf.* his *De luce* in *Die Philosophischen Werke des Robert Grosseteste*, ed. L. BAUR, Beiträge zur Geschichte der Philosophie des Mittelalters, ix (Münster, 1912), 52–54.

[159] MAIER, *Die Vorläufer* (n. 1 above), 168–169; J.E. MURDOCH, "*Mathesis in Philosophiam Scholasticam Introducta:* The Rise and Development of the Application of Mathematics in Fourteenth Century Philosophy and Theology", *Actes du Quatriéme Congrès International de Philosophie Médiévale* (Montreal, 1969), 215–254, at 217–223; J.E. MURDOCH & E.A. SYNAN, "Two Questions on the Continuum: Walter Chatton (?), O.F.M. & Adam Woodham, O.F.M." *Franciscan Studies*, xxvi (1966), 212–228, at 212–222.

[160] In 3.35–3.36 BRADWARDINE makes an unsuccessful attempt to establish a paradox about infinity.

[161] MAIER, *Metaphysische Hintergründe* (n. 90 above), 401.

[162] J.E. MURDOCH, "The Medieval Language of Proportions", *Scientific Change*, ed. A.C. CROMBIE (London, 1963), 237–271, at 251–261. But see also n. 198 below.

[163] "Quoniam autem intentio proportionis extensa est et applicatur fere omnibus adinvicem comparabilibus secundum magis et minus, ideo secundum hunc communem conceptum potest sic diffiniri: Proportio est aliquorum adinvicem comparabilium unius ad

accord with this general concept: A ratio is a certain habitude of some things that are mutually comparable one to the other. For example, of a number to a number, a magnitude to a magnitude, a sound to a sound, a time to a time, a motion to a motion, a humour to a humour, a heat to a heat, a taste to a taste. But geometry ascribes the intention of "ratio" to magnitude and has it to be defined thus: A ratio is a certain habitude of two quantities of the same genus, one to the other. I say "of the same genus" because only such are mutually comparable.

As yet the notion is rather indeterminate. In Book V of the *Elements* definitions were given for "the same ratio" and for "greater ratio", but BRADWARDINE has a strong focus on logical division, and proceeds to divide rational from irrational ratios, a subject that EUCLID had deferred to Book X.

Ratio is divided into two species which are received in comparison with proportionally diverse quantities. For some quantities are communicating or commensurable, some incommunicating and incommensurable. Commensurable quantites are those for which there is a common quantity numbering them. One quantity is said to number another if when taken according to a certain number [taken a certain number of times] it produces it [the second quantity], as a foot line [produces] a two-foot line and a three-foot line. Therefore a two-foot line and a three-foot line are communicating quantities, which a foot line numbers by Two and Three. But quantities for which there is no common quantity numbering them are called incommensurable. Of this kind are the diagonal and side of a square. According to this therefore there are two species of ratios, namely rational and irrational. A rational ratio is found (*debetur*) in commensurable quantities, and it is the only one that is found in numbers. But an irrational one fits incommensurable quantities, but in nowise numbers. Whence it is manifest that the whole consideration of ratio concerns geometry, because every ratio is of magnitude, but not every ratio is numerable.[164]

---

alterum certa habitudo. Verbi gratia, numeri ad numerum, magnitudinis ad magnitudinem, soni ad sonum, temporis ad tempus, motus ad motum, humoris ad humorem, caloris ad calorem, saporis ad saporem. Geometria autem trahit intentionem proportionis ad magnitudinem, et habet eam sic diffiniri. Proportio est duarum quantitatum eiusdem generis unius ad alteram certa habitudo. Dico autem eiusdem generis quia sola talia sunt adinvicem comparabilia" (3.1).

[164] "Dividitur autem proportio in 2 species que accipiuntur in comparatione ad quantitates proportionaliter diversas. Nam quantitates quedam sunt communicantes sive commensurabiles, quedam incommunicantes et incommensurabiles. Quantitates commensurabiles sunt quibus est una communis quantitas eas numerans. Dicitur autem una quantitas numerare aliam que secundum aliquem numerum accepta producit ipsam, ut linea pedalis lineam bipedalem et tripedalem. Sunt ergo quantitates communicantes linea bipedalis et tripedalis, quas linea pedalis secundum binarium et ternarium numerat. Quantitates vero quibus non est una communis quantitas eas numerans incommensurabiles dicuntur; cuiusmodi sunt dyameter et latus quadrati. Sunt ergo secundum hoc due proportionum species, scilicet rationalis et irrationalis. Rationalis debetur quantitatibus commensurabilibus; ipsa quoque est que debetur in numeris sola. Irrationalis vero quantitatibus incommensurabilibus convenit, numeris vero nequaquam. Unde manifestum est quod ad geometriam totaliter pertinet proportionis consideratio, quia omnis proportio est magnitudinis sed non omnis est numeralis" (3.1).

In continuing his logical division of ratio BRADWARDINE brings in the notion of denomination (*denominatio*). In the pseudo-Ciceronian *Rhetorica ad Herennium* this was defined as follows:[165]

> Denomination is [the figure of diction] that draws from close and related things an expression by which may be understood a thing that is not called by its own name.

Examples are referring to Ceres as "wheat" and to wealth as "gold". In the ARISTOTELIAN tradition the meaning was narrower and somewhat different.[166]

> Denominatives are said to be those that are called by name from something [else] with only a difference of inflection. For example, from grammar, grammarian, and from bravery, brave.

They came into their own in the category of quality.[167]

> Qualities therefore are those which we have mentioned; *qualia* are what are called according to them denominatively or from them in any other way. In many cases and indeed in almost all they are called denominatively, as white from whiteness and grammarian from grammar and just from justice, and similarly in other cases. But in some cases it is impossible for them to be called denominatively, since names for the qualities are not posited... And sometimes even when a name is posited that which is said to be a *quale* on account of it is not called denominatively. For example a good man (*probus*) is so called from virtue (*a virtute*), for what has virtue is called good, but it is not called denominatively from virtue.

The exceptions reveal a lack of fit between logic and language, and the restriction to inflectional changes of words in particular languages can seem too contingent to be of much interest. It is thus not surprising that the notion of denomination came to be much widened.[168] It is in a somewhat widened context that we may see the mathematical uses of the term. Denomination draws from discourse about one set of objects (in this case usually numbers) names for other objects, and names that convey information about the latter objects.

We have already encountered (IV.5) one reference to denomination in a mathematical context, namely where BOETHIUS was arguing for the priority of arithmetic to geometry, and held that *triangulum* and *quadratum* were de-

---

[165] *Rhet. ad Her.*, IV.xxxii.43, in [CICERO], *Ad C. Herennium de ratione dicendi*, with Engl. trn by H. CAPLAN (London & Cambridge, Mass., 1954), 334: "Denominatio est quae ab rebus propinquis et finitimis trahit orationem qua possit intellegi res quae non suo vocabulo sit appellata."

[166] *Cat.*, 1, 1a12–15, in *Aristoteles Latinus*, I.1–5, p. 5: "Denominativa vero dicuntur quaecumque ab aliquo, solo differentia casu, secundum nomen habent appellationem, ut a grammatica grammaticus et a fortitudine fortis."

[167] *Cat.*, 8, 10a27–b9, trans. from *Aristoteles Latinus*, I.1–5, pp. 27–28.

[168] See, *e.g.*, the account in R. GOCLENIUS, *Lexicon Philosophicum* (Frankfurt, 1613; repr. Hildesheim, 1964), 505–509. On paronyms (denominative terms) in medieval logic see D.P. HENRY, *The De Grammatico of St. Anselm: The Theory of Paronymy* (Notre Dame, Ind., 1964), 79–101.

nominatives of numbers. Similarly in the *Geometria* (4.0) BRADWARDINE spoke of how pyramids and columns are denominated from the number of their sides (bases excluded). Such examples, as is often the case with denomination, could suggest a participatory view in which numbers in some sense provided the forms of geometrical objects. Denomination also occurred in the algorithmic literature, as when JOHANNES DE SACROBOSCO has Ten denominated by unity, Twenty by Two, and so on.[169] Here we seem to be in the domains of the Greek πυθμήν, which in another usage MURDOCH saw as a possible ancestor of medieval denomination.[170] Reverting to BOETHIUS again, we find that a part of a number may be denominated from the number of times that it fits into the whole.[171] This usage was widespread. In a similar vein JORDANUS's *Arithmetica* defines a denominator as the number according to which a part is contained in its whole.[172] It is perhaps significant that JORDANUS speaks here of the *denominans* not the *denominatio*, and hence draws attention to the number from which the denomination is received and not to the denomination itself or its end-product, for in BOETHIUS the denomination of a sixth part was *sexta* not *senarius*. If this were so it would show a nice sensitivity to the ARISTOTELIAN requirement for a change of word-form, but in other instances this is absent, and the denomination is taken to be a number (or a fraction). We even find this in another work attributed to JORDANUS, where we meet the definitions:[173]

> The denomination of a ratio of this to that is what comes out of the division of this by that. For a ratio to be produced or composed from ratios is for the denomination of the ratio to be produced from the denominations of the ratios, multiplied one into the other.

The *De proportionibus* ascribed to CAMPANUS is similar in this regard[174] (although, as we shall see, going further in one respect), and RICHARD of Wallingford, who followed "CAMPANUS" closely came near to identifying a ratio with its denomination.[175] NICOLE ORESME exhibited the denominations of rational ratios by numbers or numbers and fractions, but he also took into account irrational ratios, and there the matter was not so simple.[176]

In the early seventeenth century RUDOLPH GOCLENIUS began his article on denomination as follows:[177]

[169] *Petri Philomeni de Dacia* ... (n.33 above), 2.

[170] T.L. HEATH, *A History of Greek Mathematics* (Oxford, 1921), i, 55–57, 115–116; MURDOCH, "The Medieval Language of Proportions" (n.162 above), 257 n.2.

[171] BOETHIUS, *De inst. arith.*, I.10, ed. FRIEDLEIN (n.112 above), 22.

[172] *Arithmetica decem libris demonstrata* ... , ed. J. LEFÈVRE D'ETAPLES (Paris, 1514), sig. aiir.

[173] BUSARD, "Die Traktate *De proportionibus*" (n.49 above), 205: "Denominacio vero proportionis huius ad illud est quod exit ex divisione huius per illud. Proporcionem produci vel componi ex proporcionibus est denominacionem proporcionis produci ex denominacionibus proporcionum altera in alteram ductis."

[174] *Ibid.*, 213.

[175] J.D. NORTH, *Richard of Wallingford. An edition of his writings with introductions, English translation and commentary* (Oxford, 1976), i, 59, n.9.

[176] *Der Algorismus Proportionum des Nicolaus Oresme*, ed. M. CURTZE (Berlin, 1868); E. GRANT, "Part I of Nicole Oresme's *Algorismus proportionum*", *Isis*, lvi (1965), 327–341.

[177] GOCLENIUS, *Lexicon Philosophicum* (n.168 above), 505.

154

Denomination signifies either the act of denominating, or the name that is drawn from something else ...

BRADWARDINE is principally interested in the act of denominating rather than in the precise name that is arrived at as a result of the process. In the case of ratios he is more interested in the possibility of a numerical description than in exactly how this description should be expressed. In particular he is not concerned with providing a one-one relation between ratios and numbers. It was, I believe, this more philosophical approach that allowed him to open the way to an extended notion of denomination of ratios. But let us follow his own reasoning. We left him at the point where he had divided rational ratios from irrational ones. He continues:[178]

A rational ratio therefore is immediately denominated by some certain number, for, since it is of commensurable quantities, it is necessary that the lesser or some part of the lesser should number the greater according to some number, on account of which Euclid says that of any two commensurable quantities the ratio of one to the other is as that of a number to a number, and this will be clearer below. This species is divided in every mode in which ratio is divided in arithmetic. For one is a ratio of equality, another of inequality. And ratio of inequality is subdivided ...

We note that the guiding idea for denomination is the BOETHIAN one of how many times a part fits into a whole. The close analogy with arithmetic allows the logical division of rational ratios to be handed over to that science. BRADWARDINE sketches out the division into ratios of greater and lesser inequality, and the division of each of these into five species. For greater inequality these are multiple, superparticular, superpartient, multiple superparticular, and multiple superpartient. We may give as examples, respectively, 3:1, 4:3, 7:5, 11:5 and 11:3. BRADWARDINE does not systematically pursue the division down to the *infimae species*, but it is clear that he does not identify these with numbers or fractions nor does he regard the denomination of a ratio to be the corresponding fraction. This appears from 3.34 where we learn that, although the greater multiple ratio has the greater denomination, the reverse is the case for superparticular ratios,

because *sesquialtera* [*e.g.* 3:2] is a greater ratio than *sesquitertia* [*e.g.* 4:3] (for *sesquitertia* is a part of *sesquialtera*), but it has denomination from a lesser number.[179]

---

[178] "Proportio igitur rationalis immediate denominatur ab aliquo certo numero; cum enim sit quantitatum commensurabilium oportet quod secundum aliquem numerum minor vel aliqua pars minoris maiorem numerat, propter quod dicit Euclides quod omnium duarum quantitatum commensurabilium est proportio alterius ad alteram tanquam numeri ad numerum, et hoc magis patebit inferius. Dividitur autem hec species secundum omnem modum secundum quem divisa est proportio in arismetica. Nam alia est proportio equalitatis, alia inequalitatis. Et proportio inequalitatis subdividitur ..." (3.1).

[179] "... quoniam sexquialtera maior est proportio quam sexquitertia, est enim sexquitertia pars sexquialtere, sed a minori numero denominationem habet."

The numbers at issue are evidently two for *sesquialtera* and three for *sesquitertia*.
So far, except for questions of nuance, the sailing has been relatively plain. We
now have to face the vexed question of irrational ratios.[180]

An irrational ratio is not in this way immediately denominated by some number
or by some numerical ratio, because it is not possible there that some part of the
lesser should number the greater according to some number. But it turns out
that an irrational ratio may be mediately denominated by number. For
example, the ratio of the diagonal [of a square] to the side is half of a double
ratio, and so other species of this ratio receive denominations by number.

We defer the question of whether BRADWARDINE means that all irrational ratios
are susceptible of numerical denomination, and explicate first the notion of mediate
denomination. This turns on the interpretation of composition of ratios. Given
three quantities a, b, and c with a greater than b and b greater than c it was standard
to say that the ratio of a to c was compounded of the ratios a to b and b to c. So far
the notion of composition is neutral, and so it remained in many treatises, but there
was a temptation to assimilate it to one of the arithmetical operations of
combination. In his version of the *Elements* CAMPANUS assimilated it to
multiplication. V. Def. 10 was,

If there are three continually proportional quantities, the ratio of the first to
the third is said to be the ratio of the first to the second duplicated.

In CAMPANUS's comment we have:[181]

Or what is the same, the ratio of the first to the third, will be as that of the first to
the second duplicated, that is, multiplied into itself.

Likewise, in the *De proportionibus* ascribed to CAMPANUS, there is the
definition:[182]

For a ratio to be divided by a ratio or for the divisor to be thrown off (*abiici*)
from the dividend is for the denomination of the dividend to be divided by the
denomination of the divisor.

But there was another tradition, found in musical works, in which the composition
of ratios was assimilated to addition. For instance (from BOETHIUS):[183]

[180] "Proportio autem irrationalis non sic immediate denominatur ab aliquo numero
aut ab aliqua proportione numerali, quoniam non est ibi possibile ut secundum aliquem
numerum pars aliqua minoris maiorem numeret. Contingit tamen mediate denominari
proportionem irrationalem a numero, ut proportio dyametri ad costam est medietas duple
proportionis, et ita capiunt alie species huius proportionis denominationes a numero" (3.1).
[181] "Siue quod idem est: erit proportio primi ad tertium sicut primi ad secundum
duplicata, hoc est in se multiplicata." See also his comment on V Def. 11.
[182] BUSARD, "Die Traktate *De proportionibus*" (n.49 above), 213: "Proportionem dividi
per proportionem aut dividentem abiici ex dividenda est denominationem dividende dividi
per denominationem dividentis."
[183] BOETHIUS, *De institutione Musica Libri Quinque*, II.11, ed. G. FRIEDLEIN (Leipzig,
1867; repr. Frankfurt, 1966), 241: "Quodsi triplum sesquitertio addas, quadruplus efficietur,
si quadruplum sesquiquarto quincuplus ..."

If you add triple to *sesquitertius* [4:3], quadruple will be produced, if quadruple to *sesquiquartus*, quintuple ...

It is this conception of composition of ratios that BRADWARDINE has, even if he does not actually use the verb *addere*.[184] It is easily extended to the multiplication of ratios by fractions, for, in the example that BRADWARDINE uses, half of the double ratio is the ratio which added to itself would produce the double ratio. But BRADWARDINE does not in fact push his extended notion of denomination to its full generality, and restricts himself to halving ratios. It was left to NICOLE ORESME to discuss multiplication of ratios by any fraction.[185] BRADWARDINE may have been limited by the term *medietas*, which suggested the finding of proportional means.[186]

We should at this point take a closer look at the term "mediate denomination" as applied to ratios. The usage may have been original to BRADWARDINE, and has been the subject of difficulties of interpretation.[187] To the account from the *Geometria* already given we add the more developed one from the *Tractatus de proportionibus:*[188]

The second grade is held by that [ratio] which is called irrational, which is not immediately denominated by some number, but only mediately, because it is immediately denominated by some ratio, which is immediately denominated by number. For example, half of the double ratio, which is the ratio of the diagonal to the side, and half of the *sesquioctava* ratio [9:8], which constitutes half of a tone.

Let us say, following this account, that the ratio X is immediately denominated by the ratio Y, which is then immediately denominated by number. One of the questions that has caused trouble is, "What is Y?" In each of the given examples only one ratio besides X is mentioned, namely that of which X is the half, and so it seems that this must be Y. Y, being rational, is then immediately denominated by number. The difficulties in interpretation have, I suggest, arisen from concentration on denomination as a name rather than as a process, and from the expectation that there should be a number or set of numbers that give a unique specification. But, as we have seen, this is not even the case for rational ratios, since both *tripla* and *sesquitertia* are denominated from Three. If we think in terms of participation an irrational ratio immediately participates in a rational ratio, which in turn immediately participates in number.

Let us now revert to the *Geometria*. BRADWARDINE continues with a logical

---

[184] *Cf.* E. GRANT, "Part I of Nicole Oresme's *Algorismus proportionum*" (n. 176 above), 340–341; Molland, "The Geometrical Background" (n. 81 above), 117.

[185] *Cf.* MOLLAND, *op. cit.*, 118.

[186] *Cf.* A.G. MOLLAND, "The Denomination of Proportions in the Middle Ages", *Actes du XIe Congrès International d'Histoire des Sciences* (Wroclaw, 1968), iii, 167–170, at 170.

[187] See MURDOCH, "The Medieval Language of Proportions" (n. 162 above), 258–261.

[188] *Tract. de prop.*, ed. CROSBY (n. 35 above), 66: "Secundum vero gradum illa tenet quae irrationalis vocatur, quae non immediate denominatur ab aliquo numero, sed mediate tantum, quia immediate denominatur ab aliqua proportione, quae immediate denominatur a numero: sicut medietas duplae proportionis, quae est proportio diametri ad costam, et medietas sesquioctavae proportionis, quae toni medietatem constituit."

division of irrational ratios, and in so doing restricts himself to ratios between lines
rather than between quantities in general. The basic distinction is the EUCLIDEAN
one (cf. X Def. 2) between lines that are incommensurable in length only and those
that are incommensurable in both length and power (*potentia*). In the former case
the squares of the lines are commensurable, but in the latter case not. He does not
embark on anything like the elaborate EUCLIDEAN classification of the irrational,
but merely sketches out the possibility of further subdivision.[189]

> Each species can be subdivided into as many species as there are ways for lines
> to be thus or thus incommensurable, for not only can lines be incommensurable
> in length only when they are as diagonal and square, but in other ways perhaps
> infinite [in number]. I speak similarly of lines incommensurable in length and
> power, because there are not only those that are taken as means between side
> and diagonal, and the means between that mean and them, and further the
> means between these and those, and so on infinitely, but also many others.

The expression is a bit garbled, but the meaning is clear. New species of irrational
ratio may be generated by forming the geometric mean between the terms of a given
irrational ratio, comparing the mean with the original terms, and repeating the
process indefinitely. But here BRADWARDINE is interested more in the possibility of
classification than in providing a careful mapping of the irrational.

BRADWARDINE's definition and logical division of ratio contains the heart of
his proportional doctrine. The succeeding four chapters read like amplification and
tidying up. But there are still two questions that we should face with their aid. The
first concerns the ontological status of ratios, which by the seventeenth century at
least had become a topic of much concern. ISAAC BARROW, for instance, reported
BORELLI as saying that ratios constitute a new species of quantity, and himself
argued vehemently against that view.[190] For ratios are certainly relations, and so
how can they go over into the category of quantity? The logicians teach that
relations only exist between *res absolutae*, and *res absolutae* cannot inhere in
relations; therefore there can be no relations between relations, as there would be if
relations could be quantities. A different view was taken by LEIBNIZ in his
controversy with CLARKE. In explicating his doctrine of space he appealed to the
analogy of ratios.[191]

> The ratio or proportion between two lines L and M, may be conceived three
> several ways; as a ratio of the greater L, to the lesser M; as a ratio of the lesser M,
> to the greater L; and lastly, as something abstracted from both, that is, as the
> ratio between L and M, without considering which is the antecedent, or which

---

[189] "Potest autem uterque species subdividi in tot species quot modis contingit lineas
sic vel sic esse incommensurabiles, nam non solum linee possunt esse incommensurabiles in
longitudine tantum dum se habent sicud dyameter et costa sed aliis modis forte infinitis.
Similiter dico de lineis incommensurabilibus in longitudine et potentia, quia non solum sunt
ille que accipiuntur medie inter costam et dyametrum, et medie inter istam mediam et illas et
iterum medie inter illas et illas, et sic in infinitum, sed etiam alie plurime" (3.1).

[190] BARROW, *Mathematical Works*, ed. WHEWELL (n. 97 above), 316–329.

[191] H.G. ALEXANDER, *The Leibniz-Clarke Correspondence* (Manchester, 1956), 71 (5th
letter, para. 47).

the consequent; which the subject, and which the object. And thus it is, that proportions are considered in music. In the first way of considering them, L the greater; in the second, M the lesser, is the subject of that accident, which philosophers call relation. But, which of them will be the subject, in the third way of considering them? It cannot be said that both of them, L and M together, are the subject of such an accident; for if so, we should have an accident in two subjects, with one leg in one, and the other in the other; which is contrary to the notion of accidents. Therefore we must say, that this relation, in this third way of considering it, is indeed out of the subjects; but being neither a substance, nor an accident, it must be a mere ideal thing, the consideration of which is nevertheless useful.

Later in the same letter LEIBNIZ again appealed to the example of ratios.[192]

Relative things have their quantity, as well as absolute ones. For instance, ratios or proportions in mathematics, have their quantity, and are measured by logarithms; and yet they are relations.

In his reply CLARKE ignored the first usage of the analogy, but with regard to the second he vigorously asserted that ratios were not quantities, for if they were, "they would be quantities of quantities; which is absurd."[193] Like BARROW, CLARKE insisted that all talk about the quantity of ratios be interpreted as referring to the related terms.

These passages make it clear that ratios were capable of producing major problems for traditional logic, but I know of no extensive fourteenth-century discussions of these issues. Nevertheless we may glean something of BRADWARDINE's attitudes. In general he treated them in accord with LEIBNIZ's third manner of conceiving them, and not in the ARISTOTELIAN sense of relatives as properties of individual subjects but with reference to something else. That he was conscious of this is at least hinted at in 3.31:[194]

By as much as some quantity is to another, by so much is the ratio of the one to the other denominated.

The proof reads:

This is clear inductively, because: if one line be equal to another, there will be an *equa* ratio between them; and, if the line be double there will be a double ratio; and, if it be incommensurably exceeding in length and power, there will be a similar irrational ratio; and always the denomination of the ratio will be like the habitude of the terms.

A similar concern seems to lie behind a rider that BRADWARDINE adds to 3.33:[195]

---

[192] *Ibid.*, 75 (para. 54).

[193] *Ibid.*, 105–107.

[194] "Quanta est aliqua quantitas ad aliam tanta denominatur proportio eius ad ipsam. Ista patet inductive, quoniam, si fuerit linea una equalis alteri, erit equa proportio inter illas, et, si dupla fuerit linea, erit dupla proportio, et si fuerit incommensurabiliter excedens in longitudine et potentia, erit proportio irrationalis consimilis, eritque semper proportionis denominatio conformis habitudini terminorum" (3.31).

[195] "Ex isto potest sumi argumentum ad probandum quod relatio sit res distincta a rebus relatis, quoniam, si linea A est maior linea B, quantitates erunt inequales, proportiones tamen sunt equales illarum ad suas medietates, ut nunc ostensum est. Ergo etc." (3.33).

From this can be drawn an argument for proving that a relation is a thing distinct from the things related, because, if line A is greater than line B, the quantities will be unequal, but the ratios of the lines to their halves are equal, as has now been shown. Therefore etc. ...

BRADWARDINE does not say whether he regards this as a valid argument, but his sympathies seem to lie in that direction. BRADWARDINE is moreover in accord with LEIBNIZ in allowing ratios to be treated as quantities. This is particularly clear in his allowing equality as well as similarity to be predicated of ratios, and in his discussion of the composition of ratios. Later ORESME was to be more explicit:[196]

Any ratio is like a continuous quantity in that it is infinitely divisible like a continuous quantity, and into two equal [parts], and into three, and into four, etc. ...

Thus the stage was well set for another point of tension between mathematics and ARISTOTELIAN philosophy.

We must now ask whether BRADWARDINE thought that his extended notion of denomination provided an adequate criterion for the equality of ratios. For CAMPANUS such an arithmetical criterion was clearly impossible:[197]

[EUCLID] could not define the identity of ratios by the identity of denominations, like an arithmetician, because, as has been said, the denominations of many ratios are unknown *simpliciter*.

CAMPANUS's explication of the EUDOXEAN criterion of equality often seems garbled, but I am not convinced that he completely misunderstood it, for in his comment on the definition of greater ratio we have the following:[198]

The ratio of the first of four quantities to the second is never greater than that of the third to the fourth, unless some equimultiples of the first and the third may be found, such that when they are related to some equimultiples of the second and the fourth, the multiple of the first will be found to exceed the multiple of the second, but the multiple of the third will not exceed the multiple of the fourth. And this can never be found unless the ratio of the first to the second be greater than the ratio of the third to the fourth, as we shall demonstrate below.

But BRADWARDINE does not even attempt to tangle with the EUDOXEAN criterion. In 3.2 he defines proportion (*proportionalitas*):[199]

---

[196] NICOLE ORESME, *De proportionibus proportionum and Ad pauca respicientes*, ed. E. GRANT (Madison, 1966), 158: "Quelibet proportio est sicut quantitas continua in hoc, quod in infinitum est divisibilis sicut quantitas continua et in 2 equalia, et in 3, et in 4, et cetera ..."

[197] "Non potuit diffinire idemptitatem proportionum per idemptitatem denominationum, sicut arithmeticus, eo quod multarum proportionum ut dictum est sunt denominationes simpliciter ignote" (V. Def. 16).

[198] "Nusquam enim est maior proportio prime 4 quantitatum ad secundam quam tertie ad quartam, quin contingat aliqua eque multiplicia ad primam et tertiam reperiri, que, cum relata fuerint ad aliqua eque multiplicia secunde et quarte, invenietur multiplex prime addere super multiplex secunde, non autem multiplex tertie super multiplex quarte. Nec usquam contingit hoc reperire quin sit maior proportio prime ad secundam quam tertie ad quartam, ut demonstrabimus infra" (V Def. 8).

[199] "Proportionalitas quoque quemadmodum dictum est in arismetica est similitudo proportionum, unde ad minus requirit duas proportiones. Dicuntur autem proportiones

Proportion as was said in *Arithmetic* is similarity of ratios, and so it requires at least two ratios. Ratios are said to be similar of which the denominations are the same, as double double, triple triple, *sesquialtera sesquialtera*, and similarly for others from the genus of rational ratios, and as half of double half of double from the genus of irrational ratios.

Similarly 3.33, which is deduced from 3.31, is the rule, that, "Ratios are similar or equal of which the denominations are equal."[200] BRADWARDINE does not explicitly assert the universality of this criterion, but nowhere does he hint that there are ratios insusceptible of denomination, even given his apparent restriction to halving of ratios, as opposed to dividing them by other numbers. I therefore incline to the view that he regarded the criterion as adequate. This may receive some support from the rather heavy weather that he makes in showing that the ratio of the diagonal to the side of the square is irrational (2.24, 3.43, 3.52). And indeed his criterion is basically adequate for the straight lines of elementary geometry, where the construction of two mean proportionals between two given straight lines is not possible.[201] But, at this stage of his career at least, there is no evidence that BRADWARDINE would have the resources to do anything like distinguishing between what were classically known as plane and solid problems. With his far more general understanding of denomination, NICOLE ORESME thought that it was probable that there were irrational ratios that were incommensurable with all rational ratios, and hence could not be expressed as a fractional multiple of them.[202] Such ratios would have no denominations.

VI.3. Quadrature

Even more basic than a criterion for the equality of ratios is one for equality between the objects from which ratios are formed. In geometry this was essentially provided by the principle of superposition (1.039). As has often been pointed out EUCLID seemed chary of applying this common notion, but BRADWARDINE revelled in its use (*cf.* 2.11, 2.21, 2.301). When applied to straight lines it immediately provides a basis for measure and the formation of ratios. But in the case of plane figures there are complications because of a derivative sense of equality – what we should call equality of area as opposed to congruence. BRADWARDINE like EUCLID introduces this new sense of equality without comment (2.19). It depends upon the first kind of equality in that equality of area between two figures may be established by the addition and subtraction of congruent figures.[203] The standard way of dealing with problems of area was to construct a square that was equal in area to the initially given figure. It is therefore not surprising that BRADWARDINE includes a chapter on quadrature at the end of the part of his work dealing with ratios, and in

---

similes quarum denominationes sunt eadem, ut dupla dupla, tripla tripla, sexquialtera sexquialtera, et sic de aliis de genere proportionum rationalium, et sicud medietas duple medietas duple de genere proportionum irrationalium" (3.2).

[200] "Proportiones sunt similes vel equales quarum denominationes sunt equales" (3.33).

[201] *Cf.* MOLLAND, "The Denomination of Proportions" (n. 186 above), 170.

[202] ORESME, *De proportionibus proportionum*, ed. GRANT (n. 196 above), 160–166.

[203] *Cf.* HEATH, *Euclid's Elements* (n. 57 above), i, 327–328.

I

his introduction to it he may be seen as justifying the special position of the square by linking mensuration of plane figures to mensuration of straight lines.[204]

> The cause in quadratures is that a square figure is of better known measure than any other figure, for when you have it that a given surface is of two square feet or of four or according to another number, you are then informed of its measure with the final assurance. On account of which geometers have been accustomed to reduce other figures to this, and not this to others.

For polygons, BRADWARDINE's strategy, (not in the actual order of his presentation in 3.61–3.64), is to resolve them into triangles, then to construct rectangles equal to the triangles, then to square the rectangles, and finally to circumscribe the squares to one another gnomonically (cf. 2.25). The squaring of rectangles (3.61) is reduced to the finding of a geometric mean, which was taught in 3.44, but solely on the authority of EUCLID. In 3.61 BRADWARDINE takes the opportunity to elucidate two ARISTOTELIAN texts in which it was said that the finding a proportional mean should form part of the definition of "squaring".[205]

The quadrature of polygons presented no real problems, but the situation was different with regard to the circle, in spite of its fundamental position in EUCLIDEAN geometry. In 1882 LINDEMANN demonstrated that it was impossible to square it by means of the procedures authorised by EUCLID's postulates. The Greeks seem to have sensed this impossibility, and their later efforts at least were of two kinds.[206] The first was to seek a quadrature by means of some higher curve, such as the quadratrix, and this in effect meant an extension of the postulates. The second was to approximate to the area of the circle by successively inscribing and circumscribing polygons of increasing number of sides. Pre-eminent in the latter field was ARCHIMEDES' *Dimensio circuli*, and it is to this work that BRADWARDINE appeals in 3.65. It had been translated twice from the Arabic – by GERARD of Cremona, and, perhaps, by PLATO of Tivoli – and from the Greek by WILLIAM of Moerbeke. [207] BRADWARDINE's quotation is in accord with the GERARD of Cremona version. Unfortunately neither the Greek nor the Arabic tradition preserves the treatise in a satisfactory form. The trouble lies with the second of its three propositions. The first in effect reduces the problem of quadrature to one of rectification, by showing that the circle is equal in area to a right-angled triangle one of whose sides is equal to the circumference of the circle. The third shows that the circumference of a circle is between 3 10/71 and 3 1/7 times the diameter. All this is in order; but the second proposition asserts that the ratio of a circle to the square on its diameter is as 11 to 14. The enunciation does not reveal that this is an

---

[204] "Causa autem in quadraturis est ista, quia figura quadrata certioris est mensure quam quecumque alia figura. Cum enim habes quod superficies data sit duorum pedum quadratorum vel 4 vel secundum alium numerum, iam certificatus es de mensura eius quantitatis certificatione ultima. Propter quod geometre alias figuras in hanc, non istam in alias consueverunt reducere" (3.6).

[205] *De anima*, II.2, 413a13–19; *Metaph.*, B.2, 996b18–21.

[206] I. THOMAS, *Selections illustrating the History of Greek Mathematics* (London & Cambridge, Mass., 1939), i, 308–347.

[207] CLAGETT, *Archimedes in the Middle Ages* (n. 55 above), i, 16–29, 30–58, ii, 157–160.

approximation, although in the proof this is indicated by the word ἔγγιστα, but as part of a clause that HEIBERG regarded as an interpolation.[208] In GERARD of Cremona's version this role is played by the even smaller word *fere*.[209] There was thus scope for all but the most attentive to assume that ARCHIMEDES had in this proposition provided a simple and exact quadrature of the circle. To a reader of CIRVELO's edition BRADWARDINE would seem to fall into this class, but in fact the relevant passage only occurs in the elaborated version.

BRADWARDINE's 3.65 asserts that the area of any circle is equal to the rectangle contained by half the circumference and half the diameter. BRADWARDINE takes ARCHIMEDES' first proposition as a postulate – because to prove it would take too long. The elaborator then adds the following:[210]

> The ratio of the line containing the circle to the diameter is *tripla sesquiseptima* [as 22:7], so that the circumference contains the diameter three times, and with that its seventh part, as is held in the foresaid booklet.

BRADWARDINE's proof then proceeds in simple form, with no explicit dependence on the added sentence, although it does assume the constructibility of a line equal to the circumference of the circle. But, as we have seen, BRADWARDINE was a bit vague on construction, and he may well have assumed the existence (in some sense) of such a line as obvious. This at least was the vehemently held position of another medieval writer on quadrature, who in what CLAGETT has called the Corpus Christi College version of ARCHIMEDES' work gave the following postulate:[211]

> The second of the postulates is that a curved line be equal to a straight line. We postulate this, although it is a principle both known *per se* and recognised by anyone of sound head. For, if a hair or a silk thread be bent around circumference-wise in a plane surface and then extended in a straight line in the same plane, who unless demented would doubt that the hair or the thread would be the same whether bent around or extended in a straight line, and would be as much afterwards as before? Again, if a circle be turned around on a plane surface with its circumference touching the plane and if it be rolled in a straight line on the plane from one of its points until it arrives at the same point of the circumference, who not out of his mind will doubt that the circumference describes a straight line equal to the circumference.

If this were BRADWARDINE's position, it may have been methodologically weak (although what reason should we assign?), and evaporated an interesting problem, but it did not involve the error of confusing an approximate value with an exact one. After BRADWARDINE's proof the elaborator has almost the last word in the chapter by performing a rather inefficient explication of a passage in ARISTOTLE's *Prior Analytics*.[212]

---

[208] ARCHIMEDES, *Opera omnia cum commentariis Eutocii*, ed. J.L. HEIBERG (2nd edn, Leipzig, 1910–15), i, 236–237.

[209] CLAGETT, *Archimedes*, i, 46.

[210] "Est autem proportio linee continentis circulum ad dyametrum tripla sesquiseptima, ita quod circumferentia continet dyametrum ter et cum hoc septimam eius partem, ut habetur in predicto libello" (3.65).

[211] CLAGETT, *Archimedes*, i, 170.

[212] *An. Pr.*, II.25, 69a30–36.

VI.4. Curvilinear angles

Finally in this section I consider a topic, which BRADWARDINE treats, but for which his doctrine of measure was inadequate. This is the question of curvilinear angles, which EUCLID admits into geometry, but only considers in any detail in Propositions 16 and 31 of Book III (15 and 30 in CAMPANUS). BRADWARDINE's treatment only diverges from CAMPANUS's in minor points. Both men are mainly interested in the paradoxes that arise from this more general conception of angle, and they consider in particular the angle between a circle and its tangent (the angle of contingency or horn-angle) and the angle between a circle and its diameter (the angle of the semicircle). In his first proposition (2.306) BRADWARDINE shows that the horn-angle is less than any rectilinear angle and that it is infinitely divisible, in the sense that any horn-angle may be divided by a greater circle tangent at the same point. (The division is not into two horn-angles, but into a horn-angle and an angle between two arcs, but BRADWARDINE does not remark on this.) The implicit criterion for one angle being greater than another is that upon superposition (with "turning over" if necessary) it should include the other in some neighbourhood of the vertex. In the second proposition (2.307) BRADWARDINE shows that the angle of a semi-circle is greater than any acute rectilinear angle, but less than a right angle; it may, he says, be increased infinitely. It may thus be greater than a rectilinear angle and less than a rectilinear one, but never equal to one. The third conclusion gives further results about angles between circles and their chords. The paradoxical features of such angles are heightened by some observations of CAMPANUS which BRADWARDINE draws upon. The first, which CAMPANUS had very pertinently added to X.1, was to the effect that any rectilinear angle was infinitely greater than any horn-angle.[213] The second two came from III.15, and involved asserting the invalidity of two seemingly harmless consequences:

It is possible to find greater than this and less than the same — therefore also [to find] equal;

and

This passes from less to greater and through all intermediates — therefore through equal.

The first is invalid because a rectilinear angle may be greater or less than the angle of a semicircle, but not equal to it. The invalidity of the second is easily seen by considering a straight line rotating about a point on the circumference of a circle. NICOLE ORESME was later to add other such paradoxes in his *Questions on Euclid*.[214]

We may see more clearly where the underlying difficulties lay by means of an anachronistic treatment. Let us consider the class C of angles in which one limb is straight and the other either straight or a circular arc. Each such angle a is either of the form $r+h$ or of the form $r-h$, where r is a rectilinear angle and h is a horn-angle.

[213] *Cf.* MURDOCH, "The Medieval Language of Proportions" (n. 162 above), 242–243. CAMPANUS is more detailed than BRADWARDINE.

[214] NICOLE ORESME, *Quaestiones super Geometriam Euclidis*, ed. H.L.L. BUSARD (Leiden, 1961), 58–62, and MURDOCH's review in *Scripta Mathematica*, xxvii (1964), 67–91, at 88–91.

(For convenience we assume that the null angle is both a rectilinear angle and a horn-angle.) Let p be the real number such that $\underline{r} = p$ right angles. Let the real number k be the measure of the radius of the circle involved in $\underline{h}$, this measure being taken with respect to some arbitrarily chosen unit line. Let q be the reciprocal of k. We take q as the measure of $\underline{h}$. (Both CAMPANUS and BRADWARDINE were necessarily vague about the measures of horn-angles.) We define a mapping f of C into the set of ordered pairs of real numbers as follows:

$$f(\underline{r}+\underline{h}) = (p, q) \qquad f(\underline{r}-\underline{h}) = (p, -q).$$

We then define:

(i) $(p, q) = (p', q')$ if and only if $p = p'$ and $q = q'$.

(ii) $(p, q) > (p', q')$ if and only if either $p > p'$, or $p = p'$ and $q > q'$.

(iii) $(p, q) + (p', q') = (p + p', q + q')$.

The mapping is homomorphic with respect to equality, "greater than", and addition, and we may take (p, q) as expressing the measure of $\underline{r}+\underline{h}$ and $(p, -q)$ of $\underline{r}-\underline{h}$. We may then say that C comprises a non-ARCHIMEDEAN set of magnitudes, for, although $(1, 0)$ and $(0, 1)$ are both measures of members of C, there is no positive integer n such that $n(0, 1) > (1, 0)$. In this way we can give precision to an assertion that any rectilinear angle is infinitely greater than any horn-angle. By varying p while keeping q fixed we may see how in a sense a continuous change does not cover all intermediates.[215]

It is hard to see how a medieval writer could have provided a full analysis of the problem. In the sixteenth century JACQUES PELETIER attempted to cut the Gordian knot by denying that the horn-angle was an angle and by equating the angle of a semicircle with a right angle.[216] This was in effect redefining the criteria for equating and ordering angles as to size. It can justifiably be regarded as arbitrary, and so it is not surprising that the controversy continued during the seventeenth century.

VII. Special Topics

VII.1. Figures of egredient angles, or star-polygons

At the end of the first part of his work BRADWARDINE includes a chapter on what he calls figures of egredient angles (*figurae egredientium angulorum*). It is tempting to suggest some vaguely occultist reason for such an interest in star-like figures, but for this there is no direct evidence. Perhaps more plausibly BRADWARDINE simply saw that an elegant theory was possible. The chapter has the interest that BRADWARDINE makes an explicit assertion of novelty of treatment:[217]

---

[215] An investigation of systems of non-ARCHIMEDEAN magnitudes with particular reference to curvilinear angles was made by VERONESE at the end of the last century; *cf.* F. WAISMANN, *Introduction to Mathematical Thinking* (London, 1951), 219–225.

[216] On this and the succeeding controversy see HEATH, *Euclid's Elements* (n. 57 above), 41–42.

[217] "De figuris egredientium angulorum dicam in hoc capitulo secundum considerationem universalem et in communi; et in hoc volo sufficere. Rarus enim est sermo de hiis, nec vidi sermonem de eis nisi solius Campani, qui de solo pentagono parum tetigit casualiter" (1.2).

In this chapter I shall speak of figures of egredient angles following a universal consideration and in general, and in this I wish to suffice, for discussion of these is rare, and I have seen no discussion of them except that of Campanus alone, who casually touched a little on only the pentagon.

BRADWARDINE's view as to the previous lack of geometrical discussion seems well borne out by the facts. In a valuable historical discussion of star-polygons, M. CHASLES drew attention to a passage in a pseudo-BOETHIAN geometry,[218] but it is very obscure. At one time S. GÜNTHER thought that he had a treatment by ADELARD of Bath,[219] but he later decided that it was by REGIOMONTANUS.[220] As a short additional corollary to I.32 CAMPANUS showed that the sum of the angles of a star-pentagon was equal to two right angles. It has been suggested that he may have derived this, directly or indirectly, from the work of THĀBIT IBN QURRA.[221] BRADWARDINE had already (1.16) used other of CAMPANUS's corollaries to this proposition in discussing the sum of the angles of ordinary polygons.

BRADWARDINE's approach to star-polygons is from the viewpoint of their genesis.[222]

A figure is said to be of egredient angles when the sides of some polygonal figure from among the simple ones are produced until they meet outside.

It is implicit that each side is to be produced in both directions and to meet another in each of these. With this definition BRADWARDINE has little difficulty in showing that the star-pentagon is the first figure (1.21). Although BRADWARDINE gives the impression that he is speaking generally, his focus tends to be on regular polygons: he does not consider pathological cases in which, for instance, a side of a pentagon produced in one direction only may meet two other produced sides. A feature of BRADWARDINE's definition is that it means that figures such as the star-hexagon are admitted; in a definition like POINSOT's in the nineteenth century[223] this would have to be regarded as two triangles rather than as a simple polygon. BRADWARDINE's definition contributes to the elegance of his theory. Star-polygons that are produced in this way from simple polygons are later referred to as those of the first order. We may proceed to higher orders.[224]

---

[218] M. CHASLES, Aperçu Historique sur l'origine et le Développement des Méthodes en Géométrie (2nd edn., Paris, 1875), 476–477; cf. M. FOLKERTS, "Boethius" Geometrie II (n. 118 above), 131–132.

[219] S. GÜNTHER, "Lo Svillupo Storico della Teoria dei Poligoni Stellati nell'Antichità e nel Medio Evo", Bulletino di Bibliografia e di Storia delle Scienze Matematiche e Fisiche, vi (1875), 313–340.

[220] S. GÜNTHER, Geschichte des mathematischen Unterrichts im deutschen Mittelalter bis zum Jahre 1525, Monumenta Germaniae Pedagogica, iii (Berlin, 1887), 247; cf. M. FOLKERTS, "Regiomontans Euklidhandschriften", Sudhoffs Archiv, lviii (1974), 149–164, at 157.

[221] G. ENESTRÖM, "Über die Geschichte der Sternvielecke im Mittelalter", Bibliotheca Mathematica, x_3 (1910), 277.

[222] "Dicitur autem figura egredientium angulorum cum latera alicuius figure poligonie de simplicibus protrahuntur in utramque partem donec concurrant exterius" (1.2).

[223] L. POINSOT, Mémoire sur les Polygons et sur les Polyhèdres (Paris, 1809).

[224] "Sicud enim primus ordo est acceptus iuxta ordinem figurarum simplicium, ita ulterius potest accipi iuxta istum ordinem alius ordo figurarum egredientium angulorum, protrahendo latera similiter ulterius usque ad iteratum concursum eorundem" (1.24).

Just as the first order is taken with respect to the order of simple figures, so further another order of figures of egredient angles may be taken with respect to this order, by similarly producing the sides further until their next meeting.

No pentagon or hexagon of the second order is possible, but BRADWARDINE appeals to a diagram to show that there is a second order star-heptagon. In 1.25 he sketches out how the process may be continued with each new order starting from the third member of the preceding order.

In addition to this tidy classification (which could be represented by a triangular array), BRADWARDINE is interested in the sum of the angles of such polygons. In 1.22 he easily shows that the sum of the angles of the star-pentagon is equal to two right angles. In 1.23 he asserts that for each succeeding member of the order the sum is increased by two right angles. For polygons with an even number of sides this is easy to show, for they may be resolved into two simple polygons. BRADWARDINE does not attempt a proof for the odd-numbered cases, but merely remarks that the result is probable (*verisimile*). In 1.25 he rises to this general speculation:[225]

> To investigate here the value of the angles of such figures would be more laborious than fruitful,[226] and so I do not pursue it. It sometimes seemed to me that all orders of figures agree in this, that the first [member] always has the value of two right angles, and a successor always adds two right angles in value over its predecessor. But although this is near to it in truth, I do not however assert it.

Despite his lack of proof, this fine general theory (even though simple) testifies to BRADWARDINE's mathematical vision, and may be held to have mapped out a research programme for others to follow.

One such was a later fourteenth-century writer, WIGANDUS DURNHEIMER, who, in what was essentially a commentary on BRADWARDINE's *Geometria*, included a greatly extended section on star-polygons,[227] and with what seems a clear dig at BRADWARDINE, prided himself on supplying preceding deficiencies:[228]

> To some there seems to be a great difficulty concerning the value of the outward-pointed angles of figures of egredient angles. For no one cared to write about the value of such angles; no one wished to undergo the labour; most rarely have I seen a discussion of them.

Among the mass of verbiage and ill-planned expression that follows there is included a quite good simple proof of the general case. It rests on the fact that each

---

[225] "De valore autem angulorum talium figurarum hic discutere laboriosum esset magis quam fructuosum. Ideo non insisto. Videbatur aliquando mihi quod omnes ordines figurarum quantum ad hoc conveniunt quod semper prima valet 2 rectos, et semper sequens addit super precedentem in valore 2 rectos. Sed quamvis hoc propinquum sit ei secundum rem tamen hoc non assero" (1.25).

[226] For the phrase c. ANSELM, *Dialogus de veritate*, in *Patriologiae Cursus Completus ... Series Latina*, ed. J.-P. MIGNE (Paris, 1844–93), clviii, 475.

[227] *MS cit.* (n. 55 above), ff. 6v–15r.

[228] *Ibid.*, f. 8r: "De valore autem angulorum egressorum figurarum egredientium angulorum magna videtur aliquibus difficultas. Nullus enim de valore talium angulorum edissere curavit; nullus enim labore subire voluit; rarissimum enim vidi sermonem de hiis."

angle of a star-polygon of a certain order is the exterior angle to a triangle in which one of the interior and opposite angles is an exterior angle of the simple polygon and the other is an angle of the star-polygon of the preceding order. It is then easy to show that the sum of the angles of the star-polygon of the original order is four right angles less than the sum of the angles of the star-polygon of the preceding order. A somewhat similar proof is given by PEDRO SANCHEZ CIRVELO, in a work that was also based on BRADWARDINE,[229] but there is no reason to suppose that he depended on WIGANDUS. Other later writers also drew on BRADWARDINE's chapter on star-polygons,[230] but we cannot include REGIOMONTANUS or KEPLER among their number.[231]

VII.2. Isoperimetry

As BRADWARDINE points out, EUCLID did not deal with isoperimetry, but frequent references were made to the subject in ancient and medieval literature. QUINTILIAN, for example, held that the sorting out of the confusion between equality of area and equality of perimeter was a prime example of the utility of geometry,[232] and it is probable that isoperimetric frauds were commonplace.[233] In astronomy a standard argument for the sphericity of the world was that the sphere was the greatest of solid figures of equal surface.[234] For SACROBOSCO this was the argument from fitness (commoditas),

> because of all isoperimetric bodies the sphere is the greatest, and of all forms the round is the most capacious. Therefore, because greatest and round, on that account most capacious. Wherefore since the world contains all things, such a form was useful and fit for it.[235]

Because of such references it was quite natural for BRADWARDINE to include a chapter (2.4) on the subject in his Geometria, but we may feel surprise at the form which the chapter took.

The standard ancient work on the subject was by ZENODORUS.[236] The original is lost, but there are extant three ancient treatments deriving from it:[237] by THEON

---

[229] CIRVELO, Cursus quattuor mathematicarum artium (n. 54 above), sig. Bi. v–ii.r.

[230] CHARLES DE BOUVELLES, Geometrie Practique (Paris, 1551), ff. 22v–28r; BROSCIUS, Apologia (n. 60 above), 16 sqq.; MS Vienna, Nat. Bibl., 5277, ff. 343v–344v.

[231] For REGIOMONTANUS see nn. 219–220 above; for KEPLER, J. KEPLER, Gesammelte Werke, ed. W. VON DYCK & M. CASPAR (Munich, 1938–), vi, 20–64.

[232] QUINTILIAN, Institutio oratoriae, I.10. 39–45, ed. F.H. COLSON (Cambridge, 1924), 136–138.

[233] Cf. S. GANDZ, "Studies in Babylonian Mathematics III. Isoperimetric Problems and the Origin of Quadratic Equations", Isis, xxxii (1940), 103–115.

[234] E.g., PTOLEMY, Almagest, I.3, in Des Claudius Ptolemäus Handbuch der Astronomie, tr. K. MANITIUS (Leipzig, 1912–3), 9. Cf. PLATO, Timaeus, 33B; ARISTOTLE, De coelo, II.4, 287a27–30.

[235] L. THORNDIKE, The Sphere of Sacrobosco and its Commentators (Chicago, 1949), 80.

[236] For a recent attempt to date him see G.J. TOOMER, "The Mathematician Zenodorus", Greek, Roman and Byzantine Studies, xiii (1972), 177–192.

[237] W. MÜLLER, "Das isoperimetrische Problem im Altertum", Sudhoffs Archiv, xxxvii (1953), 39–71. All three versions may be found in Pappi Alexandrini Collectionis Quae Supersunt, ed. F. HULTSCH (Berlin, 1875; repr. Amsterdam, 1965).

of Alexandria, by PAPPUS, and in an introduction to the *Almagest* which J. MOGENET ascribes to EUTOCIUS.[238] The last of these was translated into Latin in the twelfth or thirteenth century,[239] and from the number of manuscript copies it seems to have been widely diffused;[240] it was known to ROGER BACON.[241] The manuscript tradition has not yet been systematically studied, but we may draw attention to two manuscripts containing a work on isoperimetry ascribed to JORDANUS.[242] This seems to be a reworking of the "Eutocian" version. In his Questions on Euclid NICOLE ORESME refers to a *Liber de triangulis* for the demonstration of some isoperimetric results, but the identity of this is not known.[243]

Despite the availability of the ZENODORAN tradition BRADWARDINE's treatment is only loosely related to it. After pointing out that "isoperimetric" is a relative term, he moves on to his first conclusion:[244]

> Therefore let the first conclusion about isoperimetrics be this. Figures are isoperimetric one to the other of which the perimeters are equal.

By all his preceding discussion this should surely be a definition, but BRADWAR-DINE thinks that some proof is appropriate:

> This is clear immediately by expounding the terms. For the perimeter of a figure is the boundary or boundaries by which the figure is contained, as the periphery in a circle and three lines in a triangle. And the surface which is contained by its bound or bounds is *area* in Latin, *embodum* [*cf.* ἐμβαδόν] or *empipedum* [*cf.*

---

[238] J. MOGENET, *L'Introduction à l'Almageste*, Académie Royale de Belgique. Classe des lettres et des sciences morales et politiques. Mémoires, li, fasc. 2 (Brussels, 1956).

[239] A.A. BJÖRNBO, "Die mittelalterlichen lateinische Übersetzungen aus dem Griechischen auf dem Gebiet der mathematischen Wissenschaften", *Archiv für die Geschichte der Naturwissenschaften und der Technik*, i (1909), 385–394, at 393; CLAGETT, *Archimedes in the Middle Ages* (n. 55 above), i, 32, 630.

[240] *Cf.* THORNDIKE & KIBRE, *Catalogue of Incipits* (n. 13 above), 778, 1083.

[241] ROGER BACON, *Comm. math.*, in *Op. hact. ined.* (n. 147 above), xvi, 44.

[242] *Cf.* R.B. THOMSON, "Jordanus de Nemore: Opera", *Mediaeval Studies*, xxxviii (1976), 97–144, at 126.

[243] ORESME, *Quaest. super Geom. Eucl.* (n. 214 above), 14; *cf.* H.L.L. BUSARD, "Die Quellen von Nicole Oresme", *Janus*, lviii (1971), 161–193. There also appears to be a work on isoperimetry in MS Florence, Bib. Naz., Conv. Sopp. J.X. 40, ff. 1r–14v; see A.A. BJÖRNBO, "Die mathematischen S. Marcohandschriften in Florenz, 4", *Bibliotheca Mathematica*, xii₃ (1911–2), 193–224 at 201.

[244] "Prima igitur conclusio de ysoperimetris sit ista. Ysoperimetre sunt figure una alteri quarum perymetri sunt equales. Ista patet statim exponendo terminos. Perymeter enim figure est terminus vel termini sub quo vel sub quibus figura continetur, quemadmodum periferia in circulo et 3 linee in triangulo. Et superficies que huius termino vel terminis continetur area latine, embodum vel empipedum in greco. Et est perymeter dictio composita, sicud dyameter, a peri, quod est circa, et metros, quod est mensura, quasi mensurans circumcirca. Componitur autem ulterius perymeter cum yso verbo greco, quod idem sonat quod equale, et dicitur ysoperimeter, tra, trum, adiective, quod interpretatur equalis circummensurationis, nam yso equale, perymeter circummensuratio. Et ex hoc statim patet propositio sine discursu, quod ysoperymetre sunt figure quarum perymetre sunt equales ..." (2.41).

ἐπίπεδον] in Greek. And *perymeter* is a composite word like diameter — from *peri*, which is around, and *metros*, which is measure, as if measuring roundabout. *Perymeter* is further compounded with the Greek word *yso*, which means the same as equal, and adjectivally it is expressed as *ysoperimeter, -tra, -trum*, which is interpreted as equal in circummeasure, for *yso* is equal, and *perymeter* circummeasure. And from this the proposition is clear without argument, that figures are isoperimetric of which the perimeters are equal. ...

A peculiar argument for a geometric work, even in BRADWARDINE's own terms, but such etymologies had found their place in the commentary tradition of SACROBOSCO's *Sphere*, and BRADWARDINE's treatment certainly represents an improvement on the following effort by ROBERTUS ANGLICUS:[245]

> The meaning of the third part is clear on understanding the exposition of this word, *ysoperimetrum*; and it is said from *idos*, which is form, and *peri*, which is around, and *metros*, which is measure, as if of all measurable round forms the greatest. Which is clear, because, if there are two equal lines and a square is made from one and a circle from the other, the circle will contain more than the square.

BRADWARDINE's whole chapter seems more in accord with this tradition than with pure geometry, and we are probably justified in concluding that it was lifted with minimal revision from some other work. (Could it even be BRADWARDINE's own lost astronomical work?)[246] Among the circumstantial evidence for this is the hint at etymologies of *poligonium* and *orthogonium* in 2.42., where BRADWARDINE also misleadingly speaks as if he is introducing the word *poligonium* for the first time.

Strictly speaking BRADWARDINE's next two propositions are false, and counter-examples are easily conjured up. This is because BRADWARDINE fails to place adequate restrictions on the types of polygons of which he is speaking. Thus, while the first "EUTOCIAN" proposition is, "Of rectilinear equilateral isoperimetrics contained in circles, that which has more angles is greater",[247] BRADWARDINE's 2.42 reads, "Of all isoperimetric polygons, that which has more angles is greater."[248] For proof in this proposition and in its two successors BRADWARDINE merely produces a pair of isoperimetric polygons, one of which he shows is bigger than the other. 2.43 is, "Of all isoperimetric polygons with equal numbers of angles that which is equiangular is greater", and 2.44 is, "Of all isoperimetric polygons with equal numbers of sides and equal angles, that which is

---

[245] THORNDIKE, *Sphere* (n. 235 above), 153: "Sententia tertie partis patet intellecta expositione huius vocabuli, *ysoperimetrum*, et dicitur ab *idos*, quod est forma, et *peri* quod est circa, et *metros*, quod est mensura, quasi omnium formarum circularium mensurabilium maxima. Quod patet, quia, si fuerunt due linee equales et ex una fiat quadratum et ex alia circulus, plus continebit circulus quam quadratum." For another etymological treatment see H. HUGONNARD-ROCHE, *L'Oeuvre Astronomique de Themon Juif* (Geneva & Paris, 1973), 121.

[246] See n. 14 above.

[247] MS Cambridge, Univ. Lib., Mm. III.11, f. 195r: "Ysoperimetrorum ysopleurorum rectilineorum circulis contentorum quod plurium est angulorum maius est."

[248] "Omnium poligoniorum ysoperimetrorum quod plurium est angulorum maius est" (2.42).

equilateral is greater."[249] The three are jointly directed towards the proof of 2.45, which is that the circle is the greatest of isoperimetric figures. They there represent three tendencies which the circle realises to the highest degree. First, as ARISTOTLE says,[250] the circle is all angle; secondly it is most equal in all its curves; and thirdly its sides are most equal, since an inscribed regular polygon cuts off equal arcs. It has therefore passed so far as is possible along the three paths mapped out by the preceding conclusions, and so we conclude that it is the most capacious of plane figures, just as the sphere is the most capacious of solid ones. From wherever these arguments derive, they smack more of rhetoric than of geometrical demonstration.

VII.3. Filling place

In PLATO's *Timaeus* the small particles of the four elements were given the shapes of four of the five regular solids.[251] The remaining solid, the dodecahedron, was assigned to the "whole". ARISTOTLE did not like this type of theory: one of his objections was that it entailed the existence of a vacuum,[252] for, although a collection of cubes or of pyramids (tetrahedra) could be arranged so that there were no gaps between them, this was not the case with the other three regular solids. Similarly among regular plane figures, place could only be filled by the triangle, the square and the hexagon. The standard way of approaching the problem was to ask whether figures could be arranged about a point so that there were no gaps in its neighbourhood. In the case of plane figures there is no difficulty. PROCLUS ascribed the result to the PYTHAGOREANS,[253] and BRADWARDINE gives a satisfactory account in 1.17. But solid figures were more problematic. The main trouble was with the pyramid. By way of anticipation we may say that ARISTOTLE was in error: the pyramid does not fill place. But for the commentators the main problem was not this, but the question of how many pyramids filled place, that is, how many could be arranged around a point so that there were no gaps. This usually involved considerations of solid angles, and so we digress for a moment.

BRADWARDINE (4.0), following EUCLID's second definition in XI. Def. 11, defines a solid angle thus:[254]

A solid or corporeal angle is that which is contained by more than two plane angles which are not situated in a single surface and which meet at a single angular point.

There was a strong temptation to treat solid geometry by analogy with plane geometry, but this was not without its dangers. Let us first note a comparatively harmless instance. To his first postulate ("From any point to any point to draw a

---

[249] "Omnium poligoniorum ysoperimetrorum et equemultitudinis angulorum maius est quod est est equiangulum" (2.43). "Omnium poligoniorum ysoperimetrorum equemultitudinis laterum et equalium angulorum maius est quod equilaterum est" (2.44).

[250] *Cf. De coelo*, III.8, 307a2–3, 17–18.

[251] *Timaeus*, 53C–56C, in F.M. CORNFORD, *Plato's Cosmology* (London, 1937), 210–224.

[252] *De coelo*, III.8, 306b3–9.

[253] PROCLUS, *In Primum Euclidis* ... (n. 73 above), 304–305.

[254] "Angulus solidus sive corporeus est quem continent anguli plani plures quam duo qui non in una superficie siti ad punctum unum angularem concurrunt" (4.0).

straight line"), BRADWARDINE made the addition, "And that line to be the shortest of all those with the same ends."[255] The only occasion on which he uses the addition is in 4.21, in order to show that, if three plane angles contain a solid angle, any two of them is greater than the third.

> From the clause added to the first postulate I accept that the straight is the shortest: just as between the same ends the straight line is shorter than the curved or bent, similarly between the same lines the straightly extended surface is shorter than the curved or bent.[256]

BRADWARDINE continues by applying this type of analogical reasoning to the solid angle. This certainly does not have the degree of rigour of the corresponding EUCLIDEAN proposition (XI.21), but more insidious dangers were presented by another form of analogical argument. This concerned the quantification of the solid angle. BRADWARDINE (4.23), like CAMPANUS (XI.21), but unlike EUCLID, regarded the solid angle as having the value of the plane angles containing it. In itself this is not illegitimate, but it does suggest fallacious inferences, and these are met in discussions of filling place.

The principal medieval source for this topic was AVERROES' discussion in his "Great Commentary" on the De coelo, in the translation of MICHAEL SCOT.[257] AVERROES held that ARISTOTLE mentioned the plane figures that fill place as well as the solid ones, because the scarcity of the former is the cause of the scarcity of the latter. He also asserted that the cause of bodies filling place was that their surfaces could fill place. He expounded the reasons for there only being three plane figures with the required property, and then tried to argue analogously for solid figures. A consideration of three mutually intersecting perpendicular lines reveals that eight solid angles can come together at a point, and that each of them has the value of three right angles, that is the angle of a cube. Thus what is needed for filling place at a point is solid angles to the value of eight cubic angles. (For the plane case four right angles were needed.) The pyramid has solid angle of value two right angles, and so three pyramidal angles have the value of two cubic angles. It easily follows that twelve pyramids fill place. AVERROES shows that no combination of angles of icosohedra are equal to eight cubic angles, and asserts that the same holds for the octohedron and dodecahedron.

In the Opus tertium ROGER BACON showed himself to be a firm protagonist of AVERROES' mode of argument. After expounding his reasoning on pyramids he continued:[258]

---

[255] "Et ipsam omnium contermabilium esse brevissimam" (1.021). ARCHIMEDES had given the equivalent as an assumption in his De sphaera et cylindro, and this is reported (as a definition) in ANARITIUS, In Decem Libros... (n. 75 above), 6.

[256] "Ex clausula prime petitionis adiuncta accipio quod rectum est brevissimum: sicud inter eosdem terminos linea recta est brevior quam curva vel fracta, similiter inter easdem lineas superficies recte extensa est brevior superficie curva vel fracta" (4.21).

[257] De coelo, III, comm. 66, in ed. cit. (n. 78 above), v, f. 230r–v. ROGER BACON, Comm. math. in Op. hact. ined. (n. 147 above), xvi, 44, mentions a bock De replentibus locum. The relevant portion of the Timaeus was not included in CHALCIDIUS's translation, and so was not directly known in the Middle Ages.

[258] ROGER BACON, Opera Quaedam Hactenus Inedita, Vol. I, ed. J.S. BREWER (London, 1859), 138.

I

172

But the crowd of natural philosophers at Paris, because it does not know the terms of geometry, contradicts its author, for one fool, who had a name among the crowd, declared in public and said that Averroes lies when he says that twelve pyramids fill place, for twenty fill it, as he used to assert. But what he says is impossible....

But BACON investigated the matter more thoroughly than AVERROES, and found that by reasoning on solid angles the octohedron also should fill place, for each of its angles had the value of two and two thirds right angles, and so nine of its solid angles equalled twenty-four right angles. Thus reason has led him into apparent conflict with authority, and it was probably because of this that earlier in his chapter he had inserted one of his frequent attacks on bad translations:[259]

According to how Averroes expounds Aristotle, two corporeal figures fill place, namely the cube and pyramid. But certainty cannot be had from the text of Aristotle in Latin, because the common text is false and badly translated, and another translation is dubious.

Towards the end of the chapter BACON brings in experience to join reason and authority:[260]

Full certainty about these matters cannot be had unless bodies be made and figured according to the teaching of the thirteenth book of geometry.

This is fully in accord with his epistemology, but ironically the argument from experience was central to the case of those who held that twenty pyramids filled place. BACON may later have acquired suspicions about the cogency of AVERROES' argument, for in the more sober *Communia naturalium* he appears to have some doubts as to whether the pyramid fills place at all.[261]

I do not know the identity of BACON's "fool", but on this occasion it appears not to have been ALBERTUS MAGNUS, for in his *De caelo et mundo* ALBERT follows AVERROES' line, although without mentioning his name.[262] Later in the century the flaw in AVERROES' argument was clearly expressed by PETER of Auvergne:[263]

---

[259] *Ibid.*, 137.

[260] *Ibid.*, 139–140.

[261] *Op. hact. ined.* (n. 147 above), iv, 341–342, 363.

[262] *De caelo et mundo*, Lib. 3, Tr. 2, Cap. 7, in ALBERTUS MAGNUS, *Opera Omnia*, ed. B. GEYER (Münster, 1951–   ), v, Pars i, 238–239.

[263] THOMAS AQUINAS, *Commentarii in Quatuor Libros de Caelo Aristotelis* (Paris, 1536), 198–199: "Et quod Averrois dicit, quod angulus pyramidalis solidus est aequalis duobus rectis superficialibus, non est intelligibile. Oportet enim magnitudines aequales esse ejusdem rationis. Unde linea non est aequalis superficiei, nec aliquid istorum corporum. Angulus vero pyramidalis, et angulus superficialis eiusdem rationis non sunt, quia iste corporalis est, ille vero superficialis, quare non sunt aequales adinuicem, nec ista compountur ex illis, siquidem corpus ex superficiebus non componatur. Praeterea si angulus pyramidalis esset duo recti superficiales, tunc componeretur ex eis: quare et pyramis ex superficialibus triangulis, eadem enim est ratio. Hoc autem est falsum, et contra Aristotelis intentionem, qui vult corpora non componi ex superficialibus, et contra ipsum Commentatorem." AQUINAS's commentary was completed by PETER of Auvergne; see M. GRABMANN, *Die Werke des Hl. Thomas von Aquin*, Beiträge zur Geschichte der Philosophie und Theologie des Mittelalters, xxii, Hefte 1–2 (Münster, 1931), 263.

And what Averroes says, that the solid pyramidal angle is equal to two superficial right angles, is not intelligible. For it is necessary for equal magnitudes to be of the same *ratio;* wherefore a line is not equal to a surface nor is any of those bodies. A pyramidal angle and a superficial angle are not of the same *ratio*, because the former is corporeal and the latter superficial, and so they are not mutually equal. Nor are the ones composed from the others; certainly a body is not composed from surfaces. Moreover, if a pyramidal angle were two superficial right angles, then it would be composed from them, and therefore a pyramid would be composed from superficial triangles, for the *ratio* is the same. But this is false and against the intention of Aristotle, who held that bodies were not composed from superficial [figures], and against the Commentator himself.

The ground was thus well prepared for BRADWARDINE's discussion (4.3), and he himself added little that was new, although he did try to buttress the cube's place filling property with an arithmetical argument from the fact that a cube number multiplied by a cube number produces a cube number. His general stance is given by the cautious statement that, "According to truth the cube fills place, but according to Averroes the cube and the pyramid."[264] He does not explicitly deny that the pyramid fills place, and ends his chapter as follows:[265]

But we shall not be able for the present to attain full certainty by the way of disputation, and therefore let it be undiscussed for now.

BRADWARDINE dubs as a mere *persuasio* AVERROES' argument that the paucity of place-filling plane figures was the cause of the paucity of place-filling solids, and he isolates the fallacy in AVERROES' argument by pointing out (with reference to considerations of isoperimetry) that the following consequence is invalid:[266]

Superficial angles of twelve pyramids have the value of superficial angles of eight cubes — therefore there is as much corpulence in the former as in the latter.

He also remarks that by AVERROES' mode of argument the octohedron would fill place.

BRADWARDINE alludes to the opinion that twenty pyramids fill place, but does not develop it beyond saying that its supporters appealed to experience. His elaborator is less taciturn, and holds that the position is probable enough. He adds the intelligent remark that, if the position were true, then the twenty pyramids would form an icosohedron. Similarly an icosohedron could be imagined to be divided into twenty pyramids by lines from its vertices to its centre. If, on the other hand twelve pyramids filled place, they would form a regular solid with twelve triangular faces, and none such exists. But there still remained the possibility of eight pyramids filling place and forming an octohedron. Thus we cannot be certain that twenty fill place.

---

[264] "Dico ergo quoniam secundum veritatem cubus replet locum, sed secundum opinionem Averroys cubus et pyramis" (4.3).

[265] "Sed tamen per viam disputationis non poterimus ad plenam certitudinem pervenire pro nunc; ideo relinquatur illud ad presens indiscussum" (4.3).

[266] "Anguli superficiales 12 pyramidum valent angulos superficiales 8 cuborum — ergo tanta corpulentia est sub istis sicud sub illis" (4.3).

> But, if it were established that the pyramids into which the icosohedron was resolved in the aforesaid way were regular, then the matter would not appear dubious.[267]

With this concluding remark the elaborator came within a hair's breadth of solving the problem, for a simple reference to Proposition XIII.16 (XIII.15 in CAMPANUS) of the *Elements* would have shown him that, if a regular icosohedron was inscribed in a sphere, then the radius of the sphere is incommensurable with the edge of the icosohedron. It follows that twenty pyramids do not fill space, and a similar argument shows that neither do eight. Therefore the pyramid does not fill place at all, and ARISTOTLE was in error. But, as it was, this step is not known to have been taken until PAUL of Middelburg showed the way, in astrological prognostics for the years 1480 and 1481.[268] This long delay witnesses to the limited extent to which medieval Schoolmen actually did geometry rather than consider it.

VIII. Conclusion

By its nature an article of this kind cannot have a single sweeping conclusion, whether revisionist or not. But in order to draw some threads together I present a number of theses, not all of which I claim to have established beyond reasonable doubt.

1. BRADWARDINE's *Geometria* was in the philosophical rather than the technical mathematical tradition.
2. It was particularly related to problems of ARISTOTELIANISM.
3. Its main source was the CAMPANUS version of EUCLID, but it included chapters on star-polygons, isoperimetery, filling place, and the sphere.
4. BRADWARDINE's attitude toward mathematics was realist rather than conceptualist.
5. In the *Geometria* he tried to adapt geometry to a finite world, but in later works he moved towards a concept of infinite space.
6. He was not much troubled by the problem of geometrical exactness.
7. He did not attain a satisfactory view of the role of construction in geometry.
8. He had a strong concern for questions of order and priority among mathematical objects.
9. Scholastic disputational modes of argument impinge heavily upon his work.
10. His concern for geometrical rigour was less than in the Greek mathematical tradition; this is particularly evident when he was not following a standard mathematical authority.
11. He had a strong tendency to concentrate on the most regular case of a theorem.
12. Experience as well as deduction from first principles was a source of geometrical knowledge.
13. He carefully considered problems of measure.

---

[267] "Si tamen constaret quod pyramides in quas predicto modo resolveretur ycocedron essent regulares iam non videtur res dubia" (4.3).

[268] D.J. STRUIK, "Het Probleem 'De impletione loci'", *Nieuw Archief voor Wiskunde*, xv_2 (1926), 121–137, at 128–9, 136.

14. His philosophical approach to denomination extended the arithmetical language for speaking of ratios.
15. The *Geometria* had a steady if undramatic influence up to the sixteenth century; it may have done much to incline natural philosophers to his realist view of mathematics.
16. Nevertheless his mathematical outlook is notably different from that of the seventeenth century.

II

CAMPANUS AND EUDOXUS; OR, TROUBLE WITH TEXTS AND QUANTIFIERS *

SUMMARY. — It is generally assumed that Campanus of Novara comple-tely misunderstood the so-called Eudoxean criterion for the equality or identity of ratios. There are plausible grounds for this, but an examination of the whole of Book V of his version of Euclid's *Elements* reveals that he acquired a good un-derstanding of how the criterion actually operated, although he did not embed it in a rigorous axiomatic structure.

Since at least the time of Regiomontanus, Campanus of Novara has been berated for his treatment of proportion.[1] And indeed there are parts of his version of Book V of Euclid's *Elements* which appear to clinch the view that he completely misunderstood the so-called

---

* Membership of the Institute for Advanced Study, Princeton in the academic year 1980-1981 greatly facilitated part of the work on this paper.

[1] For Regiomontanus see M. CURTZE (ed.), *Urkunden zur Geschichte der Mathematik im Mittelalter und der Renaissance*, « Abhandlungen zur Geschichte der mathematischen Wissenschaften », XII-XIII, 1902, reprinted New York & London, Johnson Reprint 1968, p. 328. For a fine modern account of Campanus's difficulties see J. E. MURDOCH, *The Medieval Language of Proportions*, in A. C. CROMBIE (ed.), *Scientific Change*, London, Heinemann 1963, pp. 237-271.

Eudoxean theory.[2] But other parts belie this simple picture, and instead help us to produce a story in which, in a characteristically medieval fashion, understanding emerged from misunderstanding.

Campanus's initial trouble came from the texts that he received from the Adelard II version of the *Elements*.[3] Texts of definitions and of enunciations of propositions had to be treated with the reverence due to the work of an *auctor*, but sometimes the tradition did not faithfully reflect the original words. This was particularly the case with one of three definitions of Book V that we must now examine.[4]

Definition 5: Quantitates que dicuntur continuam habere proportionalitatem sunt quarum eque multiplicia aut equa sunt aut eque sibi sine interruptione addunt aut minuunt. [Quantities that are said to have a continuous proportion are those of which equimultiples are either equal or equally add over or take away from each other without a break].

Definition 6: Quantitates que dicuntur esse secundum proportionem unam prima ad secundam et tertia ad quartam sunt quarum prime et tertie multiplicationes equales multiplicationibus secunde et quarte equalibus fuerint similes vel additione vel diminutione vel equalitate eodem ordine sumpte. [Quantities that are said to be according to a single ratio, the first to the second and the third to the fourth, are those of which equal multiplyings of the first and third [compared] to equal multiplyings of the second and fourth are similar in addition or diminution or equality when taken in the same order].

Definition 8: Cum fuerint prime et tertie eque multiplicationes, itemque secunde et quarte eque multiplicationes, addatque multiplicatio prime super

---

[2] In using the standard terminology I do not intend signalling disagreement with the new view of Eudoxus's theory presented by W. R. KNORR, *Archimedes and the pre-Euclidean Proportion Theory*, « Archives Internationales d'Histoire des Sciences », XXVIII, 1978, pp. 183-244.

[3] On the Adelard and Campanus versions of the *Elements* see: M. CLAGETT, *The Medieval Latin Translations from the Arabic of the Elements of Euclid, with special emphasis on the Versions of Adelard of Bath*, « Isis », XLIV, 1953, pp. 16-42; J. E. MURDOCH, *The Medieval Euclid: Salient Aspects of the Translations of the Elements by Adelard of Bath and Campanus of Novara*, « Revue de Synthèse », LXXIX, 1968, pp. 67-94; ID., *Euclid: Transmission of the Elements*, in *Dictionary of Scientific Biography*, IV, 1971, pp. 437-459.

[4] For the text of Campanus's Book V I use *Euclidis Megarensis ... opera a Campano interprete fidissimo translata ... Lucas Paciolus ... detersit ... emendavit ...*, Venice 1509, corrected on the basis of MS New York, Columbia University, Plimpton 156, ff. 32v-49r and, as regards these three definitions, the Adelard II text as given in T. J. CUNNINGHAM, *Book V of Euclid's Elements in the Twelfth Century: the Arabic-Latin Traditions*, Ph. D. thesis, University of Wisconsin, 1972, pp. 163-164. I am grateful to Professor Marshall Clagett for the loan of photocopies of the Columbia University MS and for many useful discussions.

multiplicationem secunde, non addat autem multiplicatio tertie super multiplicationem quarte, dicetur prima maioris proportionis ad secundum quam tertia ad quartam. [When there have been equal multiplyings of the first and the third, and also equal multiplyings of the second and the fourth, and the multiplying of the first adds over the multiplying of the second, but the multiplying of the third does not add over the multiplying of the fourth, the first will be said to be of greater ratio to the second than the third to the fourth].

Definition 5 has no equivalent in the original Euclidean text, and is particularly misleading. On the other hand Campanus's Definition 6 recognisably derives from Euclid's famous Definition 5, which, in Heath's not quite literal translation, reads:[5]

Magnitudes are said to be in the same ratio, the first to the second and the third to the fourth, when, if any equimultiples whatever be taken of the first and third, and any equimultiples whatever of the second and fourth, the former equimultiples alike exceed, are alike equal to, or alike fall short of, the latter equimultiples respectively taken in corresponding order.

Heath remarks that,[6] « The difficulty in the way of an exactly literal translation is due to the fact that the words (καθ' ὁποιονοῦν πολλαπλασιασμὸν) signifying that the equimultiples *in each case* are any multiples *whatever* occur only once in the Greek, though they apply *both* to τὰ ... ἰσάκις πολλαπλάσια in the nominative and τῶν ... ἰσάκις πολλαπλασίων in the genitive ». Accordingly Heath includes two « quantifiers », but in the Latin version received by Campanus it was by no means clear that even one was to be understood.

Campanus's Definition 8 corresponds to Euclid's Definition 7:[7]

When, of the equimultiples, the multiple of the first magnitude exceeds the multiple of the second, but the multiple of the third does not exceed the multiple of the fourth, then the first is said to have a greater ratio to the second than the third has to the fourth.

Here the agreement is quite close, and in both the Greek and the Latin we may say that the requisite existential quantifier (indicating

[5] T. L. HEATH, *The Thirteen Books of Euclid's Elements*, 2nd edn., Cambridge University Press 1926; reprinted New York, Dover 1956, vol. 2, p. 114.

[6] *Op. cit.*, vol. 2, p. 120.

[7] *Op. cit.*, vol. 2, p. 114.

II

216

that only one set of multiples with the required property is demanded) is somewhat muted. Thus in these definitions Campanus's texts presented a decreasing order of corruption, and, if, as is plausibile, we see him as working from the beginning of the book to the end, then he has to tackle the worst text first.

This is a frightful mess. It is an attempt to import into Book V a separate definition of continuous proportion, that is, one obtaining in a series of (at least three) terms in which each term, except the last, has the same ratio to its successor. The text does this by analogy with the genuine Euclidean definition (which Campanus refers to as of « incontinuous proportion »), but it demands that the same multiple be taken of each of the terms instead of two sets of equimultiples, as in the definition. Whereas Euclid, properly understood, had two universal quantifiers, this definition has none explicitly, although a single one could possibly be understood. The result is a definition that reeks of vicious circularity. Despite his respect for the authorial text Campanus comes near to admitting this. His gloss indicates that « adding over » and « taking away from » are not to be interpreted merely in the sense of being greater than or less than, nor as referring to simple differences, but in a proportional way.[8]

You should not understand the multiples to relate to each other similarly in adding or taking away according to quantity of excess, but according to ratio, for otherwise the definition would be false. For equimultiples taken of any quantities of the same genus exceeding each other with equal differences also exceed each other with equal differences, and so they relate to each other similarly in adding or taking away according to the quantity of excess. But the original quantities are not continuously proportional; on the contrary there is always a greater ratio between the lesser quantities.

Campanus's interpretation is probably the best available without doing violence to the text, but the consequence is painfully clear:[9]

---

[8] « Multiplicia autem non intelligas similiter sic se habere in addendo aut minuendo quantum ad quantitatem excessus, sed quantum ad proportionem. Aliter enim diffinitio esset falsa. Nam quarumlibet quantitatum eiusdem generis equis se differentiis excedentium eque multiplicia accepta equis etiam differentiis se excedunt, unde similiter se habent in addendo et minuendo quantum ad quantitatem excessus. Nec tamen priores quantitates sunt continue proportionales; immo minorum est semper maior proportio ».

[9] « Erit itaque sensus diffinitionis premisse: Continua proportionalia sunt quarum omnia [omnium *in MS*] multiplicia equalia sunt continue proportionalia. Sed noluit ipsam diffinitionem ponere sub hac forma, quia tunc diffiniret idem per idem. A parte tamen rei est istud cum sua diffinitione convertibile ».

And so the sense of the aforesaid definition will be: Continuous proportionals are those of which all equimultiples are continuously proportional. But he did not wish to pose the definition in this form, because he would then have defined the same by the same. Nevertheless as regards reality [*a parte rei* - as opposed to verbally] this is convertible with his definition.

The one saving grace that Campanus has perhaps [10] derived here is a recognition that there is a « universal quantifier » involved.

This gloss now proceeded to colour his interpretation of the other two relevant definitions. Thus on Definition 6 we have: [11]

Similarity in adding or taking away is to be understood just as in the definition of continuously proportional [quantities], namely, not according to quantity of excess but according to ratio ... And so the sense of the definition will be: Four quantities are incontinuously proportional and the ratio of the first to the second is as that of the third to the fourth, when, if equimultiples are taken of the first and third, and also equimultiples of the second and fourth, the ratio of the multiple of the first to the multiple of the second will be as that of the multiple of the third to the multiple of the fourth. But he did not define in this form for the reason given above, although as regards reality (*a parte rei*) it is the same.

Thus the odour of circularity is still strong, and that of universal quantification weak, but in an example Campanus reveals that he does not demand that the same equimultiples be taken of the second and fourth as of the first and third. He has thus liberated himself from one of the snares presented by Definition 5.

A bigger breakthrough occurs in the comment on the eighth definition. At first Campanus tries to interpret this in line with his earlier

---

[10] See the difference in reading between the manuscript and the edition indicated in the last footnote.

[11] « Similitudo autem in addendo aut minuendo intelligatur hic sicut in diffinitione continue proportionalium, videlicet non quantum ad quantitatem excessus sed quantum ad proportionem ... Erit itaque sensus istius diffinitionis: Incontinue proportionales sunt quatuor quantitates, et proportio prime ad secundam est sicut tertie ad quartam, cum sumptis eque multiplicibus ad primam et tertiam itemque eque multiplicibus ad secundam et quartam, erit proportio multiplicis prime ad multiplex secunde sicut multiplicis tertie ad multiplex quarte. Sed non diffinivit sub hac forma propter causam predictam licet a parte rei idem sit ».

comments, and notes that there are four ways in which equimultiples can indicate that one of the original ratios was greater than the other:

(1) The multiple of the first is equal to the multiple of the second, but the multiple of the third is less than the multiple of the fourth.

(2) The multiple of the first is greater than the multiple of the second, but the multiple of the third is equal to or less than the multiple of the fourth.

(3) The multiple of the first is greater than the multiple of the second, and the multiple of the third is greater than the multiple of the fourth, « but the multiple of the first exceeds the multiple of the second more than the multiple of the third does the multiple of the fourth, according to ratio, not according to quantity of excess ».[12]

(4) The multiple of the first is less than the multiple of the second and the multiple of the third is less than the multiple of the fourth, « but the multiple of the first takes away from the multiple of the second less than the multiple of the third does from the multiple of the fourth, according to ratio, not according to quantity of excess ».[13]

But the Euclidean text appeared only to refer to the second of these ways, and so there was a problem of exegesis.

In his first answer Campanus managed a little obscurely to produce an interpretation akin to his remarks on the preceding definitions:[14]

The addition of the multiple of the first over the multiple of the second, but not of the multiple of the third over the multiple of the fourth, about which the author speaks in the definition, has latitude (*latitudinem habet*) to the four aforesaid modes and comprehends them. Thus the sense of the definition is: When, with multiples taken in the way he propounds, there is a greater ratio of the multiple of the first to the multiple of the second than of the multiple of the third to the multiple of the fourth, there will be

---

[12] « ... verumtamen plus excedit quantum ad proportionem non quantum ad quantitatem excessus multiplex prime multiplex secunde quam multiplex tertie multiplex quarte ».

[13] « ... verumtamen minus minuit quantum ad proportionem, non quantum ad quantitatem excessus multiplex prime a multiplici secunde quam multiplex tertie a multiplici quarte ».

[14] « Additio ergo illa multiplicis prime super multiplex secunde, non autem multiplicis tertie super multiplex quarte, de qua loquitur auctor in diffinitione, latitudinem habet ad istos 4 modos predictos et ipsos comprehendit. Unde sensus istius diffinitionis est: Cum, sumptis sic multiplicibus ut proponit, fuerit maior proportio multiplicis prime ad multiplex secunde quam multiplicis tertie ad multiplex quarte, erit maior proportio prime ad secundam quam tertie ad quartam. Non diffinivit autem sub hac forma propter communem causam prius dictam ».

a greater ratio of the first to the second than of the third to the fourth. But he did not define it in this form for the common reason aforesaid.

But he then moved to another, much less woolly reading, and one well in accord with the original Euclidean intent: [15]

Or we can say that the addition of the multiple of the first over the multiple of the second but not of the multiple of the third over the multiple of the fourth, about which he speaks in the aforesaid definition of greater inproportion, is properly taken as the words of the definition say, and only extends itself to the second of the aforesaid ways, even if in truth there be in each of the four ways a greater ratio of the first to the second than of the third to the fourth. Thus the sense of the definition is: If, with multiples taken in the way he propounds and with the multiple of the first being greater than the multiple of the second, it is not necessary that the multiple of the third be greater than the multiple of the fourth, then there will be a greater ratio of the first to the second than of the third to the fourth. He did not posit the remaining three modes of addition in the aforesaid definition for the reason that this is the plainest of them all, and sufficient for the said definition. For there is never a greater ratio of the first of four quantities to the second than of the third to the fourth, unless certain equimultiples of the first and the third may be found such that, when they are related to certain equimultiples of the second and the fourth, the multiple of the first will be found to add over the multiple of the second, but not the multiple of the third over the multiple of the fourth, and this may never be found unless there be a greater ratio of the first to the second than of the third to the fourth, as we shall demonstrate below on the tenth [proposition] of this [book].

---

[15] « Vel possumus dicere quod additio multiplicis prime super multiplex secunde et non multiplicis tertie super multiplex quarte, de qua loquitur in premissa diffinitione maioris inproportionalitatis, proprie accipitur prout verba diffinitionis sonant, et non se extendit nisi ad secundum quatuor predictorum modorum, licet revera quolibet istorum quatuor modorum sit maior proportio prime ad secundam quam tertie ad quartam. Unde sensus illius diffinitionis est: Cum, sumptis sic multiplicibus ut proponit, si multiplici prime existente maiori multiplici secunde non sit necessarium quod multiplex tertie sit maius multiplici quarte, tunc erit maior proportio prime ad secundam quam tertie ad quartam. Propter hoc autem non posuit reliquos tres additionis modos in predicta diffinitione, quia iste est illis omnibus magis planus, et ad dictam diffinitionem sufficiens. Nusquam enim est maior proportio prime 4 quantitatum ad secundam quam tertie ad quartam, quin contingat aliqua eque multiplicia ad primam et tertiam reperiri, que cum relata fuerint ad aliqua eque multiplicia secunde et quante, invenietur multiplex prime addere super multiplex secunde, non autem multiplex tertie super multiplex quarte. Nec usquam contingit hoc reperiri quin sit maior proportio prime ad secundam quam tertie ad quartam, ut demonstrabimus infra supra decimam huius ».

Thus Campanus's second interpretation of the definition, and as it turns out his preferred one, is modal, in terms of there being a lack of necessity in relations between the multiples. This is not quite the same as, or at least does not appear to be quite the same as, interpreting it in terms of an existential quantifier, and Campanus regards it as a matter of proof to show that one can construct a set of multiples with the required property if and only if the first ratio is greater than the second.

This proof follows on Proposition 12 (13 in Heiberg), not Proposition 10 as promised, and its technique draws heavily on that used in the proof of Proposition 8, in which it was required to show that if (in Campanus's notation) quantity BC was greater than quantity A, and D was some third quantity, then the ratio of BC to D was greater than that of A to D. The proof involved constructing equimultiples of BC and of A and a certain multiple of D such that the multiple of BC was greater and the multiple of A less than the multiple of D. Campanus appears here to have reworked and improved upon what was available to him from the tradition,[16] and he assimilated the procedure thoroughly enough to recognise its implication for other purposes.[17]

From the manner of this demonstration there appears the sufficiency of the definition of greater inproportion that the author posited in the beginning of this fifth [book]. For there is never a greater ratio of the first of four quantities to the second than of the third to the fourth, but that certain equimultiples to the first and third may be found, such that when they have been related to certain equimultiples of the second and fourth, the multiple of the

---

[16] Compare it with the corresponding passages in CUNNINGHAM, *op. cit.*, (n. 4), pp. 122-123, 170-172, 221-223, 273-275, 315-316, 363-365, and with that in MS Paris, Bibliothèque Nationale, Lat. 7373, f. 38*r-v*. The last is the translation of the *Elements* directly from the Greek, on which see J. E. MURDOCH, *Euclides Graeco-Latinus: A Hitherto Unknown Medieval Latin Translation of the Elements made directly from the Greek*, in « Harvard Studies in Classical Philology », LXXI, 1967, pp. 249-302; I am again indebted to Marshall Clagett for the loan of a photocopy. Cf. also HEATH, *op. cit.* (n. 5), vol. 2 pp. 149-153.

[17] « Ex huius autem demonstrationis modo patet sufficientia diffinitionis maioris improportionalitatis quam posuit auctor in principio huius quinti. Nusquam enim est maior proportio prime quatuor quantitatum ad secundam quam tertie ad quartam quin contingat aliqua eque multiplicia ad primam et tertiam reperiri que cum relata fuerint ad aliqua eque multiplicia secunde et quarte, invenietur multiplex prime addere super multiplex secunde, non autem multiplex tertie super multiplex quarte. Hec autem multiplicia sic reperiemus sicut demonstrabimus infra supra decimam [12 *in ed.*] huius ».

first will be discovered to add over the multiple of the second, but not the multiple of the third over the multiple of the fourth. We shall find these multiples in the way shown below on the tenth proposition of this book.

The reason for the deferment to the twelfth proposition was presumably that Campanus drew upon this in his proof, which we now present in full: [18]

From the manner of demonstration of the eighth [proposition] of this [book] and this [proposition] it will also be made manifest that if there be a greater ratio of the first of four quantities to the second than of the third to the fourth, there may be found certain equimultiples of the first and the third, such that when they shall be compared with certain equimultiples of the second and the fourth, the multiple of the first will be discovered to add

---

[18] « Ex modo autem demonstrationis octave huius et hac fiet manifestum quod si fuerit prime quatuor quantitatum ad secundam maior proportio quam tertie ad quartam continget reperire aliqua eque multiplicia prime et tertie, que, cum comparabuntur ad aliqua eque multiplicia secunde et quarte, invenietur multiplex prime addere super multiplex secunde, non autem multiplex tertie super multiplex quarte. Quod sic patet. Sit enim maior proportio AB ad C quam D ed E. Ponam ergo ut sit proportio AF ad C sicut D ad E. Eritque per hanc 12 et per 10 AF minor AB, et sit minor in quantitate FB, quam multiplicabo totiens quod proveniat quantitas maior C, que sit GH, hac conditione ut D totiens multiplicata producat quantitatem non minorem E, que sit K. Tunc ponam ut LG sit ita multiplex AF sicut GH est multiplex FB aut K D. Eritque per primam huius LH ita multiplex AB sicut K D. Deinde ponam quod M sit prima quantitas multiplex E que sit maior K, et ponam N ita multiplicem C sicut M est multiplex E. Eritque per premissas ypotheses et conversionem, diffinitionis incontinue proportionalitatis quantitas N prima multiplicium C que erit maior LG, nec erit LG minor C. Sumam ergo sub N maximam multiplicium C, aut sibi C equalem si forsan N sit prima multiplicium eius, que site O. Constabitque N ex O et C. Quia ergo LG non est minor O et GH est maior C, erit LH maior N. Quare, cum K sit minor M, patet propositum. Conversam quoque huius demonstrare possumus, videlicet quod, si contingit reperire aliqua eque multiplicia prime et tertie quaram multiplex prime addat super aliquod multiplex secunde et multiplex tertie non addat super multiplex quarte, maior erit proportio prime ad secundam quam tertie ad quartam. Quod sic probatur. Sint quatuor quantitates A prima, B secunda, CD tertia, E quarta, sintque F ad A et G ad CD eque multiplicia. Similiter H ad B et K ad E eque multiplicia. Et addat F super H, non autem addat G super K. Dico quod maior est proportio A ad B quam CD ad E. Si enim equalis, per conversionem diffinitionis incontinue proportionalitatis addet G super K, quod est contra ypothesim. Si autem minor, sit CL ad E sicut A ad B. Eritque per hanc duodecimam et decimam CL minor CD, et sit minor in quantitate LD. Ponam igitur ut MN sit ita multiplex CL, et NP multiplex LD, sicut F est multiplex A. Eritque per primam huius MP ita multiplex CD sicut F est multiplex A. Utraque igitur duarum quantitatum MP et G est eque multiplex quantitatis CD. Ergo ipse sunt equales. Nam hec illatio demonstrata est in 7 huius. Et, quia G non est maior K, non erit MP maior eadem. Sed per conversionem diffinitionis incontinue proportionalitatis MN est maior K, eo quod F est maior H. Ergo MN est maior MP, quod est impossibile. Quare relinquitur propositum ».

over the multiple of the second, but not the multiple of the third over the multiple of the fourth.

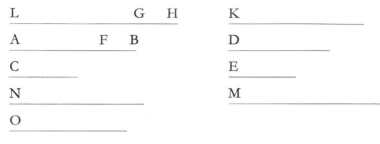

Fig. 1

This appears thus [Fig. 1].[19] For let there be a greater ratio of AB to C than of D to E. Let me posit therefore that the ratio of AF to C be as that of D to E. And by this twelfth [proposition][20] and by the tenth[21] AF will be less than AB, and let it be less by the quantity FB, which I shall multiply so many times that there comes forth a quantity greater than C, which let be GH, with the condition that D multiplied thus many times produces a quantity not less than E, which let be K. Then let me posit that LG be so much a multiple of AF as GH is a multiple of FB, or K of D. And by the first [proposition] of this [book][22] LH will be so much a multiple of AB as K is of D. Let me then posit that M be the first quantity, multiple of E, that is greater than K, and let me posit N so much a multiple of C as M is a multiple of E. By the premissed hypotheses and the conversion of the definition of incontinuous proportion, the quantity N will be the first of the multiples of C which will be greater than LG, and LG will not be less than C. Let me take therefore the greatest of the multiples of C below N or C's equal if perchance N be the first of its multiples, and let it be O. N will be composed from O and C. Because therefore LG is not less than O and GH is greater than C, LH will be greater than N. Wherefore, since K is less than M, what was proposed appears.

We can also demonstrate the converse of this, namely that if there may

---

[19] The diagrams are my own, but resemble those to be found in medieval manuscripts.

[20] In the terms of Campanus's « ekthesis », if the ratio of A to B is as that of C to D, and that of C to D is greater than that of E to F, then the ratio of A to B is greater than that of E to F.

[21] If the ratio of A to C is greater than that of B to C, then A is greater than B, and if the ratio of C to B is greater than that of C to A, then A is greater than B.

[22] If any number of quantities A, B, C, are equimultiples of D, E, F, then the aggregate of A, B, C has itself to the aggregate of D, E, F as does A to D.

be found certain equimultiples of the first and the third such that the multiple of the first adds over some multiple of the second, but the multiple of the third does not add over the multiple of the fourth, there will be a greater ratio of the first to the second than of the third to the fourth.

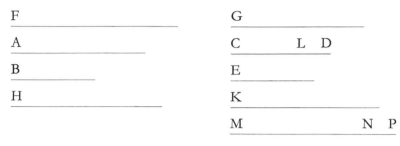

Fig. 2

This is proved thus [Fig. 2]. Let there be four quantities, A the first, B the second, CD the third, E the fourth, and let F to A and G to CD be equimultiples. Similarly let H to B and K to E be equimultiples. And let F add over H but not G add over K. I say that the ratio of A to B is greater than CD to E. For if it is equal, then, by conversion of the definition of incontinuous proportion, G will add over K, which is against the hypothesis. But if it is less let CL to E be as A to B. And by this twelfth [proposition] and by the tenth CL is less than CD, and let it be less by the quantity LD. Let me posit therefore that MN be just so much a multiple of CL and NP a multiple of LD as F is a multiple of A. By the first [proposition] of this [book] MP will be just so much a multiple of CD as F is a multiple of A. Therefore each of the two quantities MP and G is equally multiple of the quantity CD. Therefore they are equal. For this illation was demonstrated in the seventh [proposition] of this [book],[23] and, because G is not greater than K, MP will not be greater than the same, but by the conversion of the definition of incontinuous proportion, MN is greater than K, because F is greater than H. Therefore MN is greater than MP, which is impossible. Wherefore there remains what was proposed.

We note that Campanus's appeals to his Definition 6 here are quite crisp and free from the circularity that his commentary on the definition may have led us to expect. And in fact in his proof of Proposition 11 he had indicated that he now interpreted this definition in terms of

---

[23] If two equal quantities A and B are compared to a third C, then there is the same ratio of A to C as of B to C, and of C to A as of C to B.

simple excess, deficit or equality, without appeal to the opaque « similarity according to ratio ». In the proposition it was required to prove that if the ratios of A to B and of C to D are each equal to the ratio of E to F then they are mutually equal. Campanus takes equimultiples G, H, K respectively of A, C, E, and equimultiples L, M, N of B, D, F. He then argues that: [24]

By conversion of the definition of incontinuous proportion taken twice it will be the case that if K adds over N, then G adds over L and H over M, and if K takes away from N then G takes away from L and H from M, and if K is equal to N then G is equal to L and H is equal to M. Because therefore G to L and H to M hold themselves similarly in adding, taking away and being equal, with the mediation of K and N, then by the definition of incontinuous proportion A to B will be as C to D, which was proposed.

Thus by the time of Propositions 11 and 12 an increasing exposure to the Euclidean procedures has led Campanus to an essentially firm grasp of the Eudoxean criterion.

But in making this assertion I do not wish to impute complete logical purity to Campanus. There is, for instance, something very odd (in the second half of his addition to Proposition 12) about apparently proving a definition that has already been assumed.[25] Also the improvement of his understanding did not cause him to return and revise the earlier part of his book. Indeed to do so would have meant revision of the received Euclidean text, and on what basis would that be justified? The Middle Ages was quite alive to the possibility of faulty translations – a subject on which Roger Bacon was soon to ful-

---

[24] « Erit per conversionem diffinitionis incontinue proportionalitatis bis sumptam, si K addit super N quod G addit super L et H super M, et si K minuit ab N quod G minuit ab L et H ab M, et si K est equalis N quod G sit equalis L et H equalis M. Quia igitur G ad L et H ad M similiter se habent in addendo diminuendo et equando, mediantibus K e N, erit per diffinitionem incontinue proportionalitatis A ad B sicut C ad D. Quod est propositum ». On this proposition see also M. PEDRAZZI, *Analisi di una dimonstrazione di Campano da Novara alla luce della logica matematica*, « Archimede », XXV, 1973, pp. 323-327.

[25] Henry Billingsley (or perhaps John Dee) inserted the first half of Campanus's addition in his translation, *The Elements of Geometrie of the most auncient Philosopher Euclide of Megara*, London, 1570, f. 143r-v, and remarked: « Although this proposition here put by Campane needeth no demonstration for that it is but the converse of the 8. definition of this booke, yet thought I it not worthy to be omitted, for that it teacheth the way to finde out such equimultiplices, that the multiplex of the first shall excede the multiplex of the second, but the multiplex of the third shall not exceede the multiplex of the fourth ».

minate vehemently,[26] – but this did not provide license for emending them at one's own whim. The result is that, viewed simply as a deductive structure, Campanus's Book V is faulty, even if in other respects he had a sound grasp of its mathematical content. Although a very able mathematician and dealing with a work in axiomatic form, Campanus was, like most of his contemporaries, strongly imbued with what Whewell called the « commentatorial spirit of the Middle Ages ».[27] In this the aim was dialectically to shore up and recast an existing structure, rather than axiomatically to build a new (if unoriginal) free-standing edifice. There had thus been no complete revival of the Greek mathematical spirit, but ignorance and misunderstanding were not so rife as sometimes supposed.

RIASSUNTO

Si ritiene generalmente che Campano da Novara abbia completamente frainteso il cosiddetto criterio eudoxiano per l'eguaglianza o identità di rapporti. Questa opinione ha plausibili fondamenti, ma un esame dell'intero Libro V della sua redazione degli *Elementi* di Euclide rivela che egli, pur non avendo incluso tale criterio in una struttura assiomatica rigorosa, ha acquistato una buona consapevolezza di come esso debba essere effettivamente applicato.

---

[26] See, for instance, J. S. Brewer (ed.), *Fr. Rogeri Bacon Opera Quaedam Hactenus Inedita*, I, London 1859, pp. 471-473.

[27] W. Whewell, *History of the Inductive Sciences*, I, 3rd edn., London 1857, pp. 203-214.

III

SHIFTING THE FOUNDATIONS:
DESCARTES'S TRANSFORMATION OF ANCIENT GEOMETRY

SUMMARIES

*The aim of this paper is to analyse how the bases of
Descartes's geometry differed from those of ancient
geometry. Particular attention is paid to modes of
specifying curves of which two types are distinguished
- "Specification by genesis" and "Specification by
property". For both Descartes and most of Greek
geometry the former was fundamental, but Descartes
diverged from ancient pure geometry by according an
essential place to the imagination of mechanical
instruments. As regards specification by property,
Descartes's interpretation of the multiplication of
(segments of) straight lines as giving rise to a
straight line (segment), together with newer methods
of articifical symbolism, led to more concise and
suggestive modes of representation. Descartes's
account of ancient procedures is historically very
misleading, but it allowed him to introduce his own
ideas more naturally.*

*Ce mémoire a pour but d'analyser comment les
fondements de la géométrie de Descartes différaient
de ceux de la géométrie antique. Une attention
particulière est donnée aux modes de la spécification de courbes, dont deux genres sont distingués
- "spécification par genèse" et "spécification par
propriété". Pour Descartes et pour la plupart de
la géométrie grecque, c'était le premier genre
qui était fondamental, mais Descartes a divergé de
la géométrie pure des anciens en accordant à
l'imagination d'instruments mécaniques un rôle
essentiel. En ce qui concerne la spécification par
propriété, l'interprétation avancée par Descartes de
la multiplication de lignes droites (segments de
telles lignes) comme produisant (un segment d')
une ligne droite, ainsi que des méthodes plus récentes
de symbolisation artificielle, a abouti à des modes de
représentation plus concis et plus suggestifs. La des-*

cription de Descartes des procédures antiques est,
historiquement, très trompeuse, mais elle lui a
permis d'introduire ses idées propres d'une façon
plus naturelle.

INTRODUCTION

The mathematical work of Descartes is rather an enigma. It
was small in volume, but had great subsequent influence. This
suggests that it contained something radically new. But to
characterise this exactly has not been easy. A conventional
view has been to say that Descartes was inventor (or co-inventor)
of "analytical geometry". But, for various reasons, this is not
satisfactory. One difficulty is that there has been a terminolo-
gical change, and the use of algebra in geometry has come to
usurp the term "analytical geometry". But even at the beginning
of the last century John Leslie [1832] could speak favourably
of the purely geometrical analysis of the ancients [on which see
Mahoney 1968] as opposed to the algebraic analysis of the moderns.
Moreover, although they were willing to quarrel over other matters
[see e.g. Mahoney 1973, 57-60, 170-195], Descartes and Fermat, as
Milhaud [1921, 136-141] sagely noted, did not see any need to
contest priority over a new form of geometry; and indeed many
historians [see e.g. Coolidge 1963, 117-122; Schramm 1965, 89-97;
Zeuthen 1966, 192-215] have been able to emphasise how strong
were the ancient roots of "analytical geometry". It may seem that
these difficulties in characterisation could be eliminated by some
tactic such as calling Descartes's achievement the "arithmetization
of geometry", but, as Boyer [1959] has astutely argued, it can as
appropriately be labelled the "geometrization of algebra". All
this suggests the need to probe more deeply.

My aim in this paper is to contribute towards a clarification
of the nature of Descartes's work by isolating certain fundamental differences between his geometry and that of Greek antiquity, and so I shall put a strong emphasis on assessing him on
the basis of what had gone before. My particular focus will be
on problems associated with the specification of geometric curves,
and this demands a few general remarks. The geometer communicates
with words and other artificial symbols. His diagrams are intended as no more than an aid to comprehension. Thus if a
geometer wishes to speak of a particular curve, he must be able
to characterise it by means of verbal or other symbols. I shall
call a unique characterisation of a curve (which may or may not
be treated as a definition) a specification of the curve. No
more than a finite number of symbols may be used, and we meet a
type of continuum problem, for not every curve imagined as if
drawn with a "free movement of the hand" is susceptible of such
specification [1]. The modes of specification may be continually
extended and modified, but the process can reach no final

completion. We must also remember that the existence of different
modes of specification means that each mode determines its own
range of specifiable curves.

We may compare the situation with ratios.   The ratio between the diagonal of a square and its side is specifiable in
those very terms (provided we have reason for regarding it as
invariant). In modern mathematical language the same ratio is
specifiable as $\sqrt{2}:1$. In late medieval language it was specifiable
as *medietas duplae proportionis* (half the double ratio) [Molland,
1968, 117-119]. But it is not specifiable as the ratio between
two natural numbers, and hence is called irrational. In Greek
discussions of incommensurable quantities we meet the terms
ἄλογος and ἄρρητος, both of which may be translated as "inexpressible", and in the thirteenth century both Campanus and
Roger Bacon regarded the ratio between incommensurable quantities as known "neither to us nor to nature" [Molland, 1968, 116].

It is relatively easy to lay down criteria for different
kinds of specification of ratios, but with curves the situation
is more complicated. We shall find in both Descartes and the
ancients a primary distinction between different modes of specification. We may speak of this as the distinction between
specification by property and *specification by genesis*.
Specification by property lays down a property (usually a quantitative property obeyed by all the points of the curve) which
suffices to determine the curve. In Descartes this has characteristically the form of an equation. Specification by genesis
determines a curve by saying how it is to be constructed. Specifications of this kind run up against the problem of what types
of construction were regarded as acceptable at a given time. In
what follows I shall consider the different types and roles of
these two principal forms of specification in the geometry of
Greek antiquity and in that of Descartes.

I.   ANTIQUITY

We are faced with many difficulties in analysing the ancient
Greek procedures. The number of writers involved is not small,
and often because of the loss of their works we have to view them
through the eyes of reporters, who may not always give an accurate
presentation of individual nuances. We must therefore be on
our guard against assuming a single monolithic view in all details, even if there is a basic invariant core running through
all the Greek writings. Further, the issues in which we are
interested are little analysed in extant Greek writings. We
have therefore mainly to attempt to identify what was implicitly
assumed rather than to isolate explicit statements. The explicit
statements that were made often came from those whose primary
interest was more philosophical than mathematical, and we should
not be surprised to find differences between what the mathematicians

actually did and what philosophers said was proper to their
discipline. This fact has sometimes been obscured in the historiography of Greek mathematics, and its neglect is abetted by
the fact that the early parts of Euclid's *Elements* conform more
nearly to certain philosophical dicta than do its own later parts,
or other geometrical works. It is as if care were taken to show
how the most elementary and basic parts of geometry could be
made philosophically acceptable while leaving greater latitude to
the mathematician to follow his own intuitions in the higher
reaches.

In our discussions of Greek geometry we shall have to be
alive to the distinction between geometry and mechanics, and
more particularly, as pertaining to constructions, the distinction between the geometrical (γεωμετρικόs) and the instrumental
(ὀργανικόs). Contrary to what seems often to be assumed, references to instruments (including ruler and compasses) did not form
part of Greek pure geometry. But constructions were certainly
used, and indeed, as we shall see, formed the basis for the
definitions of most curves. Thus the allowable modes of construction were a principal determining factor of what was admitted
into Greek geometry. No explicit canonisation of admissible
modes is extant, and so we shall have to try to identify the
criteria from what was actually done. This will give us a
fairly firm if not precisely delimited idea of what was allowable.
We shall then consider some of the ways in which instrumental
constructions infiltrated into geometrical contexts (although
still not themselves being regarded as geometrical). We shall
then return to pure geometry and focus on some of the roles of
specification by property.

Before considering in detail geometrical construction, we
must touch on one problem that has sometimes seemed serious, but
which it is important not to exaggerate. This is the question
of the place of motion in geometry. The *locus classicus* for
the difficulty is a short passage from Plato's *Republic* [VII.9,
526C-527B], where Socrates, after admitting the incidental uses
of geometry in warfare, insisted that its higher aim was the
study of being rather than mere becoming. But this seemed to be
belied by the geometers' talking as if they were doing something,
such as squaring, applying or adding. This may be read as
casting some doubt upon the propriety of constructions in
geometry. But at that time, at least, constructions were necessary for geometry, and even if ontologically its objects were
exempt from becoming, some element of becoming was necessary for
geometric epistemology. Thus apparently Speusippus (Plato's
nephew) and others resolved the dilemma by regarding constructions
as processes of understanding "taking eternal things as if they
were in the process of coming to be" [Proclus, 1873, 77-78;
1948, 69-70; cf. Aristotle, *De coelo* I.10, 279b32-280a12 and
Becker 1927, 198] and much later in time Proclus [1873, 78-79;

1948, 70] spoke of human ideas shaping intelligible matter in
the understanding [2].

Nevertheless the emphasis on the immovable nature of
geometrical objects seems to have had some effect upon geometry,
and in the early part of the *Elements* Euclid seems wary of using
ideas of motion [Euclid 1956, 1, 224-228; Mugler 1948, 58-59].
This could square with Proclus's assertion that Euclid was a
Platonist [Proclus 1873, 68; 1948, 61-62], but perhaps more
plausibly it should be attributed to his borrowing from earlier
sets of Elements. In the first book of Euclid's *Elements* the
straight line and the circle are defined by property rather than
by genesis [Euclid 1956, 1, 153]. "A straight line is a line
which lies evenly with the points on itself." "A circle is a plane
figure contained by one line such that all the straight lines
falling upon it from one point among those lying within the figure
are equal to one another." But Euclid has to supplement these
definitions by postulates laying down when straight lines and
circles may be constructed, or, in Zeuthen's [1902, 98-100]
interpretation, when they exist. "Let the following be postulated: To draw a straight line from any point to any point.
To produce a finite straight line continuously in a straight
line. To describe a circle with any centre and distance" [Euclid
1956, 1, 154]. These definitely seem to involve some kind of
motion, and Proclus [1873, 185-187; 1948, 162-164] grasps the
nettle firmly and grounds them in motions in the imagination.
There were also in Antiquity definitions of the straight line
and circle that explicitly appealed to motion. The circle was
defined in terms of the rotation of a straight line about one of
its extremities and the straight line as that which remained
fixed on rotation when two points remained fixed [Euclid 1956,
1, 184, 168]. Hints of the latter definition can even be found
in Plato's *Republic* [Mugler 1948, 26-27].

Despite the prominence of definition by property in the
first book of Euclid's *Elements*, genetic definition was elsewhere
the norm [3]. This applies even to Euclid, for in the eleventh
book of the *Elements* he defines the sphere, cone and cylinder
by rotations of, respectively, a semicircle, a triangle and a
rectangle [Euclid 1956, 3, 261-262]. Outside Euclid's *Elements*,
spires arose from the rotation of a circle about an axis in its
plane but not passing through its centre [Proclus 1873, 119;
1948, 108]. Conic sections, as the name implies, were regularly
defined as the sections of cones by planes, and Perseus investigated the figures arising from sections of spires [Proclus 1873,
111-112, 119; 1948, 101-102, 108].   Archimedes [1910-1915, 1,
246-255; n.d. 99-102] defined conoids and spheroids by rotating
conic sections about their diameters. Archytas produced a
"certain curve" from the inter-section of the circumference of
a revolving semicircle with the surface of a half cylinder
[Eutocius 1915, 85-89; Thomas 1957, 1, 284-287].

In the above instances the rotations involved were about an axis. Apollonius [1891-93, 1, 6-7; Thomas 1957, 2, 284-286; cf. Apollonius 1961, 1] gave a more general definition of the cone (to include oblique cones) in terms of the rotation of a straight line which passes through a fixed point and moves around the circumference of a circle (whose plane does not include the point). Serenus [1896, 1-5; 1969, 1-2] was careful by analogy to extend the definition of the cylinder to include oblique cylinders. He used two equal and parallel circles and had in each rotating parallel diameters. The line joining corresponding ends of the diameters produced the surface of the cylinder.

In a trivial sense Serenus's definition of the cylinder involved two simultaneous motions that had to be correlated in some way. Other definitions involved simultaneous motions in a non-trivial sense. Later, as we shall see, Descartes would reject such curves from geometry, but the ancients seem to have had no compunction about admitting them. The spiral was of this kind, being defined by Archimedes [1910-15, 2, 44-45; n.d. 165; Thomas 1957, 2, 182-183] in terms of the uniform motion of a point along a straight line, which itself was uniformly rotating. The definition of the cylindrical helix given by Proclus [1873, 105; 1948, 95] is from the uniform motion of a point along a straight line that is moving round the surface of a cylinder. Eudoxus's generation of the hippopede [Thomas 1957, 1, 412-415] had involved the uniform rotations of two spheres which had to complete their motions in the same time.

The quadratrix of Hippias has similar features, but at least for Pappus was the cause of some difficulties. The generation given by Pappus [1965, 252-253; 1933, 192; Thomas 1957, 1, 336-339] was of this kind. In a square ABCD, B'C' moves uniformly from BC to AD, while remaining parallel to BC. In the same time AE revolves uniformly about A from AB to AD. Both motions are completed in the same time. Then the intersection of B'C' and AE traces out the quadratrix. This curve had been applied to the squaring of the circle; but as Sporus [Pappus 1965, 252-255; 1933, 193-194; Thomas 1957, 1, 338-341] had pointed out, a petitio principii was involved, for how was the quadratrix to be constructed without knowledge of the ratio of the radius of the circle to a quarter of its circumference? Pappus expounded with approval Sporus's objections, but he himself [1965, 254-255; 258-259; 1933, 194, 197] had another difficulty with the curve, namely the extent to which its genesis was mechanical (he used the adjective μηχανικός rather than ὀργανικός). What he meant by this is not transparently clear, but he seemed happier when he had analysed the curve "by means of the loci on surfaces" in terms of first the cylindrical helix and then the Archimedean spiral [Pappus 1965, 258-265; 1933, 197-201].

The whole business of the "loci on surfaces" is rather obscure [cf. Euclid 1956, 1, 15-16], and the available evidence

is scanty. We must therefore beware of drawing too many inferences from Pappus's procedures. It seems clear that Pappus regarded the spiral and the cylindrical helix as having a firmer
claim to the status of being geometrical than the quadratrix,
which could however receive authentication by being derived from
them. The constructions used in the derivation must also have
been regarded as having a fairly firm geometrical status [4].
The first derivation is from a cylindrical helix. A plectoidal
[cf. Pappus 1933, 198, n.6] surface arises from the motion along
the helix of a perpendicular from it to the axis of the cylinder.
The section of this surface by a plane that can be determined by
a property of the helix produces a curve, and the orthogonal projection of this curve onto the base of the cylinder produces the
quadratrix [5]. The production of the quadratrix from the spiral
is more complicated. A "cylindroidal surface" is formed perpendicular to the plane of the spiral and passing through the spiral.
The intersection of this with a cone gives a curved line. A
"plectoidal surface" is formed by the motion of a perpendicular
from this line to the straight line through the origin of the
spiral and perpendicular to its plane. The intersection of this
surface with a plane (determined by the spiral and inclined to
its plane at half a right angle) gives rise to another curved
line, and the orthogonal projection of this line onto the plane
of the spiral gives the quadratrix.

So far as I know, no ancient writer attempted to give a
general account of what modes of construction were acceptable
in geometry, and it would probably have been impossible to produce a universally agreed codification of the geometer's intuition. But clearly there had to be limits, since otherwise, for
instance, a very simple construction could be given for the
rectification of the circle. (The imagined motion could be a
rolling of a circle.) Our analysis has suggested that restrictions
were made to certain simple motions, and the dominant ideas seem
to have been those of rotation and of constructing straight lines
and planes. The passages from Pappus that we have just examined
suggest that in the higher reaches of geometry there may have
been standard procedures of constructing cylindroids (generalised
"cylinders") from plane curves and "plectoids" from non-planar
curves.

Pappus himself gave a rudimentary classification of curves,
or more strictly of problems, in terms of the lines used for their
solution. This classification, which Pappus attributes to much
earlier geometers, is famous and was to be given a prominent place
by Descartes. It is in terms of the geneses of the lines used,
and the passage that Pappus annexes will serve to introduce us
to the place of instrumental constructions in Greek geometrical
works:

The ancients held that there were three genera of geometrical
problems: some were called plane, some solid, and some linear.

*Those that can be solved with straight lines and circumferences
of circles are reasonably called plane, for the lines by which
these problems are solved have their genesis in a plane. Problems
that are solved by the use in their discovery of one or more sections of a cone are called solid, for in their construction it
is necessary to use surfaces of solid figures, namely conic surfaces. There yet remains the third genus which is called linear,
for lines other than those mentioned are used in the construction,
which have a varied and more intricate genesis, such as the spirals,
the quadratrixes, the conchoids and the cissoids, which have
many marvellous properties.*

*As there is this difference between problems, the ancient
geometers did not construct the aforementioned problem of the
two straight lines, which is solid by nature, following geometrical reasoning, because it was not easy to draw the sections of
the cone in a plane, but by using instruments they brought it to
a manual construction and fit preparation, as is seen in the*
Mesolabe *of Eratosthenes and the* Mechanics *of Philo and Hero.*
[Pappus 1965, 54-57; 1933, 38-39; cf. 1965, 270-271; 1933, 201-
208].

From this passage it is clear that Pappus regarded instrumental solutions as being something of a concession to human
weakness, or at least to human practical needs. Instrumental
constructions were not properly geometrical, but they could
indicate how a solution was physically to be performed. The
imagination of idealised instruments can give constructions as
exact as those of pure geometry, but they did not fit into the
canons of Greek geometry, and were strictly regarded as part of
mechanics.

In two famous passages of Plutarch we are shown Plato as
fulminating against the use of instrumental constructions in
geometry [*Quaestiones Conviviales* VIII. 2.1 in 1961, 120-123;
Vita Marcelli XIV. 5-6 in 1914-26, 4, 470-473]. Although, as
van der Waerden [n.d. 161-165] has suggested [6], these passages
may derive not from Plato but from a dialogue by Eratosthenes in
which Plato was a character, we may be sure that Plato would have
wished a definite distinction between geometry and mechanics; and,
from wherever they derive, the passages bear witness to the recognition of such a separation. Another explicit reference to
the distinction, with hints of the practical man's need of
instrumental constructions, may be found in a purported letter
of Eratosthenes to Ptolemy Euergetes. The letter (like the
other references we have so far considered) concerns the duplication of the cube, which was reduced to the problem of finding
two mean proportionals between two straight lines. After reviewing the history of the problem, the writer continued [Eutocius
1915, 90-91; Thomas, 1957, 1, 260-261; cf. von Wilamowitz-
Moellendorff 1894]: "It turned out that they all performed it
demonstratively (ἀποδεικτικῶς), but they could not do it manually

and turn it to use, except to a small extent Menaechmus, and
that with difficulty. An easy instrumental solution was, however,
found by us, by means of which we shall find, not only two means
to the given straight lines, but as many as may be enjoined."

It is in the realm of solid, and to a certain extent linear,
problems that the distinction is most apparent, for in these cases
there was likely to be considerable divergence between the geometrical and instrumental procedures. In plane problems the distinction certainly existed, but for later historians it has sometimes been obscured by the tantalisingly close analogy existing
between Euclid's first three postulates and the operations that
can be performed with a straight edge and compasses. But even
here, as de Morgan [1849, 6; cf. Euclid, 1956, 1, 246] emphasised, the analogy is not exact, for, in his words, the postulates
"do not allow a circle to be drawn with a compass-carried distance; suppose the compasses to close of themselves the moment
they cease to touch the paper." Euclid's propositions 2 and 3
of the first book are necessary to make the analogy complete.

We may glean further understanding of how even ruler-and-
compass constructions were regarded as instrumental rather than
properly geometrical from Book VIII of Pappus's *Collectio*. This
is devoted to mechanics, and Pappus included a section on instrumental problems, which he clearly specified as belonging to
mechanics. Some of these problems require only a straight edge
and compasses, although Pappus does not explicitly specify the
instruments. In association with two of them we have some rather
enigmatic remarks on the status of instrumental problems:

The so-called instrumental problems in mechanics [are those
which] *are deprived of geometrical authorities, such as those
described by one interval and that of the cylinder with both bases
mutilated, which is put forward by the architects* [1965, 1072-
75; 1933, 845].

The [problems] *among those which are especially called
instrumental are also useful and most of all when, led to something easy by analysis, they can escape the proportionate trial*
(πεῖρα) [1965, 1096-97; 1933, 860].

The first of these passages is followed by the problems of
finding the diameter of a cylinder with two mutilated bases,
which Pappus reduces to that of constructing the minor axis of
the ellipse that would pass through five given points. No instruments other than the straight edge and compasses are necessary, though the compasses have to be used on the surface of the
cylinder. The second passage is followed by a problem in which
it is demanded that seven regular hexagons be inscribed in a
given circle. Pappus reduces this by analysis to the problem
of constructing a certain triangle. He makes the problem more
complicated than it need be, but no instruments other than
straight edge and compasses are required.

It is not easy to infer much from Pappus's obscure general
statements, and possibly he was a little confused himself.

However, it seems clear that he regarded instrumental solutions
to geometrical problems as lacking in geometrical rigour, so
that in the last resort they could only be justified on the basis
of whether they worked in practice. They did not themselves fit
into the strict deductive system of geometry, but often geometrical argumentation could produce conviction that they worked.
Pappus's main difficulty in characterising their status may well
have come from a problem of specifying in general terms the
relations between geometry and mechanics.

We may derive even clearer evidence of how constructions
with simple, as well as with complicated, instruments were regarded as mechanical from a passage of Book VIII of Pappus's
Collectio that is only extant in Arabic. When reviewing Hultsch's
edition of the *Collectio,* M. Cantor [1879; cf. 1894-1908, 1,
421] suggested that the phrase "those described by one interval"
in the first of the passages that we have just quoted referred
to problems in which the compasses could only be opened to one
interval. This surmise found little favour with W. M. Kutta in
his historical study of fixed compass problems [1898, 72-74],
but the recently discovered Arabic version of Book VIII favours
Cantor's view, for it includes a group of problems in which restrictions are placed on the use of the compasses [Jackson 1970,
63-73, A43-A51; cf. 1972]. There are reasonable grounds for
attributing the passage to Pappus, or at least for assuming
that the writer put the same interpretation on "described by one
interval" as Pappus. The explicit restriction is that there "is
a given distance which must not be exceeded when we draw circles",
and the author later rephrased this in more definitely instrumental terms by saying that "we have only one small pair of compasses with which to work". But in fact, except for one problem,
only one arbitrary opening of the compasses is required, and the
exception would be easy to obviate. The author seems to have
realised this, for at times he announced that only one distance
had been used.

The broad distinction between geometrical and instrumental
procedures is clear, but puzzles can arise in some cases,
mainly it seems through lack of extant evidence. In particular
we must consider the cases of the conchoid and the cissoid. It
is clear that Pappus [1965, 54-55, 270-271; 1933, 38-39, 207-
208] and Proclus [1873, 111, 128, 356; 1948, 103, 116, 304] had
few qualms about accepting these as properly geometrical, and
yet in both cases the accounts that survive are tinged with the
instrumental. The conchoid was the invention of Nicomedes, but
his original work is lost and we have to rely on reports by
Pappus and by Eutocius. Pappus's account [1965, 242-245; 1933,
185-186; Thomas 1957, 1, 298-301] of its generation is in the
following manner [7]. *AB* is a straight line and *E* a point not
on it. Another straight line *CD* moves in such a way that *D* is
always on *AB* (i.e. *CD* is constant) and *CD* produced always passes

through *E*. The point *C* traces out the conchoid. Pappus [1965, 244-247; 1933, 187; Thomas 1957, 300-301] remarks that Nicomedes showed that the curve could be constructed instrumentally, and Eutocius [1915, 98-101] gives only an instrumental construction. This makes use of slotted rulers and pegs, and parallels exactly the genesis given by Pappus. Thus it seems that in this case Pappus may have regarded this analogue of an instrumental cons- truction as geometrical even if it fitted rather loosely into the more usual criteria [8].

The case of the cissoid is less problematic, for Diocles' construction as reported by Eutocius [1915, 67-71; Thomas 1957, 1, 270-279] is solely instrumental and does not even effect a complete genesis of the curve [9]. Let *AB* and *CD* be perpendic- ular diameters of a circle. Mark off equal arcs *EB, BZ,* with *E* on the side of *C* and *Z* on the side of *D*. Drop the perpendicular *ZH* onto *CD*. The intersection of *ED* and *ZH* is a point of the required curve. "If in this way more parallels are drawn continu- ally between *B, D,* and arcs equal to the arcs cut off between them and *B* are marked off from *B* in the direction of *C*, and straight lines are drawn from *D* to the points so obtained..., the parallels between *B* and *D* will be cut in certain points.... Joining these points with straight lines by applying a ruler we shall describe in the circle a certain curve." Both the refer- ence to the ruler and the "construction" of the curve by joining points with straight lines make clear the instrumental orienta- tion, which in any case would be expected in a work entitled, as Diocles's was, *On burning mirrors*. Diocles in fact has only given a method of constructing an arbitrary number of points on the curve and not a method of constructing the curve itself. We may suspect that a more acceptable geometrical construction (per- haps using two simultaneous motions) was discovered later, for Proclus [1873, 113; 1948, 103] reports that Geminus taught the genesis of cissoids as also of spirals and conchoids [10], but unfortunately we do not know his method.

Diocles's "construction" of the cissoid is easily trans- latable as laying down a property that each point of the curve must obey. To this extent we may regard it as leading to a specification by property of the cissoid. But, as we have seen, such specifications were not usually regarded as definitions, and would in any case need to be supplemented by an existence postulate or proof. Nevertheless specifications by property did play an important part in Greek geometrical methods, and we must now return definitely to the realms of pure geometry in order to explore some of their roles. We shall first see how certain essential properties were referred to curves, and then consider the class of locus problems and theorems.

When discussing parallel lines. Proclus referred to essen- tial properties belonging to them as such (such as the equality of the alternate angles when the parallels were cut by a straight

line). Such properties were unique to parallel lines and convertible with their definition. He added [1873, 356; 1948, 304]:

*In this way also other mathematicians were accustomed to
discourse on lines, giving the property (σύμπτωμα) of each
species. For Apollonius showed for each of the conic lines what
its property was, and Nicomedes likewise for the conchoids,
Hippias for the quadratrices, and Perseus for the spirics. For
after the genesis, the apprehension of the essential* [property]
belonging [to it] *as such* [11] *differentiates the species constructed from all others.*

The example of conic sections may show us how important the establishment of such a property was, for it would clearly be very tedious to have
to refer back to the original cone for each theorem. Thus early in his
work Apollonius [1891-93, 1, 36-53; 1961, 8-12] produces particular
planimetric properties for each of the three species of conic sections.
The simplest case is the parabola. Suppose *PM* is a diameter
(with *P* on the parabola) and *PL* the corresponding latus rectum.
Then for any ordinate *QV* to the diameter *PM*, the square on *QV*
is equal to the rectangle formed from *PV* and *PL*. Later Apollonius
[1891-93, 1, 158-165; 1961, 42-43] will show essentially how
any curve with such a property is a parabola. Thus this specification by property is unique to the parabola. We may see from
the form of this planimetric property (and the corresponding ones
for the ellipse and the hyperbola) how easy it is to read coordi-
nate geometry back into ancient works, and this part of Descartes's
method certainly had firm ancient roots.

Related to the establishment of such properties was the class
of locus problems and theorems, although in this case the emphasis was on arguing from the property to the curve. Proclus [1873,
394; 1948, 337] defines a locus (τόπος) succinctly as "a position
of a line or a surface producing one and the same property." We
frequently meet with propositions of the form that, when certain
properties of a point or line are given, that point or line is
uniquely given in position [12]. But there were also problems
without a unique solution of this kind, where, for instance,
the required point could lie anywhere on a certain line, so
that the line was the place or locus of the point, and it was
to cases of this kind that the term "locus" was most frequently
applied. Pappus, who had many relevant and no longer extant
sources available to him, and is here drawing at least partially
on Apollonius's *Plane loci,* divides loci into three classes
[1965, 660-663; 1933, 495-496]. Some are ἐφεκτικοί, when a
point is the locus of a point, a line of a line, or a surface of
a surface. Other loci are διεξοδικοί, when a line is the locus
of a point, or a surface of a line, or a solid of a surface.
Finally others are ἀναστροφικοί, when a surface is the locus of
a point, or a solid of a line. The most common form was διεξοδικοί
loci of points. Pappus subdivided these into plane, solid and
linear loci, in a way similar to that in which he had classified

problems. Plane loci comprise straight lines and circles; solid
loci comprise conic sections; all other loci are linear [13].
    A complete locus theorem must include a proof that the point
will lie on the given locus and also a proof that any point on
the locus satisfies the given condition. We find both proofs in
a proposition that Eutocius [1893, 180-185; cf. Heath 1949, 181-
188] is apparently copying from Apollonius's *Plane loci*, to the
effect that if two points are given and also the ratio between
two unequal straight lines, then the locus of a point whose
distances from the two given points is in the given ratio is a
circle. Pappus [1965, 662-671; 1933, 496-501] gives an account
of the contents of this work of Apollonius, and it is possible
to see from this some rationale (besides that of their genesis)
for treating the circle and straight line as forming a single
class, for one general proposition in particular can be looked
upon as dealing with transformations of circles or straight lines
into circles or straight lines [Steele 1936, 358-360]. But in
general we know very little of ancient locus procedures, and the
reports on Aristaeus's *Solid loci* and Euclid's *Loci on surfaces*
are even more sketchy than those on Apollonius's *Plane loci*. It
is nevertheless clear that such inferences "from property to
place" were an important part of Greek geometrical activity.
    Let us now summarise. Many may have argued that geometrical
definition should be by property rather than by genesis (for
example, Eutocius [1893, 186-187] did not regard Apollonius's
genetic definition of the cone as a definition), but in fact,
despite the privileged position of definition by property in
the first book of Euclid's *Elements*, genetic definitions of incomposite lines and surfaces tended to be the general rule.
These, together with the constructions regularly used in geometry,
demanded the imagination of certain simple motions. There seems
to have been little explicit discussion of what motions were
allowable, but rotations (understood in a broad sense) and the
construction of straight lines and planes predominated. There was
no ban on the use of two simultaneous motions.
    Although genetic definitions were usually regarded as more
basic, there was considerable interest in properties that could
give a unique specification of a curve or surface, and usually
these were in the form of some quantitative relation that had
to be obeyed by all the points of the curve or surface. For the
conic sections much use was made of fundamental planimetric properties, and the class of locus theorems dealt with what curves
answered to what properties of points. Through all this, classification of curves was based on the mode of their genesis rather
than on any properties that they possessed.
    In pure theoretical geometry there was no mention of
instruments. But practically-oriented solutions to geometrical
problems could be given by specifying how certain instruments
were to be employed. These were regarded as lacking some of the
rigour of pure geometry, and in fact as belonging to mechanics

rather than to geometry. Frequently both geometrical and instrumental solutions could be given to the same problem, and compilers
often placed them next to each other. The distinction is usually
quite clear, but a cursory reading could misconstrue it. And
in fact it has often been blurred or misinterpreted, and in
particular by Descartes.

II. DESCARTES

We may now confront Descartes's version of much of what we
have treated. We may best start with an extended quotation from
the beginning of Book II of the *Géométrie*, which is entitled
On the Nature of Curved Lines [14]:

*The ancients have well remarked that, among the problems of
geometry, some are plane, others solid and others linear, that
is to say, that some can be constructed by tracing only straight
lines and circles, while others can only be constructed by using,
at the least, some conic section, and finally others only by
using some other more compounded line. But I am surprised that
they did not beyond this distinguish different degrees among
these more compounded lines, nor can I understand why they
named them mechanical* (mechaniques) *rather than geometrical.
For in order to say that this was because there is need to use
some machine for describing them, it would be necessary for the
same reason to reject circles and straight lines, seeing that
one only describes these on paper with compasses and a ruler,
which one can also name machines. No more is it because the
instruments used for tracing them, being more compounded than the
ruler and compasses, cannot be so accurate* (si iustes); *for for
that reason it would be necessary to reject them from mechanics,
where the accuracy of works that issue from the hand is more desired
than in geometry, where it is only accuracy of reasoning that
is sought, which without doubt can be as perfect regarding these
lines as regarding the others. Neither will I say that it was
because they did not wish to increase the number of their demands,
and were content to be granted that they could join two given
points by a straight line and describe a circle with a given
centre which would pass through a given point; for they made no
scruple about further supposing, in order to treat the conic
sections, that one could cut each given cone by a given plane.
And, in order to trace all the curved lines that I intend to
introduce here, there is only need to suppose that two or more
lines can be moved, one by another* (l'une par l'autre) *and that
their intersections mark out other* [lines], *and this does not
seem to me at all more difficult. It is true that they did not
entirely receive the conic sections into their geometry, and I
do not wish to undertake to change names that have been approved
by usage, but it is, it seems to me, very clear that, taking
as one does for geometrical that which is precise and exact*

(precis & exact) *and for mechanical that which is not, and con-*
sidering geometry as a science that teaches generally how to
know the measures of all bodies, one must no more exclude the
more compounded lines than the more simple, provided that one can
imagine them to be described by a continuous movement or by
several which follow one another and of which the later are
entirely determined (entierement reglés) *by those which precede.*
For by these means one can always have an exact knowledge of
their measure. But perhaps what prevented the ancient geometers
from admitting [curves] *that were more compounded than the conic*
sections was that the first that they considered happened to be
(lit. having by accident been) the spiral, the quadratrix and
such-like, which truly belong only to mechanics and are not of
the number of those that I think must be received here, because
one imagines them described by two separate movements, which have
no ratio between them that one can measure exactly, although
they [the geometers] *afterwards examined the conchoid, the*
cissoid, and some few others which are among those [to be
received], *but because they perhaps did not sufficiently remark*
their properties, they made no more of them than the first. Or
perhaps it was that, recognising that they still knew little
regarding the conic sections, and that there even remained much
they they did not know regarding what could be done with the
ruler and compasses, they feared having to enter upon a more dif-
ficult matter.

The fundamental error in this passage is the misconstrual
of the ancient distinction between geometrical and instrumental
constructions. This leads Descartes to hold that curves higher
than the conic sections were regarded as mechanical rather than
geometrical, and he compounds this error by suggesting (very
oddly for someone who knew Apollonius's work) that even the conic
sections were not fully accepted. Having produced this analysis,
Descartes sets himself the task of making it intelligible,
and produces further misleading statements. His first explanation suggests a ruler-and-compasses restriction in ancient
works, and, although he rejects this as (in his own terms) mis-
guided, the myth of this restriction has plagued much subsequent historiography [cf. Steele 1936]. He then tries to have
Greek geometry determined by the postulates of the first book of
Euclid's *Elements*, but here he has to admit that constructions of
planes were used for the conic sections (even if he is grudging
about admitting the place of these figures in Greek geometry).
His third attempted explanation was that the spiral and quadratrix, which were not geometrical, were discovered first and only
afterwards the acceptable conchoid and cissoid. But, as we
have seen, there was no ancient compunction about admitting the
spiral and little about the quadratrix, and there could well have
been more doubt about the geneses of the conchoid and cissoid.
His fourth attempt was to suggest that the ancient geometers

wished to complete the lower reaches of geometry before moving on to the higher. But this does not in fact address itself to the same pseudo-problem, but only to the question of why more time was not spent on higher curves.

Descartes's historical errors are blatant, but his faulty exegeses allow him to introduce more naturally his own basis for geometry. This arises from the imagination of various articulated instruments in which the movements of all the parts are completely determined by the movement of one of them, and where the intersections of parts trace out curves [AT, 6, 391-395; 1954, 45-47]. The parts may all be straight lines or rulers, or one of them may be a figure already produced by a continuous movement, such as a parabola or a hyperbola. All such curves are to be received into geometry and Descartes [AT, 6, 392; 1954, 46-49] writes of those produced by one instrument that "I do not see what can prevent one from conceiving the description of the first [curve] as clearly and as distinctly as that of the circle or at least as that of the conic sections, nor what can prevent one from conceiving as well as one can the first the second, the third and all the others that one can describe, nor consequently why one should not receive them all in the same way for use in the speculations of geometry." On the other hand curves such as the spiral and the quadratrix, which arise from two simultaneous motions are to be rejected from geometry and regarded as only mechanical.

We shall have to examine later how Descartes relates this criterion for the acceptability of curves to the possibility of measure, but first we should note how the criterion goes right back to Descartes's earliest researches in mathematics. In the *Discours de la Méthode* he [AT, 6, 7; 1955, 1, 85] tells us how during his education he delighted most in mathematics, but at the time believed that "it was of service only in the mechanical arts". In the *Cogitationes Privatae* we see signs of his occupations with various practical problems of mathematics, including the invention of articulated instruments or compasses as they were generally called, for tracing curves and solving problems [AT, 10, 232-235, 238-242]. In a famous letter to Beeckman on March 26th, 1619 [AT, 10, 154-160] Descartes indicates how such generalised compasses were taking on a fundamental theoretical position in his mathematical thought. He speaks of how he has invented compasses for the division of angles into equal parts and for the solution of cubic equations. But such discoveries were suggesting to him a whole new programme for mathematical advance [AT, 10, 156-157]:

And certainly, to disclose openly to you what I am undertaking, I wish to propound not an ars brevis *of Lull but a completely new science, by which can be solved generally all questions that can be put forward in any genus of quantity, continuous as well as discrete. But each according to its nature.*

*For, as in arithmetic some questions are solved by rational
numbers, others only by surd numbers, and lastly others can be
imagined but not solved, so I hope to demonstrate that in
continuous quantity some problems can be solved with only
straight lines and circular ones, others can only be solved by
other curved lines, but such as arise from a single motion* (sed
quae ex unico motu oriuntur), *and so can be described* (duci
possunt) *by new compasses, which I do not regard as less certain
and geometrical than the common ones by which circles are described, and finally other* [problems] *can only be solved by curved
lines generated from different motions which are not subordinated
to one another, which lines are certainly only imaginary: such
is the common enough* (satis vulgata) *quadratrix. And I judge
that nothing can be imagined that cannot at least be solved by
such lines. But I hope that I shall demonstrate which questions
can be solved in this or that way and not the other, so that
scarcely anything in geometry will remain to be discovered.*

In this way Descartes had formulated a programme for
geometry from which he did not essentially diverge. But in the
Géométrie we find it far more definitely related to specification
by property. In the long passage that we quoted above we saw
how Descartes regarded the distinguishing characteristic of
geometry as opposed to mechanics as being that the geometrical
was "precise and exact". Moreover, geometry was "a science that
teaches generally how to know the measures of all bodies".
Descartes also held in that passage that one could have an
exact knowledge of the measure of curves that had been generated
in accord with his criterion of one or more determined movements.
Descartes's interpretation of what was meant by an exact knowledge
of the measure of a curve may have undergone some development,
but in the *Géométrie* he clearly explicates it in terms of equations.
"In order to understand together all those [curves] which are in
nature and to distinguish them by order into certain genera I
know nothing better than to say that all the points of those
which one can name geometric, that is to say which fall under
some precise and exact measure have necessarily some relation
(quelque rapport) to all the points of a straight line, which
can be expressed by some equation, and by one [equation] for
them all" [AT, 6, 392; 1954, 49]. Curves are then classified
according to the degree of their equations.

At the basis of Descartes's representation of curves by
equations lies the close analogy that he makes between operations
on straight lines (or, in later terminology, line segments) and
operations on numbers. In particular, by the assumption of an
arbitrarily chosen unit line, he is able to interpret the multiplication of two straight lines as given rise to a third straight
line rather than to a rectangle. This step was of fundamental
importance in making easier the representation of curves in algebraic terms. In setting up an equation for a curve Descartes

[see e.g. AT. 6, 393-394, 1954, 49-54] chose a straight line, say
AB, and a fixed point on it, say *A*. From an arbitrary point *C*
of the curve a straight line *CB* was drawn to *AB* meeting it at a
given angle. The lines *AB* and *BC* were then quantities that would
determine the position of *C*, and they were called *x* and *y*. An
equation in terms of *x* and *y* could determine the curve, by specifying a property that all its points had to obey. As we have
noted above this has close similarities to such ancient procedures
as Apollonius's establishment of *symptomata* for the conic sections.
Descartes's innovations in this regard lie in his drawing heavily
upon the traditions of algebra with the consequent assimilation
of operations on straight lines to operations on number, and in
his making this mode of representation standard and general.

Descartes held that the possibility of representing a curve
by an equation (specification by property) was equivalent to its
being constructible in terms of the determinate motion criterion
(specification by genesis) [cf. Vuillemin 1960, 77-93]. We should
note that the quasi-arithmetical operations which Descartes allows
on straight lines mean that for him an equation is what we should
call a polynomial equation: there was no place for what would later
be called transcendental functions. This follows quite naturally
from the four (or five if extraction of roots is counted) primary
operations that Descartes allows upon straight lines. In some
earlier writings we see him making use of compound ratios in
moving towards his developed doctrine of multiplication of lines
[15], and these may have played an explicit role in his original
solution of the problem of Pappus. This problem was proposed to
Descartes by Golius in 1631, and Descartes's occupation with it
seems to have played a very important role in the development of
his mature system of geometry. His original solution is lost,
but the problem forms a central theme in his *Géométrie*, and an
examination of it can give us much insight into Descartes's
geometrical procedures.

The problem is as follows [16]. There are given *n* straight
lines. From a point *C* lines are drawn making given angles with
the given lines. If *n=3* the ratio of the product of two of the
lines from *C* to the square of the third is given. If *n* is
even and greater than two the ratio of the product of *n/2* of
the lines from *C* to the product of the other *n/2* lines is given.
If *n* is odd and greater than three, the ratio of the product of
(n+1)/2 of the lines to the product of the other *(n-1)/2* lines
together with a given line is given. It is required to find
the locus of *C*. Pappus said that in the case of three or four
lines, which had been investigated by Euclid and Apollonius [cf.
Apollonius, 1891-93, 1, 4-5; 1896, lxxi], the locus was solid.
In higher cases it was linear, but there had been virtually no
study of those cases, and the curves had not in general been
more fully identified [17].

Descartes [AT, 6, 382-384; 1954, 27-32] begins his attack
on the problem with the use of his characteristic mode of

algebraic representation. He takes one of the given lines *AB*
as the reference line, and its point of intersection *A* with one
of the other given lines as the fixed point. *CB* is the line from
a possible position of *C* falling on *AB* at the given angle. He
denotes *AB* and *CB* by *x* and *y*. He then shows how the lengths of
the other lines from *C* to the given lines at the given angles can
be expressed in terms of *x* and *y* and that these expressions are
of the first degree in *x* and *y*. By multiplying these expressions
an equation may be produced, whose degree depends upon the number
of lines [AT, 6, 384-387, 396-399; 1954, 32-36, 57-65] so that,
for instance, when there are four lines the equation will be of the
second degree. Descartes holds that the locus of *C* is the curve
represented by that equation. But an error has in fact crept
in, owing to the inadequacies of Descartes's techniques for dealing with changes of sign. In each case there should be two
equations of the given degree, so that in the four line problem the
locus of *C* is not one conic section but two [18]. This error is
not so fundamental as to vitiate the rest of Descartes's treatment,
and interestingly enough he seems to have had some inkling of it
himself, for, as we shall see, he recognises two curves in one
case of the five line problem.

Descartes uses the degree of the equation as a basis for
the classification of curves, although he hints at a finer
classification on another principle by emphasizing that the circle
is simpler than the ellipse, parabola or hyperbola [AT, 6, 392-
393, 396; 1954, 49, 57]. The use of equations for classification is
an important application of specification by property, but we
should be wrong to think that the equation was for Descartes a
substitute for genetic definition. The production of an equation
did not solve Pappus's problem. The curve still had to be found.

Descartes gives most attention to the four-line locus [AT,
6, 397-407; 1954, 61-81]. From the form of the equation and with
the help of a few simple constructions, he indicates very sketchily
when the curve will be a parabola, hyperbola, ellipse or circle,
and gives such parameters as the length of the *latus rectum*. In
this he is drawing essentially on the principal planimetric
properties of the various conic sections as established by
Apollonius. But when he has achieved this he can also appeal
to Apollonius for the geometric construction of the curves from
particular sections of the cone. In this he is not being altogether consistent, for Apollonius's criteria for construction
were different from his own.

But for the higher cases there was no Apollonius to appeal
to, and Descartes was left to his own methods. He essayed no
general treatment and concentrated most of his attention on a
particular case of the five-line locus [AT, 6, 407-410; 1954,
81-86]. In this, four of the given lines are taken as parallel
with equal intervals between them. The fifth line is perpendicular and all the given angles are right angles. The product

of the perpendiculars from C to three of the parallel lines is
equated with the product of a given line (equal to the interval
between the parallel lines) and the perpendiculars from C to the
other two lines. Descartes forms the equation, and solves the
problem by showing that the same equation applies to a figure
constructed by his method of determined motions. A parabola is
constrained to move so that its axis always lies along one of the
parallel lines. A straight line is constrained to move so that
it always passes through one of the intersections of the given
lines and also through a point on the axis of the parabola fixed
relative to the parabola. The intersections of the parabola and
the straight line trace out the curve, which is in fact a cubic
curve with two branches. It was perhaps the symmetrical nature
of this problem that made Descartes realise that the complete
solution involved two cubic curves, the second being described
by reversing the direction of the parabola.

Descartes's mathematical laziness is notorious [cf. Allard
1963, 158-160, section entitled "La lassitude de Descartes envers
les Mathématiques"], and he himself frequently insisted upon it.
Very early in his treatment of Pappus's problem in the *Géométrie*
he claimed [AT, 6, 382; 1954, 27] that "it already wearies me to
write so much about it," and he frequently said that he was only
giving a sketchy treatment of particular issues in order that
others could have the pleasures of discovery or at least realise
how difficult the matter was. He had the type of mind that was
happy in producing bold general conceptions, but became bored
when it was a question of working out the detail, although he
was quite capable of doing this. Also, after his early work
in mathematics, he was far more interested in producing a
natural philosophy with a strong mathematical basis than in working
on actual problems of pure mathematics. It is thus not surprising
that the *Géométrie* can read as if it ought to have been an early
draft of itself. There are frequent obscurities and *lacunae* of
reasoning, and diverse matters that had interested Descartes at
different times of his life are sometimes thrown together with
little attempt at unification. This seems particularly so in the
case of the ovals, which Descartes saw as having application in
optics, and when treating these his criteria for geometrical
construction are more lax than his norm.

He prepared the ground for this at the end of his discussion
of Pappus's problem, where he excused himself for not considering
further higher cases. "I did not undertake to say everything,
and having explained the manner of finding an infinity of points
through which [the curves] pass I think that I have sufficiently
given the means of describing them" [AT, 6, 411; 1954, 89]. Here
Descartes's indolence seems to have led him to the brink of admitting definition by equation, but from what follows it is clear that
he regarded this mode of description as subsidiary to genesis by
determined motions [AT, 6, 411-412; 1954, 89-90]:

*It is also to the point to remark that there is a great
difference between this manner of finding several points in order
to trace a curved line, and that which one uses for the spiral
and similar* [curves] [19]: *for by the latter one does not find
indifferently all the points of the line that one is seeking, but
only those which can be determined by some measure more simple
than that which is required to compose it, and so strictly speaking
one does not find one of its points, that is to say one of those
which are so proper to the curve that they cannot be found without
it. But there is no point in the lines that serve for the question
at issue that cannot be met among those which are determined* (qui
se determinent) *in the manner just explained. And because this
manner of tracing a curved line by finding indifferently several
of its points only extends to those which can also be described
by a regular and continuous movement, one ought not to reject it
entirely from geometry.*
Thus some point-wise descriptions are allowed, but with an inferior status. Descartes also feels it necessary to make a similar
concession for certain constructions making use of strings [AT, 6,
412; 1954, 90-93]:
And one ought no more to reject that [manner of description]
in which one uses a thread or a doubled cord (une chorde repliée)
*to determine the equality or difference of two or more straight
lines which can be drawn* (tirées) *from each point of the curve
that one seeks to certain other points, or onto certain other lines
at certain angles, as we did in the* Dioptrique *in order to explain
the ellipse and the hyperbola. For, although one could not admit
any lines which resembled cords, that is to say which became sometimes straight and sometimes curved, since the ratio between
straight lines and curved ones, being unknown and even I believe
being unable to be known by men, one could conclude nothing thence
that was exact and ensured, yet because one only uses strings in
these constructions to determine straight lines, whose lengths
one knows perfectly, this ought not to make one reject them.*

Descartes points out that he has used constructions with strings
for the ellipse and the hyperbola in his optical writings [see AT,
6, 165-178], and it is in an optical context that both pointwise
descriptions and a string construction reappear in the *Géométrie*.
Descartes introduces four ovals, all of which he claims are useful
in optics [AT, 6, 424-429; 1954, 114-125; cf. AT, 10, 310-328].
In each case he gives a description by stating how an arbitrary
point is to be constructed. For a special case of one of them he
then asserts a construction using string. A rod is pivoted about
a fixed point in the plane. A string travels from the free end of
the rod, down the rod to the point where it is kept taut by a
finger, from there to a fixed point in the plane and then back to
the finger, and finally from the finger to another fixed point in
the plane, where its other end is attached. As the rod is moved
about the pivot, the finger traces out the oval. It is not

immediately obvious that this construction serves Descartes's end, and he gives no justification for it, but he is in fact right. However, string constructions had a rather peripheral place in Descartes's foundations of geometry and we must regard them as being introduced as a second-rate substitute for constructions arising from articulated instruments. And certainly pointwise descriptions must be regarded as less than a full genesis, since they do not produce all the points of the curve. The norm remained the sequence of determined movements of rigid figures.

CONCLUSION

In John Aubrey's *Brief Lives* we have an anecdote of Descartes, which Aubrey claimed to have from one Alexander Cowper [Aubrey 1898, 1, 222]:

He was so eminently learned that all learned men made visits to him, and many of them would desire him to show them...his instruments (in those dayes mathematicall learning lay much in the knowledge of instruments, and, as Sir H[enry] S[avile] sayd, in doeing of tricks), he would drawe out a little drawer under his table, and show them a paire of Compasses with one of the legges broken: and then, for his ruler, he used a sheet of paper folded double.

This story, whether true or not, can help to highlight features of Descartes's approach to geometry. He sought for clear and distinct foundations of geometry, and found it easiest to achieve these by drawing on the traditions of contemporary practical geometry. This involved reflecting on the use of instruments, but it was by no means a case of actually using them. What had to be imagined were idealised instruments, and these could be conceived, when used in a certain way, to produce the acceptable curves of geometry. This involved a radical break with the ancient vision, but Descartes disguised the nature of the break by reading his own procedures into ancient writings and implying that they used criteria of his own kind, but in a more restricted way [20].

In Descartes as in the ancients we see clearly the distinction between specification by genesis and specification by property. For him the former was certainly fundamental, but the changes he made in the latter are more immediately apparent. These were grounded in his particular "algebra of straight lines" and in his use of a standard method for representing all acceptable curves by equations. His work within the theory of equations (particularly in Book 3 of the *Géométrie*) is also highly significant, but in this paper we have been concerned with how Descartes shifted the conceptual foundations of geometry. He was very conscious that he was making changes, but whereas he gave clear characterisations of the bases of his own procedures, his account of what he was changing from is often historically misleading. In this we may sympathise, for, as we have seen, the reconstruction of

the ancient foundations is a matter of some complexity, and
Descartes was not acting as historian. But a close examination
of these foundations can show many unsuspected differences from
Descartes. A fuller historical account of how Descartes came to
make the changes that he did make would demand paying more detailed
attention to his contemporary intellectual milieu than we have done
here. But a historical explanation is not satisfactory without
a clear analysis of what has to be explained, and it is to this
end that this paper has been principally directed.

NOTES

1. For an interesting discussion of the analogous problems surrounding the "completely arbitrary" function see Becker [1927,
153-160].
2. The concept of intelligible matter in a mathematical context
is found in Aristotle, *Metaphysica* Z. 10, 1036a9-12; Z. 11,
1037a1-5; H. 6, 1045a34, but there is some doubt about the status
of the first two of these passages; see Aristotle [1957, 150,152].

3. I speak here of what Geminus [Proclus 1873, 111; 1948, 100]
would have called incomposite lines and surfaces, and do not
consider the specification of such composite lines as the perimeters of polygons. For a useful account of curves in Antiquity
see Tannery [1912].

4. My aim here is to identify the main thrust of Pappus's arguments. Particularly in the case of the first derivation, this
has meant some reconstruction and deviation from his actual
order of presentation.

5. Sporus [Pappus 1965, 254-255; 1933, 193-194; Thomas 1957, 1,
340-341] had pointed out that the original definition of the quadratrix did not produce its final point, but only the points before
the motion was completed. There is thus a limiting process involved.
The same applies to the construction of the quadratrix from the
cylindrical helix and the Archimedean spiral.

6. For fragments of Eratosthenes' *Platonicus* see Hiller [1870].
It is not certain that the work was a dialogue.

7. We only consider the first conchoid, but Pappus remarks that
there were others; cf. Heath [1921, 1, 240].

8. Nicomedes used the conchoid for the duplication of the cube,
and Eutocius [1915, 98-99; Thomas 1957, 1, 296-299] reports that
he derided Eratosthenes' discoveries as both "impracticable and

lacking in geometrical sense". Thus it may be that Nicomedes regarded the analogue of the instrumental construction as geometrical, or, less probably, that he had a completely different geometrical construction.

9. The cissoid is normally identified with the curve described by Diocles, but there is no absolute certainty; cf. Thomas [1957, 1, 270, n.a.]. It is possible, though unlikely, that the Arabic version of Diocles' work discovered by G. J. Toomer [see Toomer 1972, 190-191] contains a more geometrically acceptable genesis of the curve than that reported by Eutocius.

10. For Newton's "organic" (instrumental) construction of the cissoid, see Newton [1967-, 5, 464-466].

11. Proclus speaks of the property as τὸ καθ'αὐτὸ καὶ ᾗ αὐτὸ ὑπάρχον; cf. Aristotle, Anal. Post. I. 4, 73b26-32 and Ross's comment in Aristotle [1949, 522-523]. Pappus [1965, 234, 252; 1933, 178, 192] uses the phrase τὸ ἀρχικὸν σύμπτωμα, and gives this for the Archimedean spiral and the quadratrix. He does similarly for the conchoid, but in that case his phrase is simply τὸ σύμπτωμα [1965, 244; 1933, 186]. Apollonius [1891-93, 1, 4] spoke of the first book of his Conics as containing the γενέσεις and the ἀρχικά συμπτώματα of the conic sections.

12. Some of the propositions of Euclid's Data may be read in this way. See e.g. Euclid [1883-1916, 6, 46-55].

13. Pappus [1965, 662-663; 1933, 495-496]. Hultsch attributes this passage to an interpolator. Eutocius [1893, 184-185] also distinguishes plane and solid loci, but he sees the second group as comprising many more sections of solids than just the conic sections. He does not mention linear loci, but adds that there are also loci on surfaces. Proclus [1873, 394-395; 1948, 337-338] has the plane-solid distinction, but appears rather confused, and his whole discussion of loci seems to have been forced into a context that was not altogether appropriate. Cf. Euclid [1956, 1, 329-331].

14. Descartes [AT, 6, 388-390; 1954, 41-45]. The translations from Descartes are in general my own. I have striven for the literal, often at the expense of the elegant.

15. The steps by which Descartes struggled towards his mature form of algebraic representation cannot be considered in detail here. Among the rather scanty evidence, important pieces may be found in Regulae ad directionem ingenii 15-18 [AT, 10, 453-469; 1955, 65-77]. Compare with this Beeckman's notes from 1628-29 [AT, 10, 333-335], and see Milhaud's discussion [1921, 70-72, n.1]. In Descartes's extant letter to Golius on the problem of Pappus in

January 1632 [AT, 1, 232-235] there are puzzling references to
the motion of construction being determined by simple relations,
which are in turn explicated in terms of single ratios *(proportiones singulae)*.

16. Pappus [1965, 676-681; 1933, 506-510; Thomas 1957, 1, 488-489,
2, 600-603] had given a statement of the problem in his account of
Apollonius's *Conics*. In the *Géométrie* Descartes [AT, 6, 377-379;
1954, 16-20] takes over this account from Commandinus's translation
of the *Collectio*. In our exposition of the problem we shall,
unlike Pappus, freely allow the product of straight lines to be a
straight line, and we shall introduce the symbol n when speaking
of the number of lines.

17. A textual obscurity in Pappus's account causes difficulties
in assessing exactly what the ancients did in this regard, but
according to him it was certainly little. Cf. Pappus [1933, 508,
n.8].

18. In terms of modern "Cartesian coordinates" this may be seen
as follows. Consider a line $ax+by+c = 0$ and a point $C(l,m)$ not
on it. The perpendicular distance of C to the line is
$(al+bm+c)/\sqrt{aa+bb}$. The length of a line from C to $ax+by+c = 0$
intersecting it at a given angle ϕ is $(csc\phi)(al+bm+c)/\sqrt{aa+bb}$
Thus if we have four given lines distinguished by the subscripts
1,2,3,4, the conditions of the problem mean that $C(l,m)$ must
satisfy:

$$(a_1l+b_1m+c_1)\ (a_2l+b_2m+c_2)/\ \sqrt{(a_1{}^2+b_1{}^2)}\ (a_2{}^2+b_2{}^2)$$

$$= \pm\ k(a_3l+b_3m+c_3)\ (a_4l+b_4m+c_4)/\ \sqrt{(a_3{}^2+b_3{}^2)}\ (a_4{}^2+b_4{}^2)$$

where k is a constant determined by the given angles. Thus C
must lie on one of two conic sections, obtained respectively
by taking the plus sign and the minus sign before k. Conversely any point on either curve satisfies the required relation of
distances, and so the locus is two conic sections. Cf. [AT, 6,
724].

19. Christopher Clavius [1606, 320-322] had attempted such a
description of the quadratrix.

20. We may see Descartes's interpretation of the ancient procedures
as a natural progenitor of the great concern in the seventeenth
and eighteenth centuries with organic (or instrumental) geneses
of curves. For an account of such constructions from Antiquity
to the eighteenth century see von Braunmühl [1892].

REFERENCES

Allard, Jean-Louis 1963 *Le Mathématisme de Descartes*
    Université d'Ottawa
Apollonius of Perga 1891-93 *Quae Graece Exstant cum Commentariis
    Antiquis* Ed. J L Heiberg 2 vols Leipzig (Teubner)
_____ 1961 *Treatise on Conic Sections* Ed. in modern notation
    by T L Heath Reprint Cambridge (Heffer)
Archimedes 1910-15 *Opera omnia cum commentariis Eutocii* Ed.
    J L Heiberg 2nd ed Leipzig (Teubner)
_____ n.d. *The Works of Archimedes* Ed. in modern notation
    by T L Heath Reprint New York (Dover)
Aristotle 1928 etc. *The Works of Aristotle translated into
    English* Ed. J A Smith & W D Ross 12 vols Oxford
    (Clarendon Press)
_____ 1949 *Aristotle's Prior and Posterior Analytics* Ed.
    with introduction and commentary by W D Ross Oxford
    (Clarendon Press)
_____ 1957 *Metaphysica* Ed. W Jaeger Oxford (Clarendon Press)
Aubrey, John 1898 *"Brief Lives", chiefly of Contemporaries*
    Ed. Andrew Clark 2 vols Oxford (Clarendon Press)
Becker, Oskar 1927 *Mathematische Existenz* Halle (Niemayer)
_____ (ed.) 1965 *Zur Geschichte der Griechischen Mathematik*
    Darmstadt (Wissenschaftliche Buchgesellschaft)
Boyer, Carl B 1956 *History of Analytic Geometry* New York
    (Scripta Mathematica)
_____ 1959 Descartes and the geometrization of algebra *Am
    Math Monthly* 66, 390-393
Cantor, Moritz 1879 Review of original printing (1875) of Pappus
    [1965] *Zeitschrift für Mathematik und Physik* 24, Historisch-
    literarische Abtheilung 126-132
_____ 1894-1908 *Vorlesungen über Geschichte der Mathematik*
    2nd ed 4 vols Leipzig (Teubner)
Coolidge, Julian Lowell 1963 *A History of Geometrical Methods*
    Reprint New York (Dover)
Clavius, Christopher 1606 *Geometria practica* Mainz
de Morgan, Augustus 1849 Short supplementary remarks on the
    first six books of Euclid's *Elements Companion to the
    Almanac for 1849,* 5-20
Descartes, René 1897-1913 *Oeuvres de Descartes* Ed. Charles
    Adam & Paul Tannery 12 vols Paris This is cited as AT
_____ 1954 *The Geometry of René Descartes* ·Tr. David E Smith
    & Marcia L Latham Reprint New York (Dover) This volume
    includes a facsimile of the original (1637) French edition
_____ 1955 *The Philosophical Works of Descartes* Tr. E S
    Haldane & G R T Ross 2 vols Reprint New York (Dover)
Euclid 1883-1916 *Opera Omnia* Ed. J L Heiberg & H Menge 8
    vols and supplement Leipzig (Teubner)
_____ 1956 *The Thirteen Books of Euclid's Elements* Tr. with

introduction and commentary by T L Heath   Reprint   New York
    (Dover)
Eutocius of Ascalon   1893   *Commentaria in Conica*   Apollonius
    [1891-93, 2, 168-361].
_____   1915   *Commentarii in Libros de Sphaera et Cylindro*
    Archimedes [1910-15, 3, 1-225].
Fermat, Pierre   1891-1922   *Oeuvres*   Ed. P Tannery & C Henry
    4 vols and supplement   Paris (Gauthier-Villars)
Heath, Thomas L   1921   *A History of Greek Mathematics*   2 vols
    Oxford (Clarendon Press)
_____   1949   *Mathematics in Aristotle*   Oxford (Clarendon Press)
Hiller, E   1870   Der Πλατωνικός des Eratosthenes   *Philologus* 30,
    60-72
Jackson, D E P   1970   *The Arabic Version of the Mathematical
    Collection of Pappus Alexandrinus. Book VIII. A Critical
    Edition*   Unpublished PhD thesis, Cambridge
_____   1972   The Arabic translation of a Greek manual of mechanics
    The Islamic Quarterly 16, 96-103
Kutta, W M   1898   Zur Geschichte der Geometrie mit Constanter
    Zirkelöffnung   *Nova Acta, Abhandlungen der Kaiserlichen
    Leopoldinisch-Carolinischen Deutschen Akademie der Naturforscher*
    71, 69-101
Leslie, John   1832   Analysis   *The Edinburgh Encyclopoedia*   Ed.
    D Brewster *et al.*   The First American Edition   Philadelphia
    1, 707-711   For Leslie's authorship of the article see 18,
    xii
Mahoney, Michael S   1968   Another look at Greek geometrical
    analysis   *Archive for History of Exact Sciences* 5, 318-348
_____   1973   *The Mathematical Career of Pierre de Fermat*
    (Princeton Univ Press)
Milhaud, Gaston   1921   *Descartes Savant*   Paris (Alcan)
Molland, A G   1968   The geometrical background to the 'Merton
    School'   *British J for the Hist of Sci* 4, 108-125
Mugler, Charles   1948   *Platon et la Recherche Mathématique de
    son Epoque*   Strasbourg (Heitz)
Newton, Isaac   1967-   *The Mathematical Papers of Isaac Newton*
    Ed. D T Whiteside   (Cambridge Univ Press)
Pappus of Alexandria   1933   *La Collection Mathématique*   Tr.
    P Ver Eecke   2 vols, paginated serially   Bruges & Paris
    (Desclée de Brouwer)
_____   1965   *Collectionis Quae Supersunt*   Ed. F Hultsch   3 vols
    paginated serially   Reprint   Amsterdam (Hakkert)
Plato   1935   *The Republic*   Ed. & tr. Paul Shorey   London
    (Heinemann)
Plutarch   1914-26   *Plutarch's Lives*   With tr. by B Perrin   11 vols
    London (Heinemann)
_____   1961   *Moralia*   Vol 9 with tr. by E L Minar, F H Sandbach
    & W E Helmbold   London (Heinemann)
Proclus   1873   *In Primum Euclidis Elementorum Librum Commentarii*

III

48

Ed. G Friedlein Leipzig (Teubner)

_____ 1948 *Les Commentaires sur le Premier Livre des Eléments d'Euclide* Tr P Ver Eecke Paris (Blanchard)

_____ 1970 *A Commentary on the First Book of Euclid's Elements* Tr Glenn R Morrow (Princeton Univ Press) This volume has Friedlein's page numbers entered in the margins, and I do not cite it separately

Schramm, Matthias 1965 Steps towards the idea of function: A comparison between eastern and western science of the Middle Ages *History of Science* 4, 70-103

Scott, J F 1936 John Wallis as a historian of mathematics *Annals of Science* 1, 335-357

Serenus of Antinoeia 1896 *Opuscula* Ed. J L Heiberg Leipzig (Teubner)

_____ 1969 *Le Livre de la Section du Cylindre et le Livre de la Section du Cône* Tr P Ver Eecke Reprint Paris (Blanchard)

Steele, A D 1936 Über die Rolle von Zirkel und Lineal in der griechischen Mathematik *Quellen und Studien zur Geschichte der Mathematik, Astronomie und Physik*, Abt. B, 3, 287-369 Parts 2 and 3 of this, but for some reason not Part 1, are reprinted in Becker [1965, 146-202]

Tannery, Paul 1912 Pour l'histoire des lignes et surfaces courbes dans l'Antiquité *Mémoires Scientifiques* 11 vols Toulouse (Prival) and Paris (Gauthier-Villars) 1912-31, 2, 1-47

Thomas, Ivor 1957 *Selections illustrating the History of Greek Mathematics* 2 vols Reprint London (Heinemann)

Toomer, G J 1972 The Mathematician Zenodorus *Greek, Roman and Byzantine Studies* 13, 177-192

van der Waerden, B L n.d. *Science Awakening*, vol 1 2nd English ed. Groningen (Noordhoff)

von Braunmühl, A 1892 Historische Studien über die organische Erzeugung ebener Curven von den ältesten Zeiten bis zum Ende des achtzehnten Jahrhunderts *Katalog mathematischer und mathematisch-physikalisher Modelle, Apparate und Instrumente* Ed. Walther Dyck Munich 54-88

von Wilamowitz-Moellendorff, Ulrich 1894 Ein Weihgeschenk des Eratosthenes *Nachrichten von der Königl. Gesellschaft der Wissenschaften zu Göttingen* Philologisch-historische Klasse, 1894, 15-35

Vuillemin, Jules 1960 *Mathématiques et Métaphysique chez Descartes* Paris (Presses Universitaires de France)

Zeuthen, H G 1902 *Histoire des Mathématiques dans l'Antiquité et le Moyen Age* Tr Jean Mascart Paris (Gauthier-Villars)

_____ 1966 *Geschichte der Mathematik im 16. und 17. Jahrhundert* Reprint New York (Johnson) and Stuttgart (Teubner)

ACKNOWLEDGMENTS

Some of the themes in this paper were treated in a lecture
to the British Society for the History of Mathematics on December
15th 1972, and I am grateful for the comments then received.
For incisive criticisms of an earlier draft and pertinent suggestions, I am much indebted to Professor J. E. McGuire. I should
also like to thank: an anonymous referee and the editor for many
helpful comments; Dr. D. E. P. Jackson for making his thesis
available to me and for many useful discussions; Dr. D. Bloor
for drawing my attention to Aubrey's anecdote. A welcome opportunity for much of the work on the paper was afforded by my
tenure of an Andrew Mellon Postdoctoral Fellowship in the University of Pittsburgh.

IV

IMPLICIT VERSUS
EXPLICIT GEOMETRICAL METHODOLOGIES :
THE CASE OF CONSTRUCTION

Albert Einstein is famed for giving the opinion that, "If you want to find out anything from the theoretical physicists about the methods they use, I advise you to stick closely to one principle: don't listen to their words, fix your attention on their deeds."[1]   In like vein Alfred North Whitehead wrote:

> If often happens, therefore, that in criticising a learned book of applied mathematics, or a memoir, one's whole trouble is with the first chapter, or even with the first page.   For it is there, at the very outset, where the author will probably be found to slip in his assumptions.   Further, the trouble is not with what the author does say, but with what he does not say.   Also it is not with what he knows he has assumed, but with what he has unconsciously assumed.   We do not doubt the author's honesty.   It is his perspicacity which we are criticising.   Each generation criticises the unconscious assumptions made by its parents.   It may assent, to them, but it brings them out in the open.[2]

In this chapter I intend to use these two quotations as partial inspiration in examining the status of constructions in pure geometry from Greek Antiquity until the seventeenth century.

This will involve a search for symbiotic relationships between mathematics and philosophy.   To a large extent mathematics is what

---

(1) A. Einstein, *The World as I See It* (London, 1935), 131.
(2) A. N. Whitehead, *Science and the Modern World: Lowell Lectures, 1925* (New York, 1948), 29.

182

mathematicians do, and little formal philosophy is needed for someone to be trained by apprenticeship and example into producing new and creative mathematics, much in the way that in T. S. Kuhn's discussions of the growth of science natural scientists are trained into the paradigm that currently demarcates their discipline, and learn implicity to accept the standards that it provides.[3] On the other hand, philosophers (including mathematicians wearing philosophical hats) find much to say about mathematics, and can sometimes suggest, to the dismay of others, that a philosophical approach is necessary for major mathematical advance. This tension has spilt over into the historiography of mathematics, with strong claims and counterclaims being made for the influence of philosophy upon mathematics or *vice versa*. This study will proceed, on the (perhaps not very exciting) assumption that the truth lies somewhere between the two extremes.

THE STRAIGHT AND THE CIRCULAR[4]

In a famous passage from the *Republic* Plato has Socrates complain of contemporary geometers that,

> Their language is most ludicrous, though they cannot help it, for they speak as if they were doing something and as if all their words were directed towards action. For all their talk is of squaring and adding and applying and the like, whereas in fact the real object of the entire study is pure knowledge.[5]

This passage may be seen as relating to two issues, which I think should be more clearly separated than is often done. One concerns the role of instruments in geometry, and the other that of motion.

Let us first consider the question of instruments. The origins of geometry rest in obscurity, but it is generally and plausibly believed that it arose from practical concerns, even if these had ritual connotations.[6] Measurement of fields is not of great interest here, for it

(3) See especially, T. S. Kuhn, *The Structure of Scientific Revolutions* (2nd ed., Chicago, 1970).

(4) There is an extensive general literature on construction in Greek mathematics. See, for example, A. D. Steele, "Über die Rolle von Zirkel und Lineal in der griechischen Mathematik", *Quellen und Studien zur Geschichte der Mathematik, Astronomie und Physik*, B3 (1936), 287-369; E. Niebel, *Untersuchungen über die Bedeutung der geometrischen Konstruktion in der Antike*, Kantstudien Ergänzungshefte, 76 (Cologne, 1959); A. G. Molland, "Shifting the Foundations: Descartes's Transformation of Ancient Geometry", *Historia Mathematica*, 3 (1976), 21-49.

(5) *Republic*, 527A.

(6) A. Seidenberg, "The Ritual Origin of Geometry", *Archive for History of Exact Sciences*, 1 (1960-62), 488-527.

led naturally into problems of calculation rather than into geometry in the Greek style.   More relevant are problems where one is told to do something, such as, on a simple level, to draw a right angle.   Here, if the constructions were to be at all accurate, instruments were necessary, and among the most popular early ones were pieces of rope which could be secured at various of their points by pegs.[7]   However, it must soon have become clear that one could talk about such constructions and assess their validity without using actual ropes, and in fact the appeal to reason gave greater precision and greater generality than appeal to measurement.

The next stage would be to think it more appropriate, if one was not using ropes or other instruments, not to talk about them, and this stage had been reached by the time of Plato and Aristotle.   But then, if one was not talking about instruments or of the figures produced by them, there arose the problem of what one was in fact talking about.   This may not have bothered many working mathematicians, but they still would have had little difficulty in agreeing with Plato and Aristotle that the geometer was not talking about his diagram but about what it symbolised.[8]   That is, the pure geometer, for the tradition of practical geometry persisted, and there instructions continued to be given as to how to make and apply various instruments for the solution of problems.   But this was regarded as an activity pertaining more to mechanics than to geometry, and I wish to argue that for the pure geometer the probable practical origin of many of his constructions was virtually lost sight of, and that he was only rarely thinking in terms of the use of instruments.

But first we turn to more general considerations concerning the place of motion in geometry.   The Platonic quotation above would seem to make discussions of motion inappropriate to geometry, and Aristotle also, although he does not have a separate world of mathematicals, but considers geometrical objects as abstracted from sensible ones, still seems rather uneasy about motion.   "It is clear that some mathematical theorems consider [mathematical objects] *qua* immovable and *qua* separable from mater...   Some parts of mathematics deal with things which are immovable but presumably do not exist separately, but as embodied in matter."[9]   On the other hand, contemporary geometry obviously did rely heavily on some sort of motion.   Not only were many propositions formulated as "problems" in which it was required that something be done, i.e. constructed, but

(7) A. Seidenberg, "Peg and Cord in Ancient Greek Geometry", *Scripta Mathematica*, 24 (1959), 107-122.

(8) *Republic* 510D-E; *Posterior Analytics* I.10, 77a1-3.

(9) *Metaphysics* E.1, 1026a8-15.

184

proofs of theorems (statements of geometrical truths) regularly required auxiliary constructions.

From the philosopher's side Aristotle gave hints at an answer:

> Propositions (διαγράμματα) too in mathematics are discovered by an activity; for it is by a process of dividing-up that we discover them. If the division had already been performed, the propositions would have been manifest; as it is, they are present only potentially. Why does the triangle imply two right angles [i.e. that the angles together are equal to two right angles]? Because the angles about one point are equal to two right angles. If, therefore, the straight line parallel to the side had been drawn upwards the reason why would at once have been clear... Hence it is manifest that relations subsisting potentially are discovered by being brought to actuality; the reason is that the exercise of thought is a (bringing to) actuality.[10]

Here, as with his discussions of continuity, Aristotle enters the tricky ground that lies between thought and external reality, and this tendency is again evident when he introduces intelligible matter as a substratum for mathematical objects.

Aristotle's own views seem somewhat inchoate.[11] A more clearcut, if still philosophically problematic, picture is presented by Proclus when reporting a dispute between followers of Speusippus and followers of Menaechmus. The former had held that all geometrical propositions should be counted as theorems not problems, and that constructions of geometrical objects should be regarded "not as making, but as understanding them, taking eternal things as if they were in the process of coming to be", whereas the latter school interpreted all propositions as problems of one kind or another.

> The school of Speusippus are right because the problems of geometry are of a different sort from those of mechanics, for example, since the latter are concerned with perceptible objects that come to be and undergo all sorts of change. Likewise the followers of Menaechmus are right because the discovery of theorems does not occur without recourse to matter, that is, intelligible matter. In going forth into this matter and shaping it, our ideas are plausibly said to resemble acts of production; for the

---

(10) *Metaphysics* Θ.9, 1051a21-31; translation from T.L. Heath, *Mathematics in Aristotle* (Oxford: Clarendon, 1949), 216.

(11) On Aristotle and intelligible matter see, for instance, I. Mueller, "Aristotle on Geometrical Objects", *Archiv für Geschichte der Philosophie*, 52 (1970), 156-171, and S. Gaukroger, "Aristotle on Intelligible Matter", *Phronesis*, 25 (1980), 187-197.

> movement of our thought in projecting its own ideas is a production
> ... of the figures in our imagination and of their properties. But it
> is in imagination that the constructions, sectionings, superpositions,
> comparisons, additions, and subtractions take place, whereas the
> contents of our understanding all stand fixed, without any
> generation or change.[12]

Proclus writes as a philosopher, but he was here adjudicating between
the followers of someone who was primarily a philosopher and someone
who was primarily a mathematician.   Also the work from which the
quotation is taken is his commentary on Book I of Euclid's *Elements*,
and this should give an earnest that he meant to stay closer to
mathematical practice than many philosophers, and to be more
exegetical than prescriptive.

Let us now look at two fundamental definitions from Book I of the
Elements, which differ in character from many others in Greek geometry:
"A straight line is a line which lies evenly with the points on itself"; "A
circle is a plain figure contained by one line such that all the straight
lines falling upon it from one point among those lying within the figure
are equal to one another."[13]   Although the first of these definitions is
somewhat vague, they may both be described as definitions by property,
in which a geometrical object is defined by certain relations obtaining
between its parts.   It could happen that a definition specify an
impossible object, but here the definitions are supplemented by three
postulates laying down conditions under which straight lines and circles
may be constructed, and thus in some sense exist.

> Let the following be postulated: To draw a straight line from any
> point to any point.   To produce a finite straight line continuously
> in a straight line.   To describe a circle with any centre and
> distance.[14]

It is these postulates in particular that have given rise to the idea of the
privileged status of ruler (more strictly straight-edge) and compass
contructions in Greek geometry, but, as emphasised above, Euclid's
Elements, like other writings on pure geometry, make no reference to
instruments, and, I would argue, thoughts of instruments were hardly
even implicit.

(12) Proclus, *In Primum Euclidis Elementorum Librum Commentarii*, ed. G. Friedlein
(Leipzig, 1873), 77-79.   My translations from this are either taken from or based upon
those in Proclus, *A Commentary on the First Book of Euclid's Elemenis*, tr. G. R. Morrow
(Princeton, 1970).   This has Friedlein's page numbers in the margins, and so I do not cite
it separately.
(13) *The Thirteen Books of Euclid's Elements*, tr. T. L. Heath (2nd ed., Cambridge,
1926), I, 153.
(14) *Ibid.*, I, 154.

186

There is first the question of whether compasses in the modern sense existed at the time of Euclid, or rather when the postulates were first formulated.[15]   But this is not a very serious argument, for peg-and-cord constructions could easily be substituted.   Also we must admit that in the early philosophical tradition there was some tendency to link pure geometrical constructions to the use of instruments.   For instance, in the *Philebus* Plato has Socrates say:

> The beauty of figures which I am now trying to indicate is not what most people would understand as such, not the beauty of a living creature or a picture; what I mean, what the argument points to, is something straight, or round, and the surfaces and solids which a lathe, or a carpenter's rule and square, produces from the straight and the round.[16]

But still the general thrust of both Plato's and Aristotle's thought is to deny an instrumental basis for pure geometry, and there are even difficulties in seeing Euclid's text as faithfully reflecting instrumental procedures.

The main trouble comes with Propositions 2 and 3 of Book I: "To place at a given point (as an extremity) a straight line equal to a given straight line"; "Given two unequal straight lines, to cut off from the greater a straight line equal to the less."[17]   If one were thinking in terms of a pair of compasses or a rope, these would present no difficulty, but in fact Euclid gives quite elaborate proofs.   One would therefore, as Augustus de Morgan put it, have to "suppose the compasses to close of themselves the moment they cease to touch the paper."[18]   This is an awkward conception, and commentators have usually spoken of Euclid trying to make his conditions as rigorous as possible.   Seidenberg adhered to the view of the postulates as basically abstracting from instrumental procedures, but also suggested that Proposition 2 be read as saying, "We hereby throw away the peg and cord."[19]   I would argue that this could be extended to saying that the use of instruments was not in the forefront of Euclid's mind, but rather certain privileged figures and motions.

(15) The first three postulates are usually thought to derive from much earlier than Euclid, but in his chapter in this volume Ian Mueller argues that they may have been first formulated by Euclid himself, or at least contemporaneously with him.

(16) *Philebus* 51C.

(17) Heath, *Thirteen Books*, I, 244-247.

(18) *Ibid.*, I, 243.   Cf. J. L. Berggren, *Episodes in the Mathematics of Medieval Islam* (Berlin, 1986), 70; D. H. Fowler, *The Mathematics of Plato's Academy: A New Reconstruction* (Oxford, 1987), 291; I. Mueller, *Philosophy of Mathematics and Deductive Structure in Euclid's* Elements (Cambridge, Mass., 1981), 24-25; Seidenberg, "Peg and Cord", 119-120; Id., "Ritual Origin", 498; Id., "Did Euclid's Elements, Book I, Develop Geometry Axiomatically?", *Archive for History of Exact Sciences*, 14 (1974-75), 263-295, at 265-266.

(19) Seidenberg, "Peg and Cord", 120.

In the *Parmenides* Plato remarked somewhat laconically that, "A One, such as we have described, will have some shape, straight or round or a mixture of both."[20]   Sentiments of this kind were developed more fully by Aristotle and extended to the realm of motion: "All movement that is in place, all locomotion, as we term it, is either straight or circular or mixed from these, for these two are the only simple movements.   And the reason is that the only simple magnitudes are the straight and the circular.   Now circular [motion] is about the centre, and straight is up and down."[21]   And again, "everything that is moved locally is moved either circularly, or straight, or mixedly (ἢ κύκλῳ ἢ εὐθεῖαν ἢ ματήν)."[22]   Such notions were fundamental to Aristotle's cosmology, but also seem to have had a strong symbiotic relation with the geometry of the time, and I would suggest were more powerful than instrumental ideas in determining pure geometers' attitudes towards what were admissible constructions.   This becomes more plausible when we move outside the ambit of Book I of the *Elements* and pass to Euclid's treatment of solid geometry.   There we meet definitions of the following kind: "When, the diameter of a semicircle remaining fixed, the semicircle is carried round and restored again to the same position from which it began to be moved, the figure so comprehended is a sphere."[23]   The instrumental analogue to this is hard to find, but it is easily understood in terms of a rotation about an axis.   We should also note that we have moved on to a new sort of definition, which we may call definition by genesis as opposed to definition by property, for it is in terms of how the figure is to be constructed.

And this was in fact the standard form of definition in Greek geometry.   Euclid (or a predecessor) may have been following a particular logical penchant in presenting all his definitions in Book I by property, and, much later in time, Eutocius was to suggest that this was the only proper form.[24]   Other thinkers argued differently, and again much later in time Spinoza asserted the necessity of genetic definition:

> If the thing in question be created, the definition must... comprehend the proximate cause.   A circle should, according to this rule, be defined as follows: the figure described by any line whereof one end is fixed and the other free.[25]

(20) *Parmenides* 145B.
(21) *De Caelo* I.2, 268b17-23.
(22) *Physics* VIII.8, 261b28-29.
(23) Defn XI.14, from Heath, *Thirteen Books*, 261.
(24) *Apollonii Pergaei Quae Graece Exstant, cum Commentariis Antiquis*, ed. J.L. Heiberg (Leipzig, 1891-93; repr. Stuttgart, 1974), II, 186-187.
(25) *On the Improvement of the Understanding*, from Spinoza, *Selections*, ed. J. Wild (New York, 1930), 37-38.

IV

188

It should however be remarked that not all Euclid's definitions in Book XI are genetic, but only those that introduce essentially new "simple" shapes, rather than figures that are formed from old shapes. For instance: "An octahedron is a solid figure contained by eight equal and equilateral triangles."[26] There was then the need for "existence proofs", which in the case of the regular solids were given in Book XIII.

The motions used in the definitions in Book XI were confined to rotations about an axis, but elsewhere we find less rigid conceptions of rotation, as in Apollonius's definition of a cone:

> If a straight line indefinite in length, and passing always through a fixed point, be made to move round the circumference of a circle which is not in the same plane with the point, so as to pass successively through every point of that circumference, the moving straight line will trace out the surface of a double cone, or two similar cones lying in opposite directions and meeting in the fixed point, which is the apex of each cone.[27]

However, the notion of the circular remains, and, if this is now combined with the straight, we can produce conic sections by constructing planes to cut the cone. And many other curves were produced on similar principles.[28] Also the circular and straight motions did not have to be consecutive, but could be simultaneous, provided that they were specified to be uniform with respect to time. This occurs in Archimedes' famous definition of the spiral:

> If in a plane a straight line be drawn and, while one of its extremities remains fixed, after performing any number of revolutions at a uniform rate return again to the position from which it started, while at the same time a point moves at a uniform rate along the straight line, starting from the fixed extremity, the point will describe a spiral.[29]

No canonisation seems to have made of what was allowable, but, if we stick to the notion of the straight and the circular, we shall not go far wrong, although we should again remember that in both the ancient and the medieval (especially Arabic) traditions, ingenious instruments were devised, or at least, imagined for constructing particular curves.

(26) Defn XI.26, from Heath, *Thirteen Books*, III, 262.
(27) Apollonius of Perga, *Treatise on Conic Sections*, ed. T. L. Heath (Cambridge, 1896), 1.
(28) Cf. Molland, "Shifting the Foundations", 25-26.
(29) E. J. Dijksterhuis, *Archimedes* (Copenhagen, 1956), 264.

But the intuition of the straight and the circular is somewhat vague, and trouble could arise over particular curves. A notable example was the quadratrix. Imagine a square ABCD. A straight line moves uniformly and parallel to itself from position BC to position AD, and at the same time another straight line rotates about point A from position AB to position AD. The two motions are completed simultaneously. Then the point of intersection of the moving lines traces out a quadratrix, a curve that was used for squaring the circle. Pappus commented:

> With this Sporus is rightly displeased for these reasons. In the first place, the end for which the construction seems to be useful is assumed in the hypothesis. For how is it possible, with two points beginning to move from B to make one of them move along a straight line to A and the other along a circumference to D in equal time unless first the ratio of the straight line AB to the circumference BED is known? For it is necessary that the speeds of the moving points should be in this ratio. And how than could one, using unadjusted speeds, make the motions end together, unless this should sometimes happen by chance? But how could this fail to be irrational?[30]

Sporus's objection is intuitively cogent, and this not just on instrumental grounds, for, using instruments, it is hard to see how even just one motion could be guaranteed as uniform, while Archimedes' definition of the spiral, which demands two, seems intuitively acceptable.

Pappus remarked that this genesis of the quadratrix was more mechanical than geometrical, and it is significant that he uses the adjective μηχανικός rather than ὀργανικός, which was usual for describing instrumental constructions. However, geometrical derivations could be given from both the cylindrical helix and the Archimedean spiral.[31] This is not the place to analyse these in detail, but only to see how they extended the admissible modes of construction. The most notable features are the formation of plectoids and cylindroids. A plectoid arises from a cylindrical helix by the motion of a perpendicular from it to the axis of the cylinder, and Heath vividly compared the surface so produced to "a spiral staircase with infinitely small steps."[32] A cylindroid was formed by constructing a surface perpendi-

(30) Pappus of Alexandria, *Collectionis Quae Supersunt*, ed. F. Hultsch (Berlin, 1875-78; repr. Amsterdam, 1965), 252-254; translation from I. B. Thomas, *Selections Illustrating the History of Greek Mathematics* (London, 1939), 340. On the quadratrix cf. Molland, "Shifting the Foundations", 26-27.
(31) Pappus, ed. Hultsch, 258-265.
(32) T. L. Heath, *A History of Greek Mathematics* (Oxford, 1921), II, 381.

190

cular to the plane of an Archimedean spiral and passing through the spiral itself. Sections of these surfaces by planes were allowed, as also the orthogonal projection of curves. We can once again see the interaction between the straight and the circular, but we are also approaching the bounds of what was considered admissible.

This is also the case with the conchoid, if not with the so-called cissoid. Cissoids were referred to in Antiquity, and Proclus said that Geminus taught their geneses.[33] For long it has been conventional to see a curve described by Diocles as a cissoid, but in his recent edition of the Arabic text of Diocles' *On Burning Mirrors* G. J. Toomer has argued strongly against this identification.[34] We may thus know nothing about actual cissoids and their geneses, and Diocles' curve does not really enter into our purview, for its definition is highly instrumental, and does not even give a full definition by genesis, but only the means of constructing an arbitrary number of points on the curve.[35] The conchoid too appears to have had instrumental origins, but it was also presented in a more purely geometrical way.[36] Its genetic definition demanded the motion of a straight line in such a way that it always passed through a fixed point while a particular point on it always remained on another, fixed, straight line. It comes near to fitting our impressionistic criteria, although we should perhaps speak of the interaction of the straight and the rotatory rather than of the straight and the circular.

DIGRESSION ON RECTIFICATION

It may help us to ponder more deeply the problems of allowability if we turn aside to look at rectification. Mainline historiography of mathematics can make this seem puzzling to the tyro. On the one hand there is the idea that the rectification of a curve was first performed in about 1659, and had hitherto been widely believed to be impossible, and this view appeared to have authoritative support from both Aristotle and Descartes:

> If the [circular and the rectilinear] motions are comparable, we are confronted with the consequence... that there may be a straight line equal to a circle. But these are not comparable, and so the corresponding motions are not comparable either (Aristotle).[37]

(33) Proclus, ed. Friedlein, 118.
(34) Diocles, *On Burning Mirrors: The Arabic Translation of the Lost Greek Original* (Berlin, 1976), 24-25.
(35) *Ibid.*, 98-100; Thomas *Selections*, I, 270-279.
(36) Thomas, *Selections*, I, 298-301; cf. Molland, "Shifting the Foundations", 30-31.
(37) *Physics*, VII.4, 248b4-6.

> The ratio which is between straight lines and curves is not known, and even, I believe, cannot be known by man (Descartes).[38]

On the other hand it is well known that Archimedes had closely linked the rectification and quadrature of the circle, and had performed the quadrature of a segment of a parabola. This would seem to make the unproven denial of the possibility of rectifying curves singularly obscurantist. To attempt a resolution we may ask three different questions:

1. *Does it exist?* Averroes explicated the Aristotelian passage just quoted in terms of the impossibility of mutual superposition of straight and circular lines,[39] an argument, which, if extended, could have had drastic implications for many areas of geometry. Archimedes more subtly set up criteria for inequality:

> I assume the following:
> I.   That of the lines which have the same extremities the straight line is least.
> II. That of the other lines, if, lying in one plane, they have the same extremities, two are unequal whenever both are concave in the same direction and moreover one of them is either wholly-included between the other and the straight line which has the same extremities with it, or is partly included by and partly coincides with the other; and that the line which is included is the lesser...[40]

These, together with the intuitive possibility of arbitrary close approximation of a curved line by a polygonal line, seem to concur with common sense in allowing the possibility of equality between straight and curved — at least in the days before discussions of the real number system. But, even in Antiquity, there were plausible grounds for disagreement. Thus Proclus asked:

> Would not someone have questioned whether it is not possible that no straight lines should be equal to one another? And especially in geometrical forms that there should be inequality but no equality at all? We shall learn at least that the horn angle is always unequal, never equal, to an acute angle, that the same is true of the angle of

(38) R. Descartes, *Œuvres de Descartes*, ed. C. Adam & P. Tannery (Paris, 1897-1913), VI, 412; R. Descartes, *The Geometry of René Descartes*, tr. D. E. Smith & M. L. Latham (New York, 1954), 90; this book includes a facsimile of the original 1637 edition.

(39) *Phys.* VII, comm. 24, from *Opera Aristotelis Stagiritae* (Venice, 1560), 260v.

(40) Dijksterhuis, *Archimedes*, 145.

a semicircle, and that the transition from the greater to the less does not always proceed through equality.[41]

The horn angle was the curvilinear angle formed between the arc of a circle and a tangent to it, and the angle of a semicircle the angle between an arc and a radius.   In *Elements* III.16 Euclid demonstrated that a horn angle was less than and an angle of a semicircle greater than any acute rectilinear angle.   Paradoxes easily arise, and in the thirteenth century Campanus of Novara highlighted some similar to that given by Proclus.[42]   Vigorous controversy about their resolution continued well into the seventeenth century.[43]

But as regards the existence of equality between the straight and the curved the common sense view generally prevailed, and was robustly expressed by one medieval commentator on Archimedes' *De mensura circuli*:

> The second of the postulates is that a curved line be equal to a straight line.   We postulate this, although it is a principle both known *per se* and recognised by anyone of sound head.   For, if a hair or a silk thread be bent around circumference-wise in a plane surface, who unless demented would doubt that the hair or the thread would be the same whether bent around or extended in a straight line, and would be as much afterwards as before?   Again, if a circle be turned around on a plane surface with its circumference touching the plane and if it be rolled in a straight line on the plane from one of its points until it arrives at the same point of the circumference, who not out of his mind will doubt that the circumference describes a straight line equal to the circumference?[44]

Other writers, including Luca Valerio, Giovanni Battista Benedetti and Galileo Galilei, enjoyed the anti-Aristotelianism involved, and in such discussions frequent appeal was made to passages from Archimedes.   One of these was Proposition 18 of *On spirals*, in which Archimedes equated the length of the circumference of the first circle of a spiral with a certain straight line determined from the spiral.   In a sense this provides a rectification of the circle, but only in a sense, for the spiral came first, and determined what circle it was that was to be rectified.

(41) Proclus, ed. Friedlein, 234.

(42) *Euclidis Megarensis... Opera a Campano interprete fidissimo translata... Lucas Paciolus... detersit emendavit...* (Venice, 1509), propns III.15, 30.

(43) Cf. Heath, *Thirteen Books*, II, 39-42; A. G. Molland, "An Examination of Bradwardine's Geometry", *Archive for History of Exact Sciences*, 19 (1978), 113-175, at 163-164.

(44). M. Clagett, *Archimedes in the Middle Ages* (vol. I, Madison, 1964; vols. 2-5, Philadelphia, 1976-1984), I, 170.

2. *Can it be known?*   The relationship between construction and
existence has been a perennial theme in the philosophy and practice of
mathematics, and has generated a vast literature.   Here we need go
little beyond the uncontentious position that constructibility is often
seen as a guarantee of existence, and can, as it were, make the relevant
object known.   In this spirit Aristotle spoke of the quadrature of the
circle: "Take, for example, the squaring of the circle, supposing it to be
knowable; knowledge of it does not yet exist but the knowable itself
exists."[45]   Boethius rather unhelpfully commented that "it does not
seem to have been discovered in Aristotle's times, but was found
afterwards, and because its demonstration is long, it will be passed
over,"[46] thus succeeding in spreading confusion to the later Middle Ages.

If Boethius was referring, directly or obliquely, to an actual
attempt at quadrature, the most likely candidate would be that by
means of the quadratrix, which, as we have seen, can cogently be
accused of *petitio principii*.   The same applies to any attempt to
convert Archimedes' equation of a circumference and a straight line by
means of a spiral into a rectification, for then we should have to know
how to construct the relevant spiral, and this again involves arranging
two uniform motions to finish at the same time.   In many ways a more
plausible rectification is that provided by the anonymous medieval
commentator in terms of simply rolling a circle in a straight line along a
plane.   But we somehow feel this to be cheating, and so are again
brought up against the question of what are acceptable constructions for
solving geometrical problems, and thus providing knowledge.

3. *Can it be said?*   When discussing parallel lines, Proclus spoke of
certain essential properties belonging to them as such, which were
convertible with their definition.   He continued:

> In this way also other mathematicians were accustomed to
> discourse on lines, giving the property *(symploma)* of each
> species.   For Apollonius showed for each of the conic lines what its
> symptoma was, and Nicomedes for the conchoids, Hippias for the
> quadratrices, and Perseus for the spirics.   For after the genesis, the
> apprehension of the essential [symptoma] belonging [to it] as such
> differentiates the species constructed from all others.[47]

In the case of Apollonius's conics the symptomata were relations
between the lengths of certain straight lines, closely analogous to the

(45). *Categories* 7, 7b31-33.
(46) J.P. Migne, *Patrologiae Cursus Completus... Series Latina* (Paris, 1844-93),
LXIV, 230-231.
(47) Proclus, ed. Friedlein, 356.

equations of later "analytical" geometry.[48]   The symptomata for spirals and quadratices, as given by Pappus, were equations between the ratios of the lengths of circular arcs and those of straight lines.[49]

We shall consider Descartes's canonisation of acceptable constructions in the next section, but here we should note that he regarded it as convertible with the expressibility of a curve by a polynomial equation. The symptomata of spirals and quadratrices are not regularly translatable into such terms, and so gave Descartes a strong motivation for rejecting those curves from geometry proper.   Nevertheless, as Jules Vuillemin has amply shown,[50] Descartes was quite ready, at least on a private basis, to consider curves that were not properly geometrical.   And in general, given that equality between straight and curved could exist, there was a feeling of restlessness at its lack of expressibility.   For instance, John Wallis:

> A straight line and a curved are not such mutually heterogeneous quantities that they cannot be properly compared and be equal to one another, although it may be that the diameter and circumference of a circle are so irrational that their ratio cannot be expressed by true numbers nor even by any mode of notation yet accepted in use.[51]

And soon, more positively, James Gregory explicitly suggested a new mode of notation:

> Just as fractions never proceed from the addition, subtraction or multiplication of integers, but only from division; and incommensurable numbers never proceed from the addition, subtraction, multiplication or division of commensurables, but only from the extraction of roots; so non-analytic numbers or quantities never proceed from the addition, subtraction, multiplication, division or extraction of roots of analytic ones, but from this sixth operation, so that our invention adds another operation to arithmetic.[52]

Gregory's sixth operation involved the use of converging infinite series, but here we begin to stretch at the limits of this chapter, and so must return to the question of construction, which I hope we have now established is closely related to that of quantitative expressibility, so that, for instance, the rectification of the circle by rolling is inadmissible in that it cannot be seen to lead to any commodious form of expressibility.

(48) Apollonius, ed. Heiberg, I, 36-53; tr. Heath, 8-12.
(49) Pappus, ed. Hultsch, 234, 252.
(50) J. Vuillemin, *Mathématiques et Métaphysique chez Descartes* (Paris, 1960).
(51) John Wallis, *Opera Mathematica* (3 vols., Oxford, 1695-93-99), I, 380.
(52) James Gregory, *Vera Circuli et Hyperbolae Quadratura* (Padua, 1667), 5.

Descartes's Mechanisation of Geometry[53]

Descartes is renowned as both philosopher and mathematician, and it is not surprising that from very early on he adopted a philosophical attitude towards mathematics, as can be seen from both his correspondence with Beeckman and his *Regulae ad directionem ingenii*. This meant *inter alia* that he laid down explicit criteria for admissible geometrical constructions. In Book II of the *Geometrie* he endeavoured to introduce this in historical form by means of criticism of the ancients, but his account is distorted as a result of his insistence on interpreting their procedures in instrumental terms. In this way he can be said to have gone against the conclusion of the passage from Whitehead quoted at the beginning of this chapter: he appeared but *only* appeared to lay bare the unconscious assumptions of his predecessors. In particular, he was largely responsible for foisting on posterity the myth of the ruler-and-compasses restriction in Greek geometry.

But in the course of this he introduced his own more positive criteria, which drew on considerations of both construction and measure:

> It is, it seems to me, very clear that, taking as one does for geometrical that which is precise and exact and for mechanical that which is not, and considering geometry as a science that teaches generally how to know the measures of all bodies, one must no more exclude the more compounded lines than the more simple, provided that one can imagine them to be described by a continuous movement or by several which follow one another and of which the later are entirely determined by those which precede.[54]

The possibility of precise and exact measure is explicated in terms of polynomial equations and that of determined movements in terms of the imagination of articulated instruments in which the movement of one part determines the movements of all and where the intersections of parts trace out curves. The parts are either in the form of straight lines or of curves produced by a previous instrument.

---

(53) For some recent discussions of Descartes's geometry, see H. J. M. Bos, "On the Representation of Curves in Descartes' Géométrie", *Archive for History of Exact Sciences*, 24 (1981), 295-338; M. Galuzzi, "Recenti Interpretazioni della Géométrie di Descartes", *Scienza e Filosofia: Saggi in Onore di Ludovico Geymonat*, ed. C. Mangione (Garzanti, 1985), 643-663; E. R. Grosholz, "Descartes' Unification of Algebra and Geometry", *Descartes: Philosophy, Mathematics and Physics*, ed. S. Gaukroger (Brighton, 1980), 156-168; T. Lenoir, "Descartes and the Geometrization of Thought: the Methodological Background of Descartes' Géométrie", *Historia Mathematica*, 6 (1979), 355-379. I give a fuller discussion of some of the themes in this section in "Shifting the Foundations", 34-42.

(54) Adam & Tannery, VI, 389-390; Smith & Latham, 42.

196

In this way Descartes brought the imagination of mechanical instruments back into the heartlands of pure geometry, and his work led to a rash of publications seeking organic, that is instrumental, constructions of geometrical curves. And, however much Newton may have liked to disagree with Descartes, he had in this respect become deeply imbued with the new spirit, and so we may fittingly conclude with a quotation from the preface to the first edition of Newton's *Principia*, which can symbolise the move from the ancient intellectualist imagination of perfect simple movements to the more "practical" orientation of the seventeenth-century vision, and can allow us to speak of the mechanisation of the geometrical picture, as a companion to that of the world picture.

> To describe right lines and circles are problems, but not geometrical problems. The solution of these problems is required from mechanics, and by geometry the use of them, when so solved, is shown; and it is the glory of geometry that from so few principles brought from without, it is able to produce so much. Therefore geometry is founded in mechanical practice and is nothing but that part of universal mechanics which accurately proposes and demonstrates the art of measuring.[55]

(55) Isaac Newton, *Philosophiae Naturalis Principia Mathematica*, ed. A. Koyré & I. B. Cohen (Cambridge, 1972), I, 15.

V

THE GEOMETRICAL BACKGROUND TO THE "MERTON SCHOOL"

AN EXPLORATION INTO THE APPLICATION OF MATHEMATICS TO NATURAL PHILOSOPHY IN THE FOURTEENTH CENTURY*

AT the end of the last century Paul Tannery published an article on geometry in eleventh-century Europe,[1] which he began with the following statement:

> "This is not a chapter in the history of science; it is a study of ignorance, in a period immediately before the introduction into the West of Arab mathematics."

Despite the title of the article and the main body of its contents, Tannery's principal object was not to revel in the ignorance of the Dark Ages, but rather to attempt to throw some light on the origins of Greek geometry. He hoped, by portraying the low state of geometry in a society which was by no means uncivilized to confute the evolutionist view that theoretical geometry must develop with civilization. In the course of the article he paints a picture of eleventh-century geometry which possesses all the gloom he requires, and which, I believe, still needs little modification. He is thus able, in his conclusion, to compare two civilizations, one in which theoretical geometry did develop and one in which it did not. Historical circumstances prevented the continued observation of the medieval civilization to see how long it would have taken to develop a respectable geometry, for in the twelfth century Latin translations of ancient mathematical works started appearing in greater number. This fact in itself provided Tannery with one further argument in favour of his thesis about the origins of Greek geometry. After remarking on the appearance of the translations he continues:

> "However, it is noteworthy that, until the end of the sixteenth century, geometry remained relatively neglected in comparison with arithmetic and algebra. This gives one more reason for considering the creation of geometry by the Greeks as a fact depending far more on the genius of that people than on the degree of civilization that they had attained. Moreover, that which

---

* This paper, in an earlier form, was read to the seminar on the history and philosophy of mathematics organized by Dr. G. J. Whitrow and Dr. C. Tanner at the Imperial College of Science and Technology, London, on 21 February 1967. It has also been read by Mr. O. D. Edwards, Professor A. R. Hall, Dr. M. A. Hoskin, Mr. C. Milton, Professor J. E. Murdoch, and Dr. W. P. D. Wightman. I am very grateful for all the comments and criticisms that I have received; in particular Professor Murdoch's very detailed criticism has resulted in many changes in the final version. Nevertheless I must claim all errors and infelicities of expression as purely my own.

[1] "La Géométrie au XIe Siècle", in Paul Tannery, *Mémoires Scientifiques*, v (Paris and Toulouse, 1922), 79–102. The article was originally published in 1897.

THE BRITISH JOURNAL FOR THE HISTORY OF SCIENCE VOL. 4 NO. 14 (1968)

V

characterizes the Hellenic genius in this respect is less the fortunate accident of the original constitution of the science . . . than the interest which it aroused and the marvellous *élan*, which, intensifying more and more, lasted for more than five centuries, and which could lead an Apollonius or an Archimedes to heights that have been reached again only relatively recently."[2]

In considering this passage we omit any discussion of the validity of Tannery's attempt to throw light on the origins of Greek geometry from the vantage-point of the Middle Ages, and confine ourselves to examining his assertion of the relative neglect of geometry in the medieval period. It may be thought that nearly seventy years later, we should be able to refute this assertion, especially in view of the increased interest in medieval science which has characterized this century. But in fact no such refutation has become possible, although I think it is possible to surround Tannery's bald statement with a number of qualifications, and so give it greater precision.

Let us first look at the negative aspect. There are in the Middle Ages very few instances of any new geometrical theorems being discovered or proved. Thus the first volume of M. Clagett's study of the medieval Archimedean tradition[3] shows that there was ample interest in certain of Archimedes' works, often combined with a critical study of his procedures, but no medieval writer appears to have attacked new geometrical problems in the Archimedean spirit. Even more apparent than the medieval interest in Archimedes is the interest in Euclid. At least three different twelfth-century translators from the Arabic rendered his *Elements* into Latin,[4] and in the thirteenth century Campanus of Novara compiled what was to be the standard version for the later Middle Ages, including in it a substantial amount of comment of his own.

That the Schoolmen were deeply interested in theoretical geometry[5] there is no doubt, but there is little evidence that this interest was motivated by a desire to geometrise for themselves. We are thus left with the question as to why they felt geometry to be a worth-while study. A glance at some of the more famous medieval encomia of mathematics soon gives us a hint of the solution. Fairly early in the thirteenth century Robert Grosseteste writes:

"The usefulness of considering lines, angles and figures is of the greatest, for without them natural philosophy may not be known. Their influence is in the whole universe and in its parts absolutely. Also in related properties such as rectilinear and circular motion. Also in action and in passion . . . All causes

[2] P. Tannery, *Mémoires Scientifiques*, v, 101–102.

[3] M. Clagett, *Archimedes in the Middle Ages*, i (Madison, 1964).

[4] M. Clagett, "The Medieval Latin Translations from the Arabic of the *Elements* of Euclid, with Special Emphasis on the Versions of Adelard of Bath", *Isis*, xliv (1953), 16–42.

[5] In the Middle Ages geometry was divided into two parts: theoretical and practical (*geometria speculativa* and *geometria practica*). Practical geometry dealt with practical problems of mensuration, and numerous treatises on it are extant, but I do not consider this branch of the subject in this article.

of natural effects are to be given by lines, angles and figures, for otherwise it is impossible to know the *propter quid* in them."[6]

Later, Roger Bacon remarks:

"He who knows not [mathematics] cannot know the other sciences nor the things of this world . . . And, what is worse, those who have no knowledge of mathematics do not perceive their own ignorance and so do not look for a cure. Conversely a knowledge of this science prepares the mind and raises it up to a well-authenticated knowledge of all things."[7]

In the fourteenth century, Thomas Bradwardine says:

"[Mathematics] is the revealer of every genuine truth, for it knows every hidden secret, and bears the key to every subtlety of letters; whoever, then, has the effrontery to pursue physics while neglecting mathematics should know from the start that he will never make his entry through the portals of wisdom."[8]

In each of these three testimonies mathematics is valued principally for the power it can exercise in other intellectual pursuits. Bacon in fact, in a previously unpublished passage, actually speaks of natural philosophy as providing the main *raison d'être* of geometry:

"The geometer therefore considers the possible paths of nature, because it was for the sake of gaining knowledge of the works of nature that geometry was first and essentially established, and after that for the sake of human works. The writers on optics show us that lines and figures reveal to us the whole operation of nature, its principles and effects. The same holds in the case of celestial matters, which are considered by both natural philosophy and astronomy."[9]

The emphasis that Grosseteste and Bacon place on mathematics is closely associated with their views on the importance of optics; and the emphasis on optics in turn depends upon Grosseteste's famous light metaphysic, a doctrine which seemed to suggest that the fundamental science of the natural world should have a form analogous to that of geometrical optics.

Bradwardine's case is rather different, as we shall see, but here again the praise of mathematics takes the form of asserting its usefulness in other disciplines, and particularly in natural philosophy. Thus, although we give up the hope of finding many medieval developments in pure geometry,

---

[6] L. Baur (ed.), *Die Philosophischen Werke des Robert Grosseteste* (Münster, 1912), 59–60. (This work forms vol. ix of *Beiträge zur Geschichte der Philosophie des Mittelalters*). Cf. A. C. Crombie, *Robert Grosseteste* (2nd imp., Oxford, 1961), 110.

[7] J. H. Bridges (ed.), *The "Opus Maius" of Roger Bacon* (Oxford, 1897), i, 97. Cf. A. G. Little (ed.), *Roger Bacon: Essays* (Oxford, 1914), 167.

[8] J. E. Murdoch, *Geometry and the Continuum in the Fourteenth Century: A Philosophical Analysis of Thomas Bradwardine's Tractatus de Continuo* (microfilm, Ann Arbor, 1957), 401. Cf. J. A Weisheipl, *The Development of Physical Theory in the Middle Ages* (London and New York, 1959), 73.

[9] MS., Oxford, Bodleian, Digby 76, f. 78ar: Geometer igitur considerat vias possibiles nature, quia propter opera nature certificanda constituta est (ex *in MS*) geometria primo et per se, deinde propter opera humana. Auctores enim perspective nobis ostendunt quod linee et figure declarant nobis totam operationem nature, et principia et effectus. Et similiter patet per celestia, de quibus naturalis et astronomia communicant.

we may at least expect to find interesting applications of geometry in other fields. We may see geometry being used in this way in astronomy and in the construction of astronomical instruments; also in the discussions of the composition of the continuum that were so popular in the fourteenth century. But in this paper I shall confine myself to a consideration of certain aspects of the influence of geometry on fourteenth-century natural philosophy. In doing this I shall pay particular attention to certain features of the work of Thomas Bradwardine and of Richard Swineshead. Occasionally I shall refer to Nicole Oresme, but any full consideration of his work in this light would demand a separate article.

I take as my starting-point a geometrical work by Thomas Bradwardine written probably early in the 1320's, and usually known as the *Geometria speculativa.*[10] At the time of writing it Bradwardine had probably recently assumed his fellowship at Merton College, which he was to hold until 1335, and had not yet begun his *Tractatus de proportionibus*. The *Geometria* has the nature of a textbook, and makes no assumption of previous acquaintance with Euclid. Yet, because it is one of the few works of geometry bearing the name of a medieval author, it finds a place in most of the standard histories of mathematics. Writers on it have usually contented themselves with mentioning little more than the chapters it contains on star-polygons and on isoperimetry. These two chapters are not dependent on Euclid, and the first of them, which is largely original to Bradwardine, contains some very pleasing results about the sums of angles in star-polygons. These results are of no great profundity, and are not rigorously proved, but they do serve to show that Bradwardine was a man capable of genuine mathematical understanding and creativity. On the other hand, the conclusions that Bradwardine proposes on isoperimetry are ill-argued and some of them are false. There are reasons for regarding this chapter as taken over from an earlier work, but the propositions are not, as M. Cantor suggested, lifted directly from the medieval version of the work of Zenodorus.[11]

If one searches the *Geometria* for originality one will probably come away disappointed. But it is, after all, not the primary purpose of a textbook to be original, and therefore it seems more profitable to look for the aims the author had in writing it, and to see how he set about fulfilling them. Bradwardine himself does not tell us why he wrote the book, but

[10] Several early printed editions of this work exist, all dependent on the first one, edited by Pedro Sanchez Cirvelo and published at Paris in 1495. I have prepared a new text in my Cambridge doctoral dissertation of 1967 which is entitled: *The Geometria Speculativa of Thomas Bradwardine: Text with Critical Discussion*. It is not easy to assign a precise date to this work. Comparison with the *Tractatus de proportionibus* suggests that at times in this latter work Bradwardine was improving upon certain material in the *Geometria*. Further, Bradwardine's spell of teaching in the Faculty of Arts would seem to have been a suitable time for writing a geometrical textbook, and I am grateful to Dr. J. A. Weisheipl, o.p., for giving me his opinion on the question of dating. See pp. 16, 350, 358, 363–364 of my dissertation.

[11] M. Cantor, *Vorlesungen über Geschichte der Mathematik*, ii (2nd edn., Leipzig, 1900), 116. See my discussion of this question in *The Geometria Speculativa of Thomas Bradwardine*, (10) 321–328.

we do have some relatively early characterizations of the result. Thus, when in 1456 one Frater Fridericus copied it out as part of his mathematical collection, he remarked:

"This geometrical work contains almost all the geometrical demonstrations which the Philosopher [Aristotle] brings forth by way of example in logic and philosophy."[12]

Just under 40 years later the first editor of the work, the Spaniard Pedro Sanchez Cirvelo, described it as "gathering together all the geometrical conclusions that are most needed by students of arts and of the philosophy of Aristotle".[13] Thus, as we may have suspected, the treatise was valued for its presenting geometry as part and parcel of a larger scheme of learning, and more particularly for the help it gave in understanding Aristotle.

An examination of the work itself confirms the essential accuracy of these characterizations. Aristotle is often explicitly mentioned and the choice and display of material seems highly influenced by his works and also by other aspects of scholastic logic and natural philosophy. Sufficient elementary geometrical material is chosen to display geometry as a demonstrative science of the type described by Aristotle in the *Posterior Analytics*, but after this is done the interest in geometrical methodology falls off. Among the later topics the writer is concerned with the paradoxes presented by the horn-angle; and here, as elsewhere, he couches some of his discussion around particular logical *consequentiae* whose validity is to be examined. He devotes a chapter to the problem, arising from Averroes' commentary on the *De coelo*, as to which regular polyhedra fill space; and he gives another over to some elementary conclusions of spheric, which he illustrates on an armillary sphere. But, probably the most interesting section for our study of the relation of geometry to natural philosophy is that on proportion; to this topic is assigned the third of the book's four parts.

That the notions of ratio and proportion were much used in the Greek sciences is well known, and much of this legacy was received by the Middle Ages. In the fourteenth century, however, these notions gained such a vastly increased range, that some explanation should be sought. The following is tentatively offered.

By the beginning of the fourteenth century the works of Aristotle had been the subject of university discussion for a considerable period; and the problems of producing consistency in the system, and of finding something new to say, were producing ever more subtle interpretations.

[12] MS. Munich, Bayerische Staatsbibliothek, Clm. 14908, f. 224r: Hoc opus geometricum continet fere omnes demonstraciones geometricas quas adducit philosophus gratia exempli vel in loyca vel phylosophia.
[13] From the title page of the Paris, 1495 edition: Geometria speculatiua Thome brauardini recoligens omnes conclusiones geometricas studentibus artium & philosophie aristotelis valde necessarias.

The original Aristotelian texts were becoming far more a source of interesting questions than a corpus of knowledge aimed at producing enlightenment. The increasing subtlety of the intellectual constructions involved often made the discussions seem very remote from the actual objects discussed, and with the very hard-headed rationalist attitude of the time men could doubt the applicability of their theories to the given system of nature. There was thus an increasing tendency to discuss what is conceivable rather than what is. On these grounds the properties of the void could be discussed. None existed, but it was conceivable that it should, and therefore God could have created one. If he had done, its properties would be these. . . . This concentration on the conceivable was sometimes indicated by a writer saying that he was going to discuss a problem *secundum imaginationem*. His objects are going to be those that he presents to himself in the faculty known as the *imaginatio*.[14] Sometimes he will regard his imaginings as corresponding to actual states of affairs and sometimes not, but he will in all probability give little attention to the question of empirically testing his conclusions.

Further the *imaginatio*, in a way perhaps different from our "imagination", had, in scholastic philosophy, a very definite association with mathematics. St. Thomas Aquinas, for instance, holds that a distinguishing feature of the mathematical disciplines is that, in them, the reason judges on material given to it by the *imaginatio*, and not on material received directly from the senses, as in physics.[15] Factors supporting this view were probably the problem of geometrical exactness, and the fact that the geometer undoubtedly performs mental constructions as an essential part of his procedure. By the late thirteenth century the excessive use of the imaginative faculty could be regarded as a characteristic vice of mathematicians, and Henry of Ghent breaks off a discussion of the spatial location of angels to speak of some of his opponents as,

"those whom the Commentator characterized as having their cognitive faculty dominated by their imaginative one . . . They cannot believe that their imagination is confined to finite quantities, and therefore both the imaginings of mathematics and what is outside the heavens seem to them to be infinite . . . They cannot believe nor conceive that there is nothing outside the world, neither place nor time, nor plenum nor vacuum . . . Such people are melancholy, and make the best mathematicians, but the worst metaphysicians, for they cannot raise their minds above the spatial notions upon which mathematics is based . . . And they are inept natural philosophers . . ."[16]

---

[14] On the place of the *imaginatio* in late medieval natural philosophy see especially C. Wilson, *William Heytesbury* (Madison, 1960), 24–25, 174. Cf. also M. McLuhan, *The Gutenberg Galaxy* (London, Routledge and Kegan Paul edn., 1962), 80–81 *et passim*.

[15] S. Neumann, "Gegenstande und Methode. Der Theoretischen Wissenschaften nach Thomas von Aquin aufgrund der Expositio super Librum Boethii de Trinitate", *Beiträge zur Geschichte der Philosophie des Mittelalters*; XLI, Heft 2 (1965), 132–135.

[16] Quodlibet II, questio 9: *Quodlibeta Magistri Henrici Goethals a Gandavo doctoris Solemnis* (Paris, 1518), f. 36r. Cf. R. Klibansky, E. Panofsky and F. Saxl, *Saturn and Melancholy* (London, 1964), 338–339.

If Henry were disturbed by these instances of mathematicism, he would probably have been horrified by what happened in the next century, for then, when men had more to imagine, they had correspondingly more to treat mathematically. One of the most impressive results of this development is the increased attention given to quantities that are not spatially extended. Such are the speeds of motions, the intensity of heat in a body—and also the degree of charity in a man. Some intensive qualities had for long been the subject of ontological discussion under the general heading of the intension and remission of forms, but with little attempt being made towards a systematic quantification. Now, in the fourteenth century, these intensities were viewed as if they were continuous quantities, that is magnitudes. This alone would have sufficed to bring them under the domain of geometry, which in the Middle Ages claimed to deal with magnitudes generally; but it seems that we may go further and say that intensities were imagined as geometric straight lines, which were indeed the paradigm examples of magnitudes in the *Elements*. In the second half of the fourteenth century Nicole Oresme wrote:

"Every measurable thing, numbers excepted, is imagined in the manner of continuous quantity. Therefore, for their measurement it is necessary to imagine points, lines and surfaces, or their properties . . ."[17]

This statement of Oresme's lies at the heart of his doctrine of "Configurations of intensities", and is more developed than those to be found in earlier writers. But I believe that in this statement, as in many other instances, Oresme is merely making clearly explicit what had been implicit in other writers. Such making explicit is by no means trivial, for, by identifying the essence of what his predecessors had been doing, he was able to make clear the ground for further development.

The predecessors upon whom Oresme is depending most strongly in this connection are almost certainly the members of the so-called "Merton School",[18] a group of writers on natural philosophy who flourished in Merton College, Oxford, during the first half of the fourteenth century. Foremost among them in time is Thomas Bradwardine, whose *Geometria* has already been brought under discussion, and whose *Tractatus de proportionibus* of 1328 is one of the most important documents emanating from this school. Junior to him were John Dumbleton, William Heytesbury, Richard Swineshead and Roger Swineshead.[19] Richard Swines-

[17] M. Clagett, *The Science of Mechanics in the Middle Ages* (Madison and London, 1959), 368; cf. p. 347.
[18] To marshal the evidence concerning the extent to which Oresme was acquainted with Mertonian works would be outside the scope of this article. M. Clagett (*op. cit.* in *n. 17*, p. 331) says that the "distinctive vocabulary and principal theorems" of Mertonian kinematics passed to Italy and France about 1350. For our purposes it is only necessary to assume that Oresme had a certain familiarity with the spirit of the Mertonian methods, and this could easily have been obtained merely by hearsay.
[19] For the distinction between Roger Swineshead and Richard Swineshead see J. A. Weisheipl, "Roger Swyneshead, o.s.b., Logician, Natural Philosopher, and Theologian" in *Oxford Studies presented to Daniel Callus* (Oxford, 1964), 231–252.

head's work in particular is of amazing subtlety and sophistication and eminently qualified him for his position as the *bête noire* of many humanists. Until the time of Oresme the Mertonian methods do not seem to have become fashionable at Paris, and Richard de Bury, the famous bibliophile and friend of Bradwardine, was able to write in about 1344:

> "Alas! by the same disease which we are deploring, we see that the Palladium of Paris has been carried off in these sad times of ours, wherein the zeal of that noble university, whose rays once shed light into every corner of the world, has grown lukewarm, nay, is all but frozen. There the pen of every scribe is now at rest, generations of books no longer succeed each other, and there is none who begins to take place as a new author. They wrap up their doctrines in unskilled discourse, and are losing all propriety of logic, except that our English subtleties, which they denounce in public, are the subject of their furtive vigils."[20]

Presumably Richard had no eye for the Paris developments that could be associated with the name of John Buridan, but, if he had lived long enough, he would surely have found satisfaction in the works of Oresme, wherein, I think, we may see the high-point of this mathematical tradition, and certainly its most systematic exposition.

Let us now return to its content. As one of its main concerns was with non-spatially extended quantities, then even if these quantities were imagined as straight lines, the immediate interest is not with the configuration of these lines. The fundamental question is rather, "How much?", and with this question are raised problems of measurement—of theoretical measurement rather than of actual physical measurement, for the latter was rarely attempted in medieval natural philosophy. Scholastic discussions of this type rarely make use of units. The failure to introduce these greatly simplifying devices meant that the fundamental principles of measurement were kept more firmly in mind, and so the Schoolmen clearly saw that, in most cases, measurement rested upon the comparison of two objects of the same genus with respect to size. Such comparison gives rise to a ratio (*proportio*), and hence we are driven back to geometry.

The place of proportion in Greek geometry is well known and one of its most striking features is the definition of equal ratios, given in Euclid's *Elements*[21] and usually ascribed to Eudoxus. We may without much distortion paraphrase this by saying that $A:B$ is equal to $C:D$ if and only if for all positive integers m and n,

$$mA \overset{>}{\underset{<}{=}} nB <=> mC \overset{>}{\underset{<}{=}} nD.$$

This definition, partly as a result of the obscurity of the translation,

[20] Richard de Bury, *Philobiblon, the Text and Translation of E. C. Thomas*   . (Oxford, 1960), 104–107.
[21] Book V, definition 5.

was not understood in the Middle Ages,[22] and in his version of the *Elements* Campanus flounders hopelessly in search of suitable general criteria of the equality of ratios.[23] But the situation was not altogether desperate, for there existed a large class of ratios, whose equalities and inequalities could be directly inferred from the terms in which they were described. I mean of course the rational ratios, those subsisting between commensurable quantities. The theory of such could be directly taken over from arithmetic, for each ratio between commensurable quantities corresponded to a ratio between numbers. The principal medieval authority on numerical ratios was the *Arithmetica* of Boethius, in which the various species and subspecies of ratio are carefully and laboriously enumerated.[24] At the end of this logical division we have a series of descriptions of individual ratios, ranging from the relatively simple *dupla* and *sesquialtera* to more cumbersome expressions of the type exemplified by *quadrupla sesquiquarta* and *triplex superquadripartiens quintas*.[25] The fact that fractions were not used by Boethius in representing numerical ratios did not contribute to ease in managing them. However, the specification of ratios by numerically based names, or denominations, does immediately give more information about them than do mere relations of equality and ordering, which is all that can be deduced from the Eudoxean criteria.[26] Thus an approach to the study of ratios based upon their numerical descriptions is better suited for practical purposes. In this spirit Roger Bacon, in his *Communia Mathematica*, complains of the obscurity introduced into Euclid's fifth book by the lack of an initial logical division of ratio.[27] The only stumbling-block in the way of the arithmetical approach to the general study of ratio was the existence of irrational ratios. Both Campanus and Bacon had to admit that these were known neither to us nor to nature. "In talibus non est nota proportio, nec nobis nec naturae."[28]

In his *Geometria speculativa* Bradwardine, whether knowingly or not, follows Bacon's recommendation that the study of proportion be based on the logical division of ratios. He thus soon separates rational from irrational ratios, and, with a brief summary of the procedure to be adopted, consigns the former class to arithmetic to be fitted there with denominations. He then returns to irrational ratios and remarks:

[22] J. E. Murdoch, "The Medieval Language of Proportions" in A. C. Crombie (ed.), *Scientific Change* (London, 1963), 251 sqq.

[23] Comment on Book V, definition 5.

[24] Boethius, *De Institutione Arithmetica Libri Duo . . .*, ed. G. Friedlein (Leipzig, 1867), 45–72.

[25] Thus 2:1 is called *dupla proportio*; 3:2, *sesquialtera*; 17:4, *quadrupla sesquiquarta*; 19:5, *triplex superquadripartiens quintas* (or, in the elliptical form actually given by Boethius, *triplex superquadripartiens*).

[26] It is of course no part of the aim of Book V of the *Elements* to provide numerical specifications of ratios.

[27] Roger Bacon, *Opera hactenus inedita*, xvi (Oxford, 1940), 80.

[28] Campanus, comment on Book V, definition 3. Cf. Roger Bacon, *op. cit.* in *n. 27*, 79–80. following the reading of MS. *siglum D*.

V

"An irrational ratio, however, is not in this way immediately denominated by a number or even by a numerical ratio, for it is not possible in that case that any part of the smaller quantity should number the greater according to some number. It may happen, however, that an irrational ratio be mediately denominated by number. For example the ratio of the diagonal of a square to its side is a half of the double ratio, and in this manner other species of such ratios receive denominations by number."[29]

The general import of this statement is clear: Bradwardine is claiming the possibility of introducing numerical description for certain irrational ratios. His method for so doing has its basis in the medieval development of an ancient mathematical principle, which probably took its origin in Greek musical theory,[30] and of which hints are to be found in Euclid's *Elements*.[31] The principle has to do with the composition of ratios, and the basic idea lying behind it is that the result of compounding the ratio $A:B$ with the ratio $B:C$, where A is greater than B and B is greater than C, is the ratio $A:C$. We may write:

$$(A:B) + (B:C) = (A:C).{[32]}$$

In doing this we have introduced the arithmetical terminology of addition, but this is in essential accord with fourteenth-century practice. Although the actual verb *addere* does not appear to have been used in this connection before the time of Oresme,[33] the other terminology that Bradwardine employs shows clearly that it was already latent in his conception.[34] Once again Oresme gives clear expression to the notions of his predecessors; and in the long disquisition on the denomination of

---

[29] A. G. Molland, *The Geometria Speculativa of Thomas Bradwardine* (see note 10), 121: Proportio autem irrationalis non sic immediate denominatur ab aliquo numero licet ab aliqua proportione numerali, quoniam non est ibi possibile ut secundum aliquem numerum pars aliqua minoris maioris numeret. Contingit tamen mediate denominari proportionem irrationalem a numero, ut proportio dyametri ad costam est medietas duple proportionis, et ita capiunt alie species huius proportionis denominationes a numero.

[30] P. Tannery, *Mémoires Scientifiques*, iii (Paris and Toulouse, 1915), 70–73; Á. Szabó, "Die Frühgriechische Proportionenlehre im Spiegel ihrer Terminologie", *Archive for History of Exact Sciences*, ii (1962–66), 251–255.

[31] Book V. definitions 9, 10; Book VI, proposition 23.

[32] It may be helpful for the reader at this point to turn to the appendix to this article, for the terminology that I am adopting is at variance with that used in most of the modern literature on the subject. The justification for my convention will become more apparent in the course of the article, but it should be remarked here that if we, like the Schoolmen, do not regard a ratio as a number, then we are free to define addition of ratios in any way we please, providing of course that the operation which we select satisfies the associative and commutative laws. By speaking of the compounding of ratios as addition we get closer to word-for-word correspondence with medieval language, and we no longer have to accuse medieval mathematicians of using such terms as *dupla* in two senses in the same sentence. (On the subject of this choice of convention see my review of E. Grant's edition of Oresme's *De proportionibus proportionum* and *Ad pauca respicientes* in *Annals of Science*, xxii (1966), 296–297). In the symbolism that I have adopted I have tried to ease the path of the modern reader by placing the signs for operations upon ratios in Clarendon (or bold-face) type.

[33] E. Grant, "Part I of Nicole Oresme's *Algorismus proportionum*", *Isis*, lvi (1965), 340–341.

[34] See, for example, H. L. Crosby (ed.), *Thomas of Bradwardine: His Tractatus de Proportionibus* (Madison, 1955), p. 78, ll. 293–310. There Bradwardine makes it quite clear that he is going to use the terms *duplus, triplus, quadruplus* in such a way that doubling, tripling or quadrupling a ratio will for us correspond to squaring, cubing or raising to the fourth power the fraction that we form from the ratio.

ratios included in his *De proportionibus proportionum*, he bases his argument on the assertion that a ratio may itself be regarded as a continuous quantity so far as division into parts is concerned.[35] The division is effected by the introduction of means between the terms of the ratio.

From the definition of the addition of ratios there easily follows that of multiplication and division of a ratio by an integer.[36] Thus in the passage quoted above Bradwardine divides the double ratio by 2 to give the ratio of the diagonal of a square to its side. We may write this as,

$\frac{1}{2} \cdot (2A : A)$, where A is any continuous quantity, or perhaps as $\frac{1}{2} \cdot (2 : 1)$.

This allows the first incursion of number into the field of irrational ratios, and Bradwardine does not go much further than this. But Nicole Oresme develops the notion much further and makes it clear that any ratio expressible in the form $\frac{p}{q} \cdot (A : B)$, where $A:B$ is a rational ratio, is denominable by number.[37]

This theory is often referred to as Oresme's doctrine of fractional exponents.[38] This, although in some ways illuminating, is, I believe, historically misleading, for it suggests to us that ratios are in fact numbers, and that a fairly general notion of irrational numbers is being introduced into theoretical mathematical discussions. But a reading of medieval texts makes it quite plain that a ratio was not regarded as a number. It was a relation subsisting between two objects, which, although susceptible of numerical description, was logically and ontologically quite distinct from number. Numbers could be both added together and multiplied together, but ratios were only susceptible of the one operation of combination that came to be known as addition. To a certain extent, as Oresme saw,[39] ratios partook of the nature of continuous quantity, but continuous quantities were certainly not numbers, and usually only received determination as to size from a process of mutual comparison. In adopting a notation reminiscent of that used in discussing vectors, I hope to obviate such confusions, and to sit closer to the actual medieval procedures.

We may compare the medieval operations on ratios with the corresponding modern ones on fractions by noting that the ordered group of real numbers under addition is isomorphic to the ordered group of positive real numbers under multiplication. By doing this we may see that the medieval procedures were justified, but in fact they did not achieve

[35] Nicole Oresme, *De proportionibus proportionum and Ad pauca respicientes*, ed. E. Grant (Madison, Milwaukee, and London, 1966), 158.
[36] We may think of it as scalar multiplication.
[37] Nicole Oresme, *op. cit.* in n. 35, 160.
[38] See e.g. H. Wieleitner, "Zur Geschichte der gebrochen Exponenten", *Isis*, vi (1924), 509–520, and E. Grant, *op. cit.* in n. 33, 340–341.
[39] See note 35.

V

the generality that such a comparison suggests. In particular the scholastic attempts to deal with ratios of lesser inequality, that is ratios in which the first term is less than the second, ran into unexpected difficulties, and even Oresme's account is incoherent.[40] We may associate this with the lack of a concept of negative number.

But despite this deficiency the medieval developments did extend the language of mathematics sufficiently far to allow the Schoolmen to speak with confidence on a wide range of quantitative problems of natural philosophy. The fact that irrational ratios were, previous to this development, inexpressible may seem to us trivial, as rational approximations are clearly sufficient to express any empirical observation. But, as I have already remarked, the Schoolmen were not dealing with material directly received from the senses, but rather with material pictured in the *imaginatio*, and here the distinction between the commensurable and the incommensurable can seem of the highest importance. It is in this spirit that Nicole Oresme, in his attacks on certain astrological practices, expends so much effort on considering whether or not the celestial motions are mutually commensurable.

But the development of the notion of composition of ratios did not only contribute to solving the problem of denominating ratios. It also played a prominent role in determining the form in which proposed quantitative laws of nature should be expressed. This is particularly evident in the law of motion enunciated by Bradwardine in his *Tractatus de proportionibus*. It was at the time universally agreed that the speed of a motion depended upon what we may call the force causing the motion and the resistance acting against it. Further, Aristotle had spoken of a proportion being involved.[41] However, the Aristotelian text seemed obscure and Bradwardine set himself the task of finding the true law. To do this he first put forward and systematically refuted four erroneous theories. He continues: "Now that these mists of ignorance, these windy arguments have been dispersed it remains that there should shine forth the light of the knowledge of truth."[42] This knowledge proposes to us a fifth opinion, but unfortunately its light is not yet burning with sufficient brilliance

---

[40] Nicole Oresme, *op. cit.* in n. *35*, 150–155, 321–322; A. Maier, *Die Vorläufer Galileis im 14. Jahrhundert* (Rome, 1949), 90, no. 20. A detailed examination of Oresme's difficulties would be out of place here, but basically he is trying to deal with ratios of lesser inequality by analogy with the procedures adopted for ratios of greater inequality. The obvious analogy would lead to such results as 1 :9 being double 1 :3, but Oresme regards it as too much of a *verborum abusio* that the lesser should be double the greater. He therefore adopts a different procedure (which involves 1 :3 being double 1 :9), but the operation of addition which he defines (or at least indicates) on this basis is non-commutative: he does not explore the consequences. If he had been familiar with negative numbers he would not have regarded it as unreasonable that the lesser should be double the greater, for twice −4 is −8. In fact, if we extend the precise mathematical analogy between ratios of greater inequality and positive real numbers, then the ratio of equality corresponds to zero and ratios of lesser inequality correspond to negative numbers.

[41] *Physica* IV. 8, 215b1–216a7; VII. 5, 249b27–250b10.

[42] H. L. Crosby, *op. cit.* in n. *34*, 110.

to make Bradwardine's initial statement transparently clear. It is only by examining the results that Bradwardine deduces from his law that we get a true picture of what he meant. In Oresme's clearer statement the law is that "The speed follows the ratio of the power of the mover to the thing moved, or to the power of the thing moved"[43]—that is, the speed is proportional to the ratio of force to resistance. We symbolize the law as follows:

$$V \sim (F : R),$$

where $\sim$ may be read as "is proportional to". The meaning in a special instance is that, if we double the ratio of force to resistance, we double the speed, where doubling of the ratio has the customary fourteenth-century meaning.[44] In general we may say that if V_1 is associated with F_1 and R_1, and V_2 is associated with F_2 and R_2, then,

$$V_1 : V_2 = (F_1 : R_1) : (F_2 : R_2).[45]$$

The full generality of this expression was not achieved by Bradwardine, and in particular he does not appear to have spoken clearly of ratios between ratios. However, the particular deductions he performs show that he meant the same thing.

As far as I know, Miss A. Maier was the first modern writer to emphasize the significance of Bradwardine's law,[46] and in her exposition of it she gave a modern translation in terms of V being proportional to $log \, F/R$. As a result of her efforts Bradwardine's achievement has gained an established place in standard works on the history of science, but the logarithmic expression of it has all too often led writers to speak of the complicated nature of Bradwardine's "function". In fact the reverse is true. Bradwardine chose the least complicated expression available to him, for, given the conditions to be satisfied, what could be simpler than saying that the speed is proportional to the ratio of the force to the resistance? In his *Two New Sciences*, Galileo makes Salviati ask,

"When . . . I observe a stone initially at rest falling from an elevated position and continually acquiring new increases of speed, why should I not believe that such increases take place in a manner which is exceedingly simple and rather obvious to everybody?"[47]

[43] Nicole Oresme, *op. cit.* in *n. 35*, 262: Velocitas sequitur proportionem potentie motoris ad mobile seu ad resistentiam eius. Cf. Bradwardine in H. L. Crosby, *op. cit.* in *n. 34*, 110: Proportio velocitatum in motibus sequitur proportionem potentiae motoris ad potentiam rei motae. Bradwardine's writing of *proportio velocitatum* instead of *velocitas* obscures his statement.

[44] See nn. 32, 34, and the appendix to this article.

[45] Thus, if F_1 is as 9, F_2 as 3, R_1 as 4, R_2 as 2, we have $(F_1 : R_1) : (F_2 : R_2) = (9 : 4) : (3 : 2) = 2 : 1 = V_1 : V_2$.

[46] A. Maier, *Die Vorläufer Galileis im 14 Jahrhundert* (Rome, 1949), 86–95. For an earlier discussion of Bradwardine's law see M. Clagett, *Giovanni Marliani and Late Medieval Physics* (New York, 1941), 130–137. Although Clagett does not in this work emphasize the novelty of Bradwardine's view, I am unable to agree with Maier's opinion that "Clagett hat Bradwardines Lehre völlig missverstanden" (*op. cit.*, 108, n. 55).

[47] Galileo Galilei, *Dialogues concerning Two New Sciences*, tr. H. Crew and A. de Salvio (Dover reissue of 1914 edition), 161.

V

If Bradwardine had had his Salviati, we should not be surprised to hear him asking the same question about the speed of a motion in relation to its force and resistance. It is only through changes in mathematical language that Bradwardine's law no longer strikes us with its simplicity. The concept of simplicity is therefore often dependent upon the mathematical grammar in use at a given time.

It is probably the "exceedingly simple and rather obvious" formulation of Bradwardine's law that caused it to be so unobtrusively accepted by other fourteenth-century writers, who rarely make even the most indirect reference to Bradwardine in justification of their procedures. And, further, when at the end of the fourteenth century, Blasius of Parma launched an attack upon it, his objections were based on his view that Bradwardine erred in his notion of the composition of ratios.[48] This highlights the fact that to scholastic natural philosophy of this type the coherence of the mathematical expression of a theory was as much of importance as its correspondence with empirical observation. And in fact the concepts of force and resistance, although precisely mathematized theoretically, were empirically very vague.

The introduction of Bradwardine's law into Merton College greatly increased the range and subtlety of the problems its scholars were able to discuss. Contemporary with Bradwardine's work there were numerous discussions of a type now labelled kinematic. In these, time was also treated as a continuous quantity with seeming disregard to the famous but rather obscure Aristotelian definition of time as the number of motion according to before and after.[49] Out of discussions of this nature grew the now famous "Merton theorem of uniform acceleration", and in the work of Richard Swineshead we see the situation complicated by his discussing conjointly dynamical and kinematical problems—that is, problems involving forces and resistances varying with time. As an example of the approach adopted, I shall remark briefly on one of the tracts included in his *Liber calculationum* which is entitled *De loco elementi*.[50]

One of Swineshead's main objects in this piece is to consider one aspect of the question as to whether a body may be treated as the sum of its parts, a question which, as we shall see, is pregnant with consequences as to the possibility of a mathematical treatment of nature. Swineshead considers a body falling through the Centre of the World, and asks whether, in its fall, the part of the body that has already passed the Centre will resist the progress of the fall. He first assumes that it will, and launches into a long and highly sophisticated discussion of the implications of such a view. As a result of his assumption, he is able to regard the body as a

[48] A. Maier, *op. cit.* in *n. 46*, 104–107.

[49] *Physica* IV. 11, 220a24–25.

[50] A new text of this tract may be found in M. A. Hoskin and A. G. Molland, "Swineshead on Falling Bodies", *British Journal for the History of Science*, iii (1966–67), 150–182. In the early printed editions of the *Liber calculationum* it appears as Tractatus XI.

straight line divided at the Centre of the World. The force will be proportional to the length that has not yet passed the Centre, and the resistance will be proportional to the length on the other side of the Centre. A vacuum is assumed, as this provides the most difficult condition affecting the result he wishes to establish. The body is also assumed to be perfectly heavy, although the proof is later extended to cover the case of mixed bodies.

The first part of his argument involves the establishment of numerous results of the proportional algebra, results that depend intimately upon the addition view of the composition of ratios. Armed with these he is able to move on to prove his main result, namely that in no finite time will the body be able to reach the Centre so that its midpoint coincides with the Centre of the World. For this he offers two rigorous proofs. In the first and simpler one he divides the distance between the centre of the body and the Centre of the World into an infinity of parts, such that the first represents half the distance, the second half the remainder, and so on. He shows that each such part takes longer to be traversed than did the preceding one. The result follows.

The second argument[51] is much more difficult, although Swineshead characterizes it as being shorter. It also makes use of far more of the mathematical preliminaries than did the first one. If we described the first argument as employing a step-function, then the second would be typified as dealing directly with the original continuous function, without replacing it by any more tractable one. The argument consists of a number of *consequentiae* and quasi-syllogisms, and in it Swineshead seems to be struggling towards the attainment of some sort of logic of continuously varying quantities, which would provide formal rules for making inferences about such quantities. The argument is of course almost entirely in ordinary language, and brings home forcefully the enormous advantages that were to accrue from the development of mathematical symbolism and the calculus.

The complicated nature of the problem for ordinary language discussion follows from the fact that the speed of the body depends upon the force and resistance, while these themselves depend upon the position which the body has so far reached. There is a great danger of circular reasoning.

When he has proved that his assumption leads to the conclusion that the body would take an infinite time to reach the Centre, Swineshead is able to regard the assumption itself as sufficiently refuted. The motion of the body was natural, and Nature does not organize her affairs in such a way that desires she has implanted are incapable of fulfilment. Therefore, in this respect at least, the body does not act as the sum of its

51 M. A. Hoskin and A. G. Molland, *loc. cit.*, 161–163, 176–177.

parts. It remains to develop the alternative position, that the body acts as one whole, in such a way that each of its parts contributes to the fulfilment of the natural *appetitus* of the whole body. Each part, regardless of its position, urges the complete body to the position where its centre coincides with the Centre of the World.

In Swineshead's portrayal of this second position we notice a sharp change of outlook. The first position had been treated almost purely mathematically, and the geometrical influence was immensely strong. But Swineshead's arguments for the second view no longer have this flavour; they are rather far more reminiscent of the arguments used by St. Thomas Aquinas when he was asking how a man could love God more than himself.[52] The analogy has ceased to be geometrical and has become biological or sociological.

Medieval writers in their discussion of motion may not have sought much for empirical confirmation or refutation of their views, but they were quite alert to the possibility of refuting a view by showing it inconsistent with other principles. And the view refuted might be the view that a particular method of quantification is valid. Despite the fourteenth-century habit of quantifying almost everything seen or unseen, there always remained the possibility of a particular quantification being rejected and the use of geometry withdrawn. Scientific concepts were not yet sufficiently well developed for quantification in any given instance to appear either obviously possible or obviously impossible.

With the graphical diagrams of Nicole Oresme the influence of geometry upon natural philosophy was to become far more apparent, but in this study of certain Mertonian methods I hope to have shown that such influence was very strong before his time; and I have in fact suggested that Oresme's diagrams should be viewed historically as materializations of the imaginings of the Mertonians. The work of the Mertonians and its development by Oresme thus provide one very clear reason why geometry was valued by the Schoolmen, while they still, as Tannery noted, did little to develop the subject.

"Every day, Sancho," said Don Quixote, "you grow less simple and wiser."

"Yes", replied Sancho, "for some of your worship's wisdom must stick to me. Since lands of themselves barren and dry, with mucking and tilling come to yield good fruit. I mean that your worship's conversation has been the muck, which has been cast upon the sterile ground of my dry wit, and the time of my service and communion with you has been the tillage. And so I expect to bear fruit of my own, which may be a blessing, and won't disgrace me, I hope, or slither off the paths of good breeding you have beaten in this parched understanding of mine."[53]

[52] Quodl. I, art. 8.
[53] Miguel de Cervantes Saavedra, *The Adventures of Don Quixote*, tr. J. M. Cohen (Penguin edn., 1950), 539.

The pure fields of geometry were not much cultivated in the Middle Ages, but at least some of their ancient produce was spread as muck upon the lands of scholastic natural philosophy. The fruits so produced may have been fair in themselves, but their greatest use was probably in providing new muck for future generations.

APPENDIX

In this appendix I attempt to portray in a relatively formal manner some of the main threads in the theory of ratios most generally assumed in the fourteenth century. I try to keep close to the spirit of fourteenth-century procedures, but also to achieve greater clarity by employing a symbolism that would not have been familiar to the Schoolmen, but one which I hope does not distort their reasoning to too great an extent. The choice of such a symbolism presents certain difficulties, because, as was explained in the text of the article, medieval writers speak of addition of ratios where a modern writer would be inclined to speak of the multiplication of the corresponding fractions. As should be clear from the foregoing article, there are very good reasons for retaining the medieval expression, and accordingly I use a plus sign to render medieval talk of the addition of ratios, but, to obviate confusion, I place it in bold-face type. I adopt a similar policy in regard to other operations on ratios.

It must be emphasized that I can claim no more for this appendix than that it may prove useful as an aid to reading either this article or original medieval texts.

A ratio (mathematically speaking) is a certain relation between two quantities. We write the ratio of A to B as $A:B$.

We do not provide a general definition for the equality of ratios, but we state that, in the case of ratios between (positive whole) numbers:

$$m : n = p : q \text{ if and only if } \frac{m}{n} = \frac{p}{q}$$

Further, if A and B are any quantities, we say that:

$$A : B = m : n \text{ if and only if } nA = mB$$

From now on we confine our attention to ratios of greater inequality—that is ratios $A:B$ where $A > B$.

We introduce "addition" of ratios by saying that:

$$(A : B) + (B : C) = (A : C)$$

In the case where $A : B = B : C$ we have:

$$(A : B) + (A : B) = (A : C)$$

We write:

$$2. (A : B) = A : C$$

$$\frac{1}{2}. (A : C) = A : B$$

In a similar way we achieve the general expression $\frac{m}{n}. (A : B)$, where m and n are any (positive whole) numbers.

Thus, for example, we have:

$$(5 : 3) + (3 : 2) = 5 : 2$$
$$2 . (3 : 2) = 9 : 4$$
$$\frac{3}{2} . (25 : 9) = 125 : 27$$

We also speak of ratios between ratios and say that:

$$(A : B) : (C : D) = m : n \text{ if and only if } A : B = \frac{m}{n} . (C : D)$$

For example:

$$(125 : 27) : (25 : 9) = 3 : 2.$$

Corrigendum: pp. 120–21, it is a little misleading to say 'Galileo makes Salviati ask...'. In fact Galileo is making Salviati quote (or have quoted) Galileo asking... The original is accordingly in Latin not Italian. This in no way affects the point that I was trying to make.

VI

RICHARD SWINESHEAD
AND CONTINUOUSLY VARYING QUANTITIES

If we can take one of the principal rallying cries of seventeenth century experimental philosophy to be, « Things not words », then perhaps the corresponding slogan for fourteenth century mathematical natural philosophy should be, « Imaginations not words » ; for it was characteristic of this period to treat physical problems *secundum imaginationem* [1]. As I have argued elsewhere [2], this method of treatment may be closely associated with the use of mathematics in natural philosophy, for mathematics, and particularly geometry, was held to receive its material from the imaginative faculty, and much of the fourteenth century « mathematical physics » may be seen as the projecting of geometric imaginations onto physical objects. The method did not confine itself to spatially extended quantities, but also brought under its sway such things as the intensities of heats, the speeds of motions, and time.

When the geometric method entered into scholastic discussions, it had as its colleague and rival the logical method. Geometry cannot of course depend solely upon the imaginative faculty : it needs words to describe and relate the imaginations, just as experimental philosophy cannot go to the extreme of abolishing words in the manner satirised by Swift in his account of Gulliver's visit to the Academy of Lagado. But it may be questioned whether the language of medieval logic was the best adapted for geometrical discussions. Certainly logic's demand for rigorous argument was all to the advantage of geometry, and its precise use of words allowed very difficult mathematical concepts to be handled. But on the other hand medieval logic was conducted in terms of ordinary language, and medieval Latin was over-rich in technical terms. One may note in this connection the medieval insistence upon retaining each member of a pair of contraries, such as heat and cold, or intension and remission. Medieval logic was also much concerned with analysing the « properties of terms », and the ways in which words could be used in different contexts [3]. Thus the tendency was to take the primary focus off the imagined geometric figures and onto the words used in discussing them. In pure geometry this is not so dangerous, as there is no large technical

128

vocabulary, but in problems of natural philosophy it could be very damaging.

One can see the influence of scholastic logic in many pure geometric works ([4]), and a converse influence of geometry upon logic may also be suggested ([5]), but to view a really major encounter of Geometry and Logic one should perhaps turn to one of the most important works of fourteenth century natural philosophy, Richard Swineshead's *Liber calculationum* ([6]). One of the main difficulties in Swineshead's work for the modern reader is that, after he sees how Swineshead is basing himself upon a relatively simple geometric imagination, he then has to follow the author through a morass of difficulties in which seemingly cavilling objections are raised and answered at great length. In all this the attention is focussed primarily upon the words and the geometric model seems to have been forgotten. At other times, however, Geometry and Logic walk happily hand in hand, and the resources of precise verbal argument are used to elucidate quite complex mathematical problems. It is one of these that I wish principally to discuss in this paper.

It occurs in the tractate of the *Liber calculationum* that is entitled *De loco elementi*. Swineshead is discussing a thin uniform rod that is falling through the Centre of the Earth, and he wishes to show that, if the part of the rod that has already passed the Centre resists the fall of the whole rod, then the centre of the rod will take an infinite time to reach the Centre of the Earth. His first main argument for this was discussed by Michael Hoskin and myself when we recently re-edited the tractate, but we did not provide any analysis of the second, which is the one that concerns me now ([7]). In some ways it is the more ambitious, for, if we were to describe Swineshead's procedure in the first argument as employing a step function, we should say that in the second he was dealing directly with the original continuous function.

There is often a temptation to represent Swineshead's arguments by means of an artificial symbolism. In general this is impractical because of the richness of his conceptual apparatus, but for this short argument I think that it may be our best procedure. I shall therefore try to present the main lines of his argument with the aid of a notation that is primarily based upon the sort of sentence structure that he himself uses. We shall need three classes of symbols, corresponding respectively to verbs, adverbs, and nouns.

Verbs

Only one symbol is required : δ for « decreases ».

Adverbs.

We need both adverbs qualifying one verb and adverbs relating two. Let there be the following correspondences : U for « uniformly in proportion » ; S for « more and more slowly in proportion » ; E for « as swiftly in proportion as » ; M for « more swiftly in proportion than ». All the adverbs here are further qualified by the phrase « in proportion ». This means that, for instance, $U(\delta(x))$ implies that x loses equal ratios in equal times, and $\delta(x) \ E \ \delta(y)$ implies that in the same time x and y lose equal ratios.

Nouns.

Various lower case letters will be introduced for particular nouns. But we also need a sign to move from « x decreases » to « the rate of decrease of x ». We use a superscript bar for this, giving $\overline{\delta(x)}$.

In reconstructing Swineshead's argument we first isolate the premises. He accepts as intuitively evident that :

$$\delta(\overline{\delta(x)}) \ E \ \delta(x) \quad \rightarrow \quad U(\delta(x)) \ \dots\dots\dots\dots\dots \ (1)$$

From this he holds that it follows that :

$$\delta(\overline{\delta(x)}) \ M \ \delta(x) \quad \rightarrow \quad S(\delta(x)) \ \dots\dots\dots\dots\dots \ (1a)$$

In the mathematical preliminaries he has established that, if $x > y$, x decreases, and $x + y$ remains constant, then :

$$\delta(x : y) \ M \ \delta(x - y) \ \dots\dots\dots\dots\dots\dots \ (2)$$

He uses Bradwardine's law, and, if we denote speed by v, force by f, and resistance by r, this becomes for retarded motions :

$$\delta(v) \ E \ \delta(f : r) \ \dots\dots\dots\dots\dots\dots \ (3)$$

(In contemplating propositions (2) and (3) we must remember that it was then the custom to regard as *adding* ratios what we should now call *multiplying* fractions ([8]).)

We now move on to the particular case and Swineshead's reasoning on it. Let the length of the part of the rod that has not passed the Centre be a, and that of the remainder b. Let $a - b = d$. Then the force is as a and the resistance as b. Therefore, by (3) :

$$\delta(v) \ E \ \delta(a : b) \ \dots\dots\dots\dots\dots\dots \ (4)$$

But the speed is proportional to the rate of decrease of d, a fact that Swineshead establishes by a short argument. Therefore :

$$\delta(v) \ E \ \delta(\overline{\delta(d)})$$

Therefore, by (4) :

$$\delta(\overline{\delta(d)}) \ E \ \delta(a : b)$$

But, by (2) :

$$\delta(a : b) \ M \ \delta(d)$$

Therefore :

$$\delta(\overline{\delta(d)}) \ M \ \delta(d)$$

130

Therefore, by (1a) :

$$S(\delta(d))$$

From this the required result, that the rod would need an infinite time for its centre to reach the Centre of the Earth easily follows.

When we reflect upon this argument we are at first struck by the very high degree of mental tenacity and ingenuity that Swineshead has displayed in this, for him, very difficult problem. But coupled with our admiration is also an awareness that, although this is the sort of problem that in later times would be attacked with the techniques of the calculus, Swineshead's way was not one which could lead to this method ([9]). Even in the form in which we have symbolised it, his method does not seem easily susceptible of development or generalisation ; and when we remember that Swineshead was himself using ordinary language and only drawing upon a small part of his range of technical terminology, we can feel even more convinced that he had nearly reached his limit. The refinement of ordinary language may be suggestive for future developments, but for rapid progress mathematics must rely upon an artificial language created very much *ab initio*.

NOTES

([1]) See C. WILSON, *William Heytesbury* (Madison, 1960), 24-25, 174.

([2]) A.G. MOLLAND, " The Geometrical Background to the ' Merton School ' ", *Bristish Journal for the History of Science*, IV (1968-9), 108-125.

([3]) See I.M. BOCHENSKI, *A History of Formal Logic*, tr. and ed. I. Thomas (Notre Dame, Indiana, 1961) 251 *et passim*.

([4]) M. CLAGETT, " Archimedes and Scholastic Geometry " in *Mélanges Alexandre Koyré* (Paris, 1964), I, 40-60. See also pp. 17-20 of my Cambridge Ph. D. dissertation (1967), *The Geometria Speculativa of Thomas Bradwardine*.

([5]) Cf. W.J. ONG, *Ramus, Method, and the Decay of Dialogue* (Cambridge, Mass., 1958), ch. 4.

([6]) I have used the Venice, 1520 edition, and, for the portion particularly discussed later in the paper, the new edition of the 11th tractate in M.A. HOSKIN and A.G. MOLLAND, " Swineshead on Falling Bodies ", *British Journal for the History of Science*, iii (1966-7), 150-182. It is tempting but perhaps rash to see the meeting of Logic and Geometry in Swineshead's work as a clash between predominantly oral modes and predominantly visual ones ; cf. M. McLUHAN, *The Gutenberg Galaxy* (London, Routledge and Kegan Paul, 1962), 80-81 *et passim*.

([7]) See n. ([6]). The text of the argument occurs on p. 176-177 and our English rendering on pp. 161-163. I have also referred to the argument in the article cited in n. ([2]).

([8]) See my article cited in n. ([2]).

([9]) For other ways in which Swineshead may be associated with the calculus, see C.B. BOYER, *The Concepts of the Calculus* (New York, 1949), ch. 3.

VII

John Dumbleton and the Status of Geometrical Optics

The varying fortunes of the principle "To save the phenomena" have shown clearly the difficulties that arose in assimilating astronomical theories of a mathematical and observational type within the context of Aristotelian philosophy.[1] These difficulties led thinkers such as Thomas Aquinas to stress extravagantly the hypothetical nature of any mathematical astronomical theory, and views similar to those of Aquinas were later to be insinuated misleadingly into the preface of Copernicus's *De revolutionibus* and were to plague the fortunes of Galileo. Less dramatically a similar difficulty was sometimes found in incorporating the work of the *perspectivi*, or writers on geometrical optics, within the Aristotelian theory of vision.[2] It is one occurrence of this difficulty that I wish to discuss in this paper.

At the end of the extant part of his *Summa logice et philosophie naturalis* (probably written at Oxford in the 1340s) John Dumbleton gives a

---

1. See Pierre Duhem, *SOZEIN TA PHAINOMENA: Essai sur la Notion de Théorie Physique de Platon à Galilée* (Paris, 1908), translated as *To Save the Phenomena* (Chicago & London, 1969), and Jürgen Mittelstrass, *Die Rettung der Phänomene* (Berlin, 1962).
2. See, for example, S.Sambursky, "Philoponus' Interpretation of Aristotle's Theory of Light", *Osiris*, 13 (1958), 114-126. The relevant part of Philoponus's commentary on the *De anima* was not available in Latin in the Middle Ages: see Jean Philopon, *Commentaire sur le De anima d'Aristote: Traduction de Guillaume de Moerbeke*, ed. G.Verbeke (Louvain & Paris, 1966), lxxxvii-xcviii.

long and involved discussion of vision.[3] The text bristles with obscurities, but not so much as to prevent the main points from standing forth. Dumbleton's principal object is to argue against the existence of visual rays emitted from the eye, and so he gives many complicated and often repetitive arguments to confute the views of Empedocles, Plato, Grosseteste and Roger Bacon, and to establish the view of Aristotle, Alhazen, Averroes, Avicenna and Albertus Magnus that vision is purely passive. Visual rays had been used especially by the *perspectivi* (whom Dumbleton usually cites as a class), and for this reason Alhazen, as a mathematical writer, was a particularly valuable ally, but his support still presented certain difficulties.

In the first book of his *Optica* Alhazen had argued strenuously against there being anything sent out from the eye in vision. The mathematicians may make great use of visual rays, but, Alhazen says, "In demonstrations they only use imaginary lines, and they call them radial lines."[4] However, he immediately continues: "And now we have shown (*declaravimus*) that vision does not grasp anything from things seen except by the paths (*verticationes*) of those lines." It could probably seem to many that Alhazen was doing some hasty back-stepping here, for, although he has said that visual rays are only imaginary lines, he straightway claims that these imaginary entitites are essential in optical explanations. Such a difficulty had faced another Arabic thinker, Averroes, and he held that the lines of the *perspectivi* were essential to vision but had as their

3. I have used the version in MS Vatican, Lat.6750, ff.193v-202r. For the last chapter (ff.200v-202r) I have collated this with MS Cambridge, Gonville and Caius, 499/268, ff.161r-162v, and MS London, British Museum, Royal 10.B.XIV, ff.224r-226r, but still have not achieved a completely satisfactory text. On Dumbleton see J.A.Weisheipl, "The Place of John Dumbleton in the Merton School", *Isis*, 50 (1959), 439-454, and "Ockham and Some Mertonians", *Mediaeval Studies*, 30 (1968), 163-213, pp.199-207.
4. *Opticae Thesaurus Alhazeni Arabis Libri Septem...*, ed. F.Risner (Basel, 1572), prop. I.23, p.15. See D.C.Lindberg, "Alhazen's Theory of Vision and its Reception in the West", *Isis*, 58 (1967), 321-341.

subiectum the diaphonous medium, which could by its nature receive form and colour in this way.[5]

The question of the status of the geometrical figures used by the *perspectivi* seems throughout to be intertwined with Dumbleton's discussion of visual rays, but in the last chapter, when he seems fairly confident that he has disposed of the existence of such rays, the problem becomes central. He opens the chapter by saying that, since so many philosophers have said that vision by reflection and refraction needs to be completed by lines, triangles and visual rays, these may not be purely fictitious. In the chapter he devotes much attention to the optical principle that the angle of reflection is equal to the angle of incidence. Alhazen had argued for this principle from experimental evidence,[6] but Dumbleton is disturbed that he has not demonstrated it. He notes that some would at this point say that, just as a similar generates a similar, so the intention (*intentio*) caused by a visible object leaves the mirror by an angle similar to that by which it arrived. But Dumbleton is not in fact convinced that the equality of angles of incidence and reflection is sufficient for vision, but in trying to establish exceptions he seems to neglect Alhazen's precept that reflection takes place in the plane perpendicular to the mirror.[7] Anyway, Dumbleton does not seem convinced that his argument has demolished geometrical optics, and he speaks of the great harmony that exists between vision and geometry, so that the *perspectivi* often provide the right answer, which cannot be found otherwise. Geometers are rather like those who think that numbers are the principles of all things, and so they seek to show the causes of many things by their own art as a testimony to its sufficiency.[8]

---

5. Averroes, *Compendia Librorum Aristotelis Qui Parva Naturalia Vocantur*, ed. A.L.Shields & H.Blumberg (Cambridge, MA, 1949), 28. Cf. Averroes, *Epitome of Parva Naturalia*, tr. H.Blumberg (Cambridge, MA, 1961), 15, 79.
6. *Opticae Thesaurus* (n.4), IV.10-12 (pp.108-109).
7. *Ibid.*, IV.13 (pp.109-111).
8. ... geometrici propria arte in eius sufficientie testimonium multorum ostendere causas petunt.

4

Dumbleton then gives an example of how the principle of the equality of angles shows how the point of reflection moves when the object moves, and in so doing he displays, as in other places, the paucity of his geometrical competence.

After this he reverts to the justification of the principle. Alhazen has not demonstrated it, and therefore it is necessary to proceed by analogy with natural philosophy, where we begin with what is known to the senses. We thus argue from the effect, but we are not to assume that we are led to the cause. Rather the situation is similar to the use of lines and instruments in measuring the height of an object, and so "neither the cathetus nor the visual rays is a cause of vision in any genus of cause, but by such imagined lines we can measure where a thing seen by reflection appears."[9] This state of affairs is not unique to optics, for in the science of weights a cricle is imagined with respect to which one object may be said to be heavier than another *secundum situm.*[10] But this does not mean that an object is actually heavier or lighter on account of its position on a balance, for its form remains unchanged.

The introduction of statics suggests to Dumbleton the possibility of using an anlaogy to elucidate the cause of vision by reflection, and he goes on to speak of instruments by means of which great weights may be lifted, and those which enable one weak man to overpower many strong ones. Marvellous things may be effected instrumentally that could not be achieved by the agent or the instrument alone. So in optics we may conceive the medium that reflects the intention caused by the visible object as being an instrument. Later he appeals to Aristotle's principle of art imitating nature as justification for

---

9. ... nec cathetus nec radius visualis est causa visionis in alico genere cause sed per tales lineas ymaginatas possumus mensurare ubi apparet res visa per reflectionem.

10. Cf. E.A.Moody & M.Clagett, *The Medieval Science of Weights* (2nd printing, Madison, 1960), 128 sqq. *et alibi.* Dumbleton's reference is to *auctor de ponderibus.*

arguing from artificial objects.[11] Unfortunately Dumbleton's explantion of reflection can tell us little about the quantitative aspects of the process. However, the idea of instrumental causality as a solution to his problem seems to have fascinated him, and he uses it to speak of how the soul moves the body,[12] before he finally proceeds to a rather crude discussion of refraction in terms of the differing densities of media, in the course of which he becomes involved in a rather uninteresting sophism that need not detain us.

At times it is difficult to preserve one's patience with Dumbleton. His arguments are often long, rambling and inconclusive, and one suspects that not all the obscurities of expression are due to textual corruption. His intellect certainly does not seem to be of the calibre of some of his Mertonian contemporaries. But with all that we must remember the difficulties that faced him in this discussion, for, like Copernicus when confronted with homocentric spheres and Ptolemaic astronomy,[13] Dumbleton was caught between two different modes of explanation. One seemed philosophically fairly satisfactory but not empirically so, and the other had the reverse characteristics. But while Copernicus had the ability to move a long way towards a resolution of his dilemma, Dumbleton was unable to do much more than minimise the significance of geometrical optics while rather shamefacedly admitting its power.

At the beginning of his *Traité de la lumière* Christiaan Huygens reviewed some of the results of geometrical optics, and then continued:[14]

---

11. Probably a reference to *Physica* II.2, 194a21-23.

12. Cf. Thomas Aquinas. *In Aristotelis Librum de Anima Commentarium*, ed. A.M.Pirotta (4th edn, Turin, 1959), lib.II, lect.IX, n.348 (p.90) *et alibi*.

13. Nicolaus Copernicus, *De Revolutionibus Orbium Coelestium, Libri VI* (Nürnberg, 1543), sig. iiiv; *Three Copernican Treatises*, tr. E.Rosen (New York, 1959), 57.

14. Christiaan Huygens, *Oeuvres Complètes* (The Hague, 1888-1950), XIX, 459. Translation from Christiaan Huygens, *Treatise on Light*, tr. S.P.Thompson (Dover reissue, New York, 1962), 1.

The majority of those who have written touching the various parts of optics have contented themselves with presuming these truths. But some, more inquiring, have desired to investigate the origin and the causes, considering these to be in themselves wonderful effects of Nature. In which they advanced some ingenious things, but not such that the most intelligent folk do not wish for better and more satisfactory explanations.

Dumbleton had the courage to take the "more inquiring" path. The fact that he by no means provided such satisfying explanations as Huygens depends in part on the fact that Huygens had a very different underlying philosophy.

VIII

Cornelius Agrippa's mathematical magic

THIS is a disreputable subject, and demands an apologia, if not an apology. The first part of this is easy, for in recent years great, and sometimes exaggerated, emphasis has been placed on the role of magic in the emergence of modern science. It is hence readily seen to be a worthy object of scholarly study, but it is not so clear that this tolerance should immediately be extended to its mathematics, for this has tended to embarrass even those writers most sympathetic to the magical tradition.[1] Nevertheless it was enthusiastically accepted by many intelligent men of the Renaissance, and this in itself demands empathy and explanation. But, even so, is Agrippa a satisfactory choice as its representative? He was certainly not the most original or systematic thinker of his era, and indeed is someone easily accused of charlatanry. However, these very features, together with the wide diffusion of his works, help to ensure that he accurately reflects the spirit of the age. By the same token, we shall not need to linger over the problem of sincerity posed by the fact that his magical 'encyclopedia' *De occulta philosophia* was published only shortly after his *De incertitudine et vanitate scientiarum et artium* in which he had roundly attacked magic.[2] A first, and much shorter, version of the former work had been completed in 1510, but in this article I shall only concern myself with its final form of 1533.[3]

1. Devices

The *De occulta philosophia* is divided into three books, dealing respectively with natural, mathematical and ceremonial magic, which in turn correspond

---

[1] See e.g. F. Yates, *Giordano Bruno and the hermetic tradition* (London 1964; repr. New York, 1969), p. 324.

[2] Cf. C.G. Nauert, *Agrippa and the crisis of Renaissance thought* (Urbana, 1965), pp. 32–33; D.P. Walker, *Spiritual and demonic magic from Ficino to Campanella* (London, 1958), pp. 90–91; Yates, *op. cit.* (note 1), p. 131.

[3] A facsimile of the 1510 manuscript is published in Agrippa, *De occulta philosophia*, ed. K.A. Nowotny (Graz, 1967). My references will be to Agrippa, *Opera* (Lyon [?], n.d.; repr. Hildesheim, 1970). On the printing history of *De occulta philosophia* and other matters of Agrippan bibliography see J. Ferguson, 'Bibliographical notes on the treatises *De occulta philosophia* and *De incertitudine et vanitate scientiarum* of Cornelius Agrippa', *Publications of the Edinburgh bibliographical society*, *12* (1925), pp. 1–23, and Nauert, *op. cit.* (note 2) pp. 32–33, 106, 112–113, 335–338.

(albeit somewhat loosely) to the three-fold division of the world into elemental, celestial and intellectual. Book II begins with a panegyric on mathematics:

The mathematical disciplines are so necessary and cognate to magic that, if anyone should profess the latter without the former, he would wander totally from the path and attain the least desired result. For whatever things are or are effected in the inferior natural virtues are all effected and governed by number, weight, measure, harmony, motion and light, and have their root and foundation in these.[4]

Agrippa's first examples of the power of mathematics do not at first glance appear particularly magical. They concern the making of automata, of things which, although lacking natural virtues, are yet similar to natural things. Tradition had handed down quite a copious list of these, and Agrippa cites examples attributed to Vulcan, Daedalus, Archytas, and Boethius.[5] Of similar kind were simulacra produced by optical means in the manner taught by Apollonius and Witelo, and Agrippa claims for himself the knowledge of how to make something that can seem suggestive of the telescope:

And I have come to know how to make two alternate mirrors in which, when the sun is shining, everything that is illuminated by its rays is clearly discerned at remote distances of several miles.[6]

It was knowledge of mathematics and natural philosophy that led to the construction of all these, and the same had been true for greater marvels in Antiquity, such as the Caspian Gates and the Pillars of Hercules, of which now only vestiges or reports remained:

Although all these seem to be in conflict with nature itself, yet we read that they were made, and to this day we discern their traces. The crowd say that suchlike were the work of demons, since the arts and the artificers have perished from memory, and there are not those who bother to understand and examine.[7]

So far we do not seem to be straying from the history of technology as ordinarily understood, but, after brief references to magnetism, Agrippa makes it clear that there is more to his mathematics than to ours:

And here it is appropriate for you to know that just as by natural things we acquire natural virtues, so by abstract, mathematical and celestial things we receive celestial virtues, namely motion, life, sense, speech, foreknowledge and divination, even in less well disposed matter, such as that fashioned not by nature but only by art. And in

---

[4] De occulta philosophia II.1 (Opera, I, p. 153); cf. De incertitudine et vanitate scientiarum et artium XLI (Op. , II, p. 89).

[5] De occ. phil. II.1 (Op., I, pp. 153–154). Cf.De inc. et van. XLIII (Op., II, pp. 91–92), and J.P. Zetterberg, 'Mathematicall magick' in England: 1550–1650 (Ph.D. thesis, University of Wisconsin, 1976), pp. 34–35.

[6] De occ. phil. II.1 (Op. I, p. 154). Cf. Deinc. et van. XXVI (Op. II, pp. 60–61).

[7] De occ. phil. II, 1 (Op. I, p. 155).

this way images that speak and predict the future are said to be made, as William of Paris narrates about the speaking head forged at Saturn's rising, which they say spoke with human voices.[8] He who knows how to choose suitable matter that is best fitted to be the patient, and also the strongest agent will produce indubitably more powerful effects. For it is a general axiom of the Pythagoreans that just as mathematicals are more formal than physicals so they are more actual, and just as they are less dependent in their being so also are they in their operation, and among all mathematicals, as numbers are more formal so also are they more actual; to them are attributed virtue and efficacy for both good and evil, not only by the philosophers of the heathens but by the theologians of the Hebrews and Christians.[9]

With this emphasis on the power of number Agrippa has reached the heartland of his mathematical magic, and can leave behind his consideration of mechanical and optical devices, whose construction was subjected to geometry rather than to arithmetic.

2. Numbers

At this point it is necessary to emphasize as strongly as possible that Agrippa's conception of number was very different from our own. For him, as for the preceding philosophical and pure mathematical tradition, a number was a collection of units. In this conception fractions and surds were not properly numbers, for true numbers were very definitely discrete entities, to be contrasted with the continuous quantities that were the concern of geometry. Agrippa was conscious that other views were possible, but insisted that his concern was with

rational and formal number, not the material, sensible or vocal number of the merchants, about which the Pythagoreans, the Academics and our Augustine care nothing.[10]

It is only when this is clear that we can hope to make sense of Boethius' assertion (highlighted by Agrippa) that numbers provided the exemplar for the Creation, or realize how significant was Kepler's break with this numerological tradition in asserting that, on the contrary, geometry was God's archetype.[11]

In talking of formal numbers Agrippa and his like were asserting the existence of entities that were both outwith the soul and distinct from the

[8] Cf. L. Thorndike, *History of magic and experimental science* (New York, 1923–58), II, p. 351.

[9] *De occ. phil.* II.1 (*Op.* I, pp. 155–6).

[10] *De occ. phil.* II.2 (*Op.* I, p. 157).

[11] Boethius, *De institutione arithmetica* I.2, ed. G. Friedlein (Leipzig, 1857; repr. Frankfurt, 1966), p. 12; cf. Agrippa, *De occ. phil.* II.2 (*Op.* I, p. 156). C.G. Jung and W. Pauli, *The Interpretation of nature and the psyche* (London, 1955), pp. 159–167; J.V. Field, 'Kepler's Rejection of numerology', *Occult and scientific mentalities in the Renaissance*, ed. B. Vickers (Cambridge, 1984), pp. 273–296.

VIII

numbered objects, whereas opponents of magic such as Descartes would be equally insistent that numbers were no different from the things being counted.[12] Although separate, formal numbers were yet manifested in all sorts of collections in the world, and it is here that the modern reader has a particular difficulty in rendering numerology intelligible, for the question immediately comes to mind of where a particular collection, say a flock of sheep of which some members are beginning to stray, ends. In one sense this difficulty is by no means new, and Plotinus, for example, emphasized that not every group of ten men that you counted formed a true decad, but only something like a choir or an army.[13] However, in the present time we are faced with the additional problem that our conception of the physical world does not allow numerous finite and well-defined sets of things of the same kind. In Agrippa's day the situation was very different, and it is enlightening to remember how even somewhat later Kepler struggled to provide a geometrical rather than a numerological answer to the question of why there were precisely six planets.[14] The reason we do not ask this question is not so much that we think that Kepler had the wrong number, but that we think that the number is basically accidental, whereas for Kepler it was embedded in God's original design for the universe.

Agrippa devotes several chapters of his *De occulta philosophia* to discussing particular manifestations of the smaller numbers at various levels of his hierarchical universe. Many of the results are presented in tabular form, and we may conveniently read down the scale of Two (*binarius*).[15] In the archetypal world this is represented by names of God of two letters each (in Hebrew): *Iah* (from jod and hev) and *El* (from aleph and lamed). In the intellectual world we have two intelligible substances, angel and soul, and in the celestial world two great luminaries, Sun and Moon. In the elemental world two elements, namely earth and water, give rise to the living soul, and the lesser world has two principal seats of the soul, heart and brain. Finally, when we reach the infernal world, we find that there are two leaders of the demons, Behemoth and Léviathan, and two things which Christ threatens to the damned, namely weeping and gnashing of teeth. Quotation of part of the surrounding text will make it clear that this list includes only some of the mysteries of Twoness.

Plutarch writes that the Pythagoreans called unity Apollo, the dyad strife and boldness, the triad justice, which is the highest perfection, but nor is this without many mysteries. Hence two tables of law in Sinai, two cherubims facing the mercy

[12] R. Descartes, *Regule ad directionem ingenii* XIV, in *Oeuvres de Descartes*, ed. C. Adam and P. Tannery (Paris, 1897–1913), X, pp. 445–446.

[13] *Enneads* VI.6.16.

[14] Cf. Field, *op. cit.* (note 11).

[15] I use capitals to distinguish the nouns *binarius*, *ternarius*, etc. from the adjectives *duo*, *tres*, etc.

seat with Moses, two olives pouring out oil in Zecharia,[16] two natures in Christ, divine and human. Hence two appearances of God were seen by Moses, front and rear.[17] Also two testaments, two commands of charity, two first dignities, two first peoples, two genera of demons, good and bad, two intellectual creatures, angel and soul, two great luminaries, two equinoxes, two poles, two elements giving rise to the living soul, earth and water.[18]

As usual the reasoning connecting together the different manifestations of the number, and relating these to any of its mathematical properties is rather loose, and even Agrippa's meaning is sometimes obscure.

We may complement our vertical tour of the manifestations of Two by a horizontal trip along the manifestations of the first twelve numbers at the celestial level.[19] We find that there is one king of the stars, two great luminaries, three quaternions of signs and of houses and three lords of triplicities, four triplicities of signs, four groups of stars and planets related to the elements and four qualities of celestial elements, five erratic stars, six planets deviating from the ecliptic in the breadth of the zodiac, seven planets, eight visible heavens, nine mobile spheres, ten spheres of the world, twelve signs of the zodiac and twelve months. Eleven does not appear on the list, because:

just as it transgresses ten, which is of law and commands, so it falls short of twelve, which is of grace and perfection. It is therefore the number of sinners and penitents. Hence in the tabernacle there were ordered to be made eleven blankets of hair-cloth,[20] which is the dress of penitents and bewailers of their sins. Wherefore this number has no communion with divine things, nor with celestial ones.[21]

In his discussion of the celestial manifestations of number, Agrippa makes quite a lot of capital from a relatively small investment. Much of the discussion depends either directly or indirectly on their being just seven planets with certain differentiae between them. The other main theme is the division of the zodiac into twelve signs. This was somewhat less natural, but relatively few in Agrippa's time would have regarded it as purely conventional in the way that Nicole Oresme had suggested in the fourteenth century, although it was standard to hold that the division was in need of justification.[22]

The hierarchy and numerology in Agrippa's universe are combined with an elaborate system of relations and correspondences between its elements. These may be on one level, as when:

[16] *Exodus* XXXI.18, XXV.20; *Zechariah* IV.12.

[17] *Exodus* XXXIII.11, 22–23.

[18] *De occ. phil.* II.5 (*Op.* I, pp. 162–163).

[19] *De occ. phil.* II.4–14 (*Op.* I, pp. 161–200).

[20] *Exodus* XXXVI.14–17.

[21] *De occ. phil.* II.14 (*Op.* I, p. 196).

[22] S. Caroti, 'Nicole Oresme, Quaestio contra divinatores horoscopios', *Archives d'histoire doctrinale et littéraire du moyen age*, *43* (1976), pp. 201–310, at pp. 251–252. Cf. *Supplementum ficinianum* ed. P. O. Kristeller (Florence, 1937; repr. 1973), II, pp. 41–42.

Mercury, Jupiter, Sun and Moon are friends to Saturn, and Mars and Venus his enemies. All the planets are friends of Jupiter except Mars, and so all except Venus hate Mars. Jupiter and Venus love Sun, while Mars, Mercury and Moon are hostile. All except Saturn love Venus. Friends of Mercury are Jupiter, Venus and Saturn, enemies Sun, Moon and Mars. Jupiter, Venus and Saturn are friends of Moon, and Mars and Mercury enemies.[23]

Alternatively there may be correspondences between different levels and kinds of thing. The most famous of these are probably those that subordinate different parts of the body to different signs of the zodiac and also to different planets, but the system also extends to elements, metals, precious stones, animals, plants, etc., etc..[24] Moreover, the relationships are mirrored at the various different levels:

And of what sorts are the friendships and enmities of the superiors so also are the inclinations of the things subordinated to them among the inferiors[25]

We are thus drawn irresistibly towards the image of a series of structure-preserving mappings.

At this point there is the temptation to go further and speak more generally in terms of structuralism or of abstract algebra. As regards the former, there do seem to be definite affinities between Agrippa's thought and structuralism, but I am not sure how illuminating it would be to describe him as a proto-structuralist or to use modern structuralist techniques to analyse his system. The question of abstract algebra is related but tighter, and an attempt has been made to portray geomancy, a divinatory technique on which Agrippa himself wrote,[26] in group-theoretic terms.[27] However, the group involved was rather trivial, and in general there is something absurd in trying to assimilate Agrippa and his like, as regards aims, methods and attitude, to modern algebraists. But with all this said, there does seem to be a certain similarity of mental *set* involved, which may perhaps be explicated by the counterfactual speculation that, if it had been Renaissance magic that developed into modern science, the appropriate mathematics would have been more akin to abstract algebra than to the infinitesimal calculus. It would have been a mathematics that concentrated on discreteness rather than on continuity.

3. Magic squares

But let us return to Agrippa, and this time to a rather more complex example of his numerology, namely the role of magic squares.

23 *De occ. phil.* I.17 (*Op.* I, p. 33).
24 *De occ. phil.* I.22–32 (*Op.* I, pp. 43–59).
25 *De occ. phil.* I.17 (*Op.* I, p. 34).
26 *In geomanticam disciplinam lectura* (*Op.* I, pp. 500–526).
27 M. Pedrazzi, 'Le figure della geomanzia: un gruppo finito abeliano', *Physis*, *14* (1972), pp. 146–161.

There are also handed down by the mages certain mensules of numbers, distributed among the seven planets, which they call the holy tables of the planets, distinguished with very many and great virtues of celestials, inasmuch as they represent the divine rationale of celestial numbers, impressed on celestials by the ideas of the divine mind through the mediation (*ratio*) of the soul of the world and the sweetest harmony of the celestial rays, according to the ratio of effigies that consignify the supramundane intelligences, which can only be expressed by the signs of numbers and characters, for material numbers and figures only have power in the mysteries of hidden things representatively through formal numbers and figures, inasmuch as these are governed and informed by divine intelligences and numerations . . .[28]

The 'mensules' are in fact magic squares, of which one is associated with each of the seven planets: a 3 by 3 one for Saturn, 4 by 4 for Jupiter, and so on, up to 9 by 9 for the Moon.[29] In close conjunction with this each planet also has three characteristic diagrams.

Let us look at the example of Saturn. Agrippa describes the situation thus:

The first of these 'mensules', assigned to Saturn, consists of a square Three, containing nine individual numbers and in each line three, which, in whatever direction and along each diameter, constitute fifteen; the total sum of the numbers is forty-five. Over this are set by divine motions names that fill up the aforesaid numbers, with an intelligence for good and a demon for evil. From the same number is elicited the sign or character of Saturn and his spirits, which we shall annex to his table below. They say that this table engraved on a lead plate with Saturn favourable aids birth, makes a man secure and potent, and brings about the success of petitions to princes and powers, but, if it is made with Saturn unfavourable, it hinders building and planting and suchlike, dispossesses a man of honours and dignities, engenders strife and discord, and scatters armies.[30]

Associated with Saturn are various names, whose numerical values in Hebrew characters correspond to the magic square, being either 3, 9, 15 or 45.[31] For example, the intelligence of Saturn is called Agiel, which Agrippa forms from the Hebrew characters yaleph, gimel, jod, aleph, lamed, and accordingly has numerical value $1 + 3 + 10 + 1 + 30 = 45$. Similarly the name of the demon, Zazel, is formed from zain, aleph, zain, lamed, and has value $7 + 1 + 7 + 30 = 45$.

Saturn himself and his two spirits also have characteristic diagrams associated with them (see Fig. 1), which are in some way derived from the magic square. K. A. Nowotny has proposed an elaborate explanation of this

---

[28] *De occ. phil.* II.22 (*Op.* I, pp. 215–216).

[29] On ways of associating magic squares with the planets see W. Ahrens, 'Magische Quadrate und Planetenamulette', *Naturwissenschaftliche Wochenschrift*, N.F. *19* (1920), pp. 465–475. See also I. R. F. Calder, 'A note on magic squares in the philosophy of Agrippa of Nettesheim', *Journal of the Warburg and Courtauld Institutes*, *12* (1949), pp. 196–199, and M. Folkerts, 'Zur Frühgeschichte der magischen Quadrate in Westeuropa', *Sudhoffs archiv*, *65* (1981), pp. 313–338.

[30] *De occ. phil.* II.22 (*Op.* I, p. 216).

[31] *De occ. phil.* II.22 (*Op.* I, p. 219).

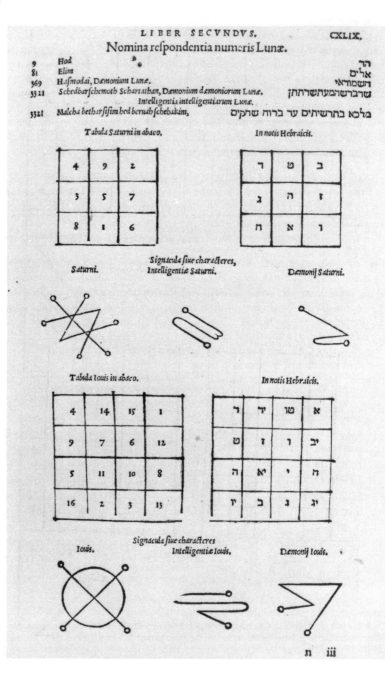

FIGURE 1. H. C. Agrippa, *De occulta philosophia, Liber secundus*, CXLIX, 1510. By courtesy of the British Museum.

derivation,[32] which I do not find convincing in all its details. Nevertheless it does seem clear from his work that the principal rationale for the formation of the characters of Saturn's two spirits (and also the spirits of the other planets) is to join the numbers in the magic square that correspond to the Hebrew letters of the spirit's name. (A number greater than nine may be reduced to one of one digit by adding together its digits, which is equivalent to division by nine and considering only the remainder.) Thus the geometrical figures have an arithmetical origin, which enhances their power, for, as Agrippa later remarks, 'Geometrical figures arising from numbers are thought to be of no less powers.'[33]

Agrippa should not be thought of as deploying any purely mathematical originality in his treatment of magic squares; in this respect his work is almost certainly completely derivative.[34] His concern is more with using the magic squares and associated names, numbers and figures to provide a set of meaningful denominations for the planets. When Alice tentatively asked Humpty Dumpty whether a name had to mean something, she received the testy answer: 'Of course it must: my name means the shape I am—and a good handsome shape it is, too. With a name like yours, you might be any shape, almost'. Again, with the computerization of libraries, we are being asked to focus on bar codes, names which possess only denotation, as well as on shelf marks, which, in systems such as Dewey, are also connotative. Agrippa was firmly in the tradition which believed that things had their correct names, which reflected their true natures and were thus possessed of considerable power. He may without much exaggeration be thought of as putting forward a scientific programme in which the properties of things would be derived from such names, although the programme of course remained vague, and had little hope of being significantly realized.

4. Occult virtues

Finally, instead of following Agrippa through all the other topics of Book II, I wish to turn to the question of occult virtues.[35] These played a key role, at least rhetorically, in the transition to modern science, and can provide a test case for a programme of mathematization. They were traditionally defined as properties of an object that did not derive in any direct way from the elements that constituted it. There was dispute over their causation, but quite frequently they were assigned irreducibly to a body's specific substantial

---

[32] K.A. Nowotny, 'The construction of certain seals and characters in the work of Agrippa of Nettesheim', *Journal of the Warburg and Courtauld Institutes, 12* (1949), pp. 46–57.

[33] *De occ. phil.* II.23 (*Op.* I, p. 216).

[34] I am grateful for Dr. J. Sesiano's opinion on this question.

[35] Cf. K. Hutchison, 'What happened to occult qualities in the scientific revolution?', *Isis, 78* (1982), pp. 233–253, for a somewhat different view of these.

form, and thus had the character of brute inexplicable facts. In the four-teenth century Nicole Oresme had directed his doctrine of configurations of qualities to the issue. In this doctrine causal efficiency was assigned to the pattern of variations of intensities of qualities across a subject, and Oresme suggested that by means of it

there could be briefly assigned a general rationale of certain occult virtues and marvellous effects or experiments whose causes are otherwise unknown.[36]

The programme is to make the virtues mathematically intelligible. In similar but stronger vein, Descartes held it as a major virtue of his mathematico-mechanistic programme that it showed the way to finding the causes of the 'wonderful effects which are usually referred to occult qualities',[37] and accu-sations of resorting to occult qualities soon became a standard form of abuse from mechanically inclined philosophers.

Agrippa had a considerable interest in occult virtues, and in a passage that appears heavily dependent on Albertus Magnus enumerates opinions on their causation.

Alexander the Peripatetic, not deviating from his qualities and his senses, thinks that they arise from elements and in fact from their qualities, which could perhaps be thought true, except that the qualities are of the same species, but many operations of stones agree neither in genus nor in species. Therefore the Academics, together with their Plato, attribute the virtues to the formative ideas of things, but Avicenna reduces such operations to intelligences, Hermes to stars, and Albert to the specific forms of things.[38]

Unlike Albertus, Agrippa held that, rightly understood, none of these opin-ions deviated from the truth.

In the first place, God, the end and origin of all virtues, presents a sigil of ideas to his ministers the intelligences, who, like faithful executors, consign, like instruments, whatever is entrusted to them to the heavens and stars, which are meantime disposing the matter to receive those forms which, as Plato says in the *Timaeus*, reside in the divine majesty through the stars, that are to be drawn out. The giver of forms distributes them through the ministry of the intelligences, which he sets over his works as mistresses and custodians, to whom there is entrusted in the things commit-ted to them such a faculty that every virtue of stones, herbs, metals and all the rest is from these presiding intelligences. Thus form and virtue arise first from the ideas, then from the guiding and governing intelligences, afterwards from the disposing aspects of the heavens, next from the disposed complexions of the elements, corre-

---

[36] *Nicole Oresme and the medieval geometry of qualities and motions. A treatise on the uniformity and difformity of intensities known as Tractatus de configurationibus qualitatum et motuum*, ed. M. Clagett (Madison, 1968), p. 236.

[37] R. Descartes, *Principia philosophiae* IV, 187, in *ed. cit.* (note 12), VIII-1, p. 314.

[38] *De occ. phil.* I.13 (*Op.* I, p. 26). Cf. Albertus Magnus, *Book of minerals*, II.i.1–4, tr. D. Wyckoff (Oxford, 1967), pp. 55–67.

sponding to the influences of the heavens by which the elements are disposed. Therefore operations of this kind occur in the inferior things by expressed forms, but in the heavens by disposing virtues, in the intelligences by mediating reasons (*rationes*), in the archetype by exemplary ideas and forms, and it is necessary that all these come together in the execution of the effect and virtue of any thing. There is therefore a virtue and wonderful operation in every herb and stone, but greater in a star, beyond which also from the presiding intelligences each thing obtains many for itself, but most of all from the supreme cause, to whom all things mutually and consummately correspond.[39]

The image is of diffusion of power through the hierarchies of the universe, and we later learn that this diffusion is mediated by the spirit of the world and the rays of the stars.[40]

All this leads us to expect an imprinting of the characteristics of the higher things upon the lower, and in particular we should count on seeing a reflection of the magic squares and other 'true names' of the planets in corruptible things. In this way Agrippa could be portrayed as following a valiant (even if futile) programme for making occult virtues intelligible by revealing their, so to speak, genetic codes. But unfortunately there is very little of this in the texts themselves. Instead Agrippa is concerned to emphasise the very limited intelligibility of the virtues:

They are called occult properties, because their causes are hidden, so that the human intellect cannot fully investigate them, wherefore philosophers arrived at the greatest part of them by long experience more than by the search of reason.[41] . . . It is clear then that the occult properties in things are not from elemental nature, but heavenly implanted, hidden to our sense. They proceed from the life and spirit of the world by the stars' rays, which by us can only be investigated by experience and conjectures.[42]

We may thus perhaps dejectedly conclude that Agrippa's mathematical magic is indeed a disreputable subject, but less because it was obvious nonsense than because he failed to push his programme to anywhere near its limits.

[39] *De occ. phil.* I.13 (*Op.* I, p. 27).
[40] *De occ. phil.* I.14 (*Op.* I, pp. 28–30).
[41] *De occ. phil.* I.10 (*Op.* I, p. 21).
[42] *De occ. phil.* I.15 (*Op.*, I, p. 30).

ANCESTORS OF PHYSICS

Early Physics and Astronomy: A Historical Introduction. OLAF PEDERSEN and MOGENS PIHL (Macdonald and Janes, London, and American Elsevier, New York, 1974). Pp. 413. £10·95.

Let us start with some banausic details. This work derives from a Danish original: *Historisk indledning til den klassike fysik*, i: *De eksakte naturvidenskaber i oldtid og middelalder* (Munksgaard, Copenhagen, 1963). I take this description from a review,[1] since reprehensibly the publishers of the English version give no more than the first half of the title, and that only on the dust jacket, which will not be available to most library readers of the volume. The point is important, because the original description reveals an intent that is not immediately apparent from the English version. The book was seen as the first volume of a larger work, whose centre of interest was to be the physics of a later period. Such an aim almost inevitably casts a character over the work different from what it would have had if otherwise conceived. Much of this character remains in the English version.

In their preface the authors write: "Long teaching experience has convinced us of the need for a book which might serve not only as a first introduction but also as a practical guide to a more detailed study". This immediately brings to mind two comments. The first concerns the price. Even by today's standards, £10·95 is a ridiculous figure for a textbook of this nature, and should effectively prevent the book from being where it belongs—on students' shelves. The second relates to the authors' curious omission of any footnotes. This will make it far more difficult than necessary for the student to identify an intriguing quotation or investigate further a particular point of information. But this defect is partially remedied by the authors' adoption of two other devices. The first is a long bibliography, which will be very useful, but would have benefited from more thorough updating and adaptation to the English-speaking reader. Its partitioning is sometimes rather irritating, as when three closely related works by Duhem appear in three different sections. The second device is a series of short biobibliographies, which form as it were a mini-version of Sarton's much maligned but still invaluable *Introduction to the history of science*. These will provide the student with a very good immediate source of reference, but I think that their value would have been enhanced if rather more attention had been given to citing recent journal articles and to indicating where English translations of primary materials could be found. To the average student this would have been more useful than repetitious mentions of standard reference works, and a concern with the location of critical editions of Greek authors.

As to scope the authors rather disarmingly say, "Much is left out, and each of the twenty chapters is nothing more than an essay illustrating one important theme in the complex pattern of the whole field".[2] More thematically they point out that "the main emphasis of the book is on the mathematical description of nature as it gradually emerged in astronomy and also, to a lesser extent, in mechanics and physics".[3] The end-product remains a book of very wide coverage, which includes much that is not available in similar form elsewhere. Nine pages are devoted to pre-Greek science, 159 to the Greeks, 107 to the Middle Ages, and fortyone to the Renaissance. In reviewing the Danish version L. Rosenfeld wrote, "It may sound very strange, but this is in fact the first text-book on history of science written according to sound standards of both historical and scientific scholarship".[4] This opinion is hyperbolic, and unfair to other writers. But the book does indeed have very strict standards, and it is hard to find a statement that can be unambiguously labelled false. This is a rare virtue in a work of such range. Moreover its chapters on the history of astronomy are particularly fine for giving an introductory treatment at some depth. This alone makes the book a very valuable addition to the literature.

But in general the book's many merits are best appreciated by consulting the volume itself. Here I think that it may be more profitable to devote the remainder of this essay to a meditation taking its starting point from a feeling of dissatisfaction that the book produced in me. (The absence of such a feeling would be disquieting, in suggesting that perfection had been attained.) By following this course I shall hope to indicate one route whereby a more rounded historical picture may be achieved. I shall not stick very closely to the text, but shall treat of various themes relevant to the book's ambit, and shall sometimes go into more detail than would have been appropriate in the book itself.

I. FORM AND MATTER

Whatever the ontological defects of the Aristotelian distinction between form and matter, its appeal is clearly shown by the variety of ways in which it has been adopted and adapted in other fields. Even when a different terminology is used, the need for an analogous distinction often remains, as may be witnessed by the logical oppositions between intension and extension, connotation and denotation, sense and reference. I wish here to use the form—matter opposition in referring to scientific theories. I shall not attempt to be rigorous, but on the formal side the emphasis will be on how a theory actually appeared integrally to the minds of its propagators,[5] whereas the material side will be more concerned with particular implications that may be drawn from the theory. Viewed in this light, I would hold that Pedersen and Pihl, in common with much modern historiography in this area, undervalue the formal aspect in comparison with the material. Conversely, in modern economic discussions the outsider is often bemused by the formal aspect, and demands material exemplification by asking what the concepts 'really mean' in practical terms.

The temptation towards 'material historiography' can be abetted by certain kinds of positivist attitudes, and by judging too much from the standpoint of modern physical science. In the latter, accuracy of prediction is a *sine qua non*, and early theories can often seem to be characterized principally by their inaccuracies. But this approach can all too easily lead to neglect of the early search for a unified system of the world, which still remains an important part of the scientific quest. It is customary to dub histories written from the viewpoint of the present state of science as Whiggish, but this can sometimes be too facile a condemnation, for Whiggery exists at various levels, and when eliminated at one may reappear at another. Nevertheless we may guard ourselves against some of its grosser distortions by attention to the dangers of presenting past theories in modern scientific language.

II. THE PROBLEM OF MATHEMATICAL TRANSLATION

Two radically different approaches to the historiography of mathematics are indicated by the following quotations:[6]

(i) We will now refer to a law which is of great significance to the history of the sciences. Science as a whole and the individual sciences in particular are conceived of as being in a progressive development. If the history of science x at time t is written, the form that science has achieved at time t serves as metascience. To illustrate this law we notice that in a modern history of mathematics, modern methematics serves as the metascience (Karl Dürr).

(ii) We West-Europeans may put our scientific notion of number to perform the same tasks as those with which the mathematicians of Athens and Baghdad busied themselves, but the fact remains that the theme, the intention and the methods of the like-named science in Athens and Baghdad were quite different from those of our own. *There is no mathematic but only mathematics.* What we call "the history of mathematics"—implying merely the progressive actualizing of a single invariable ideal—is in fact, below the deceptive surface of history, a complex of self-contained and independent developments, an ever-repeated process of bringing to birth new form-worlds, and appropriating, transforming and sloughing alien form-worlds, a purely organic story of blossoming, ripening, wilting and dying within the set period. The student must not let himself be deceived. The mathematic of the Classical soul sprouted almost out of nothingness, the historically-constituted Western soul, already possessing the Classical science (not inwardly, but outwardly as a thing learnt), had to win its own by apparently altering and perfecting, but in reality destroying the essentially alien Euclidean system. In the first case, the agent was Pythagoras, in the second Descartes. In both cases the act is, at bottom, the same (Oswald Spengler).

Despite his exaggerations and gross errors of fact my sympathies are with Spengler in his first attempt to get at the form, as opposed to Dürr's almost complete emphasis on the matter. Neither book was devoted to the history of mathematics, and it may be that in the history of logic (with which he was dealing) Dürr's method could be less objectionable. But in the history of mathematics it is very dangerous. This is largely because it allows unrestricted translation of past mathematics into modern mathematical terms. Such translation is ever tempting, often done, and sometimes justified. But on many occasions it can greatly mislead.

As a radical example, we may consider the case of Bradwardine's law. Bradwardine's original statement of this was, "Proportio velocitatum in motibus sequitur proportionem potentiae motoris ad potentiam rei motae",[7] which may be translated literally into English as, "The ratio of speeds in motions follows the ratio of the power of the mover to the power of the thing moved". But it can also be translated, and in a sense impeccably translated, into the form:

$$V = k \log \frac{F}{R},$$

where V is the speed, F the force (or power of the mover), and R the resistance (or power of the thing moved), and k is a constant. The rationale for this is clearly displayed by Pedersen and Pihl (pp. 232–3).[8] But in this translation something very odd has happened, and from the formal side we do not even wish to speak of the meaning being preserved. A modern mathematician contemplating a logarithmic relation is clearly doing something very different from a medieval mathematician viewing a very simple relation between a speed and a ratio. I shall try to show later how closer attention to form may elucidate probems about the origins of Bradwardine's law.

The above example was extreme, but more insidious dangers may lurk where the translation appears more innocuous. Thus, we may see little harm in rendering talk of the square of a straight line a in terms of the symbol a^2. But the formation of this symbol can immediately suggest the formation of such symbols as a^7, $a^{\frac{1}{2}}$, a^0, which in their turn can seek for the appropriate concepts.[9] This extension was not suggested by the original geometric formulation, and the translation can sometimes leave us wondering over the pseudo-problem of why early writers did not make generalizations that in the new symbolic formulation seem obvious. Similarly, if we are told that a Renaissance algebraicist solved a cubic equation, we bring to mind something of the form $ax^3 + bx^2 + cx + d = 0$, and often this is done for us by historians of mathematics. But the original formulation was not like this, and we are in danger of losing contact with what was going on. (It may be that in this instance the danger is not so great as in some others, but we cannot *a priori* be confident of this.) Difficulties of this kind arise from the fact that to a large extent mathematics is itself a language, and advances in mathematics are often linguistic advances, which can be disguised by too ready translation. We may remember the commonplace that the correct formulation of a mathematical problem is frequently more than halfway towards its solution.

But the pointing out of a historiographical difficulty is by no means equivalent to its resolution. Whatever the dangers of translation into modern terminology, we cannot altogether dispense with it, for this could easily lead to the position of accepting only collections of primary sources as history. To lay down general rules for the acceptability of translations is impossible, and probably the most important thing is that the reader be made aware of the principles used in the translation and the particular distortions liable to arise in individual cases. But we may note that there are at least three different ways in which modern mathematics may be used in describing past mathematics:

(1) The way that we have been discussing, which may be called material translation. The past work is presented in what are taken to be logically equivalent modern terms.

(2) Artificial notation is used to present the essential structure of past argumentation. This may involve creating a notation specifically for the purpose in hand, and making it fit as closely as possible the sentence structure of the original.[10] Whereas this method can reveal readily the strategy of past arguments, it is open to the dangers of the suggestiveness of symbols.

(3) The resources of modern mathematics can be used to show that past arguments were not completely incoherent. A notable recent example of this is A. Robinson's use of non-standard analysis to show how talk of infinitesimals can be made respectable.[11] This may alert the historian to a more sympathetic attitude towards pre-Weierstrassian mathematicians, but the dangers of distortion are evident.

All these modes have their place and their dangers in the historiography of mathematics. But in the case of astronomy or physics it may be thought that it is over-pedantic to dwell so much on the dangers. Surely mode (1) will suffice, provided that it does not obscure the underlying physical concepts? Often indeed it will, especially when the mathematics involved was unremarkable for its time. Pedersen and Pihl, for example, give (pp. 211–13) such a presentation of Jordanus's treatment of the inclined plane, which does not distort the physical basis of the argument. But I shall hope to show that there are other cases in which, even if the focus of interest is elsewhere, more attention to mathematical form can be historically illuminating.

III. DIVISIONS OF KNOWLEDGE

Form is very context sensitive. With their material emphasis, Pedersen and Pihl somewhat neglect the intellectual contexts of the work that they consider. This is even apparent from the title of the English version, which suggests two well-defined, and perhaps equipollent, areas of study in Antiquity and the Middle Ages that can appropriately be labelled "astronomy" and "physics". But things were not really that simple, and the Danish title, which displays the book as dealing with ancestors of later, so-called classical, physics is better, even if it does some violence to the comparative degree of independence that astronomy has retained after the establishment of classical physics.

Pedersen and Pihl do not in this volume explicitly discuss the problem of locating the ancestors of physics. But the Greek cultural ambience is clearly of the utmost importance, and more particularly the characteristic forms of Greek philosophy and mathematics. Because of his immense influence on Late Antiquity and the Middle Ages, it is convenient to place a particular focus on the time of Aristotle. We may distinguish four relevant forms of endeavour:

(1) Pure mathematics. Of particular importance was the existence of an axiomatic system of geometry.

(2) Methodology. The work that comes immediately to mind is Aristotle's *Posterior analytics*, in which geometry provides the prime example of a demonstrative science. Perhaps also the *Topics* should be given more consideration than is sometimes done.

(3) Philosophy of nature, or physics in the Aristotelian sense. This has many differences from later physics, and does not square easily with the analyses of science given in the *Posterior analytics*.[12]

(4) What Aristotle called the more physical of the branches of mathematics.[13] By his time these included optics, astronomy, some form of mechanics, and musical theory[14], but no independent works are extant from so early a date.

In an article on medieval science,[15] which appeared before the Danish version of the book but was more contextually sensitive than the book, Pedersen regarded (4), which by then were often referred to as *scientiae mediae*, as of particular importance on the road to physics. Two of these, astronomy and music, formed part of the traditional quadrivium, and, while not neglecting influences such as those from philosophy and the mechanical arts, Pedersen concluded that, "Il me semble juste de dire qu'il y a un chemin du quadrivium à la physique".[16] Pedersen's aim was to stress continuity, and there are attractions in focusing on the 'middle sciences' for this end, since they have definite similarities with later physics. In some cases, admittedly, it could seem that experience had only a general role in establishing their first principles. This had been the case with geometry, a feature that allowed

Plato to use a geometrical example in arguing for anamnesis,[17] and it is particularly striking in Archimedes's *On the equilibrium of planes*. This example put Ernst Mach at some pains to uncover hidden assumptions in the establishment of the law of the lever.[18] On the other hand, optics, astronomy, and music all, to varying degrees, had to rely on more detailed observations, and indeed musical theory provided a *locus* for discussions of the proper balance between reason and the senses in such sciences.[19] A notable feature of the middle sciences was that they lived relatively independent lives in Antiquity and the Middle Ages, having, as it were, little paradigms of their own, and developing (perhaps sometimes regressing) within their own traditions. But for the birth of a new physics, more radical attempts at creation, transformation and unification were needed.

Among the many important influences on this process, physics in the Aristotelian sense had a multi-faceted role, which is still in need of much elucidation. We may point here to three aspects. First, although Aristotle gave to mathematics a high place in providing *propter quid* explanations in the middle sciences,[20] his general attitude to the discipline was rather ambivalent. In particular, he had some difficulty in locating the middle sciences in his division between mathematics and physics,[21] a difficulty that continued to be felt by his medieval commentators.[22] Moreover, incompatibilities were seen between Aristotle's doctrines and those of the middle sciences. The case of Ptolemaic astronomy *versus* Aristotelian cosmology is well known, but there were also difficulties in reconciling geometrical optics with the Aristotelian theory of vision.[23] Sometimes the result was an instrumentalist interpretation of the middle sciences, but at others the tensions were more fruitful.

Secondly, although there are grounds for calling Aristotle's physical treatises more philosophical than scientific in approach, they are still much concerned with problems in the foundations of physics, whether understood in the ancient or the modern sense, problems such as the nature of time and space (or place), the difficulties raised by continuity, the relation of the whole and the part, and of one and many, theoretical questions of measure, and the appropriate conceptual structure for the analyses of motion. These discussions should be given more weight than is often done, for it is not *a priori* obvious what foundations are the appropriate ones to choose, even if subsequent pedagogy can make them appear common sense. By examining such conceptual problems we get added insight into how past problem situations could appear far more difficult to those facing them than they do from the viewpoint of a particular later solution. Moreover, such analyses can help us to characterise more justly the essential differences between older and newer physics.

Thirdly, a notable omission from the established middle sciences was one dealing with sublunary motion. For this the obvious source to turn to was Aristotle, even if in many aspects he seemed merely to throw out hints. The lack of a proper mathematical science seems to have been felt, and we may see works as diverse as Proclus's *Institutio physica*[24] and Bradwardine's *Tractatus de proportionibus* as attempts to respond to the need. Fourteenth century Europe in particular saw a major upsurge in attempts to mathematize not only motion but the intensities of qualities. In this movement Oresme's *Tractatus de configurationibus qualitatum et motuum* is a particularly bold and original work and in it Oresme seems very consciously to be striving towards the creation of a new middle science.[25] Such developments allow us to sympathize with the judgement of J. Gagné (in a study of the medieval middle sciences taking its starting-point from Pedersen's article cited above) that, "L'histoire des sciences intermédiaires nous renvoie plutôt à un autre courant historique, plus sourd, mais non moins important, au contraire, dans lequel c'est la physique du type aristotélicien qui cherche la mathématique, comme si la physique avait aussi cherché le *Quadrivium*".[26] A closer analysis of the relevant problems in their own contextual settings may help us to see more clearly into the vexed question of the influence of fourteenth century work upon Galileo and others.

IV. ASTRONOMY AND ITS HISTORY

Great literature and great philosophy are often held to transcend time, and, by their treating of unchanging themes of perennial interest, to be worthy of an approach that need pay little regard to their historical origins. The existence of such views allows for the frequent arguments that take place between literary historians and literary critics, and between different types of historians of philosophy, as to the proper means of treating past writings. Science is at first glance radically different. The works of the past are rarely held to maintain a culturally transcendent value *as works of science*, Lord Snow even suggested as a criterion for dividing "the two cultures" that scientists did not need past works.[27] "Science is cumulative, and embodies its past." This is not completely false, but is open to attack from various quarters. At the moment I wish only to draw attention to certain peculiarities of the relation that astronomy has had to its past. Astronomy for the most part cannot strictly be called an experimental science. The means of putting nature to the test are usually absent, and the astronomer has to wait for nature in her own good time to reveal herself. Once a revelation has been made it cannot be repeated at will, and so the record of a past observation can acquire an importance far greater than the record of a simply repeatable experiment. In particular, the means for rejecting past observations as erroneous are not at all simple. An example is given by Pedersen and Pihl (pp. 184–5)[28] when they discuss how observations made in the ninth century seemed to contradict the value given by Ptolemy for the precession of the equinoxes. One strategy in this situation was to reject Ptolemy's value, but since the determination of the rate of precession necessarily depended on using very old observations, this was not the obviously correct solution. An alternative was to assume that the rate of precession varied, and this Thābit ibn Qurra provided for with his theory of trepidation. Much later, but in the same problem situation, Copernicus revealed himself a strong partisan of accepting ancient observations.[29] "If an yone . . . thinks that the ancients are untrustworthy in this regard, surel y the gates of the art are closed to him. Lying before the entrance, he will dream the dreams of the disordered about the motion of the eighth sph ere and will receive his deserts for supposing that he must support his hallucination by defaming the ancients." Later still, consultation of ancient records was an important part of the investigation of perturbations of planetary motions, and in recent times interest in supernovae has led to enquiries as to when they may have appeared in the past.[30]

Examples of this kind illustrate a type of dependence on astronomy on its history that is rare in other physical sciences. Conversely historians of astronomy have frequent recourse to the present state of the subject by using tables for past planetary positions computed on the basis of modern theory. To these relations we may add the fact that there is a far closer identity of aims and methods between ancient and modern computational astronomy than is the case with most other sciences. Moreover, there is little need for a concern with basic ontology. All these factors make it possible for there to be astronomical dialogue across the ages, in which problems of translation do not become inextricably entangled with conceptual problems. This may do much to account for the style of approach adopted by many of the most distinguished modern historians of early astronomy. We may characterise this as (1) thoroughly material in emphasis, (2) strongly internalist, the relevant boundaries being those of astronomy as a mathematical science, and (3) demanding the highest scholarly standards in paleography and philology, and in the handling of the relevant mathematical techniques. Work in this tradition has greatly advanced our knowledge of early astronomy, and many of the results are reported by Pedersen and Pihl. But the excellence of the third characteristic can all too easily lead to the assumption that the first two represent the only acceptable approach to the subject. The result is that historiographies that should be complementary are regarded as antagonistic.

This is nowhere better illustrated than in the case of Copernicus, and in particular in his insistence on uniform circular motion. Pedersen and Pihl draw on recent work to show how there had been concern for this among Arabic astronomers, and how some of Copernicus's techniques were anticipated by Nāṣir al-Dīn al-Ṭūsī and Ibn al-Shāṭir.[31] In a fairly balanced account they point out Copernicus's objections to Ptolemy as given in the beginning of the *Commentariolus*, but seem rather embarrassed about them, for they continue (p. 302), "It is worth noticing, however, that Copernicus also had more rational motives for adhering to uniform circular motions". This begs the question of what is to be regarded as rational in this context. O. Neugebauer took a stronger line, and had little patience with Copernicus's objections to the equant, which he clearly regarded as an example of philosophical prejudice.[32] By a very material mode of treatment he was able to show how in a sense Copernicus did not even succeed in removing the equant. N. Swerdlow was less dismissive, but in his effort to avoid anything 'philosophical' he propounded a justification that is much in need of explication.[33] "The principle of uniform circular motion as Copernicus uses it is a mechanical principle about the rotation of a sphere and nothing more. It should not be understood as a philosophical, much less metaphysical, principle about the motion proper to the substance of the heavens. Speculations about such things do not belong to the domain of mathematical astronomy." It is not at all obvious what is to be understood by 'mechanical principle' in this context, nor what grounds Copernicus would have for holding it. Moreover, it is surely illegitimate to impose on Copernicus a dogmatic conception of what does and does not belong to 'mathematical astronomy', and to demand that he be influenced by nothing from outside.

In fact much of the trouble seems to come from an insistence on the immunity of astronomy from outside interference. This could take support from accounts such as those by Aquinas and Osiander in which astronomical hypotheses seem only to be constrained by empirical evidence. But this was not the universal view. For instance, the classical account of Geminus had demanded that the astronomer go to the physicist for his first principles, and had even hinted at a road from astronomy to physics: "It will be necessary to go further and examine in how many different ways it is possible for these phenomena to be brought about, so that we may bring our theory concerning the planets into agreement with that explanation of the causes which follows an admissible method".[34] Copernicus's work shows clearly that his approach was very much within this tradition, and that he sought for a harmony between physics and astronomy. But the accepted form of physics at the time was Aristotelian, and this would not do as it stood. Copernicus retained from it the principle of natural motions, but regrounded and reformulated it. Uniform circular motion, which for Aristotle had been the natural motion only of the heavenly spheres, became basic throughout the universe, and rectilinear motions were relegated to the pathological cases in which a part was separated from the whole.[35] In this, as has so often been the case, Copernicus was being both Aristotelian and anti-Aristotelian at the same time. Neugebauer has denigrated Copernicus's astronomy, and his physics in itself was even less successful. But, by treating the two in combination, Copernicus pointed the way to the eventual subjection of astronomy to a new physics.

V. JORDANUS DE NEMORE, GERARD OF BRUSSELS, AND JOHANNES DE TINEMUE

Melchisedec was without father, without mother, and without descent. While the historian will allow theories to be without descent, he is rightly sceptical about allowing them to be without parents. But sometimes a material approach can disguise real problems of ancestry. Pedersen and Pihl (p. 209) say that Jordanus "was perhaps a Dominican; his life-story is still unclear, and several writings have been wrongly ascribed to him". They place Gerard of Brussels in the first half of the thirteenth century and remark (p. 218) that his *Liber de motu* "was the first Mediaeval treatise entirely devoted to kinematic questions". These are fairly standard judgements, but they do not bring to the reader's attention the very troubling problems concerning the cultural matrix of these figures. These problems have been spasmodically admitted by historians, but I think that they will appear much more serious when all the works of the Jordanus corpus are considered together and in comparison with Gerard's work. Works of these men are often found in the same manuscript codices, and sometimes in association with the *De curvis superficiebus* of Johannes de Tinemue, which also presents problems of origin. In this section I shall give a sketch of some of the difficulties raised by the works of these three men.

Heiberg had stated that the *De curvis superficiebus* was without doubt a translation from the Arabic.[36] Clagett, who has twice edited the treatise, was more cautious. In his first edition he was led to the conclusion that it was a translation, probably from the Arabic.[37] In the second edition he shifted to the view that it was a translation from the Greek.[38] His principal ground for regarding it as a translation was the degree of familiarity that the author displayed with Archimedean procedures, and, in particular, he seemed to have a more intimate knowledge of the *De sphaera et cylindro* than would have been available from Latin sources. Clagett toyed with the hypothesis that he may have been a Latin writer familiar with Greek texts, but was disinclined to accept it.[39] However, in reviewing Clagett's work G. J. Toomer[40] was a firm partisan of a Latin origin, and he even suggested an allusion to Ovid. "The fact is that there is nothing in the style to mark the work as a translation, and much to mark it as an original composition." But he still admitted the strong Archimedean influence. The name of the author is of little help to us, and even the expansion *Tinemue* is uncertain.[41] Clagett has noted a possibility of identifying him with an English canonist John of Tynemouth,[42] who was a clerk to Hubert Walter,[43] but in the absence of further evidence, this remains very speculative. The only firm *terminus ante quem* is provided by the *De triangulis* (or *Philotegni*) of Jordanus and the *De motu* of Gerard, which both cite it and which were both in existence by 1260.[44] The question of a *terminus post quem* is completely open.

Gerard's *De motu*[45] depends quite heavily on the *De curvis superficiebus*, but the central theme of his work is the equating of motions according to axiomatic criteria, for which no clear rationale is given. It is hard to see how this could have appeared out of the blue with no pre-existent tradition of discussing such questions. No such tradition is apparent in Latin, and it would seem more plausible to expect it to have grown up in the late Greek geometrical ambit, for the *De motu* as it stands is far more a mathematical work than a philosophical one, and is in marked contrast to later Latin works on motion. However, Gerard's control of the relevant mathematical techniques does not seem altogether firm, and this again suggests his drawing upon earlier work. Of him as a person we have virtually no evidence, although the cognomen *de Brussel/de Bruxella*[46] suggests a Latin origin. It has been suggested that he may be identified with the equally shadowy Gernardus, the author of *Algorithmus demonstratus*.[47]

For many reasons, not least the size of the corpus, the Jordanus problem is more complicated. We may first note the difficulty that has crept in through the attempted identification of Jordanus de Nemore with Jordanus of Saxony, the second Master-General of the Dominicans. For this the lack of evidence is glaring, particularly in places where one may expect to find it, such as in a letter from Grosseteste to Jordanus of Saxony.[48] The strongest evidence is provided by the fourteenth century chronicler Nicholas Trivet, who wrote, "In this year [1222] at the third General Chapter of the Friars Preacher held at Paris, there was appointed as successor to Blessed Dominic in the Mastership of the Order of Friars Preacher Brother Jordanus, German by nationality from the Diocese of Mainz, who, since he was held to be great at Paris in the secular sciences, and particularly in mathematics, is said to have written two very useful books, one on weights [*de ponderibus*] and one on given lines [*de lineis datis*]".[49] Trivet does reveal attempts to ascribe works of the Jordanus corpus to Jordanus of Saxony, but he seems to express doubts about their veracity, and may even attribute them, as we can do, to a desire for hagiography. Moreover the tradition is rather vague, for although there is a *De numeris datis* in the corpus, there is no work that can plausibly be described as *De lineis datis*. Other direct evidence for the identification is scanty and later. Neither does the name Jordanus add much support, for, although it may not have been common,[50] we may at least identify a Jordanus of Melbourne who was a member of the *familia* of Thomas Becket, and said to have been for his time *non mediocris scientiae*,[51] and a Jordanus *fisicus* who seems to have been a member of Hubert Walter's household.[52] There is nothing original in rejecting the identification of Jordanus de Nemore and Jordanus of Saxony,[53] but the existence of the hypothesis has all too easily led to the assumption that if the first Jordanus was not the second he was someone like him. But in fact, when the hypothesis is rejected, the person of the mathematician becomes as shadowy as that of Johannes or Gerard, and the problem of dating almost as acute. With regard to this we have a *terminus ante quem* of 1259–60 for several of the works,[54] and a possible *terminus ante quem* of 1215–16 for two of the algorithmic works.[55] We may get some idea of the *terminus post quem* from the citations of the *Liber de similibus arcubus* of Aḥmad ibn Yūsuf (Ametus filius Iosephi), on the assumption that Jordanus was using a translation by Gerard of Cremona.[56]

The statical works ascribed by Jordanus have hitherto come in for most attention. There are three closely related works, but this is not unusual, for throughout the corpus multiple versions are common. These are $E = $ *Elementa Jordani super demonstrationem ponderum*, $P = $ *Liber de ponderibus*, and $R = $ *De ratione ponderis*.[57] We can here only give a rough account of the similarities and differences between the versions. The postulates and enunciations of the propositions of E correspond very closely with those of P (except that the latter has four propositions derived from another work). Let us call these postulates and enunciations the skeleton. The skeleton also corresponds quite closely with the early part of R, but R is a much longer work. It is divided into four parts, and the last two propositions of the first part and the whole of the last three parts have little correspondence to E or P. That the problem of sources and relations has been serious can be seen by the following synopsis of views. Duhem, Moody, Clagett and Maier all agree in not ascribing P to Jordanus.[58] Duhem took it to be a Peripatetic transformation of E. Clagett seemed to favour either this hypothesis or that P was a translation from Arabic and E a transformation of it by Jordanus. Moody suggested that the skeleton was received in translation and that Jordanus composed E on its basis. Maier on the other hand held that the skeleton was composed by Jordanus and that both E and P were the works of commentators. As regards R, Thurot over a hundred years ago had written, "Quant à l'ouvrage de Jordanus lui-même il me parait traduit de grec, et pourrait bien dériver du traité de Ptolémée Περὶ ροπων".[59] Duhem at first, much to Sarton's annoyance, dubbed its author "Précurseur de Léonard de Vinci",[60] but later came to the conclusion that, whereas its first part was of medieval Latin origin, its last three parts were a translation from Greek via Arabic.[61] Moody ascribed it to Jordanus,[62] and Clagett with rather more caution inclined to the view that it was by Jordanus or a near contemporary.[63]

The problems even in this one part of the corpus are clearly many. Closer study of the rest of the corpus will intensify them, but may also help towards a resolution. There is still much editing to be done,[64] particularly as works often exist in more than one version. It is usually possible to identify a pristine version, which lacks the "commentatorial spirit"[65] that characterizes so many medieval reworkings of mathematical treatises. Among the statical treatises both E and R appear to be pristine. The pristine versions of other works present similar problems of sources, for, while many aspects of their mathematical form may be seen as natural developments of parts of Greek mathematics, it is almost inconceivable that they should arise independently.

As one example we may cite the facility with which Jordanus uses the Greek mathematical language of givenness, which is found so frequently in, for example, the work of Pappus. The statements involved infer from the fact that, if certain things and/or relations are given and certain conditions hold, then something else is given. The wide variety of contexts in which Jordanus applies this mathematical style suggests that he is drawing upon a rich tradition. For these and similar problems we may feel the temptation that has existed with regard to the statical works—to regard at least some of them as translations. But for this there is a troubling lack of evidence, and the fact that Jordanus cites, for example, the *Liber de similibus arcubus*, which existed in translation from Arabic,[66] and the *Liber de ysoperimetris*, which existed in translation from Greek,[67] suggests a Latin origin for the corpus.

The purpose of this section has been to point up a problem rather than to provide a resolution. For what it is worth, I am tempted to regard all three authors as writing in Latin, but moving or having moved in a Greek cultural ambience, perhaps in twelfth century Sicily or Byzantium, where they acquired some of the spirit of Greek mathematical procedures. Their works would then be drawing heavily on Greek mathematical works, many no longer extant, but would not be mere translations. We could perhaps compare their practice with how Boethius used Greek sources in compiling his *Arithmetica* and *Musica*. I say a Greek rather than an Arabic ambience, largely because of the particular sort of austerity of mathematical style that they adopt, although this could be disputed. But, whatever the truth of conjectures of this kind may be, it is at least clear that in the present state of scholarship it is dangerous to assume that these works were a direct product of medieval Latin culture. And the fact that they inspired little further constructive work in the same spirit suggests that they fell on unfruitful soil. We cannot allow them to have the Melchisedecian character of lack of parentage, but, in a telling sense, they share his lack of descent.

VI. THE ORIGINS OF BRADWARDINE'S LAW

In the last section we saw how formal considerations may reveal the existence of a problem or make a problem appear more serious. In this section I wish to show conversely how a formal approach may come near to dissolving a problem. I take as example Bradwardine's "law of motion" (whose mathematical form we considered in section II), and the view that it had a pharmacological origin.

This view took root when Clagett drew attention to what he saw as mathematical similarities between Bradwardine's law and al-Kindī's work on grades of medicine, and tentatively suggested influence.[68] M. McVaugh developed the thesis, and proposed Arnald of Villanova, who presented al-Kindī's approach in a clearer form, as an intermediary.[69] Later D. Skabelund and P.

Thomas suggested Walter of Odington's treatment of intensities in alchemy as providing a link between Arnald and Bradwardine.[70] The whole thesis has gained a certain amount of acceptance, but recently a protest has been entered by S. Drake.[71] While I am in general sympathy with the spirit of Drake's attack, I cannot accept his view in its entirety, particularly when it comes to characterizations of medieval proportional theory.

I shall be arguing less from the implausibility of a pharmacological influence on Bradwardine than from lack of need to postulate it, but we should note that the relevant passages from al-Kindī, Arnald of Villanova and Walter of Odington did not achieve the generality of formulation found in Bradwardine's law, nor do they display much linguistic similarity to it. This militates against influence. My positive thesis will be that Bradwardine's law derives quite naturally from Aristotle and the commentaries of Averroes, by means of a more rigorous mathematical approach, reinforced by the analogy of musical theory. All these sources are referred to by Bradwardine, whereas his *Tractatus de proportionibus* includes no reference to pharmacology or alchemy.

Much secondary literature on the history of science would suggest that the manner of variation of speed with respect to force and resistance was a topic of major concern to Aristotle. But in fact there are few places where he alludes to it,[72] and he never gives a systematic treatment. The customary form $V = \text{const.} \times \dfrac{F}{R}$ is developed by Pedersen and Pihl (p. 122), but it has to be remembered that this is anachronistic in more than one way. Materially it is an extrapolation from what Aristotle said, and formally it uses an un-Aristotelian mathematical language, and suggests that Aristotle was propounding a first principle of a science. Aristotle himself gives no sign of doing this, and does not even present a uniform terminology. But by the time of Averroes's commentaries on the relevant passages there had been a change, for Averroes introduces into his arguments general statements, which make use of the language of active and passive powers, and look far more like laws of motion. For example: "The speed proper to any motion follows the excess of the power of the mover over the power of the thing moved";[73] or, "Speed and slowness are only according to the ratio of the power of the mover to the power of the thing moved".[74] These statements are quoted by Bradwardine,[75] and, together with others, clearly helped to determine the linguistic form of his own expression,[76] "The ratio of speeds in motions follows the ratio of the power of the mover to the power of the thing moved".

The major difference between Averroes and Bradwardine is one of intent rather than of material disagreement. Then as now proportional language could be either vague or precise. Averroes's language was vague, whereas Bradwardine's central aim was to produce a mathematically coherent theory. Thus he had to deal with apparent contradictions between Averroes's

ANCESTORS OF PHYSICS   69

expressions, and to decide what was the true mathematical position. To this end he critically considered five possible positions, of which he rejected the first four, and accepted the fifth. "There does not seem to be any position by which the ratio of speeds in motions can be saved, except one of those already given. But the first four have been destroyed; therefore there only remains the fifth true one".[77] Bradwardine's arguments employ reason, experience and authority. Reason is used to examine whether a position is internally inconsistent or leads to absurdity. The experiences appealed to are those that would be common at the time, and do not make any use of precise measurements. (There is an interesting reference to the behaviour of a mechanical clock.[78]) The principal authorities were Aristotle and Averroes. Their statements were subjected to a searching examination of a kind more appropriate to the lawyer than the historian. Apparent contradictions were only apparent, and, when they were reconciled, Bradwardine's own position emerged as the true interpretation of the authorities.

Of the five positions considered by Bradwardine, one has a different character from the rest. The first three rejected positions and his own position all propose precise mathematical relationships determining speed. But the fourth position holds that, "There is no ratio nor any excess of motive power to resistive power, and therefore the ratio of speeds in motions does not follow any ratio or excess of motive power to the power of the mobile, but some dominion and natural relation of the mover to the moved".[79] This opinion hacks at the very roots of Bradwardine's endeavour by denying the possibility of mathematization, on the grounds that powers are not quantified. Bradwardine's first argument against it reveals the influence of musical theory.[80] "But this position can be rejected, because if there were no ratios between powers on account of their not being quantities, then for the same reason there would be no ratios between sounds. And so the modulation of the whole of music would perish". Thus the existence of one mathematical science can give confidence in the possibility of another. But we may go further, and suggest another kind of musical influence on Bradwardine. The central problem that the proponents of the pharmacological thesis were trying to solve was the origins of the 'exponential' nature of Bradwardine's law. If we adhere more closely to Bradwardine's original form, the question is why Bradwardine regarded the composition of $A:B$ and $B:C$ (where $A>B>C$) as giving rise to $A:C$, and why he interpreted this (implicitly if not explicitly) as addition. To the question posed thus the pharmacological answer is less plausible, for *inter alia* that tradition had less talk of ratios. On the other hand Bradwardine's addition view of ratios is central to the musical tradition,[81] and this could easily have provided a specific source for Bradwardine, if the language were not commonplace by his time. We may even see a tight analogy between Bradwardine's law and a fundamental (if unexpressed) principle of musical theory, for whereas the former held that speed varied with the ratio between powers, the latter assumed that the interval between two sounds varied as the ratio associated with them. Pedersen and Pihl (p. 221) raise the question of why there seems to have been so little astronomical influence on Mertonian concern with motion. May it not be that a sublunary member of the quadrivium seemed a more appropriate stimulus to mathematical physics?

VII. FORM AND THE GLASS BEAD GAME

In one crucial respect Bradwardine diverged from the musical tradition. For, although the latter was sometimes rather vague about the conceptual underpinning of its ratios, it did provide various means (some admittedly severely faulty) of empirically determining them, of which the standard was the division of the monochord.[82] Bradwardine was faced with the problem of quantifying powers that were in a strict sense indivisible. His conceptual solution to this does not give complete satisfaction,[83] and methods for empirically measuring the ratios between powers are almost completely absent. This makes the material aspect of his law very flimsy, and it may be more accurate to describe it as empirically meaningless rather than as empirically false. The same disability afflicted many other fourteenth century attempts at mathematical science, and the resulting tensions are exhibited particularly forcibly in the work of Oresme. His capacity for producing striking innovations is shown particularly in his renowned doctrine of configurations, but even in his principal work on the subject he had to admit that the empirical basis was weak,[84] and in other works he gives signs of despair of the possibility of attaining an exact mathematical knowledge of nature.[85] There are times when he seems to play with beautiful conceptions for which no fit subject could be found. Such concern with disembodied forms can be fascinating, but it may easily pall and seem sterile when no means of escape into something richer are apparent. This is not to say that fourteenth century work in this tradition was without subsequent influence, but it may do much to explain why it is so difficult to give a clear and definitive account of the nature of this influence.

It may seem that a similar charge of sterility could be brought against the historian who puts such an emphasis on the formal aspects of past science as I have been advocating. An obsession with ghosts of departed theories is surely as unlikely to lead anywhere as a mania for listing past 'positive discoveries'. This charge would hold water if the 'formal historiography' were regarded as an end in itself, but this it should never be. Not only is there always need for concern with the material infra-structure, but the establishment of how past theories appeared to their original holders should reveal more clearly how they fitted into the more general cultural, social and philosophical frameworks of their times. This in turn may make clear to us which of their aspects were genuinely innovatory and which simply represented the obvious way of doing things. We should then be able to see what factors cry out for explanation in more dynamic historical terms. Neglect of the initial re-creation of past thought can easily lead and has often led to the attempt at solving pseudo-problems while neglecting genuine ones. In this subject at least the Glass Bead Game must be played before it can properly be transcended.[86]

REFERENCES

1. By L. Rosenfeld in *Centaurus*, x (1964–65), 60.
2. Preface, unnumbered page.
3. *Ibid.*
4. See ref. 1.
5. We remember that for Aristotle the rational soul received the forms of objects. *De anima*, III. 4, 429a10–430a9.
6. K. Dürr, *The propositional logic of Boethius* (Amsterdam, 1951), 19–20; O. Spengler, *The decline of the West*, tr. C. F. Atkinson (New York, 1945), i, 60–61. Most of Spengler's chapter "The meaning of numbers" is reprinted in *The world of mathematics*, ed. J. R. Newman (London, 2nd imp., 1961), iv, 2312–47 Our quotation is at 2319–20.
7. Thomas Bradwardine, *Tractatus de proportionibus*, ed. H. L. Crosby (Madison, 1955), 110.
8. On the mathematical interpretation of Bradwardine's law see also A. G. Molland, "The geometrical background to the 'Merton School' ", *British journal for the history of science*, iv (1968–69), 108–25.
9. For the importance of 'devices' leading to concepts see R. L. Wilder, *Evolution of mathematical concepts* (Transworld Student Library edn, London, 1974), 110 *et passim*.
10. I have used this policy in "Richard Swineshead and continuously varying quantities", *Actes du XIIe Congrès International d'Histoire des Sciences* (Paris 1970–71), iv, 127–30.
11. See, for instance, A. Robinson, "The metaphysics of the calculus", *Problems in the philosophy of mathematics. Proceedings of the International Colloquium in the Philosophy of Science, London, 1965*, vol. i, ed. I. Lakatos (Amsterdam, 1967), 28–40, reprinted in *The philosophy of mathematics*, ed. J. Hintikka (London, 1969), 153–63,
12. On the methods and concerns of Aristotle's *Physics* see the very illuminating article by G. E. L. Owen, "Τιθέναι τὰ φαινόμενα", *Aristote et les problèmes de la méthode* (Louvain, 1961), 83–103, reprinted in *Aristotle*, ed. J. M. E. Moravcsik (London, 1968), 167–90.
13. *Physica*, II. 2, 194a6–11.
14. *Ibid.*, and see *Anal. post.*, I. 7, 75b14–16, I. 9, 76a22–25, I. 12, 77a40–b2, I. 13, 78b35–79a13.
15. O. Pedersen, "Du quadrivium à la physique: Quelques aperçus de l'évolution scientifique au Moyen Age", *Artes liberales: Von der Antiken Bildung zur Wissenschaft des Mittelalters*, ed. J. Koch (Leiden and Cologne, 1959), 107–23.
16. *Ibid.*, 123.

17. *Meno*, 81E–86A.
18. E. Mach, *The science of mechanics*, tr. T. J. McCormack (4th edn, Chicago and London, 1919), 8–20. *Cf.* E. J. Dijksterhuis, *Archimedes*, tr. C. Dikshoorn (Copenhagen, 1956), 291–304.
19. *Cf.* I. Düring, *Ptolemaios und Porphyrios über die Musik* (Göteborg, 1934), 23–24; Boethius, *De institutione musica*, V. 3 (ed. G. Friedlein (Leipzig, 1867, reprinted Frankfurt, 1966), 354–5); M. Dickreiter, *Der Musiktheoretiker Johannes Kepler* (Berne and Munich, 1973), 61–68.
20. See particularly *Anal. post.*, I. 13, 78b31–79a16.
21. *Physica*, II. 2, 193b22–194a11.
22. J. Gagné, "Du *quadrivium* aux *scientiae mediae*", *Actes du Quatrième Congrès International de Philosophie Médiévale* (Montreal and Paris, 1969), 975–86.
23. *Cf.* S. Sambursky, "Philoponus' interpretation of Aristotle's theory of light", *Osiris*, xiii (1958), 114–26, and A. G. Molland, "John Dumbleton and the status of geometrical optics", *Actes du XIIIe Congrès International d'Histoire des Sciences* (Moscow, 1974), iii–iv, 125–30.
24. Ed. with German translation by A. Ritzenfeld (Leipzig, 1912). The partial twelfth century Latin translation is edited by H. Boese, *Die mittelalterliche Übersetzung der* ΣΤΟΙΧΕΙΩΣΙΣ ΦΥΣΙΚΗ *des Proclus* (Berlin, 1958).
25. *Cf.* A. G. Molland, "Nicole Oresme and scientific progress", *Miscellanea mediaevalia*, ix (1974), 206–20, at 208–13.
26. Gagné, *op. cit.* (ref. 22), 986.
27. C. P. Snow, "The case of Leavis and the serious case", *Times literary supplement* (1970), 737–40. *Cf.* P. B. Medawar, *The hope of progress* (London, 1972), 107: "Science . . . in some sense comprehends its history within itself"; but Medawar insists that he is speaking of "scientific endeavours and accomplishments" and not of the "history of scientific ideas".
28. See also B. R. Goldstein, "On the theory of trepidation according to Thābit b. Qurra and al-Zarqāllu and its implications for homocentric planetary theory", *Centaurus*, x (1964–65), 232–47.
29. L. Prowe, *Nicolaus Coppernicus* (Berlin, 1883–84; reprinted Osnabrück, 1967), ii, 177. Translation from E. Rosen, *Three Copernican treatises* (2nd edn, New York, 1959), 99.
30. See, for example, B. R. Goldstein, "Evidence for a supernova of A.D. 1006", *The astronomical journal*, lxx (1965), 105–14.
31. They do not discuss the question of influence. On this see W. Hartner, "Copernicus, the man, the work, and its history", *Proceedings of the American Philosophical Society*, cxvii (1973), 413–22, at 420–1.
32. O. Neugebauer, "On the planetary theory of Copernicus", *Vistas in astronomy*, x (1968), 89–103.
33. N. M. Swerdlow, "The derivation and first draft of Copernicus's planetary theory. A translation of the Commentariolus with commentary", *Proceedings of the American Philosophical Society*, cxvii (1973), 423–512. A gentle protest against Swerdlow's attitude in this regard is entered by Hartner, *op. cit.* (ref. 31), 416, n. 7.
34. M. R. Cohen and I. E. Drabkin, *A source book in Greek science* (Cambridge, Mass., 1948), 91. On the relation of Copernicus to 'saving the phenomena' see J. Mittelstrass, *Die Rettung der Phänomene* (Berlin, 1962), 197–206.
35. See especially *De revolutionibus*, I. 8. Oresme had made similar moves in discussing the possibility of the rotation of the Earth while commenting on

Aristotle's *De coelo*. See Nicole Oresme, *Le livre du ciel et du monde*, ed. A. D. Menut and A. J. Denomy (Madison, 1968), 526–28.

36. Archimedes, *Opera omnia cum commentariis Eutocii*, ed. J. L. Heiberg (2nd edn, Leipzig, 1910–15), vol. iii, p. xcviii.

37. M. Clagett, "The *De curvis superficiebus Archimenidis*: A medieval commentary of Johannes de Tinemue on Book I of the *De sphaera et* cylindro of Archimedes", *Osiris*, xi (1954), 295–346, at 295–9.

38. M. Clagett, *Archimedes in the middle ages* (Madison, 1964–), i, 440–2.

39. *Ibid.*, 441, n. 8.

40. *Speculum*, xlii (1967), 362–5.

41. Clagett, *op. cit.* (ref. 37), 296; *op. cit.* (ref. 38), 440.

42. Clagett, *op. cit.* (ref. 38), Addenda and Corrigenda.

43. A. B. Emden, *A biographical register of the University of Oxford to A.D. 1500* (Oxford, 1957–59), iii, 1923. *Cf.* C. R. Cheney, *Hubert Walter* (London, 1967), 164–6.

44. *Jordani Nemorarii Geometria vel de triangulis*, ed. M. Curtze (Torun, 1887), 21; MS Edinburgh, Royal Observatory, Crawford Library, no. 1, [f. 6v]. The manuscript is unfoliated; the numbers that I give assume that the text starts on f. 1r. The version of the *De triangulis* in the manuscript is substantially different from that in Curtze's edition, and is probably a more accurate reflection of the original work. M. Clagett, "The *Liber de motu* of Gerard of Brussels and the origin of kinematics in the West", *Osiris*, xii (1956) 73–175, at 121. For the dating of the works of Jordanus and Gerard see below.

45. Edited by Clagett, *op. cit.* (ref. 44). Some important new points of interpretation are made in E. D. Sylla, "The Oxford calculators and the mathematics of Motion, 1320–1350. Physics and measurement by latitudes" (Unpublished Ph.D. thesis, Harvard University, 1970), Appendix B, B1–B14. Sylla's exegeses are on the whole very convincing, but I cannot altogether agree with her general characterization that "What Gerard does is to find average or mean velocities" (B1). This seems to introduce concepts that were not in his mind.

46. Clagett, *op. cit.* (ref. 44), 104; MS *cit.* (ref. 44), [f. 52v].

47. Clagett, *op. cit.* (ref. 44), 106.

48. Robert Grosseteste, *Epistolae*, ed. H. R. Luard (London, 1861), 131–3.

49. Nicholas Trivet, *Annales sex regum Angliae qui a comitibus Andegavensibus originem traxerunt*, ed. Thomas Hog (London, 1845), 211; "Hoc anno, in capitulo fratrum Praedicatorum generali tertio, quod Parisiis celebratum est, successor beati Dominici in magisterio ordinis fratrum Praedicatorum factus est frater Jordanus, natione Teutonicus, dioecesis Maguntinae; qui cum Parisiis in scientiis saecularibus et praecipue in mathematicis magnus haberetur, libros duos admodum utiles, unum de Ponderibus, et alium de Lineis datis, dicitur edidisse".

50. *Cf.* E. Jamison, *Admiral Eugenius of Sicily*, (London, 1957), 158.

51. *Materials for the life of Thomas Becket Archbishop of Canterbury*, ed. J. C. Robertson (London, 1875–85), iii, 526; D. Knowles, *The episcopal colleagues of Archbishop Thomas Becket* (Cambridge, 1951), 26.

52. Cheney, *op. cit.* (ref. 43), 163; *Cartulary of the Priory of St Gregory, Canterbury*, ed. A. M. Woodcock, Camden 3rd Series vol. lxxxviii (London, 1956), 5.

53. For discussions of the identification of the two Jordanus's see: Jordanus, *ed. cit.* (ref. 44), iv-vi; P. Duhem, *Les origines de la statique* (Paris, 1905–6), i, 104–5; E. A. Moody and M. Clagett, *The medieval science of weights* (2nd printing, Madison, 1960), 121–2; J. E. Hofmann, "Ueber eine Euklid-Bearbeitung, die

dem Albertus Magnus zugeschrieben wird", *Proceedings of the International Congress of Mathematicians, 1958* (Cambridge, 1960), 554–66, at 561–2; M. Clagett, "Jordanus de Nemore", *New Catholic encyclopedia* (New York, 1967), vii, 1103–4; E. Grant, "Jordanus de Nemore", *Dictionary of scientific biography*, vii (New York, 1973), 171–9, at 172; R. B. Thomson, "Jordanus de Nemore and the University of Toulouse", *British journal for the history of science*, vii (1974), 163–5.

54. Richard of Fournival's library contained several works from the corpus, and Richard died before 1260. See Items 43, 45, 47, 48, 59 of his *Biblionomia* (or library catalogue) as given in A. Birkenmajer, *Études d'histoire des sciences et de la philosophie du moyen âge* (Wroclaw, 1970), 166–73. As Clagett has noted in *Isis*, lxiv, (1973), 392, Item 43 can be identified with the Edinburgh manuscript cited in ref. 44 above. J. E. Murdoch, "The medieval language of proportions", *Scientific change*, ed. A. C. Crombie (London, 1963), 237–71, at 258, has shown how Campanus of Novara took over some definitions from Jordanus's *Arithmetica* in his version of the *Elements*, and Murdoch has also been able to fix a *terminus ante quem* of 1259 for this version: "The medieval Euclid: salient aspects of the translations of the *Elements* by Adelard of Bath and Campanus of Novara", *Revue de synthèse*, lxxxix (1968), 67–94, at 73, n. 18.

55. MS Oxford, Bodleian, Savile 21 has a probable date of 1215–16 and contains two algorithmic works from the corpus, quite possibly copied by Grosseteste. See S. H. Thomson, *The writings of Robert Grosseteste* (Cambridge, 1940), 32, and R. W. Hunt, "The library of Robert Grosseteste", *Robert Grosseteste*, ed. D. A. Callus (Oxford, 1955), 121–45, at 133–4.

56. Jordanus, *ed. cit.* (ref. 44), 21; MS *cit.* (ref. 44), [ff, 6v, 7v, 8v]. An Arabic and a Latin version of the *Liber de similibus arcubus* are edited by H. L. L. Busard, and P. S. van Koningsveld, "Der *Liber de arcubus similibus* des Ahmed ibn Jusuf", *Annals of science*, xxx (1973), 381–406. Another (probably derivative) Latin version is edited in Jordanus, *ed. cit.* (ref. 44), 48–50.

57. All these are edited in Moody and Clagett, *op. cit.* (ref. 53).

58. Duhem, *op. cit.* (ref. 53), i, 128–30; Moody, in Moody and Clagett, *op. cit.* (ref. 53), 145–6; M. Clagett, *The science of mechanics in the middle ages* (Madison, 1959), 73, 84; Maier's review of Moody's and Claggett's work in *Isis*, xlvi, (1955), reprinted in A. Maier, *Ausgehendes Mittelalter* (Rome, 1964–67), ii, 453–8.

59. C. Thurot, "Recherches historiques sur le principe d'Archimède", *Revue archéologique*, 2nd series, xix, (1869), 42–49, 111–23, 294–9, 354–60, at 117.

60. Duhem, *op. cit.* (ref. 53), i, 134–6. *Cf.* G. Sarton, *Introduction to the history of science* (Baltimore, 1927–48), ii, 614.

61. Duhem's later thesis is expounded in P. Duhem, *Études sur Léonard de Vinci* (Paris, 1906–13), i, 311–16; Duhem, *op. cit.* (ref. 53), ii, 318–23; P. Duhem, *Le système du monde* (Paris, 1913–59), i, 388–93.

62. Moody and Clagett, *op. cit.* (ref. 53), 171–2.

63. Clagett, *op. cit.* (ref. 58), 73–74, 80.

64. We may note two recent editions: B. B. Hughes, *The De numeris datis of Jordanus de Nemore: A critical edition, analysis, evaluation and translation* (Ph.D. thesis, Stanford University, 1970); R. B. Thomson, *Thirteenth century mathematical astronomy: De plana spere Iordani* (D. Phil. thesis, Oxford University, 1974). Thomson's thesis contains a valuable bibliography of Jordanus's writings.

65. For the phrase *cf.* W. Whewell, *History of the inductive sciences* (3rd edn, London, 1857), i, 203–14.
66. See ref. 56 above.
67. MS *cit.* (ref. 44), [ff. 1v, 7r]. On the translation of the work see A. A. Björnbo, "Die mittelalterlichen lateinische Übersetzungen aus dem Griechischen auf dem Gebiet der mathematischen Wissenschaften", *Archiv für die Geschichte der Naturwissenschaften und der Technik*, i (1909), 385–94, at 393.
68. Clagett, *op. cit.* (ref. 58), 439, n. 35.
69. M. McVaugh, "Arnald of Villanova and Bradwardine's law", *Isis*, lviii (1967), 56–64.
70. D. Skabelund and P. Thomas, "Walter of Odington's mathematical treatment of the primary qualities", *Isis*, lx (1969), 331–50.
71. S. Drake, "Medieval ratio theory *vs* compound medicines in the origins of Bradwardine's Rule", *Isis*, lxiv (1973), 67–77. A fuller discussion of Drake's views on this and related matters must await another occasion.
72. See especially *Physica*, IV.8, 215a33–216a7, VII.5, 249b30–250a15; *De coelo*, I.6, 273b31–274a10.
73. *Physica*, VII, comm. 35 (*Opera Aristotelis Stagiritae* (Venice, 1560), vol. iv, f.266v): ". . . velocitas propria unicuique motui sequitur excessum potentiae motoris super potentiam moti . . .".
74. *De coelo*, II, comm. 36 (*ed. cit.*, vol. v, f 125v): "velocitas . . . et tarditas non sunt nisi secundum proportionem potentiae motoris ad potentiam moti".
75. Bradwardine, *ed. cit.* (ref. 7), 86, 110.
76. *Ed. cit.*, 110. Latin given at ref. 7 above.
77. *Ed. cit.*, 112.
78. *Ed. cit.*, 98.
79. *Ed. cit.*, 104.
80. *Ed. cit.*, 106.
81. See for instance Boethius, *De inst. musica*, II. 11 (*ed. cit.* in ref. 19, p. 241), and other parts of that work.
82. *Cf.* Cohen and Drabkin, *op. cit.* (ref. 34), 294–9, and Boethius, *De inst. mus.*, I.4, I.10–11, IV.1, IV.18 (*ed. cit.*, 188–91, 196–8, 301–2, 348–9).
83. Bradwardine, *ed. cit.* (ref. 7), 106–10.
84. *Nicole Oresme and the medieval geometry of qualities and motions. A treatise on the uniformity and difformity of intensities, known as Tractatus de configurationibus qualitatum et motuum*, ed. M. Clagett (Madison, 1968), 404.
85. On the tensions in Oresme *cf.* Molland, *op. cit.* (ref. 25), and my essay review of Grant's edition of the *De commensurabilitate vel incommensurabilitate motuum celi* in *British journal for the history of science*, vi (1972–73), 311–13.
86. *Cf.* Hermann Hesse, *The glass bead game (Magister ludi)*, tr. R. and C. Winston (Harmondsworth, 1972). Originally *Das Glasperlenspiel* (1943).

X

Colonizing the world for mathematics: the diversity of medieval strategies

There is nothing new about trying to make the world mathematical, and the work of Marshall Clagett in particular has shown that numerous such efforts were made in the Middle Ages. In this chapter, I shall try to get some sense of the diversity of medieval strategies by making use of the metaphors of begetting (usually parthenogenetically)* and colonizing. History cannot be forced into a straitjacket, but the rough outlines of the story are that long ago arithmetic went colonizing and begat geometry and music to rule over the new territories. Geometry later declared a considerable degree of independence from arithmetic, and also colonized on its own and begat astronomy, optics, and mechanics. In the Middle Ages all six of these tried to colonize, but little successful begetting occurred. Logic also appears as a character, but in a less clear-cut way. A recurrent theme will be the tension between holism and atomism, of the extent to which a whole may be understood in terms of a set of determinate parts.

Arithmetic I
Arithmetic must be accounted the oldest mathematical science, and it is hard to conceive of human society without an ability to count and perform simple operations of addition and subtraction, and even of multiplication and division. Again, at an early stage there must have been a need for rudimentary measurements of lengths, heights, and areas, that is to say, the expression of the size of these in numerical terms. Thus, arithmetic may be said to have given rise to geometry. By the time of the philosophical Greeks, arithmetic (in its pure state)

---

* Begetting is usually regarded as a male affair, while the mathematical sciences were traditionally female. In this chapter no sexist overtones are intended: The metaphors are loose and mixed.

was conceived of as dealing with discrete collections of abstract units. (This had the effect of meaning that fractions were not properly numbers.) From this more formal standpoint, arithmetic among the Pythagoreans was able to colonize part of the realm of sound, and so engender the science of music, because of the association of the principal musical consonances with simple whole number ratios.

Geometry I

Geometry may originally have conformed nearly to its etymological meaning of the measurement of fields, but among the Greeks a particularly pure form was developed in which it was conceived as dealing generally and abstractly with continuous quantity. With the discovery of incommensurability, it was found to be not so subservient to arithmetic as was once thought, and henceforth there was a considerable chasm between the continuous and the discrete, and geometry had to develop many of its own special methods. Nevertheless numbers could not be completely banished from geometry, and it was usually allowed that arithmetic retained a certain priority. For instance, at the beginning of his *Geometria speculativa*, Thomas Bradwardine wrote that "Geometry is subsequent to arithmetic in a certain way, for it is of posterior order, and the properties of numbers are of service in magnitudes."[1]

In Greek pure geometry the range of figures that could appear was determined by the permissible constructions, which were sometimes, as in Euclid's *Elements*, enumerated in the postulates. In the plane geometrical part of that work the only lines to appear are either straight ones or circular arcs. In works by Archimedes, Apollonius, and others the range was widened but still nowhere nearly approached the extent of variation that could be seen (at least apparently) in nature or in freehand drawing. In fact, most of the figures of Greek geometry may be regarded as built up from a series of rotations about axes.[2] To Plato it seemed that the consequent "purity" of geometry signified that its objects were not sensibly based but existed in a separate realm of mathematicals. Aristotle on the other hand insisted that the objects of geometry had no separate existence but were derived by a process of abstraction from sensible things: for him, too, the geometer was not speaking of his diagrams but of what they symbolized.[3] The separation, whether real or mental, of the objects of geometry meant that there was no guarantee that nature herself could be captured in the limited net provided by human mathematics, even in its most sophisticated forms.

Nevertheless it was part of the Greek genius to attempt the feat, and so there arose what Aristotle called "the more physical of the branches of mathematics,"[4] which in the Middle Ages were often called "middle sciences." Plato is reputed to have posed the problem: "By the assumption of what uniform and ordered motions can the apparent motions of the planets be accounted for?"[5] Whatever the truth of this may be, the question was answered by Eudoxus in terms of a series of uniformly rotating spheres. Later astronomical theories were more complicated, in order to achieve a better fit with the observed data, but in all there was the implicit assumption that the heavenly bodies behaved in ways similar to what a geometer was doing when he performed his constructions, and certainly not in a capricious or wholly unpredictable fashion. Likewise in optics, visual rays were proposed and postulated to travel in straight lines, except in certain circumstances that had to be investigated. Once again a quite good fit with observation was obtained, but there had to be the initial confidence that nature, at least in some of her parts, would succumb to mathematics. Mechanics took its starting point more in the realm of human constructs, and so needed less initial confidence. We may, however, note that whereas Aristotle said that only "lines, surfaces, bodies, and also, besides these, time and place" were, strictly speaking, continuous quantities,[6] statics also treated weight as one, and so for that matter did Aristotle himself![7] Again, although music was traditionally regarded as a child of arithmetic, it still made the crucial assumption (remarked upon below) that pitch could be treated as a continuous quantity.

Optics
In both the Neoplatonic and the Christian traditions light had for long been a potent symbol of divine causal action, but for us it is convenient to start with Robert Grosseteste's metaphysics or philosophy of light. As David C. Lindberg has pointed out, this had at least four components: epistemological; metaphysical or cosmogonical; etiological or physical; theological.[8] Only the second and third need concern us here, and they may be seen as pulling in somewhat different directions. Let us first consider Grosseteste's cosmogony. The principal source is the short treatise *De luce*, which he began as follows:

> First corporeal form, which some call corporeity, I judge to
> be light (lux), for light of itself diffuses itself in every
> direction, so that from a point of light a sphere of light as
> great as is possible (*quamvis magna*) is suddenly generated,
> unless something shady comes in the way. Corporeity is
> what the extension of matter in three dimensions necessarily
> follows, but, since each, namely corporeity and matter, is
> itself a simple substance lacking any dimension, it was
> impossible for form that was in itself simple and lacking
> dimension to induce dimension in every direction into matter
> that was similarly simple and lacking dimension, except by

multiplying itself and diffusing itself suddenly in every
direction, and in its diffusion extending matter.[9]

In this process of multiplication the matter farther from the center
became more rarefied, and multiplication was brought to a halt with a
still finite sphere as a result of matter's limited capacity for rarefaction.
The extremity of this sphere was the firmament, and Grosseteste then
proceeded to discuss the formation of the other spheres, but we may
ignore that here.

Grosseteste's scheme asserts that extension itself is a product of the
self-multiplication of light. Although the sphere produced was finite,
the multiplication had to be infinite, "for a simple thing finitely rep-
licated does not generate a quantity (*quantum*), as Aristotle shows in
De caelo et mundo, but it is necessary that it be infinitely multiplied
to generate a finite quantity."[10]

Although Grosseteste invokes the authority of Aristotle, he is in fact
adopting a profoundly un-Aristotelian position, for Aristotle was ad-
amant that continua were not composed of indivisibles, but could only
be divided into other continua which were then susceptible of similar
division in a never-ending process. The idea that continua have ultimate
components may be seen as holding out an earnest that wholes may
be fully understood in terms of their parts, an attitude more characteristic of seventeenth-century mechanism than of Aristotelian
holism.[11]

Grosseteste was by no means unique in the Middle Ages in holding
a compositionist view of continua, but his type of stance became far
more widespread in the seventeenth century. Grosseteste showed some
awareness of the type of tradition he was in when he said, with regard
to his production of quantity from the multiplication of light, that "This,
as I believe, was the understanding of the philosophers who posited
all things to be composed from atoms, and said that bodies were composed from surfaces, and surfaces from lines, and lines from points".[12]
It would be absurd to try to make Grossesteste into either an ancient
or a seventeenth-century mechanist; but his conception does at least
make the physical universe at heart more like a collection of undiffer-
entiated discrete objects, and so places a quasi-numerical structure at
the heart of physical reality. It also makes geometry once again more
subservient to arithemetic, and fittingly the treatise ends with a piece
of numerology, although this probably does not derive in any direct
way from his attitude toward continuity.

The physical side of Grosseteste's philosophy of light was more conventionally geometrical, and attempted the assimilation of a whole
range of natural effects to the laws of geometrical optics.

All causes of natural effects have to be given by lines,
angles and figures for otherwise it is impossible for the
reason why (*propter quid*) in them to be known. This is

manifest thus. A natural agent multiplies its virtue from itself right into the patient, whether it acts on sense or on matter. This virtue is sometimes called species, sometimes similitude, and it is the same whichever way it is called, and the agent will send the same into sense as into matter or a contrary, in the way it sends the same hot (*calidum*) into touch as into cold, for it does not act by deliberation or choice, and so it acts in one way whatever it meets, whether sense or something else, whether animate or inanimate, but the effects are diversified on account of the diversity of the patient.[13]

Grosseteste then proceeds to discuss in a rather sketchy way how different strengths of action result from the different orientations of the lines along which the virtues travel, and also the circumstances in which their rays are reflected or refracted.

In all this Grosseteste is not completely reducing physics to mathematics, but he does continually assert the superiority of the latter, and gives the impression that the physicist is a mere underlaborer to the mathematician, to whom belongs the privilege of providing the best *propter quid* explanations. Thus at the beginning of his treatise on the rainbow he wrote, "Consideration of the rainbow is for both the perspectivist and the physicist, but it is for the physicist to know the fact (*quid*), the perspectivist the reason why (*propter quid*), on account of which Aristotle in the book of *Meterorologica* did not set forth the reason why, which is for the perspectivist, but compressed the fact about the rainbow, which is for the physicist, into a brief discourse."[14] However, as Lindberg has emphasized, Grosseteste's actual optical knowledge was very limited,[15] and so, to an even greater extent than with many other medieval attempts at mathematization, his schemes remained merely programmatic.

Grosseteste's most important follower in essaying a generalized optics was Roger Bacon, whose faith in the potency of mathematics paralleled Grosseteste's own. "Demonstration by cause is necessarily far more powerful than demonstration by effect, and Aristole holds this in the book of *Posterior Analytics*. Therefore, since in natural things demonstration by cause is had along mathematical paths, and demonstration by effect is had along natural [philosophical] paths, the mathematician is far more powerful in relation to natural things than the natural philosopher himself."[16] But Bacon did not follow Grosseteste's philosophy of light in all its ramifications, and, in particular, omitted the cosmogonical aspect. Instead, he insisted that light was an accident and not prior to quantity.[17]

Where Bacon most enthusiastically followed Grosseteste was in the doctrine of the multiplication of species, and this he developed in far greater detail. He was particularly aided in his enterprise by having assimilated more thoroughly than had previous Latin scholars the optical theories of Alhazen, which were to dominate subsequent optics until the time of Kepler.[18] Most of Bacon's discussion of the geometry of the multiplication of species is based on optical examples, but he is insistent that the doctrine is of far wider application and essential for a proper understanding of natural effects.

> These species bring about every alteration in the world and in our bodies and souls. But, because this multiplication of species is unknown to the crowd of students, and only to three or four Latins, and that [only] in optics (*in perspectivis*), that is in the multiplication of light and colour for vision, therefore we do not perceive [as such] the wonderful actions of nature that are all day brought about in us and in things in front of our eyes, but we judge them to be brought about either by a special divine operation, or by angels, or by demons, or by chance and fortune. But it is not so, except insofar as every operation of a creature is in some way from God. But this does not preclude the operations being brought about by natural reasons, because nature is an instrument of divine operation.[19]

The heavens and the human rational soul are particularly important sources of species. The species of the former account for astrological influences, while those of the latter, especially when conjoined with appropriate heavenly influences, can produce all sorts of marvelous effects. "By this power bodies are healed, venomous animals are put to flight, brutes of all kinds are called to hand, both serpents from caves and fish from the depths of the waters."[20] In this way the doctrine of multiplication became a cornerstone in Bacon's program of naturalizing phenomena that were often accounted magical.[21]

In his major treatise on the subject, the *De multiplicatione specierum*, Bacon gives quite a detailed account of how species are actually multiplied.[22] Species of corporeal objects are of a bodily nature but are not themselves individual bodies. Instead, the individual parts of the medium are successively assimilated to the nature of the emitting object. Each part of the medium acts upon the next, in order to draw out the relevant potentiality, so that the species are transmitted rectilinearly (unless impeded) in a stepwise fashion. This has often reminded scholars of later wave theories of light, and certainly Bacon's scheme merits at least a superficial comparison with how Huygens has pulses of light transmitted from particle to particle. Also, by concentrating on individual parts of the medium and analyzing the motion into a series of discrete units, Bacon suggests how wholes may be understood in terms of their parts, and thus veers in this instance toward an atomistic stance.

Bacon's account also imbeds the mathematics of transmission firmly in the nature of physical things. This was not to be the case with a later compatriot, John Dumbleton, who pursued a long, rambling inquiry into the status of the lines, angles, and figures employed by the perspectivists, and came to the conclusion that these were mere fictions useful for predicting where an image seen, for example, by reflection, would appear.[23] Dumbleton's case may have been extreme, but Bacon's vision of mathematizing nature on the analogy of optics seems to have attracted few significant followers until the time of John Dee.[24]

Astronomy
Being made of the fifth element, the heavens behaved on radically different principles from the sublunary regions, and so astronomy had less scope for colonization than, say, optics or music. Nevertheless, it did have some influence on the ways in which a more general mathematical science could be conceived. One locus for this was the question of the status of the epicycles and eccentrics used in mathematical astronomy, a topic considered by Edward Grant in Chapter 7. Were they mere mathematical fictions useful for saving the phenomena, or did they correspond to actual orbs in the sky? These questions raised in explicit form the problem of the extent to which one was justified in holding that one's mathematical imaginings represented the actual structure of nature, and gave much scope for conflict between what I have elsewhere called realist and conceptualist attitudes on the question of the relation of mathematics to nature.[25] It is interesting to note that in this instance Roger Bacon, usually so firmly realist, seems to have wavered toward the conceptualist pole,[26] even though he held astronomy to be one of the principal reasons for the formation of geometry: "The authors of perspective show us that lines and figures declare the whole operation of nature, its principles and effects, and this is similarly evident through celestial things, which are considered by both natural philosophy and astronomy."[27]

One writer who emphatically asserted the real existence of epicycles was Nicole Oresme, who went on to suggest that angels or intelligences may not be needed for moving the heavens, and in doing so, invoked a memorable mechanical analogy:

> Perhaps, when God created [the heavens], he placed in them motive qualities and virtues, just as he placed weight in terrestrial things, and placed in them resistances against these motive virtues. And these virtues and resistances are of another nature and matter from any sensible thing or quality that is here below. And the virtues are moderated, tempered and harmonised against the resistances, so that the movements are made without violence. And, except for the

X

52

> violence, this is in some way similar to when a man has
> made a clock, and leaves it to go and be moved by itself; so
> did God leave the heavens to be moved continually
> according to the ratios that the motive virtues have to the
> resistances, and according to the established decree.[28]

This image can suggest that similar mathematical laws may apply both to the celestial regions and to sublunary machines. This could in turn open the prospect of mathematizing the sublunary world by treating it mechanically.[29] Also, John Buridan's suggested extension of impetus to the heavens[30] could invite a closer connection between celestial and sublunary motion, and hold out the promise of making the latter more precisely mathematical.

Mechanics

For the Middle Ages we must understand this as confined essentially to statics and hydrostatics, and not yet as extending to considerations of motion. Although there was a vigorous tradition, deriving largely from treatises associated with the name of the enigmatic[31] Jordanus de Nemore, this science effected little colonizing in the Middle Ages, despite Nicolaus Cusanus's enthusiastic encomia of weight as a means of getting experimental and quantitative knowledge of a whole range of phenomena.[32] Much of the trouble arose from the fact that in the Aristotelian tradition, weight was a concept lacking in independence and almost always had to be considered in conjunction with its contrary lightness. Pure elemental fire was absolutely light, and pure elemental earth was absolutely heavy, but in all sublunary bodies there was a mixture of elements, and so a warring combination of weight and lightness. That this did not preclude mathematization is shown by quite a striking passage in which Bradwardine applied his law of motion to the conception.

> All mixed bodies of similar composition will be moved with
> equal speed in a vacuum, for in all such the movers are
> proportional to the resistances. Therefore by the first
> conclusion of this chapter, all such will be moved equally
> swiftly. From this also you will know that, if two unequal
> mixed heavy bodies of similar composition are suspended in
> a balance in a vacuum, the heavier will go down, for let A
> and B be two such heavy bodies, A greater and B less, and
> let C be the heaviness (*gravitas*) of A, and D similarly the
> lightness of the same. Let E be the heaviness of B, and F
> the lightness of the same. Then C, D, E, F are four
> proportionals, and C is the greatest, F the least. Therefore,
> by the eighth supposition of the first chapter, C and F
> gathered together exceed D and E brought together. And C

> and *F* strive to raise B, and only D and E resist. Therefore,
> by the second part of the ninth conclusion, B will ascend,
> and A descend.[33]

The second part of this passage makes it clear that, while a mathematical statics on these assumptions is possible, it will be considerably more complicated than ordinary statics.

Bradwardine's earlier conclusion, that bodies of similar composition would fall equally swiftly in a vacuum, can look notably "modern," but its very modernity made it unacceptable to even such a figure as Nicole Oresme.

> I suppose that the speed of a motion is according to the
> ratio of the motive virtue to the resistance, and hence, if
> these ratios are equal in two moved bodies, they will be
> moved with equal speeds. Then I take, for example, two
> bodies of fine silver of which one is quadruple the other in
> size (*qualité*), and I posit that in the smaller one the heavy
> (*pesans*) elements with regard to the light ones are as 6 to 1,
> and then in the big one, which is of a similar mixture, they
> will be as 24 to 4, which is such a ratio as 6 to 1. And then,
> by the supposition made above, the small and the big will be
> moved downwards with the same speed, if other things are
> equal, and consequently the two bodies weigh equally, and
> this is manifestly false. Therefore elements are not in their
> proper form in mixed bodies.[34]

Oresme's conclusion, that elements change their forms when entering into mixtures, effectively rules out the possibility of mathematizing heaviness and lightness. Ironically, among the culprits in backing up the Aristotelian association of weight with speed of descent was the Jordanus statical tradition, where we meet the postulate "That which is heavier descends more rapidly," and the conclusion "Among any heavy bodies, the ratio of speed in descending and weight, taken in the same order, is the same . . . ," although Bradwardine held that the latter was being misinterpreted.[35]

Music

According to Aristotle, the Pythagorean association of number with music was a potent factor in making them extrapolate and hold "the whole heaven to be a musical scale and a number."[36] In so doing they introduced the seductive doctrine of the music of the spheres. Aristotle admitted the seductiveness, but rejected the theory. Boethius, on the other hand, regarded this type of *musica mundana* as very important, and there had also been hints of it in Plato's *Timaeus*.[37] Thus, in the twelfth century, before the translation of Aristotle's *De caelo*, it had reasonable authority, although it was by no means clear what the actual quantities were that the musical ratios were between. Even later, Aristotle's criticisms did not completely destroy the doctrine, for it could be held that the music was not perceptible to the senses but of an intellectual nature. This was basically the strategy of Nicole Oresme, who, after providing a substantial discussion of what sorts of ratios might be involved and how, went on to affirm a close relationship between human, celestial, and divine music.[38] But, even though he went into some detail, Oresme did little to try and tie the doctrine in with the theories of mathematical astronomy. Kepler was probably the first to take that task seriously.

Plato, in the *Timaeus*, provided further intimations of musical structure in the world in his accounts of the bonding of elements and of the formation of the World Soul,[39] but his expression was laconic in the extreme and very difficult to interpret precisely, and in any case the influence of the *Timaeus* declined dramatically after the twelfth century. I therefore move to a less obvious but arguably more significant example of musical influence to be found in a fourteenth-century work, the *Tractatus de proportionibus* of Thomas Bradwardine.[40]

This work contains his by now famous proposal for a quantitative law of motion, which, translated literally, reads: "The ratio of speeds in motion follows the ratio of the power of the mover to the power of the thing moved."[41] In seeking to establish his own position, Bradwardine examined and rejected four other positions, the last of which is the following: "There is no ratio nor any excess of motive power to resistive power, and so the ratio of speeds in motions does not follow any ratio or excess of motive power to power of the mobile, but a certain dominion and natural relation of mover to moved."[42] The nub of this is to assert that powers, not being quantities, cannot properly be compared quantitatively, and so the search for any mathematical relation between them is otiose. Bradwardine's opening objection to the position is the following:

> If there were no ratio between powers on account of their not being quantities, there would not be a ratio between sounds, and then the whole modulation of music would perish, for the *epogdous* or tone consists in a sesquioctaval ratio, the *diatesseron* in a sesquitertial, the *diapente* in a sesquialteral, the *diapason*, which is composed from *diatesseron* and *diapente*, in a double, *diapson cum diapente* in a triple, and *bis diapason* in a quadruple ratio.[43]

Although music was regarded as subordinate to arithmetic, Bradwardine's argument points out that it also includes an implicit quantification of pitch in the manner of a continuous quantity. And if pitch, then why not powers? The very existence of music as a mathematical science thus gave confidence in the possibility of extending mathematics' domain.

But there was also, I would maintain, a linguistic influence from music that allowed Bradwardine to formulate the law in the way he did. The law, as quoted above, appears very simple in expression, but modern writers have often spoken of its logarithmic or exponential nature. The paradox depends on a shift in mathematical language. In the ancient Greek and medieval mathematical traditions there is quite frequent talk of compounding ratios together.[44] If A is greater than B and B greater than C, the result of compounding the ratio of A to B with that of B to C was the ratio of A to C. Our natural tendency is to interpret this as multiplication, and this was sometimes done in the Middle Ages. However, in musical works, such as that by Boethius, it was regularly regarded as addition. This was fairly natural, since ratios corresponded to intervals, and compounding ratios corresponded to combining intervals, or adding them together.

For long this interpretation of compounding ratios remained unobtrusive and innocent, but Bradwardine and later Nicole Oresme developed its consequences in an extensive and systematic manner. For instance, doubling a ratio now corresponded to what we would call squaring a fraction, and halving it to taking a square root. If we symbolize Bradwardine's law itself by saying that it asserts that V (speed) is proportional to the ratio of F (power of the mover) to R (power of the thing moved), then in modern terms this translates into V being proportional to the logarithm of F/R. This translation in itself suggests what a potent weapon was available for creating a rich mathematical account of the natural world, and this promise was well borne out in the work of such figures as Richard Swineshead, even though the mathematical physics thus created had very vague empirical reference.

Arithmetic II

The one area of direct medieval colonizing by arithmetic that I shall consider is numerology. To us this can seem one of the most baseless of traditional superstitions, but when the world was conceived to contain determinate numbers of things of the same kind (four elements, seven planets, etc.) and was also thought of as the product of design, it was perfectly reasonable to seek a rationale for the particular numbers chosen. As Boethius said,

> All things whatsoever that were fabricated from the first age
> of nature seem to have been formed on the rationale of
> numbers, for this was the principal exemplar in the mind of
> the framer, for hence is obtained the number of the four

X

56

elements, hence the succession of times, hence the motion of the stars and revolution of the heavens.[45]

Aristotle attacked the arithmeticism of the Pythagoreans, but still gave a numerological explanation for there being just three dimensions:

> For, as the Pythagoreans say, the world and all that is it is determined by the number three, since beginning and middle and end give the number of an 'all,' and the number they give is the triad. And so, having taken these things from nature as (so to speak) laws of it, we make further use of the number three in the worship of the Gods.[46]

The peculiar position of this number was further enhanced with the advent of the Christian doctrine of the Trinity, but, despite the abundance of numerology in medieval theological and devotional literature, it made curiously little impact on the major works of natural philosophy.[47] That was to be far more a Renaissance trait, exemplified in profusion in works such as Henry Cornelius Agrippa's *De occulta philosophia*.[48]

Geometry II

An obvious starting point for seeking direct geometrical colonizing would seem to be Plato's theory of geometrical atomism.[49] In this, four of the five regular solids gave their shapes to the small particles of the four elements, while the fifth, the dodecahedron, was in a vaguer way assigned to the "whole." If accepted, Plato's theory would surely have given great confidence in the possibility of mathematical science, for it promised that from the smallest parts outward, nature was mathematically designed. But this was not to be. Aristotle launched a vigorous attack on the theory,[50] and Plato's own account was not included in Chalcidius's incomplete Latin translation of the *Timaeus*. Thus the main source of medieval knowledge of the theory was Aristotle's criticism, and this was universally or almost universally accepted, either tacitly or, in such writers as Albertus Magnus, with delight.[51] More effort was spent in considering a mathematical difficulty that arose from Aristotle's criticisms, about filling space with regular polyhedra.[52]

Far more mileage can be obtained by considering the geometrization of qualities, a subject that has received great attention in recent years.[53] For Aristotle, "A quantity does not seem to admit of a more and a less. Four-foot for example: one thing is not more four-foot than another."[54] Moreover, unlike the term "four-foot," "'large' or 'small' does not signify a quantity but rather a relative."[55] On the other hand, "Qualifications [but, it turns out, not all of them] admit of a more and a less; for one thing is called more pale or less pale than another, and more just than another."[56] In all this Aristotle seems to be making a

big gap between quantities and qualities, but in fact it was the ability
of qualities to admit a more and a less, to be intended and remitted,
that opened the way for their quantification, for there is a strong temptation to ask, "How much more?" or "How much less?" This happened at an early stage in the pharmacological tradition, and Roger
Bacon explicitly used a straight line to represent the range of intensities
of, say, heat in a drug.[57]

In the natural philosophical tradition the ontological problems associated with intension and remission had received considerable attention from thirteenth-century thinkers, but in the fourteenth century
there was a tendency to emphasize the logical and quantitative aspects
of the question,[58] and with this we regularly find ranges of intensity
being assimilated to straight lines. This tendency reached its zenith in
Nicole Oresme's *De configurationibus qualitatum et motuum*, which
attempts a thoroughgoing mathematization of the world. In Oresme's
conception the degree of intensity of a quality at each point of a subject
was represented by a perpendicular proportional in length to the degree
of intensity at that point. In the case of a linear subject this resulted
in a sort of graph, and in a two-dimensional subject, a relief map. For
a body one should by analogy have a four-dimensional figure. This
option was not available to Oresme, and so he settled for, as it were,
superimposed relief maps. In this way he was postulating how the entire
qualitative makeup of a body may be mathematically represented. But
he did not stop with mere representations: His configurations were
meant to have explanatory power in a way similar to ancient atomism.

> It is manifest that bodies have different powers (*diversimode
> potest*) in their actions according to the difference of their
> figures, on account of which the ancients who maintained
> that bodies were composed of atoms said that the atoms of
> fire were pyramidal on account of its vigorous activity.
> Thus, according to the difference in the pyramids, bodies
> can pierce more or less, and, according to this or that
> sharpness, it is certain that they can cut more or less
> strongly, and so for other actions and figures. And, since it
> is thus for the figures of bodies, it seems reasonable for it to
> be able to be spoken conformably about the aforesaid
> figurations of qualities, so that there is a quality whose
> particles are proportional in intensity to small pyramids, and
> on account of this it is more active, other things being equal,
> than an equal quality that was either simply uniform or
> proportional to another, not so penetrating, figure. Or, if
> there were two qualities of which the one's particles were
> proportional to sharper pyramids than the other's particles,
> the quality that corresponded to the sharper pyramids

would, other things being equal, be more active, and
similarly for other figures.[59]

In this Oresme is appealing to mathematics to provide *propter quid* explanations, and proposing the formation of a science of qualities that would be subalternate to geometry. Although he did not develop it much, a particularly important area of application of the doctrine was in the explanation of occult virtues,[60] those properties of things that did not follow directly from their elemental constitution, and hence often seemed brute facts, incapable of being rendered fully intelligible. Oresme's suggestion was that, if the configurations of the qualities be taken into consideration as well as the ratios, then the virtues succumb to a mathematical rationale. In this he may be compared directly with Descartes, who held it to be a major benefit of his mechanical philosophy that it showed the way to discovering the causes of the "wonderful effects that are usually referred to occult qualities."[61] A major difference between the two is that, although Descartes's mechanistic explanations are often fantastical, he stuck to his program tenaciously, whereas Oresme showed far less confidence in the possibility of grounding his doctrine empirically, and may ultimately have abandoned it.[62] The urge to beget a new middle science was strong, but the territory did not seem sufficiently subdued.

We may also use Oresme as preeminently representative of the general geometrization of motion.[63] Oresme treated motions analogously with qualities, and held that "intensity of speed" was to be graphed over both time and the parts of the moving body. This and the work of related writers, notably the Mertonians, can suggest that there were being developed sophisticated techniques for dealing with "instantaneous velocity," thus putting the fourteenth century well on the way to the seventeenth. I have argued elsewhere that there is a very real sense in which these thinkers can be seen as occupying a halfway house between Aristotle and the likes of Galileo,[64] but it is important to recognize how different was their approach from that of their seventeenth-century successors, a difference that largely arose from their holistic attitudes. In the seventeenth century there was a strong tendency to regard motions as being built up from the instantaneous velocities of individual mass points, but in the Middle Ages the primary focus was on the whole motion of the whole body, from the beginning to the end. This resulted in treating speed as something like a five-dimensional object, as is at least apparent from an otherwise not very clear passage from Oresme:

There is a twofold difformity of speed, subjective and
temporal, which, as regards the purpose in hand, differ in
this, that subjective punctual speed, just like punctual
quality is to be imagined by a straight line, and linear

> subjective speed is to be imagined by a surface or superficial
> figure, but the speed of a surface is to be imagined by a
> body, and similarly the speed of a body by a body, entirely
> in the same way as was said about the figuration of
> qualities. . . . But instantaneous punctual speed is imagined
> by a straight line, and temporal punctual speed is to be
> imagined by a surface, but the temporal speed of a line is
> imagined by a body, and similarly superficial and corporeal
> [speeds] are imagined by a body because there is not
> available (*non contingit dare*) a fourth dimension, as was
> said [above].[65]

This conception can easily cause problems in comparing motions together. The so-called Merton Rule, which equates a uniformly difform
motion with a uniform motion, follows from a simple equation of areas,
but a similar equation leads to Oresme's assertion that "A uniform
speed that lasts for three days is equal (*est equalis*) to a speed three
times as intense that lasts for one day,"[66] contrary to one's intuitive
understanding of what it is to be speedy.

Moreover, even the concept of intensity of speed is not as unambiguously quantified as one might have expected. Oresme held that
intensity of speed was to be measured by the amount of the particular
"perfection" that was being gained or lost as a result of the motion.
"I say therefore that universally that degree of speed is unqualifiedly
more intense or greater at which in an equal time there is gained or
lost more of that perfection following (*secundum*) which the motion is
made."[67] But this means that intensity of speed can depend on how
the perfection is described. For instance, in a rectilinear motion of
descent:

> The speed of motion is measured by the space traversed,
> but the speed of descent by nearness to the centre. Thus it
> is possible that A and B be moved equally swiftly but not
> descend equally swiftly, in that A is moved along a direct
> line to the centre and B along an oblique line, and so A
> descends more swiftly than B, and yet B is moved equally
> swiftly. Similarly, since descent is measured by the ratio of
> nearness to the centre, it happens that what is moved
> uniformly or regularly along a direct line from the centre
> descends difformly, because it nears the centre more swiftly
> when near than when far away, but with there always
> remaining an equal speed of motion.[68]

In similar circumstances Richard Swineshead would try to deploy the
resources of rational argument in order to determine which was the
correct quantification, but Oresme was more inclined to revel in the
multiplicity of possibilities. "According to the multiple denominations,

speed is multiply varied or denominated.''[69] In this way it can often seem that it is language rather than nature that is being quantified, and so despite the intensity of his geometrical vision, mathematics can for Oresme remain very much on the surface of things.

Oresme spoke of his graphical representations as imaginations. This was appropriate, for in the Middle Ages there was a close association between geometry and the imagination, since it was in the imaginative faculty that geometrical objects were ''viewed.'' Moreover, the imagination was often associated with the positing, contrary to Aristotle, of an infinite space outside the heavens, and such a space was often referred to as imaginary, not in order to deny its existence but to assert that it was pictured in the imagination.[70] The two themes were brought together by Henry of Ghent, who distrusted the imagination, and described some of his opponents as

> those of whom the Commentator says that in them the imaginative virtue dominates over the cognitive virtue, and so, as he says, they do not believe demonstrations unless the imagination accompanies them, for they cannot believe that there is neither plenum nor vacuum nor time outside the world, nor can they believe that there are here non-corporeal beings that are neither in place nor in time. They cannot believe the first because their imagination does not stop in finite quantity, and so mathematical imaginations and what is outside the heaven seem to them infinite. But in this it is not right to believe the imagination. . . . Therefore such people are melancholy and make the best mathematicians, but the worst metaphysicians, because they cannot extend their understanding beyond site and magnitude, on which mathematicals are founded . . . , and they make inept natural philosophers.[71]

With this connection it should not surprise us that two of the most notable fourteenth-century proponents of an infinite space were the mathematicians Thomas Bradwardine and Nicole Oresme; and I have suggested elsewhere that geometrical exigencies were a major factor in bringing Bradwardine to this view, even if theological considerations have to be given at least equal weight.[72] In both the doctrine of configurations and in the assertion of infinite space we seem to have clear examples of how imaginative representations of the world can affect one's view of the actual constitution of the world – in these instances casting it in a geometrical mode.

Logic

This section needs to be included, but it must either be very long or very short. The former option would involve a disproportionate amount of space and lengthy time for research and reflection, and so it has to be the latter. The reason logic has to be considered is that in important fourteenth-century traditions of natural philosophy the urge to mathematize was inextricably bound up with what later ages would regard as the most futile of logic-chopping exercises – *quisquiliae* in the typical humanist view of Richard Swineshead. The context must be seen as the scholastic disputation, where one had to use logical, and especially dialectical, techniques to examine an opponent's arguments. At first there was little mathematics involved, but with the fourteenth-century tendency to move from ontological issues to descriptive ones, which were usually concerned with things that were in principle more accessible to the senses, the question "How much?" more and more frequently raised its head. Not that the Schoolmen went out and empirically measured things, but they did give much attention to the theory of how things that were not directly measurable, such as speeds or intensities of qualities (cf. above, under "Geometry II") should be quantified and "denominated." Such contexts could often give rise to quite complicated logico-mathematical arguments,[73] but if one tries to make diagrams of their forms, one often finds the need to see certain propositions as reinforcing the arrows that represent the passage from one assertion to another.[74] Dialectic has infiltrated into the demonstrative arguments that are normally characteristic of mathematics, and this is one reason for approving of Leibniz's description of the tradition as "semi-mathematical."[75] In the work of a Swineshead or an Oresme one can feel that knowledge is very much the aim, but in a text such as Themo Judei's "Question on the Motion of the Moon," one can easily wonder whether one is not descending simply into sophisticated sophistry.[76]

Afterword

The seventeenth century saw the world mathematized in a far more effective way than had the Middle Ages. The process involved many people, but among the most outstanding were Galileo and Descartes. From his Pisan days onward, Galileo had been strongly influenced by "the superhuman Archimedes, whose name I never mention without a feeling of awe."[77] The researches of Marshall Clagett have amply demonstrated the extent of Archimedes' penetration into the Middle Ages, but they also serve to highlight how in the sixteenth century there arose a far greater tendency not only to admire Archimedes and invoke his authority, but to emulate him and advance beyond what he had achieved.[78] It was the tradition of mechanics, with its statical and hydrostatical works, that was most influential on Galileo. However, as we have seen, mechanics did little colonizing in the Middle Ages. This helps to explain how it was that in the seventeenth

62

century the mathematization of the world picture was intimately bound up with its mechanization.[79]

Complementary to the Archimedean influence was the emphasis on experimentation. This is not the place to investigate the precise role that experiments played in Galileo's achievement, but only to note how Galileo was wont to present his quantities in such a way that one could see how at least in principle they were empirically measurable. Cannonballs may not have followed his theoretical parabolic trajectory exactly, but at least this curve could be compared with their actual paths in a more direct and precise way than could, for example, Bradwardine's law be tested against nature.[80]

Descartes wrote that Galileo "only sought the reasons of certain particular effects without having considered the first causes of nature, and so built without foundation."[81] There is some justice in this stricture (if so it should be described), and at the ontological level, at least, Descartes was the more radical thinker. His program involved seeing extension as the only essential property of matter, and so virtually identifying matter and space. He was thus able to claim to Mersenne that his physics was nothing but geometry,[82] although he did notably little technical geometry within the context of his natural philosophy. Descartes's strategy is basically a wholesale and direct colonization by geometry, but even here mechanics played a substantial part, for the imagination of mechanical instruments formed an essential part of Descartes's conception of geometry, and his mathematization of natural philosophy was abetted by comparisons of animals, and so on, with mechanical automata.

In the Middle Ages optics and music made considerable efforts to increase their territory, but in the seventeenth century they were far overtaken by mechanics, although Kepler allowed them to flex their muscles in his celestial physics, and even Newton contemplated a musical theory of colors.[83] Nevertheless, in order to see them make significant and lasting inroads, we probably have to wait for the theory of electromagnetic waves and for wave mechanics.

Notes

1 A. G. Molland, "The Geometria Speculativa of Thomas Bradwardine: Text with Critical Discussion" (Ph.D. dissertation, Cambridge University, 1967), 59.

2 Cf. A. G. Molland, "Shifting the Foundations: Descartes's Transformation of Ancient Geometry," *Historia Mathematica* 3 (1976):25–27.

3 *Anal. Post.* I.10.76b40–77a3.

4 Aristotle, *Physics* II.2.194a7–8.

5 M. R. Cohen and I. E. Drabkin, *A Source Book in Greek Science* (Cambridge, Mass.: Harvard University Press, 1948), 97.

6 Aristotle, *Categories* 6. 4b22–23, 5a38–39.

7 For example, in *Phys.* IV.8.

8 D. C. Lindberg, *Theories of Vision from al-Kindi to Kepler* (Chicago: University of Chicago Press), 1976. Cf. Lindberg, "On the Applicability of Mathematics to Nature: Roger Bacon and his Predecessors," *British Journal for the History of Science* 15 (1982):12.

9 *Die philosophischen Werke des Robert Grosseteste, Bischofs von Lincoln*, ed. L. Baur. Beiträge zur Geschichte der Philosophie des Mittelalters, IX (Münster: Aschendorff, 1912), 51.

10 Ibid., 52.

11 Cf. A. G. Molland, "The Atomisation of Motion: A Facet of the Scientific Revolution," *Studies in History and Philosophy of Science* 13 (1982):31–54.

12 Grosseteste, *Philosophischen Werke*, ed. Baur, 53–54.

13 Ibid., 60.

14 Ibid., 72.

15 Lindberg, *Theories of Vision*, 94–102.

16 *The "Opus Maius" of Roger Bacon*, ed. J. H. Bridges (Oxford, 1897–1900; repr. Frankfurt, 1964), I, 188–189.

17 *Roger Bacon's Philosophy of Nature: A Critical Edition, with English Translation, Introduction, and Notes, of De multiplicatione specierum and De speculis comburentibus*, ed. D. C. Lindberg (Oxford: Clarendon Press, 1983), 14; *Opera hactenus inedita Rogeri Baconi*, ed. R. Steele et al. (Oxford: Clarendon Press, 1905–40), XVI, 62–63.

18 Cf. Lindberg, *Theories of Vision*, 107–116.

19 *Fr. Rogeri Bacon Opera quaedam hactenus inedita*, ed. J. S. Brewer (London, 1859; repr. Kraus Reprint, 1965), I, 99–100.

20 Bacon, *The "Opus Maius,"* I, 395.

21 Cf. A. G. Molland, "Roger Bacon: Magic and the Multiplication of Species," *Paideia*, forthcoming.

22 Bacon, *De multiplicatione*, ed. Lindberg, passim.

23 A. G. Molland, "John Dumbleton and the Status of Geometrical Optics," *Actes du XIIIe Congrès International d'Histoire des Sciences* (Moscow: Nauka, 1974), III–IV, 125–130.

24 *John Dee on Astronomy: Propaedeumata Aphoristica (1558 and 1568)*, ed. and tr. Wayne Shumaker, int. J. L. Heilbron (Berkeley: University of California Press, 1978); N. H. Clulee, "Astrology, Magic, and Optics: Facets of John Dee's Early Natural Philosophy," *Renaissance Quarterly* 30 (1977):632–680.

25 A. G. Molland, "An Examination of Bradwardine's Geometry," *Archive for History of Exact Sciences* 19 (1978):131, and "Mathematics in the Thought of Albertus Magnus," in *Albertus Magnus and the Sciences*, ed. James A. Weisheipl (Toronto: Pontifical Institute of Mediaeval Studies, 1980), 467.

26 Cf. P. Duhem, *To Save the Phenomena*, tr. E. Doland and C. Maschler (Chicago: University of Chicago Press, 1969), 38–40, and Grant's Chapter 7 in this volume.

27 MS Oxford, Bodleian, Digby 76, fol. 78ar: "Auctores enim perspective nobis ostendunt quod linee et figure declarant nobis totam operationem nature, et principia et effectus, et similiter patet per celestia, de quibus naturalis et astronomia communicant." Fols. 69r–79r of this manuscript contain some geometrical writing following immediately after a version of Bacon's *Communia mathematica* (edited by Steele in Bacon, *Opera*

hactenus inedita, XVI). I have little doubt about Bacon's authorship of these unpublished passages, and hope soon to publish an edition of them.

28 Nicole Oresme, *Le livre du ciel et du monde*, ed. A. D. Menut and A. J. Denomy (Madison: University of Wisconsin Press, 1968), 288. The clock image is not original to Oresme, but goes back at least to Cicero *De natura deorum* 2.34–38; cf. Oresme, *Livre du ciel*, 282.

29 For a suggestive study of the relationship between clocks and other automata on the one hand and mechanical philosophy on the other, see D. J. de Solla Price, "Automata and the Origins of Mechanism and Mechanistic Philosophy," *Technology and Culture* 5 (1964):9–23.

30 Iohannes Buridanus, *Quaestiones super libris quattuor de caelo et mundo*, ed. E. A. Moody (Cambridge, Mass.: The Mediaeval Academy of America, 1942), 180–181; cf. M. Clagett, *The Science of Mechanics in the Middle Ages* (Madison: University of Wisconsin Press, 1959), 524–525.

31 Cf. A. G. Molland, "Ancestors of Physics," *History of Science* 14 (1976):64–67, and M. Clagett, *Archimedes in the Middle Ages* (Madison: University of Wisconsin Press, 1964; Philadelphia: American Philosophical Society, 1976–1984), V, 145–146.

32 *Idiota de staticis experimentis*, in Nicolaus de Cusa, *Opera omnia* V, (Hamburg: Felix Meiner, 1983), 219–241.

33 Thomas Bradwardine, *Tractatus de proportionibus*, ed. H. L. Crosby (Madison: University of Wisconsin Press, 1955), 116.

34 Oresme, *Livre du ciel*, 670.

35 E. A. Moody and M. Clagett, *The Medieval Science of Weights* (Madison: University of Wisconsin Press, 1952), 128, 154, 174. Cf. Bradwardine, *Tractatus de proportionibus*, 100–104.

36 *Metaph.* A5. 986a2–3; cf. *De caelo* II.9.290b12–291a27.

37 Boethius, *De institutione arithmetica libri duo. De institutione musica libri quinque . . .* , ed. G. Friedlein (Leipzig, 1867; repr. Frankfurt: Minerva, 1966), 187–188; *Timaeus* 36D.

38 Oresme, *Livre du ciel*, 476–486.

39 *Timaeus* 31b–32C, 35B–36B.

40 On what follows, cf. Molland, "Ancestors of Physics," 67–70.

41 Bradwardine, *Tractatus de proportionibus*, 110.

42 Ibid., 104.

43 Ibid., 106.

44 On all this, cf. Molland, "Examination of Bradwardine's Geometry," 150–160, and E. D. Sylla, "Compounding Ratios: Bradwardine, Oresme and the First Edition of Newton's *Principia*," *Transformation and Tradition in the Sciences*, ed. E. Mendelsohn (Cambridge: Cambridge University Press, 1984), 11–43.

45 Boethius, *De institutione arithmetica*, p. 12.

46 *De caelo* I.1.268a11–16.

47 Cf. V. F. Hopper, *Mediaeval Number Symbolism* (New York: Columbia University Press, 1938; repr. New York: Cooper Square, 1969).

48 Cf. A. G. Molland, "Cornelius Agrippa's Mathematical Magic," forthcoming in a volume edited by C. Hay.

49 *Timaeus* 53C–56C.

50 *De caelo* III.8.306b3–307b23.

51 Cf. Molland, "Mathematics in the Thought of Albertus Magnus," 474–475.

52 Molland, "Examination of Bradwardine's Geometry," 170–174.

53 See, for instance, A. Maier, *An der Grenze von Scholastik und*

Naturwissenschaft (Rome, 1952), 255–384; *Nicole Oresme and the Medieval Geometry of Qualities and Motions. A Treatise on the Uniformity and Difformity of Intensities, known as Tractatus de configurationibus qualitatum et motuum*, ed. M. Clagett (Madison: University of Wisconsin Press, 1968); E. Sylla, "Medieval Quantification of Qualities: The Merton School," *Archive for History of Exact Sciences* 8 (1971):9–39.

54 *Cat.* 6.6a19–20.
55 *Cat.* 6.5b27–28.
56 *Cat.* 8.10b26–27.
57 *Opera hactenus inedita*, IX, 144–149. Clagett, *The Science of Mechanics*, 334, doubts the authenticity of the ascription of this work to Bacon.
58 Cf. A. Maier, *Zwei Grundprobleme der scholastischen Naturphilosophie*, 3rd ed. (Rome: Edizioni di Storia e Letteratura, 1968), 74–109.
59 Oresme, *De configurationibus*, 226.
60 Ibid., 234–238. Cf. A. G. Molland, "The Oresmian Style: Semi-Mathematical but also Semi-Holistic," *Université de Nice, Cahiers du Séminaire d'Epistémologie et d'Histoire des Sciences* 18 (1985):7–12. A fuller version of this paper is scheduled to appear in a volume edited by P. Souffrin.
61 *Principia philosophiae* IV.187, in *Oeuvres de Descartes*, ed. C. Adam and P. Tannery (Paris, 1897–1913), vol. 8, pt. 1, p. 314.
62 Cf. A. G. Molland, "Nicole Oresme and Scientific Progress," *Miscellanea Mediaevalia* 9 (1974):213.
63 On what follows, cf. Molland, "Atomisation of Motion."
64 Molland, "The Oresmian Style."
65 Oresme, *De configurationibus*, 292.
66 Ibid., 406.
67 Ibid., 276.
68 Ibid., 278.
69 Ibid., 280.
70 On medieval theories of infinite space, see especially E. Grant, *Much Ado about Nothing: Theories of Space and Vacuum from the Middle Ages to the Scientific Revolution* (Cambridge: Cambridge University Press, 1981), chap. 6.
71 Quodlibet II, questio 9, in *Quodlibeta Magistri Henrici Goethals a Gandavo Doctoris Solemnis* (Paris, 1518), fol. 36r.
72 Molland, "Examination of Bradwardine's Geometry," 132–136.
73 Cf. A. G. Molland, "Richard Swineshead and Continuously Varying Quantities," *Actes du XIIe Congrès International d' Histoire des Sciences* (Paris, 1971), 127–130.
74 Cf. Molland, "Examination of Bradwardine's Geometry," 147–148.
75 *Leibnizens mathematische Schriften*, ed. C. I. Gerhardt (Halle, 1849–63). Erste Abtheilung, IV, 13–14.
76 H. Hugonnard-Roche, *L'Oeuvre astronomique de Themon Juif* (Geneva: Minard, 1973), 251–411. Cf. my review in *Journal for the History of Astronomy* 7 (1976):68–69, where I remark on Themo's delight in displaying intellectual pyrotechnics, to the possible detriment of a disinterested search for knowledge.
77 *Le opere di Galileo Galilei. Nuova ristampa della edizione nazionale* (Florence: Barbera, 1968), I, 300; Galileo Galilei, *On Motion and on Mechanics*, tr. I. E. Drabkin and S. Drake (Madison: University of Wisconsin Press, 1960), 67.

78 Cf. A. G. Molland, "Archimedean Fortunes," *History of Science* 19 (1981):143–147.
79 The phraseology is from the title of E. J. Dijksterhuis, *The Mechanization of the World Picture* (Oxford: Clarendon Press, 1961).
80 Cf. A. R. Hall, *Ballistics in the Seventeenth Century* (Cambridge: Cambridge University Press, 1952), 79–101, and M. Segre, "Torricelli's Correspondence on Ballistics," *Annals of Science* 40 (1983):489–499.
81 *Oeuvres de Descartes*, II, 380.
82 Ibid., II, 268.
83 *The Optical Papers of Isaac Newton*, ed. A. E. Shapiro (Cambridge: Cambridge University Press, 1984–), I, 544–547; I. Newton, *Opticks* (New York: Dover, 1952), 154, 225.

XI

ROGER BACON AS MAGICIAN*

The practice of magic was much in vogue in the Renaissance and even the word had gained a limited respectability. Thus in 1558 when Giambattista della Porta published his collection of curiosities of art and nature he did so under the title *Magia naturalis*, and even in the next century the far more sober Bishop John Wilkins was to publish a book entitled *Mathematicall Magick*.[1] Such works indicate essential similarities between magic and science in that each has as part of its aim the application of not readily apparent knowledge to practice. But we should not think that the widespread acceptance of natural magic in the Renaissance meant that the term had become a synonym for what we should now call science,[2] for we still have to bear in mind such pictures as those of Marsilio Ficino chanting his Orphic hymns,[3] of John Dee conversing with spirits through his medium Edward Kelly,[4] and of Tommaso Campanella and Pope Urban VIII closeted together and performing secret rites to ward off the plague.[5]

Writers on various types of magic were wont to look back to earlier workers in the tradition. Foremost among these were the supposed ancient practitioners of *prisca magia* such as Zoroaster, Orpheus, Pythagoras, Plato, and Hermes Trismegistus, but there is at times mention of more modern figures. Thus in his *Apologia* of 1487 Pico della Mirandola listed Alkindi, Roger Bacon, and William of Auvergne as *iuniores* who had detected the nature of good non-demonic magic.[6] These names are often repeated, together with those of such

---

* For helpful advice and criticism at various stages in the preparation of this paper I should like to thank especially Dr. N. W. Fisher, Dr. R. K. French, Dr. C. H. Lohr, the late Professor J. M. Lothian, Mr. M. P. McDiarmid, Professor J. E. McGuire, Dr. J. N. Mattock, and Dr. M. J. W. Pittock.

[1] First ed. 1648; republished in J. Wilkins, *The Mathematical and Philosophical Works* (Reprint of 2nd ed.; London 1970) II 89-246.

[2] D. P. Walker, *Spiritual and Demonic Magic from Ficino to Campenella* (London 1958) 75-76, writes, 'The activities designated by the term natural magic all had a strong tendency to become indistinguishable from some other activity more properly called by another name; magic was always on the point of turning into art, science, practical psychology, or, above all, religion.'

[3] Walker, *op. cit.* 12-24.

[4] See e.g., the article on Dee in *Biographia Britannica* III (London 1750) 1633-45.

[5] Walker, *op. cit.* 205-210.

[6] G. & G. F. Pico della Mirandola, *Opera quae extant omnia* (Basel 1601) I 80-81. Cf. G.

Reprinted by permission from *Traditio* 30 (1947), 445–60, Fordham University Press, New York.

446

other medieval figures as Albertus Magnus, Arnald of Villanova, Cecco d'Ascoli, Michael Scot, Peter of Abano, and Ramon Lull, but usually the references are brief, and sometimes an author contents himself with a mere list of medieval magicians.[7]

We must suspect that the somewhat arid discussions of this kind were given more body by a rich legendary tradition, which in particular would dwell on the supposed deeds of these men and not solely on their writings; and indeed in nineteenth-century Italy orally transmitted folklore about Michael Scot was still current.[8] In turning to consider such legends we restrict our attention to Roger Bacon. Here we find that our major legendary sources are reduced to essentially two. The first is a prose romance written probably in the late-six-teenth century and entitled *The Famous Historie of Fryer Bacon. Containing the Wonderfull Things that he did in his Life: also the Manner of his Death; with the Lives and Deaths of the two Coniurers, Bungye and Vandermast. Very Pleasant and Delightfull to be Read.*[9] This work, which I shall hereafter call the *Famous Historie,* formed the basis for Robert Greene's play *The Honorable Historie of frier Bacon, and frier Bongay,* and the play contains no new legendary material of interest. The second source is much earlier, but much shorter. It occurs in a recital of deeds of Franciscans written in Dubrovnik in 1384-85 by one Peter of Trau.[10] In this Bacon is not explicitly spoken of as a magician,

---

Pico della Mirandola, *De hominis dignitate* (ed. E. Garin; Florence 1942) 152, and see pp. 23-24 of Garin's introduction.

[7] See e.g. H. C. Agrippa, *De occulta philosophia* ([Cologne] 1533) sig.aa.iii; J. Wierus, *De praestigiis daemonum* (5th ed. Basel 1577) 154, 880-881; M. del Rio, *Disquisitionum magicarum libri sex* 1.3, 1.5.q.4 (3rd ed. Mainz 1606) I 21-22,' 185 *et passim;* G. Naudé, *Apologie pour tous les Grands Personnages qui ont esté faussement soupçonnez de Magie* (Reprint of 1st ed. Paris 1625; London 1972); L. Thorndike, *A History of Magic and Experimental Science* (New York 1923-58) II 549-551, 888-890; IV 498, 520, *et passim.* On Bacon more particularly see also e.g. del Rio, *Disq. mag.*1.4.q.1, 1.5.q.1 (I 83, 152-4 in 3rd ed.); Thorndike, *Hist. Mag.* VI 244-6, 431, 467; W. F. McNeir, 'Traditional Elements in the Character of Greene's Friar Bacon,' *Studies in Philology* 45 (1948) 172-179.

[8] J. Wood Brown, *An Enquiry into the Life and Legend of Michael Scot* (Edinburgh 1897) 222-228.

[9] I use the edition in *Early English Prose Romances* (ed. W. J. Thoms, 2nd ed.; London 1858) I 179-250. The first edition known of was in 1623, but the work must have been available to Robert Greene whose *Friar Bacon and Friar Bungay* was written by 1592. See McNeir, *op. cit. (supra* n. 7) 172 n. 1.

[10] MS Oxford, Bodl., Canon. Misc. 525 fol. 202ᵛ-203ᵛ: Qualiter fratres minores fuerunt phylosophi naturales capitulum quartum . . . (203ʳ) . . . Item frater Rogerius dictus Bachon Anglicus magis reali phylosophie studens quam scribende mirasa [sic] operatus est in ea experimenta. Nam tante subtilitatis in naturali phylosophia extitit ut magis eius mirabilibus experimentis (quibus nulla verior scientia) quam scripture stilo aut doctrine verbo insistens, pontem ultra triginta miliaria longum naturaliter condempsans, super mare a terra firma in Anglie insulam per ipsum inde illuc cum tota sua comitiva transiens, aliquando fecit, ipsum post eius salubrem transitum similiter destruens, rarefaciendo naturaliter. Huiusmodi etiam cum semel in Anglia cuidam ioculatori, de ipso nugas facienti, cyrothecam quam secum portabat dedisset excuciendam ad quamdam, integramque in domo coram omnibus stabiliret [sic] columpnam, ipseque eam excuciente primo percuteret ad eam eiusdem aeris simili condempsatione, sic fecit eius manum dextram qua sic excuciebat

but as one who was more interested in performing experiments in real philosophy than in writing or teaching. Nevertheless the deeds recounted are of a type
that would later be termed magical. Both these accounts probably had a
strong basis in oral tradition,[11] and we may suspect that the uncertainties of
orally transmitted stories formed the background to the volte-face made by the
bibliographer John Bale. In his *Summarium* of 1548 he described Bacon as a
'juggler and necromantic mage' who was said to have performed great marvels at Oxford 'not by the power of God but by the operation of evil spirits.'[12] But about ten years later, in his *Catalogus*, Bale wrote of Bacon, 'He
was possessed of incredible skill in mathematics, but devoid of necromancy,
although many have slandered him with it.'[13]

Bale's experience may provide us with a salutary warning of the dangers of
dealing with legendary material; on the other hand the excavations of Troy
and Knossos may warn us of the complementary dangers of its complete neglect.
I intend, therefore, in this article to select three themes from the legendary tradition and to use them as starting points in attempting an investigation of the
historical Bacon's activity. The legends themselves can of course offer us only the
slenderest evidence, but they may well serve to give a valuable orientation to our

---

cum dicta cyrotheca absorberi quod omnibus eidem viderentur immers[um?] collumpne. Et
per fortitudinem condempsationis ipsius aeris taliter eandem materiam fecit stringi, quod
idem ioculator vehementer aclamaret(?) misericordiam, promittens se nunquam de fratre
truphari, per ipsius aeris similem rarefactionem liberatus sit. De similibus et maioribus
idem Rogerius mencionem facit in sua epistola ad papam Clementem quartum ad laudem
Dei amen. Qualiter fratres minores fuerunt perspectivi capitulum quintum. . . . Item
prephatus frater Rogerius Bachon, qui tante huiusmodi scientie plenitudine (203ᵛ) redun-
dabat, ut delectatione experimentorum eius, obmissis doctrinis et scriptis componendis,
aliquando in universitate Oxonie duo specula composuit patentia, in quorum altero quilibet
omni hora diei et noctis poterat accendere candelam, in altero vero videre quid agebant
homines in quantumcumque remotis constituti partibus. Et quia ad experimentum primi
studentes plus stabant candelas accendendo quam in libris studendis, et in secundo multi,
visis suis consanguineis et amicis mori, infirmari, aut aliter impediri, de universitate rece-
dentes studium destruebant, eiusdem universitatis communi consilio utrumque est fractum.
Igitur quot qualia et quanta mirabiliora hic in hijs, scilicet phylosophia et perspectiva, com-
posuisset et conscripsisset scientiis, ex quo tam stupendis in eis instabat experimentis ad
laudem Dei amen.' In certain places the manuscript readings seem highly corrupt, but the
nature of the marvelous tricks is quite clear. Cf. A. G. Little, 'Description du manuscrit
Canonic. Miscell. 525 de la Bibliothèque Bodléienne à Oxford,' *Opuscules de critique historique* 1 (1903) 251-297 esp. 287-8.

[11] The extant reports of oral tradition about Bacon are mainly of topographical interest.
See e.g. Anthony Wood, *Survey of the Antiquities of the City of Oxford* (ed. A. Clark; Oxford
1889-99) I 425-427; Thomas Hearne, *Remarks and Collections* 24 Dec. 1723, 23 Sep. 1724
(Oxford 1885-1921) VIII 148, 271.

[12] John Bale, *Illustrium maioris Britanniae scriptorum . . . summarium* ([Ipswich] 1548)
fol. 114ᵛ: '. . . prestigiator ac Magus necromanticus, non in virtute Dei, sed in operatione
malorum spirituum Oxonii ad nasum eneum, scholasticorum domicilium, mirabilia magna
fecisse traditur.'

[13] John Bale, *Scriptorum illustrium maioris Brytannie . . . catalogus* (Basel 1557-59) I
342: 'Accessit ei in Mathesi peritia incredibilis, sed absque Necromantia: quamuis ea a
multis infametur.'

investigation. We shall have always to remember that legends about a particular person often use that person merely as a vehicle for tales derived from another source, as is witnessed by many modern anecdotes about eccentrics. But when this is so, the person about whom the anecdote is told usually presents certain features that make him a fit subject for it.[14] Thus the very existence of the Bacon legends may be held to give us *prima facie* evidence that he indulged in activities which could give plausibility to the stories about him. It is also possible that the mass of alchemical writings (many, but not all, spurious) attributed to Bacon[15] helped to make him a fit subject for magical legends, and probably there was a two-way effect with legends encouraging false attributions which themselves reinforced legends. The question of what, if any, alchemy Bacon practised will be outside the scope of this article.

In recent years there has been little attempt to reconstruct what Bacon actually did, but interest in his activities survived longer than did the magical tradition. Already in the sixteenth century there were attempts to dissociate him from magic, and John Dee wrote a work (now lost) to demonstrate that Bacon's deeds did not depend upon the action of demons.[16] In 1625 Gabriel Naudé included him among the great men to be defended against charges of magic[17] and by 1679, the Royal Society of London was showing interest in his works and wishing to see more of them printed.[18] Roger Bacon was being transformed from a magician into a hero of experimental science.[19] Out of this grew the popular picture of him as a lone figure struggling desperately to illuminate a darkened age, a picture which does not yet seem to be wholly dead. But from the middle of the nineteenth century Bacon became the object of more intensive and wide-ranging critical study and much re-evaluation has taken place. He has been dethroned from his position as a man three hundred years ahead of his time and shown to

---

[14] The Virgil legends, on which see J. W. Spargo, *Virgil the Necromancer* (Cambridge Mass. 1934), seem to be an exception, but this is probably explained by the legends growing up long after Virgil's death.

[15] See A. G. Little, 'Roger Bacon's Works with References to the MSS. and Printed Editions,' *Roger Bacon: Essays* (ed. A. G. Little; Oxford 1914) 375-425 and D. W. Singer, 'Alchemical Writings attributed to Roger Bacon,' *Speculum* 7 (1932) 80-86. J. Pits, *Relationum historicarum de rebus anglicis tomus primus* (Paris 1619) 369, also ascribes some apparently magical works to Bacon.

[16] C. H. Josten, 'A Translation of John Dee's "Monas Hieroglyphica" (Antwerp 1564) with an Introduction and Annotations,' *Ambix* 12 (1964) 84-221 at 122-124; J. Crossley, 'Autobiographical Tracts of Dr. John Dee' in *Chetham Miscellanies* 1 (1851) (= *Remains Historical and Literary Connected with the Palatine Counties of Lancaster and Chester* vol. 24) 75; cf. 26. On aspects of Dee's relation to Bacon see N. H. Clulee, 'John Dee's Mathematics and the Grading of Compound Qualities,' *Ambix* 18 (1971) 178-211.

[17] Naudé, *op. cit.* (*supra* n. 7) 488-495.

[18] T. Birch, *The History of the Royal Society of London* (London 1756-7) III 470-474, 477, 479; cf. IV 156.

[19] For a scholarly and still very useful account, written largely from this standpoint, see the article on Bacon in *Biographia Britannica* I (London 1747) 341-364. For other early treatments of Bacon see J. Ferguson, *Bibliotheca Chemica* (Glasgow 1906) I 63-66. Bacon cannot of course be taken to be an experimental scientist in the modern sense; see N. W. Fisher and S. Unguru, 'Experimental Science and Mathematics in Roger Bacon's Thought,' *Traditio* 27 (1971) 353-378.

have been in many ways a typical Scholastic thinker. His fulminations against
reliance upon authority have been compared with the very uncritical way in
which he himself used authority. His errors and superstitions have been emphasized, and the stories of his persecution by the Church brought down to size.
As essential tools for these tasks a mass of unedited material has been published,
and difficult problems of chronology and bibliography tackled.[20] Such exercises
are by no means complete,'but I think that we are now justified in approaching
for a while older traditions of Bacon scholarship and using the modern work
to consider what may be inferred about the actions of this man, who still shines
through his writings as an individual[21] and attractive figure who poses many
problems about the life and thought of his times.

I. The Brazen Head

In the fifth chapter of the *Famous Historie* it is related how Bacon found that
he could surround England with a wall of brass for her greater protection if he
made a brazen head and heard it speak.[22] The construction of the head seems
to have been relatively easy, but making it speak was far more difficult, and
no books proved of any use to Bacon and his collaborator Bungay.[23] They
therefore sought the advice of a devil who, under constraint, informed them of the
operations necessary and emphasized how essential it was that they should hear

---

[20] Among important studies of Bacon we may note: E. Charles, *Roger Bacon* (Paris 1861);
Roger Bacon: Essays (ed. A. G. Little; Oxford 1914); L. Thorndike, *A History of Magic and
Experimental Science* II (New York 1923) 616-691; R. Carton, *L'Expérience physique chez
Roger Bacon* (Paris 1924); T. Crowley, *Roger Bacon: The Problem of the Soul in his Philosophi-
cal Commentaries* (Louvain and Dublin 1950); S. C. Easton, *Roger Bacon and his Search for
a Universal Science* (Oxford 1952). Among major editions may be noted: *Opera quaedam
hactenus inedita* (ed. J. S. Brewer, London 1859); *The 'Opus Maius' of Roger Bacon* (ed.
J. H. Bridges; Oxford 1897-1900); *Opera hactenus inedita* (ed. R. Steele et al., Oxford 1905-40);
Moralis Philosophia (ed. E. Massa; Zurich 1953). For an extended bibliography on Bacon
see F. Alessio, 'Un secolo di studi su Ruggero Bacone (1848-1957),' *Rivista critica di storia
della filosofia* 14 (1959) 81-102.
[21] Even Thorndike (*Hist. Mag.* II 678) who was much concerned to stress Bacon's similarities to his contemporaries writes, 'There is no other book quite like the *Opus Maius* in
the Middle Ages, nor has there been one like it since.'
[22] *Famous Historie* (205-211 Thoms).
[23] There was a thirteenth-century Oxford Franciscan called Thomas Bungay, on whom
see A. B. Emden, *A Biographical Register of the University of Oxford to A. D. 1500* I (Oxford
1957) 305. A. G. Little and F. Pelster, *Oxford Theology and Theologians* (Oxford 1934) 75
note that 'No contemporary evidence to justify the tradition of Bungay's close association
with Roger Bacon has yet come to light.' However, there seems to have been another Friar
Bungay in the fifteenth century with a definite reputation as a magician, for when describing
the Battle of Barnet of 1471 the chronicler Robert Fabyan wrote, 'Of the mystes and other
impedimentes whiche fyll vpon the lordes partye, by reason of the incantacyons wrought by
fryer Bungey, as the fame went, me lyst not to wryte.' See his *The New Chronicles of England* (ed. H. Ellis, London 1811) 661. It therefore seems that the legendary tradition has
conflated the two to produce a composite figure who can both be contemporary with Bacon
and vie with him in magical practices. Little weight can be attached to the ascription of a
De magia naturali to Thomas Bungay in Bale, *Catalogus* I 347.

the head when it did speak. The process recommended was long and arduous and the moment of speaking uncertain, so that it eventually fell out that the head uttered its few words while the friars were asleep and the stupidity of Bacon's servant Miles prevented them from being awakened before the head disintegrated in a vast explosion. The project thus failed.

Various rationalizations of this story have been attempted. In the seventeenth century Sir Thomas Browne thought he had the answer and wrote:

> Every ear is filled with the story of Frier *Bacon*, that made a brazen head to speak these words, *Time is,* Which though they want not the like relations, is surely too literally received, and was but a mystical fable concerning the Philosophers great work, wherein he eminently laboured: implying no more by the copper head than the vessel wherein it was wrought, and by the words it spake, then the opportunity to be watched, about the *Tempus ortus,* or birth of the mystical child, or Philosophical King of *Lullius*: the rising of the *Terra foliata* of Arnoldus, when the earth, sufficiently impregnated with the water, ascendeth white and splendent. Which not observed, the work is irrecoverably lost. . . . Now letting slip this critical opportunity, he missed the intended treasure. Which had he obtained, he might have made out the tradition of a brazen wall about *England.* That is, the most powerfull defence, and strongest fortification which Gold could have effected.[24]

This explanation — that the story is an allegorical account of an alchemical process — certainly has the merit of taking into account all the facets of the legend, including the wall of brass and the missed opportunity, and Bacon himself admitted that he was wont to write on alchemy in *aenigmata*.[25] But there are still reasons for being suspicious of it.

These stem mainly from the fact that stories of artificial speaking heads were very common and attached themselves to, among others, Virgil, Gerbert, Robert Grosseteste, and Albertus Magnus.[26] Thus it seems that a romance writer would be liable to add a speaking head to a story of any magician, and so there is little reason for supposing anything specific in Bacon's career to suggest the legend. We, therefore, have to consider the explanation of the widespread medieval notion of these devices, and it is rather implausible to suggest that, in the first half of the twelfth century when William of Malmesbury was writing of Gerbert's speaking head,[27] he was in fact retailing an alchemical allegory. We thus seek another explanation.

One such has been suggested by Lynn White, backed up by archaeological evidence,[28] for there survive certain medieval sufflators or fire blowers shaped in the form of human heads.[29] Water was put into these vessels and they were

---

[24] Thomas Browne, *Pseudodoxia epidemica* 7.17 (ed. C. Sayle, *Works* [Edinburgh 1904-07] III 72).

[25] *Opus tertium* (ed. A. G. Little, *Part of the Opus Tertium* [Aberdeen 1912] 77-86).

[26] See the fine survey of legends of speaking heads in A. Dickson, *Valentine and Orson* (New York 1929) 200-216. Legends of artificial heads, of course, had one ancestor in those of oracular severed heads; our task is to find other progenitors.

[27] William of Malmesbury, *De gestis regum Anglorum* 2.172 (ed. W. Stubbs [London 1887-89] I 202-203).

[28] L. White, *Medieval Technology and Social Change* (London 1964) 90-92.

[29] F. M. Feldhaus, 'Ein Dampfapparat von vor tausend Jahren,' *Prometheus* 25 (1913-14) 69-73; W. L. Hildburgh, 'Aeolophiles as fire-blowers,' *Archaeologia* 94 (1951) 27-55. The

then placed near a fire. After a sufficient interval the water boiled and a mixture of air and steam was blown out of the mouth of the vessel onto the fire causing it to burn more fiercely. Presumably these ingenious devices made some kind of noise when in operation, and they may even have been designed with this end in view, for a similar machine described by Hero of Alexandria was designed to blow a trumpet or imitate birdsong.[30]

This rationalization of the brazen-head stories seems to possess sufficient verisimilitude to make us think that we are on the right track, but the mention of Hero suggests an extension of the argument, for a legend would seem less likely to arise from a device primarily intended to be useful than from one concocted purely for purposes of ostentation. Several of these were designed in antiquity and Hero's *Pneumatica* in particular presents us with numerous mechanical toys and temple devices, including machines for pouring libations on an altar when a fire is lit under it, singing birds, drinking animals, and such-like.[31] The elaborate embellishments made both to medieval water clocks and early mechanical clocks[32] suggest that men of the Middle Ages had tastes very similar to Alexandrian Greeks in these matters, and recent writers have argued for a far greater degree of mechanical ingenuity in the Latin Middle Ages than is commonly assumed.[33] In particular, by the end of the thirteenth century

---

oldest specimen which Feldhaus describes in some detail is made of bronze. This would have been included under the term 'brass' up to the eighteenth century. Roger Bacon's discussion of *aes* and *orichalcum* shows that for him the distinction between these terms was not that between modern 'bronze' and 'brass'; see J. M. Stillman, *The Story of Alchemy and Early Chemistry* (Dover ed.; New York 1960) 266-269. The action of human shaped sufflators was described by Albertus Magnus, *De meteoris* 3.2.17 (*Opera omnia* II [ed. P. Jammy; Lyons 1651] 100).

[30] Hero of Alexandria, *Pneumatica* 2.35 (ed. W. Schmidt, *Opera quae supersunt omnia* I [Leipzig 1899] 316-322).

[31] On the later tradition of Hero's *Pneumatica* see M. Boas, 'Hero's *Pneumatica*. A Study of its Transmission and Influence,' *Isis* 40 (1949) 38-48. Until very recently it has been assumed that two at least partial Latin translations were made during the Middle Ages; see A. Birkenmajer, 'Vermischte Untersuchungen zur Geschichte der mittelalterlichen Philosophie,' *Beiträge zur Geschichte der Philosophie des Mittelalters* 20 Heft 5 (1922) 19-31, and C. H. Haskins, *Studies in the History of Mediaeval Science* (Ungar ed.; New York 1960) 181-183. However, E. Grant, 'Henricus Aristippus, William of Moerbeke and Two Alleged Mediaeval Translations of Hero's *Pneumatica*,' *Speculum* 46 (1971) 656-669, has put forward strong arguments for doubting whether any such translation was made at that time. Nevertheless it will be clear from what follows that the tradition of such devices as are described in the *Pneumatica* did pass to the Middle Ages. Roger Bacon, *Communia mathematica* 3.2.2 (ed. Steele, *Op. hact. ined.* XVI 44), mentions a *De conductibus aquarum*. This is probably the fragmentary Latin translation of the *Pneumatica* of Philo of Byzantium (ed. W. Schmidt, *Heronis Alexandrini Opera omnia* I 458-489). The devices in this fragment are not as ostentatious as Hero's, but are related; cf. A. G. Drachmann, *Ktesibios, Philon and Heron* (Copenhagen 1948) 45-47.

[32] See e.g. A. P. Usher, *A History of Mechanical Inventions* (Revised ed.; Cambridge, Mass. 1954) 187-210.

[33] See e.g. M. Sherwood, 'Magic and Mechanics in Medieval Fiction,' *Studies in Philology* 44 (1947) 567-592, and D. J. de S. Price, 'Automata and the Origins of Mechanism and Mechanistic Philosophy,' *Technology and Culture* 5 (1964) 9-23.

the Castle of Hesdin in Artois had a very large collection of trick machinery
to entertain the unwary guests.[34] It seems probable that devices of this
kind would have become famous, and they may even have formed part of the
equipment of some medieval jugglers, although the reports of jugglers' activities
concentrate more on their producing optical illusions.[35]

However that may be, there were at least sufficient devices for reinforcing, if
not initiating, brazen-head legends, and it may be that speaking tubes or other
means of localizing sound were used. We have no definite evidence for associating
any of these devices with Bacon himself, but it is certain that he, like other
practically minded philosophers, would have been fascinated by such machines[36]
and could even have designed some for himself and displayed them to his colleagues.

II. Optical Devices

Our next selection of legendary material has a far more definite connection
with Bacon himself, and we shall be able to compare it with several passages
from his own writings. It concerns various marvelous optical devices. In the
Famous Historie we read that 'It did chance that the King of England (for
some cause best knowne to himselfe) went into France with a great armie,
where after many victories, he did beseige a strong towne and lay before it full
three moneths, without doing to the towne any great damage, but rather received
the hurt himselfe.'[37] Eventually the king announced that he would give a
substantial reward to anyone who could capture the town for him. Friar Bacon
heard of this and journeyed to France. When he reached the king he made a
long speech about the marvels that may be performed by art without the use
of magic, part of which reads as follows:

> Physicall figurations are farre more strange: for by that may be framed perspects
> and looking-glasses, that one thing shall appeare to be many, as one man shall appeare
> to be a whole army, and one sunne or moone shall seem divers. Also perspects may be
> so framed, that things farre off shall seem most nigh unto us: with one of these did
> Iulius Caesar from the sea coasts in France marke and observe the situation of the
> castles in England. Bodies may also be so framed that the greatest things shall appeare
> to be the least, the highest lowest, the most secret to bee the most manifest, and in
> such like sort the contrary. Thus did Socrates perceive, that the dragon which did
> destroy the citie and countrey adioyning, with his noisome breath, and contagious in-
> fluence, did lurke in the dennes between the mountaines: and thus may all things that
> are done in cities or armies be discovered by the enemies. Againe, in such wise may
> bodies be framed, that venemous and infectious influences may be brought whither

---

[34] Sherwood, *op. cit.* 587-591.

[35] In Geoffrey Chaucer, *Squieres Tale* 209-211 (ed. W. W. Skeat, *Complete Works* [Oxford
1894] IV 467) an onlooker says that the horse of brass on which the knight has appeared
'is rather lyk/ An apparence y-maad by som magyk, / As Iogelours pleyen at thise festes
grete.'

[36] Compare the famous lists of possible mechanical devices given by Bacon in *Communia
mathematica* 3.2.2 (43-44 Steele) and *Epistola de secretis operibus artis et naturae* 4 (ed. J. S.
Brewer, *Op. quaedam hact. ined.* 532-3).

[37] *Fam. Hist.* (211-2 Thoms).

a man will: in this did Aristotle instruct Alexander; through which instruction the poyson of a basiliske, being lift up upon the wall of a citie, the poison was convayd into the citie, to the destruction thereof: also perspects may be made to deceive the sight, as to make a man beleeve that hee seeth great store of riches, when that there is not any. But it appertaineth to a higher power of figuration, that beams should be brought and assembled by divers flexions and reflexions in any distance that we will, to burne any thing that is opposite unto it, as it is witnessed by those perspects or glasses that burne before and behinde.[38]

This quotation would not have been made at such length were it not for the fact that the author of the romance has lifted the speech almost verbatim from one of Bacon's own works, the *Epistola de secretis operibus artis et naturae*,[39] and so this is what Bacon himself believed could be done. According to the author of the *Famous Historie*, after Bacon had finished his speech, he used his perspect glasses to show the king the town that he was besieging as if at close range, and on the following morning he brought the glasses again into play, this time to burn down various buildings in the town so that the king was able to take it with the minimum of resistance.[40]

This pair of uses for optical instruments is also found in the 1385 Peter of Trau account of Bacon, where we read:

He was so complete a master of optics that from love of experiments he neglected teaching and writing, and made two mirrors in the University of Oxford: by one of them you could light a candle at any hour, day or night: in the other you could see what people were doing in any part of the world. By experimenting with the first, students spent more time in lighting candles than in studying books; and seeing in the second their relations dying or ill or otherwise in trouble, they got into the habit of 'going down' to the ruin of the university: so by common counsel of the University both mirrors were broken.[41]

To these accounts we may add another optical story reported by Roger's namesake Francis, who wrote, 'They have an old tale in Oxford, that Friar Bacon walked between two steeples: which was thought to be done by glasses, when he walked upon the ground.'[42]

When we move from these legends to considering what Bacon in fact did, we must first of all try to find out what equipment he had. That he was not niggardly in his expenditure on learning may be gathered from his references to the two thousand pounds that he had spent in the twenty years prior to 1267 or 1268 on books, instruments, experiments, and other expenses necessary for the pursuit of wisdom.[43] We may thus feel certain that he would have acquired

---

[38] *Fam. Hist.* (213-4 Thoms).

[39] *Ep. de sec. op.* 5 (534-5 Brewer).

[40] *Fam. Hist.* (215-6 Thoms).

[41] See *supra* n. 10. Translation from A. G. Little, 'Roger Bacon,' *Proceedings of the British Academy* 14 (1928) 265-296 at 267.

[42] Francis Bacon, *Sylvia sylvarum* 8.762 (ed. J. Spedding, R. L. Ellis and D. D. Heath, *Works* II [London 1857] 586). Cf. Robert Burton, *Anatomy of Melancholy* 1.3.3 (ed. F. Dell and P. Jordan-Smith [New York 1927] 364) and I. d'Israeli, *Amenities of Literature* (London 1842) III 192.

[43] *Opus tertium* 17 (ed. J. S. Brewer, *Op. quaedam hact. ined.* 59).

what optical instruments were available, but these may not have been many. In particular, at the time of writing the works for the pope around 1267, it does not seem that Bacon had a large range of lenses, for, when he gets down to practical details instead of merely saying what can be done, he speaks of a crystal sphere or hemisphere or else of a round glass filled with water.[44] We may feel certain that he possessed instruments of this kind, and in fact he sent a crystal ball to the pope,[45] but probably they exhausted his range of lenses. However, towards the end of the thirteenth century eyeglasses came into use in Italy,[46] and so it may be that before the end of his life a wider supply of lenses became available to Bacon.

On the question of burning mirrors we may produce more definite evidence, for, at the time of writing the works for the pope Bacon was particularly interested in the construction of one such by Petrus Peregrinus, whose experiments on magnetism have given him lasting fame. Bacon mentions Peter's endeavors in this connection four times in the *Opus maius* and *Opus tertium*.[47] On the third occasion he briefly announces the completion of the task, and on the fourth he goes triumphantly into more detail:

> I have mentioned already that this type of congregation [of rays] can be made by reflection and that a mirror has been made, a model and sign, as it were, of this wonder of nature, so that the possibility of such a work may be seen. But it was with great expenses and labour that it was made, for its contriver was set back by the sum of 100 Parisian pounds and he worked at it for many years laying aside study and other necessary occupations. But he would not have given up the labour for the sake of a thousand marks, both on account of the most beautiful power of wisdom which he recognised, and for the reason that in future he can make better mirrors at less cost, because he has learned by experience what he previously did not know. Nor is it any wonder if he spent so much and laboured so hard in this first work, because never has any Latin known how to achieve this before him; and it is indeed a wonder that he dared to approach such an unknown and such an arduous business. But he is the most wise of men and nothing is difficult to him unless it be because of lack of money. Certainly if the citizens of Acre [*Aconenses*] and those Christians who are beyond the sea had twelve such mirrors they could drive the Saracens from their lands without any shedding of blood, and there would be no need for the lord king of France to set out with an army to take that land. . . .[48]

Both the theory and the practice of the construction of parabolic burning mirrors had been treated by the Arabic writer Ibn al-Haitham, known to the Latins as Alhazen, and his work on the subject had been translated into Latin

---

[44] E.g. in *Opus maius* 4.2.2 (I 113 Bridges).

[45] *Op. tert.* 32 (111 Brewer).

[46] See E. Rosen, 'The Invention of Eyeglasses,' *Journal of the History of Medicine* 11 (1956) 13-46, 183-218.

[47] *Op. mai.* 4.2.2 (I 116 Bridges); *Op. tert.* 13, 33, 36 (47, 113, 116 Brewer). On Petrus Peregrinus and his relation to Bacon see E. Schlund, 'Petrus Peregrinus von Maricourt,' *Archivum Franciscanum historicum* 4 (1911) 436-455, 633-643; 5 (1912) 22-40 and A. C. Crombie, *Robert Grosseteste and the Origins of Experimental Science* (2nd imp.; Oxford 1961) 204-210.

[48] *Op. tert.* 36 (116 Brewer).

under the title *De speculis comburentibus* and circulated anonymously.[49] It
seems from a remark of Bacon's in the *Opus maius* that Peter was using this
work in constructing his burning mirror, although he perhaps only had available
a defective version.[50] In what is probably a very late work Bacon refers to
Alhazen's tract in some detail and then gives a résumé of his own experiences in
having burning mirrors constructed:

> I have had many burning mirrors made in which as if through models the goodness
> of nature may be manifested, and they are not of great cost when compared with the
> quantity of useful and splendid works [obtainable]; for the first mirror made cost sixty
> Parisian pounds, which is equivalent to about twenty pounds sterling, but afterwards
> I had a better one made for ten Parisian pounds, that is five marks sterling, and later
> still, when carefully experienced in these matters, I perceived that better ones could be
> made for two marks or twenty *solidi*, . . . but great and subtle consideration is needed.[51]

Thus it seems that up to 1267 Bacon did not have any curved mirrors of much
use, but that after this period he acquired several. In this later period of his
life he would still have had the crystal balls and glasses of water of his younger
days and may even have acquired some more sophisticated lenses. Laden with
all this apparatus he would almost certainly have done something with it, but
we are not provided with many natural philosophical works from the later
period of Bacon's life, so that we have once again to indulge in a certain amount
of conjecture.

But first we must emphasize the general spirit that Bacon and his contemporaries had in regard to optical devices. This spirit is well exemplified by the
passage already quoted which the author of the *Famous Historie* lifted from the
De secretis operibus artis et naturae, and many similar utterances are to be found
in the *Opus maius*. Bacon has very much an eye to the deceits that may be
performed with optical instruments.[52] To this end he regards 'broken mirrors'
as particularly efficacious, for, by means of such, multiple images may be produced.[53] It is interesting to note that Bacon regards even this as a case of art
perfecting nature, for, as Pliny related, under certain atmospheric conditions

---

[49] J. L. Heiberg and E. Wiedemann, ' Ibn al-Haiṭams Schrift über parabolische Hohlspiegel,'
Bibliotheca Mathematica 10₃ (1910) 201-237.

[50] *Op. mai.* 4.2.2 (I 116 Bridges). Cf. S. Vogl, *Die Physik Roger Bacos* (Erlangen 1906) 71.

[51] MS London, Brit. Mus., Royal 7.F.viii fol. 4ᵛ: 'Multa enim specula feci fieri comburentia
in quibus tanquam per exemplaria potest bonitas nature manifestari nec sunt magni sumptus
secundum quantitatem utilium operum et magnificorum. Primum enim speculum factum
constitit 60 libras parisiencium que valent circiter 20 libras sterlingorum sed postea feci
fieri melius pro 10 libris parisiencium scilicet pro v marcis sterlingorum et postea diligenter
expertus in hiis percepi quod melioria possent fieri pro duabus marcis vel 20 solidis . . . sed
magna consideratio et subtilis requiritur in hac parte.' Cf. Charles, *op. cit. (supra* n. 20)
305. A. G. Little *op. cit. (supra* n. 15) lists the work from which this quotation is taken as a
recension of the *De multiplicatione specierum.* This it probably is, but Bacon seems to have
intended it to form part of the fifth part of his *Compendium studii theologiae,* which may
have been his last projected attempt at a grand synthesis: see Charles, *op. cit.* 90-91. From
Comp. stud. theol. 1.2 (ed. H. Rashdall [Aberdeen 1911] 34) we learn that the first part of
this work was being written in 1292.

[52] *Op. mai.* 5.3.3.3-4 (II 164-6 Bridges).

[53] *Op. mai.* 5.3.1.6, 5.3.3.3 (II 145-6, 164 Bridges).

several suns and several moons may be seen. This is spectacular, but Bacon is also interested in using the principle to multiply men and armies so that the infidels may be scared out of their wits. Probably Bacon had experimented with fragmented plane mirrors to produce minor illusions of this sort and we have good evidence that similar tricks were being performed by the jugglers of the time.

Not much study seems to have been made of the non-literary and non-musical activities of these medieval entertainers, but it is quite clear that they had a large repertoire of what we should now call conjuring tricks, including at times optical illusions.[54] From the fourteenth century we have references to such illusions by Chaucer,[55] and probably at the end of the thirteenth century, Thomas Cabham had spoken of a class of jugglers who 'make as it were certain images to be seen, by incantations or otherwise.'[56] For more detail we have to move to the sixteenth century where we are given a very full first-hand account of a magical séance by Benvenuto Cellini,[57] for which an explanation was later proposed by Sir David Brewster,[58] who suggested that the spirits were in fact images projected by concave mirrors onto the clouds of smoke that the magician had produced. Such images could be made to move around in the smoke, and it only needed the powers of imagination of those present in the mysterious midnight atmosphere to produce a convincing and terrifying effect. But back in the thirteenth century Witelo, in his *De natura demonum*, had written of how the appearance of demons could be produced by optical means, and Nicole Oresme later associated this with the practices of jugglers.[59]

Thus it seems certain that in Bacon's time jugglers were making use of optical illusions, and Bacon himself would have been very interested, for he certainly thought it relevant to include in the paean of praises that he accorded Petrus Peregrinus the fact that he examined 'the illusions and devices of all the jugglers.'[60] Peter of Trau too related a rather obscure story of how Bacon got the better of a juggler who had been making fun of him, though this was not by optical means.[61]

As we have seen, the legendary tradition concentrated on Bacon's being able to see distant things as if near and on his burning of objects. It seems certain that Bacon was able to use both mirrors and crystal balls to do such things as

---

[54] The best study from this point of view seems still to be J. Strutt, *Glig-Gamena Angel-Deod or The Sports and Pastimes of the People of England* (London 1801) 152-160. Many jugglers' conjuring tricks are discussed in Reginald Scot, *The Discoverie of Witchcraft* 13 (ed. M. Summers [London] 1930); optical illusions are mentioned in ch. 19 on p. 179. On the possible importance of jugglers to the history of technology see J. Needham, *Clerks and Craftsmen in China and the West* (Cambridge 1970) 58-59.

[55] See particularly *Squieres Tale* 208-227, *Frankeleyns Tale* 410-423, 533-541 (IV 467 494, 497-8 Skeat). See also Skeat's discussion of the etymology of 'etregetour' in III 273.

[56] E. K. Chambers, *The Mediaeval Stage* (Oxford 1903) II 262: 'alii qui . . . et faciunt videri quasi quaedam fantasmata per incantationes vel alio modo.'

[57] Benvenuto Cellini, *Life* 1.13 (ed. R. H. H. Cust [London 1927] I 242-247).

[58] D. Brewster, *Letters on Natural Magic addressed to Sir Walter Scott* (London 1832) 68-76.

[59] M. Clagett, *Nicole Oresme and the Medieval Geometry of Qualities and Motions* (Madison, Wis. 1968) 358, 484-5.

[60] *Op. tert.* 13 (47 Brewer): 'omnium joculatorum illusiones et ingenia.'

[61] See *supra* n. 10.

lighting candles by the sun's rays, but there was nothing new in this.[62] The ability to see distant objects as if near is far more problematic. In the *Opus maius* he speaks of the possibility of combining both mirrors and perspect glasses to this end, but very similar passages are to be found in the writings of Robert Grosseteste, and Bacon's source could have been purely literary.[63] Nevertheless it seems very probable that even by the time of the *Opus maius* Bacon had experimented with combinations of crystal balls and flasks of water and observed a large, though distorted, magnification. Whether later in life he tried to produce any refinements of such an experience (possibly using mirrors) is difficult to say, but we may consider one piece of evidence.

In 1579 Thomas Digges published *An Arithmeticall Militare Treatise named Stratioticos*. . . . This work had been begun by Thomas's father, Leonard, and at the end of it in a short memoir of his father's doings Thomas wrote:

> He was able by *Perspectiue Glasses* duely scituate vpon conuenient *Angles*, in such
> sorte to discouer euery particularitie in the Countrey rounde aboute, wheresoeuer the
> *Sunne* beames might pearse: As sithence *Archimedes*, (*Bakon* of *Oxforde* only excepted)
> I haue not read of any in *Action* euer able by meanes natural to performe the like.
> Which partly grew by the aide he had by one old written booke of the same *Bakons
> Experiments*, that by straunge aduenture, or rather *Destinie*, came to his hands, though
> chiefelye by conioyning continual laborious Practise with his *Mathematical* Studies.[64]

In his *Pantometria* Leonard Digges had said that he had written at length on the 'miraculous effectes of perspectiue glasses,'[65] but this work seems never to have been published. The crucial point for us in the *Stratioticos* passage is the book of Bacon's that Leonard used. R. Steele says simply that it 'is no longer known to exist,'[66] while F. R. Johnson seems to assume that it is the *Opus maius*.[67] Certainly it is in Part V of the *Opus maius* that Bacon writes of the possibility of combining mirrors or perspect glasses in order to see at a distance, and this may have been enough to influence Leonard Digges. Nevertheless, although this part of the *Opus maius* often circulated separately,[68] 'Bacon's Experiments' seems rather an odd title for it. It is, therefore, quite possible that Digges was referring to some other more detailed work that is now either lost[69] or still surviving in manuscript under a perhaps confusing title, for the

---

[62] C. Singer, 'Steps Leading to the Invention of the First Optical Apparatus,' *Studies in the History and Method of Science* II (ed. C. Singer, Oxford 1921) 385-413 at 386-7.

[63] *Op. mai.* 5.3.3.3-4 (II 165-6 Bridges); Robert Grosseteste, *De iride* (ed. L. Baur, *Die philosophischen Werke* [Münster 1912] 74). Cf. Little, *op. cit.* (*supra* n. 41) 274, and E. Rosen, 'Did Roger Bacon Invent Eyeglasses?' *Archives internationales d'histoire des sciences* 7 (1954) 3-15.

[64] *An Arithmeticall Militare Treatise named Stratioticos . . . . Long since attempted by Leonard Digges Gentleman. Augmented, digested and lately finished by Thomas Digges, his Sonne* (London 1579) 189-190.

[65] *A Geometrical Practice, named Pantometria . . . framed by Leonard Digges Gentleman, lately finished by Thomas Digges his sonne* (London 1571) sig. G.i^v-G.ii^r.

[66] R. Steele, 'Roger Bacon and the State of Science in the Thirteenth Century,' *Studies in the History and Method of Science* II (ed. C. Singer, Oxford 1921) 121-150 at 147.

[67] F. R. Johnson, *Astronomical Thought in Renaissance England* (Baltimore 1937) 178-9.

[68] Little, *op. cit.* (*supra* n. 15) 382-4.

[69] In 1682 Robert Plot thought that it might have been in the custody of Thomas Allen; see Birch, *op. cit.* (*supra* n. 18) IV 156.

chaotic state of Bacon's manuscript legacy has been the despair of bibliographers since the time of Leland.[70]

These features of the work of Bacon and of Leonard Digges have often been discussed by writers on the history of the telescope, though sometimes in terms dependent upon the later existence of the telescope. I have tried as far as possible to avoid anachronism by considering this aspect of Bacon's activity within the context of what Renaissance writers would have called natural magic. In general Bacon's optical pursuits may be seen as exemplifying very favorably his repeated insistence on the value both of probing the secret causes of nature and applying the theoretical knowledge gained to practical ends, for besides the 'prophecies of future discoveries,' which we have noted, and the practical work, which we have attempted to reconstruct, Bacon wrote at length on the theory of the transmission, reflection, and refraction of rays, and indeed — like Grosseteste — he had grounds for regarding optics as almost the basic science of nature, for other 'species' were 'multiplied' in the same way as light, and this was the fundamental mode for the transmission of the forces of nature.

III. Forbidden Magic

The activities that we have so far discussed would not have been termed magical by Bacon himself, although they would fall within the domain of the natural magic of a later age.[71] Our final theme brings us to the gates of what in all ages would have passed for magic and concerns the raising of spirits, a subject which has a large place in the *Famous Historie*. We do not need to go into details, but may cite as one example a contest between Bacon and the German conjuror Vandermast.[72] At the close of a banquet Vandermast raises the spirit of Pompey for the delectation of the English king. Bacon promptly replies by producing the ghost of Julius Caesar. The two spirits fight; Caesar kills Pompey; Bacon wins the contest.

When describing such incidents the imagination of a romance writer will obviously roam far and wide, but the general theme of necromantic activities gives us occasion for re-examining Bacon's attitude to magical practices. This subject has been considered with some thoroughness by Thorndike,[73] who draws upon a wealth of relevant texts, but his account is somewhat vitiated by his apparent assumption that the domain of magic is given *a priori*, and he seems to hold that it includes anything 'occult.' Now, although this may be a useful general characterization (which could be held to include much of modern science) it must here be supplemented by a consideration of Bacon's own definition of magic, for otherwise it is illegitimately easy to hold with Thorndike that Bacon 'fails in his attempt to draw the line between science and magic.'[74]

---

[70] On some of the difficulties which arise from Bacon's method of writing see F. Picavet, *Essais sur l'histoire générale et comparée des théologies et philosophies médiévales* (Paris 1913) 218-224.

[71] Bacon seems never to have used the term *magia naturalis*, but it had been used earlier by William of Auvergne e.g. in *De legibus* 24 (*Opera omnia* [Paris 1674] I 69).

[72] *Fam. Hist.* (217-8 Thoms). I am unable to identify a historical source for Vandermast. In Greene's play he has the Christian name Jacques. The name may represent a corruption of that of some figure such as the Cracovian Jakob Randersacker, on whom see Thorndike, *Hist. Mag.* IV 457, 482.

[73] Thorndike, *Hist. Mag.* II 659-677.　　　　[74] *Ibid.* 666.

In his attempt to divide philosophy from magic, or, as he more frequently says, true mathematics from false mathematics, Bacon's main criterion seems to be whether one is morally or theologically justified in holding certain beliefs or indulging in certain practices. If a practice is licit, it is not magic; if it is illicit and has to do with the misuse of knowledge, it is magic.

Bacon discusses the characteristics of false mathematics in several of his writings. One of the fullest descriptions is in his introduction to the pseudo-Aristotelian *Secretum secretorum*.[75] There we learn that false mathematicians have two main faults. The first is that they believe that everything happens of necessity. This is the doctrine of astrological determinism and need not concern us here. The second is that they make use of demons. In some cases these are made to appear sensibly, especially on polished surfaces, such as the finger nail of a virgin boy or a sword; they then give information either verbally or by visual impression. In other cases the demons act invisibly, as in the divinatory practices of geomancy, hydromancy, aeromancy and pyromancy. The information that they give may be either true or false, and they are of course chiefly motivated by spite. The calling upon such malicious spirits will increase mightily as the day of Antichrist approaches.

All this is very clear, and if one wants to play safe one will keep well away from any practices that may involve the action of demons. But Bacon is precluded from this course by other of his principles, for one of his most central doctrines is that there are many marvels of art and nature that can and should be investigated and applied to the utmost good of Christendom. This is surely going to mean that he will have to approach very near to forbidden ground, and there is evidence that in fact he does.

When calling upon their demons necromancers were wont to make much use of songs and incantations, but Bacon believes that there are also marvelous natural powers produced by the human voice when backed up by the action of the rational soul.[76] To make use of these one will have to perform actions very close to those of the magician, who himself may be using natural powers when he thinks that he is employing the service of demons. Bacon recognises the danger very clearly and writes: 'It is therefore necessary to be very cautious in one's decisions in these matters, for a man may easily fall into error, and many do err in both directions, for some decline every operation, while others go to excess and fall into magic.'[77] Bacon himself gives some evidence of favoring the rasher policy, for he praises Petrus Peregrinus for his investigations 'of the experiments, prophecies, and songs of old women and of all magicians.'[78] It is probable that Bacon himself proceeded in this manner, and one of the few contemporary references that we have to him shows him listening to one Peter of Ardene giving an account of how he attended five séances at which a certain Spanish master called up his demon, who answered the questions that those present put to it.[79] We could not feel confident that Bacon's curiosity never led

---

[75] *Tractatus brevis et utilis ad declarandum quedam obscure dicta in libro Secreto secretorum Aristotelis* 3 (ed. Steele, *Op. hact. ined.* V 6-8).

[76] *Op. mai.* 3.14; 4 (III 122-5, I 395-9 Bridges); *Ep. de sec. op.* 3 (529-532 Brewer).

[77] *Ep. de sec. op.* 3 (531 Brewer).

[78] *Op. tert.* 13 (47 Brewer): 'experimenta vetularum et sortilegia, et carmina earum et omnium magicorum.'

[79] *Liber exemplorum* (ed. A. G. Little; Aberdeen 1907) 22.

him to attend such a séance himself. Indeed he may have gone to see whether the effects were the result of optical illusions.

A similar situation applies in the case of forbidden books. Bacon both fulsomely condemns such books and also asserts that many of them contain portions of genuine wisdom.[80] The implication is clearly that, although they are in general to be eschewed, the pioneer investigator is under an obligation to examine them and extract those things that are licit.

Thus underneath Bacon's vigorous condemnations of magic we may see evidence of an acute personal dilemma, and his natural curiosity, combined with the policy to which he was committed, may at times have led him to over-step the mark. In trying to form a probable picture of his activities in this direction we must remember the context in which his works were appearing, for when writing to the pope or issuing a work for general release it would not have been prudent to accuse himself of forbidden practices. And it is noteworthy that it is in the *Epistola de secretis operibus artis et naturae*, which has the form of a private letter, that Bacon lays himself most open to the charge of dabbling in magic, even though he still explicitly condemns it there. In general there seems a fair degree of probability that Bacon performed certain actions that could easily have led his less educated contemporaries to believe that he was a full-blooded magician. We should also expect any suspicion of trafficking with spirits to escape the pen of the Franciscan chronicler Peter of Trau, who was anxious to present a favorable if slightly quixotic picture of Bacon. Despite all this we must still admit that there is no evidence that Bacon was imprisoned on the grounds of suspected necromancy.[81]

* * *

The course of this paper has been marked by the frequent occurrence of tentative arguments, and we have had again and again to content ourselves with the exploration of possibilities and the assertion of probabilities: certainty has usually eluded us. This state of affairs cannot give complete satisfaction, but in this field it is one that we may be doomed to live with. Nevertheless I think that we have established that the historical Bacon was not altogether unsuitable vehicle for the legends about him, although we must admit that our knowledge of the origin and development of the legendary tradition remains scanty.[82] But even if the genetic connection between the historical Bacon and the legendary Bacon is tenuous, this does not preclude us from inclining to the view that the former was not merely an armchair philosopher but went some way towards meriting his later classification as a magician.

---

[80] *Ep. de sec. op.* 3 (532 Brewer).

[81] Easton, *op. cit. (supra* n. 20) 126-143, 192-202, has very plausibly suggested that Bacon's troubles arose from his holding Joachite views. Cf. F. Heer, *The Intellectual History of Europe* (London 1966) 135-8. Anthony Wood, *op. cit. (supra* n. 11) II 401 suggested that he may have been condemned for the work *De victoria Christi contra Antichristum*. T. Tanner, *Bibliotheca Britannico-Hibernica* (London 1748) 63 n.s, following Leland gives the *incipit* of this as 'Nec sum propheta, nec filius prophetae.'

[82] It is curious that in his *Summa logicae et philosophiae naturalis*, which was written probably in the 1340s in Oxford, John Dumbleton referred to Bacon as 'unus qui Bakun cognominatur' (MS Vatican, Vat. Lat. 6750, fol. 194vb).

NICOLE ORESME AND SCIENTIFIC PROGRESS

In the recent growth of historical interest in late medieval natural philosophy the work of Nicole Oresme has been much studied, but an adequate assessment of his place in the history of science remains difficult to achieve, although there is increasing emphasis on the need to consider him in the context of his own time. This will mean devoting more attention to his own views of scientific development and of his place within it. In this paper I shall consider in this light two of Oresme's most polished and individual Latin works, the *Tractatus de configurationibus qualitatum et motuum* and the *Tractatus de commensurabilitate vel incommensurabilitate motuum celi*.

But first we may gain some orientation by treating briefly one particular theme that has been much studied, namely Oresme's speculations on the possible diurnal spin of the Earth. In his *Livre du ciel et du monde*, which was completed in 1377, Oresme gave strong arguments in favour of attributing such a spin to the Earth. K. Michalski traced Oresme's thoughts on the subject through two earlier works and wrote[1]:

Lorsqu'on compare entre eux les trois commentaires de Nicolas d'Oresme, c'est-à-dire le commentaire latin sur le *De sphaera*, le commentaire latin sur le *De caelo et mundo*, enfin le commentaire français sur le même ouvrage, on s'aperçoit qu'il proclame avec une conviction croissante, la théorie du mouvement rotatoire de la terre autour de son axe.

Michalski well revealed the development in Oresme's thought, but it is difficult to hold that it represented an increasing conviction of the Earth's motion, for in the *Livre du ciel et du monde* Oresme concluded his arguments by abruptly rejecting it[2]:

Et nientmoins touz tiennent et je cuide que [le ciel] est ainsi meu et la terre non: Deus enim firmavit orbem terre, qui non commovebitur, nonobstans les raisons au contraire, car ce sont persuasions qui ne

---

[1] K. Michalski: La Physique Nouvelle et les Différents Courants Philosophiques au XIVe Siècle. Originally published 1928 and reprinted in: K. Michalski: La Philosophie au XIVe Siècle: Six Etudes. Ed. K. Flasch (Opuscula Philosophica 1). Frankfurt 1969. Pp. 205—277. The passage cited is on pp. 263—268 and the quotations from p. 263.

[2] Nicole Oresme: Le Livre du ciel et du monde. Ed. A. D. Menut & A. J. Denomy. Madison, Milwaukee & London 1968. Pp. 536—538.

concludent pas evidanment. Mais consideré tout ce que dit est, l'en pourroit par ce croire que la terre est ainsi meue et le ciel non, et n'est pas evidant du contraire; et toutevoies, ce semble de prime face autant ou plus contre raison naturelle comme sont les articles de nostre foy ou touz ou pluseurs. Et ainsi ce que je ay dit par esbatement en ceste maniere peut aler valoir a confuter et reprendre ceulz qui voudroient nostre foy par raysons impugner.

This argument parallels closely that used by Berkeley in the *Analyst*, where he argued that the versions of the calculus presented by Newton and Leibniz were thoroughly lacking in rigour. The work was addressed to an "infidel mathematician", and Berkeley wrote thus[3]:

Whereas then it is supposed that you apprehend more distinctly, consider more closely, infer more justly, conclude more accurately than other men, and that you are therefore less religious because more judicious, I shall claim the privelege of a Freethinker; and take the liberty to inquire into the object, principles, and method of demonstration admitted by the mathematicians of the present age, with the same freedom that you presume to treat the principles and mysteries of Religion; to the end that all men may see what right you have to lead, or what encouragement others have to follow you.

Berkeley was quite prepared to admit the truth of conclusions reached by the calculus. His concern was with the logic of the demonstrations, which he held to be insufficient. Similarly we can see Oresme admitting with Aristotle that the Earth was stationary while reproaching him for his insufficient arguments; and Oresme's principal objections to Aristotle in the *Livre du ciel et du monde* are that Aristotle often held things to be necessarily so when God could have made them otherwise[4]. We should note also that an acceptance of the motion of the Earth would have placed great difficulties in Oresme's way and rendered valueless much of the rest of his commentary on the *De coelo*, for a stationary Earth is fundamental in Aristotelian cosmology, and as subsequent history was to show the "escape from the Aristotelian predicament"[5] could only be performed against almost insurmountable difficulties.

[3] The Works of George Berkeley Bishop of Cloyne. Ed. A. A. Luce & T. E. Jessop. London et al. 1948—57. Vol. 4, p. 65.

[4] Cf. the important article by E. Grant: Late Medieval Thought, Copernicus, and the Scientific Revolution. In: Journal of the History of Ideas 23 (1962) 197—220. Grant there considered Oresme's treatment of the motion of the Earth in the light of Tempier's condemnations of 1277 and the influence of nominalism. He contrasted Oresme's assertion of the hypothetical nature of arguments on this question with Copernicus's conviction that the Earth really did move. See also E. Grant: Physical Science in the Middle Ages. New York et al. 1971. P. 90. There Grant says of Copernicus's belief, "This is the stuff of error, fantasy, and scientific revolutions."

[5] Cf. C. B. Schmitt: A Critical Survey and Bibliography of Studies on Renaissance Aristotelianism 1958—1969. Padua 1971. Pp. 129—132.

Oresme wrote of his *Livre du ciel et du monde*[6], "Je ose dire et me faiz fort que il n'est honme mortel qui onques veist plus bel ne meilleur livre de philosophie naturele que est cestui, ne en ebreu, ne en grec ou arabic ne en latin, ne en françois." But to the modern reader it may seem that its chief mark of originality is the degree of scepticism that it displays, and scepticism by itself is insufficient for scientific advance, since an old view will rarely be rejected completely in the absence of a new candidate to take its place. However, in some of Oresme's earlier works the situation is not so clear-cut and we can see signs of interesting tensions.

I. Tracratus de configurationibus qualitatum et motuum[7]

In the opening sentences of this work Oresme gives some idea of how he viewed it[8]:

Cum ymaginationem meam de uniformitate et difformitate intensionum ordinare cepissem, occurrerunt michi quedam alia que huic proposito interieci ut iste tractatus non solum exercitationi prodesset

---

[6] Oresme: op. cit. (supra n. 2). P. 730.

[7] Edited in M. Clagett: Nicole Oresme and the Medieval Geometry of Qualities and Motions. A Treatise on the Uniformity and Difformity of Intensities, known as Tractatus de configurationibus qualitatum et motuum. Madison, Milwaukee & London 1968 (= De config.). See also L. Thorndike: A History of Magic and Experimental Science. New York 1923—58. Vol. 3, pp. 424—433; D. B. Durand: Nicole Oresme and the Medieval Origins of Modern Science. In: Speculum 16 (1941) 167—185; A. Maier: Zwei Grundprobleme der scholastischen Naturphilosophie. 3rd ed. Rome 1968. Pp. 81 —109; A. Maier: An der Grenze von Scholastik und Naturwissenschaft. 2nd ed. Rome 1952. Pp. 289—343; A. Maier: La Doctrine de Nicolas d'Oresme sur les "Configurationes Intensionum". Reprinted in: A. Maier: Ausgehendes Mittelalter. Rome 1964—67. Vol. 1, Pp. 335—352; A. G. Molland: Oresme Redivivus. In: History of Science 8 (1969) 106—119.

The question of dating Oresme's works is fraught with difficulties. See Thorndike: op. cit. vol. 3, pp. 399—402; M. Clagett: The Science of Mechanics in the Middle Ages. Madison and London 1959. P. 338 n. 11; Clagett in De config. pp. 122—125. However we can be confident that the De configuationibus and De commensurabilitate preceded the Livre de divinacions, which was Oresme's first work in French. In De config. pp. 645—648 (cf. p. 125 n. 12) Clagett has attempted a relative ordering of all Oresme's works. In this the De configurationibus is placed six works later than the De commensurabilitate. E. Grant has given an admittedly tenuous argument for supposing the De configurationibus to precede the De proportionibus proportionum and a fortiori the De commensurabilitate: see Nicole Oresme: De proportionibus proportionum and Ad pauca respicientes. Ed. E. Grant. Madison, Milwaukee & London 1966. Pp. 13—14. From my view of the treatises I am inclined to place the De configurationibus prior to the De commensurabilitate, but the point is not crucial.

[8] De config. p. 158.

sed etiam discipline. In quo ea que aliqui alii videntur circa hoc confuse sentire et obscure eloqui ac inconvenienter aptare studui dearticu-
latim et clare tradere et quibusdam aliis materiis utiliter applicare.

The word "disciplina" must here be taken as meaning demonstrative
science with overtones of mathematics[9], and "exercitatio" probably has
connotations of disputation[10]. Oresme's claim for his work is in fact
reminiscent of Aristotle's characterisation (in Boethius's translation) of
dialectical reasoning as useful for »exercitatio", for "obviationes" and
for "secundum philosophiam disciplinae"[11]. It may be that Oresme was
making a conscious allusion, and the connections between dialectical
reasoning and the demonstrative sciences in Aristotelian thought is
rather obscure[12]. In any case Oresme was clearly expressing a hope that
his treatise would be useful for demonstrative science, and, as we shall
see, he was probably aiming at the creation of a new science.

The most immediately striking feature of the treatise is the "graphical" representations employed in it. These start from the assumption
that the intensity of a quality is quantifiable and can therefore be
represented as a straight line. In the case of a linear subject Oresme
represented the intensity of the quality at any point by a straight line
perpendicular to the subject, and the ratio of the lines at any two points
was the same as the ratio of the intensities at those points. By these
means the whole quality was represented by a plane figure with its base

---

[9] See M. D. Chenu: Notes de lexicographie philosophique médiévale. Disciplina.
In: Revue des Sciences Philosophiques et Théologiques 25 (1936) 686—692. In
Aristotelian translations "disciplina" is found rendering at times "ἐπιστήμη", "μάθημα"
and "μάθησις": see the indices to: Aristoteles Latinus V 1—3 Topica. Ed. L. Minio-
Paluello & B. G. Dod. Leiden 1969, and to other volumes of Aristoteles Latinus.
Cf. also Boethius: In Topica Ciceronis Commentaria 1 (J. P. Migne: Patrologiae
Latinae Tomus LXIV. Paris 1860. P. 1045) and Boethius: De trinitate 2 (The Theolo-
gical Tractates. The Consolation of Philosophy. London & Cambridge Mass. 1918.
P. 8). In his Livre de éthiques Oresme says "et entent par discipline science speculative".
Quoted by Clagett in De config. p. 437 from Nicole Oresme: Le Livre de ethiques
d'Aristote. Ed. A. D. Menut. New York 1940. P. 103.
[10] H. Rashdall has noted the use of the word "exercitium" as a synonym for
"disputatio" in the context of university statutes: see H. Rashdall: The Universities
of Europe in the Middle Ages. Ed. F. M. Powicke & A. B. Emden. London 1936.
Vol. 3, p. 398 n. l. In De config. p. 437 Clagett attempts to give "exercitatio" the
sense of an exercise "leading to a determining of the truth", but he has misread:
The De Moneta of Nicholas Oresme and English Mint Documents. Ed. C. Johnson.
London et al. 1956. P. 1, where the word is "excitari" not "exercitari". Oresme had
(almost certainly earlier) treated of configurations in disputed question form in his
Questiones super geometriam Euclidis of which the relevant portions are re-edited by
Clagett in De config. pp. 521—575.
[11] Topica 1.2, 101 a 25—101 b 14 (Aristoteles Latinus V 1—3, p. 7).
[12] See for instance J. M. Le Blond: Logique et Méthode chez Aristote. 2nd ed.
Paris 1970. Pp. 3—56 and P. Wilpert: Aristoteles und die Dialektik. In: Kant-Studien
48 (1956—7) 247—257.

on the subject, and if, for example, the quality was uniform, the resulting figure was a rectangle. Two-dimensional subjects led in a similar way to "relief maps" in three dimensions, but a three-dimensional subject demanded an infinity of such maps, for Oresme would not allow a fourth dimension. In all this Oresme may be seen as developing along lines similar to his contemporaries and predecessors, for a quantitative treatment of qualities had become fashionable[13], and this naturally led to their representation as straight lines, for such were the paradigm examples of continuous qualities.

Except for the ability he has gained to represent the quantity of the whole quality of a subject unequivocally by the area or volume of the achieved figure[14], Oresme is thus far only new in being clearer and more highly developed than his predecessors. But the clarity that he achieved in representing extended qualities by geometrical figures suggested to him a crucial extension of his doctrine, which appears to show that he was indeed attempting the creation of a new mathematical science. The new step is introduced thus[15]:

Manifestum est corpora in actionibus suis diversimode posse secundum varietatem figurarum eorundem corporum, propter quod antiqui ponentes corpora componi ex athomis dixerunt athomalia ignis fore pyramidalia propter eius activitatem fortem. Unde secundum diversitatem pyramidum possunt corpora magis aut minus pungere; et secundum aliam et aliam actutiem, certum est quedam fortius aut minus fortiter posse secare, et ita de aliis actionibus et figuris. Et cum ita sit de figuris corporum, videtur rationabile conformiter posse dici de predictis figurationibus qualitatum; ut videlicet sit aliqua qualitas cuius particule sint in intensione proportionales parvis pyramidibus, et propter hoc illa sit activior, ceteris paribus, quam equalis qualitas uniformis simpliciter aut que esset proportionalis alteri figure non ita penetrative ...

Oresme is proposing to explain the varying activities of equally intense qualities by means of the geometrical shapes of the configurations representing them. In doing this he seems to be making the science of qualities subalternate to geometry, so that it will be the business of the lower science to know the "quia" through the senses and of the higher to

[13] See Maier: An der Grenze (n. 7 supra), pp. 257—288; De config. 50—73; E. Sylla: Medieval Quantification of Qualities: The "Merton School". In: Archive for History of Exact Sciences 8 (1971) 9—39. Cf. A. G. Molland: The Geometrical Background to the "Merton School". In: British Journal for the History of Science 4 (1968—9) 108—125, pp. 114, 123.
[14] De config. 1.4, pp. 172—176. Oresme gives little heed to the empirical interpretation of equality of qualities, although he does imply that equality of "velocitates totales" implies equality of distances traversed (De config. 3.8, p. 414).
[15] De config. 1.22, p. 226.

know the "propter quid", for in the *Analytica posteriora* Aristotle had said[16]:

Alio autem modo differt propter quid ab ipso quia quod est per aliam scientiam utrumque speculari. Huiusmodi autem sunt quecumque sic se habent ad invicem, quod alterum sub altero sit, ut perspectiva ad geometriam et mechanica ad steriometriam et armonica ad arismeticam et apparentia ad astrologiam. Fere autem univoce sunt quedam harum scientiarum, ut astrologia mathematica et que navalis, et armonica mathematica et que secundum auditum. Hoc enim ipsum quidem quia sensitivorum est scire, propter quid autem mathematicorum; hii enim habent causarum demonstrationes, et multototiens nesciunt ipsum quia, sicut universale considerantes multototiens quedam singularium nesciunt propter inconsiderationem.

Oresme refers to the role of experience when he goes on to emphasise that this shows that equal qualities can act differently, and so there is something to explain[17]:

Nam expertum est qualitatem uniformiter extensam in subiecto, ut puta caliditatem, aliter agere et tactum aliter immutare quam equalis qualitas cuius una particula esset intensa, alia remissa, alia intensa, et sic alternatim secundum particulas subiecti, ita ut illa qualitas esset difformis et iuxta ymaginationem positam ad modum parvarum pyramidum figurata. Unde forsan propter hoc verum est illud quod solet dici, videlicet quod alique qualitates sunt pungitive ut aliquis sapor vel odor vel frigus vel calor, ut calor qui est in pipere. Et inveniuntur quandoque due qualitates eiusdem speciei et eque intense et tamen una est magis activa et magis pungitiva quam alia, cuius causa potest assignari secundum ymaginationem prius dictam . . .

So far Oresme has been relatively tentative and has clearly admitted that the justification for his doctrine rests upon an analogy with how bodies act differently according to their differing corporeal shapes. But as the treatise progresses he shows more and more confidence in the potentialities of the doctrine for explaining a wide range of properties and interactions between objects. We need not consider these in detail, but we may note how Oresme produced a picture in which the qualitative configuration of a body took on a similar reality to its corporeal shape[18]:

---

[16] Anal. post. 1.13, 78 b 35—79 a 6 (Aristoteles Latinus IV 1—4 Analytica Posteriora. Ed. L. Minio-Paluello & B. G. Dod. Bruges & Paris 1968. P. 300). I have quoted the William of Moerbeke recension since there are some obscurities in the James of Venice versio communis (pp. 31—32), although these should not have caused confusion in the Middle Ages.

[17] De config. 1.22, pp. 226—228.

[18] De config. 1.24, p. 232.

Ex philosophia naturali et per experientiam manifestum est omnia corpora naturalia preter quatuor elementa et aliqua mixta ex elementis ipsis in imperfectione propinqua certas sibi determinare figuras, sicut sunt animalia et plante et aliqui lapides et partes istorum. Determinant etiam sibi certas qualitates eis naturales quas quidem qualitates preter figurationem quam habent a subiecto necesse est figurari figuratione quam habent ab earum intensione secundum ymaginationem premissam. Oportet igitur quod predicta corpora naturalia vel forme ipsorum determinent sibi certam figurationem suarum qualitatum radicalium seu complexionalium et sibi naturalium, ut sicut forma leonis exigit aliam corpoream figuram quam forma aquile, ut satis patet primo de Anima, ita calor naturalis leonis sit secundum intensionem aliter figurabilis quam calor aquile vel falconis, et ita de aliis.

We can see how passages like this led A. Maier to assert that for Oresme, "La grandeur intensive n'est pas autre chose qu'une dimension spatiale, invisible sans doute, mais saisissable par la pensée humaine"[19].

Oresme's world in this treatise is a mathematical one[20], but far more parameters are involved than would later be the case for Descartes and others, for besides shape, size and motion, we have to consider the configuration of the various qualities which inform bodies. Even in the case of motion we have to consider what difformities there are in its intensity (or speed) through time, for Oresme believed that, for example, the ability of the stingray to shock depended upon the figuration of its speed[21].

Oresme's programme is an ambitious attempt at scientific advance within a basically Aristotelain framework. But the connection between the geometrical and the empirical sides of his doctrine remained weak. In particular Oresme did not specify any procedure for actually measuring the intensity of qualities, and even if this difficulty could have been surmounted there would have remained the difficulty of attempting to reconstruct the configuration of intensities over a whole body. Oresme showed himself well aware of such weaknesses when he wrote[22], "Verumptamen proportio intensionum non ita de proprie vel ita faciliter attingitur per sensum sicut proportio extensionum." Thus without a firm empirical basis Oresme's imagination could be no more than a likely story, and unless there were clear avenues for providing a stronger

---

[19] Maier: La Doctrine ... (supra n. 7), pp. 342—343.

[20] Cf. Durand: op. cit. (supra n. 7), p. 180: "If we were in the mood of Duhem, looking for a precursor, we might say, here is the forerunner of Descartes indeed, not merely as the inventor of analytical geometry, but as the initiator of the conception that all natural phenomena may be mathematically reduced to magnitude, figure and motion."

[21] De config. 2.10, p. 294.

[22] De config. 3.5, p. 404. Cf. pp. 48—49 and Maier: Zwei Grundprobleme (supra n. 7), p. 85.

base the doctrine could not have seemed worthy of further development. Thus, although the idea of graphical representations was to continue, and the subject "latitudines formarum" to enter some university curricula[23], the attempt to use configurations to provide "propter quid" explanations seems to have died with Oresme; and we may even go further and suggest that this treatise was its first and last manifestation, for Oresme seems never to have reverted to the attempt, and may well have become sceptical of the possibility of attaining knowledge by this route[24].

II. Tractatus de commensurabilitate vel incommensurabilitate motuum celestium[25]

In the prologue to this work Oresme draws on Seneca's *De otio* and Cicero's *De natura deorum* for testimonies to the value of contemplation of the heavenly bodies, and he manages to extend Seneca's praise of Zeno and Chrysippus to commendation of early discoverers of astronomical knowledge[26]:

---

[23] See e. g. S. Günther: Geschichte des mathematischen Unterrichts im deutschen Mittelalter bis zum Jahre 1525 (Monumenta Germaniae Paedagogica 3). Berlin 1887. Pp. 181—182, 198—199, 209—211, 216.

[24] In De config. p. 137 Clagett notes four occasions on which Oresme cites his De configurationibus, but on none of these is Oresme making any appeal to the distinctive features of the configuration doctrine. See G. W. Coopland: Nicole Oresme and the Astrologers. A Study of his Livre de Divinacions. Liverpool 1952. Pp. 60, 92 and Nicole Oresme: Le Livre de Politiques d'Aristote. Ed. A. D. Menut. In: Transactions of the American Philosophical Society 60 (1970) Part 6, pp. 349, 355.

Our suggestion gains weight if Oresme's Questio contra divinatores horoscopios and the annexed Quodlibeta really have the date 1370 which is given by the two extant manuscripts. Thorndike: op. cit. (supra n. 7) p. 402 accepted this date, but Maier: Zwei Grundprobleme (supra n. 7), p. 251 expressed some doubts. In De config. p. 129 Clagett noted that the Quodlibeta treated of problems where one would expect the configuration doctrine to be employed but where it was not. He wrote, "Hence we must conclude either (1) that by 1370 Oresme had completely abandoned, or had little confidence in, the configuration doctrine as a possible explanation, or (2) that the work was written prior to his application of the doctrine to specific phenomena. My inclination is to accept the latter conclusion, and therefore to mistrust 1370 as the composition date." I cannot ascribe very much weight to this argument, but the question of the dating of the Quodlibeta requires further study.

[25] Edited in E. Grant: Nicole Oresme and the Kinematics of Circular Motion. Tractatus de commensurabilitate vel incommensurabilitate motuum celi. Madison, Milwaukee & London 1971 (= De comm.). See also A. Maier: Metaphysische Hintergründe der Spätscholastischen Naturphilosophie. Rome 1955. Pp. 28—30 and V. Zoubov: Nicole Oresme et la Musique. In: Mediaeval and Renaissance Studies 5 (1961) 96—107.

[26] De comm. p. 172.

»Zenonem et Crisippum maiora egisse", affirmat Seneca, "quam si duxissent exercitus, gessissent honores, leges tulissent. Quas non uni civitati, sed toti humano generi tulerunt." Si enim bella gerere, novas leges condere pulchrum est nonne magis commendandi sunt qui plus-quam Herculea audacia superum agressi sunt orbem et ausi mente conspicua scandere celum eterna ipsius decreta primi pronunciare mortalibus; quorum speculatione nihil post deum melius, nihil dulcius.

We might think that the value Oresme places on the first revelations of the "decreta" of the heavens to humans would be a prelude to his announcing further progress. But in fact he, like Seneca in *De otio*[27], has doubts about the possibility of fulfilment of man's natural desire for knowledge[28]:

Quatinus scilicet iocunditatem celestis plausus aspiceret, quam mira celeritate moderatur orbis conversio, quam rato ordine celi constantia mutabilis perseverat, qualitercumque anniversarias vicissitudines perpetuis motibus renovare videtur, quorum ratio et proportio licet per omne temporis seculum lateant et nulla possint subtilitate aut humana diligentia deprehendi, hec tamen impossibilitas nec generat fastidium nec diffidentiam parit, nam quod[29] de hoc capere possumus mentem reficit et allicit atque ad ultra inquirendum incitat et quadam suavi violentia mortalium corda sursum propellit.

Thus, although knowledge cannot be obtained, it is good for the human mind to seek it. Oresme's argument is reminiscent of the reply that Galileo made Salviati give to Simplicio's argument that God may have arranged things differently from what Salviati thought[30]:

An admirable and angelic doctrine, and well in accord with another one, also Divine, which, while it grants to us the right to argue about the constitution of the universe (perhaps in order that the working of the human mind shall not be curtailed or made lazy) adds that we cannot discover the work of His hands. Let us, then, exercise these activities permitted to us and ordained by God, that we may recognize and thereby so much the more admire His greatness, however much less fit we may find ourselves to penetrate the profound depths of His infinite wisdom.

Galileo is clearly being ironic, and after all he thought that he had made a genuine advance in knowledge, but Oresme seems to be in a dilemma. He is imbued with a strong desire for knowledge, but thinks

---

[27] Seneca: De otio 5.7 (Moral Essays vol. 2. Ed. J. W. Basore. London & New York 1932. P. 194).

[28] De comm. p. 174. Here as elsewhere I have taken the liberty of altering the punctuation in the published text.

[29] With MSS FL, for Grant's "quidem".

[30] Galileo Galilei: Dialogue concerning the Two Chief World Systems — Ptolemaic and Copernican, tr. S. Drake. Berkeley & Los Angeles 1962. P. 464.

XII

that his problem is unanswerable, and so falls back on traditional accounts of the value of contemplating the stars. The stated purpose of the work is to offer a middle course, but we may doubt whether he fully succeeds[31]:

Ne igitur tam nobili studio cupientes insistere aut pro nimia difficultate diffidant aut temeraria presumentes audacia seipsos et alios decipient credentes sapere de siderum motibus que sciri nequeunt ab homine, hunc libellum edidi de commensurabilitate motuum celi.

The treatise was written after the *De proportionibus proportionum* and the *Ad pauca respicientes,* which have relations to it[32]. Oresme claims that the new work will contain some conclusions that he has found since his earlier treatises. He asserts his ignorance of anyone having treated the more fundamental conclusions (principaliores), and thus once again indicates a desire to traverse new ground.

After the prologue the work falls into three parts. The first proceeds on the assumption of the commensurability of the celestial motions, and the second on the assumption that some of them are incommensurable. Two motions are taken to be commensurable if commensurable angles are described about the centre or centres in equal times. The most striking feature of assuming the commensurability of the motions of several bodies is that at some time in the future they will return to precisely the positions that they now occupy. The accomplishment of such a return Oresme calls a revolution (revolutio)[33]. In the first two parts of the work Oresme competently proves a number of theorems and solves a number of problems concerning the possibility of various types of conjunction, on the basis of his two different assumptions. But the details of this need not concern us. Of more relevance to our purpose is the third part of the work, for here is faced the real problem, as to whether or not the celestial motions are commensurable.

Oresme introduces the matter thus[34]:

Cum de tribus propositis duo utrumque pertransissem ex duabus ypothesibus contradictoriis utrumque conditionaliter concludendo quid sequitur si omnes motus celi sint invicem commensurabiles, et quid si aliqui sint incommensurabiles; restat tertium quod plus appetit intellectus, non plene quietatus donec cathegorice sit conclusum et quousque suppositum fiat notum, scilicet an sint commensurabiles an non.

But at this point the style changes radically[35]:

[31] De comm. p. 174.
[32] These have also been edited by Grant. See n. 7 supra.
[33] De comm. p. 178.
[34] De comm. p. 284.
[35] Ibid.

Sed dum suspenso animo hoc expedire proponerem, ecce mihi, quasi sompniatori, visus est Apollo, musis et scientiis comitatus, meque talibus increpat verbis: "Pessima", inquit, "tua est occupatio, afflictio spiritus est et labor interminabilis[36]. An nescis quod rerum mundi proportiones noscere[37] precisas humanum transcendit ingenium, quod cum de sensibus[38] queris a sensibus debes incipere, quibus nequit deprehendi precisio punctualis."

Apollo draws on the authority of al-Battāni to emphasise the inability of the senses to detect minute differences of motions, and points out that, when mathematics is applied to the sensible world, sensible principles must be used[39]: "Sic ergo eorum proportio ignota est nec ad eius notitiam te perducet arismetica nec geometria, que cum ad sensibilia applicantur sensibilibus principiis innituntur." Oresme admits that his own powers will not lead him to an answer, and permits himself one cry of complaint[40]: "Sed o dii immortales, qui noscitis omnia, cur fecistis quod homines natura scire desiderant, et fraudato desiderio vel frustrato nobis absconditis optimas veritates?" But then, as if shocked by his own termerity, he launches into assertions of the rightness of things[41], before beseeching Apollo to reveal to him the solution of the problem of commensurability.

But instead of replying himself Apollo calls on the muses and sciences to respond, and immediately two contradictory answers are produced with Arithmetica asserting the commensurability of the motions and Geometria that some of them are incommensurable. When they had thus as it were entered their suits at law (factaque quasi litis contestatione)[42] Apollo ordered that each defend her case with reasons.

The result is interesting. While Oresme is careful that neither sister produce conclusive arguments in favour of her position, his sympathies clearly lie with Geometria. But bound up with Geometria's arguments for commensurability are arguments in favour of the continual emergence of novelty in the world, whereas her sister's are much more in favour of tradition. Thus Geometria emerges as Oresme's spokeswoman not only on the particular issue but on the whole question of progress. She is also in accord with him in emphasising the distinction between probability and truth.

[36] Cf. Ecclesiastes 1.13—14, 17.
[37] With MSS FLP for Grant's "nosce".
[38] With MSS AFLPR for Grant's "sensibilibus".
[39] De comm. p. 286.
[40] Ibid. I read "noscitis" with MS F for Grant's "noscis".
[41] There seems to be a discontinuity here. Could it be that the fellows and masters of Paris University, to whom Oresme submitted the work (De comm. p. 174), demanded some excision of his complaint?
[42] De comm. p. 288.

A central part of Arithmetica's case is that rational ratios are better
than irrational ones, which are in fact absurd (surde)[43], and that therefore the highest bodies in the world must move commensurably with
rational ratios between their motions. Geometria on the other hand is
more impressed with the notion of plenitude, and is constantly asserting
that the more variety there is the better. Thus a mixture of rational and
irrational ratios is better than rational ratios by themselves[44]:

> Nam sive irrationalis proportio sit nobilior sive non, earum tamen
> congrua commixtio pulchrior est singularitate uniformi. Sic enim vide-
> mus in aliis. Unde mixtum ex elementis melius est optimo elemento, et
> celum insignius quam si essent stelle ubique per totum. Ymo universum
> est perfectius propter corruptibila et etiam propter monstra. Cantus-
> que consonantiis variatus dulcior quam si fieret continue optima con-
> sonantia, scilicet dyapason, et pictura variis distincta coloribus specio-
> sior colore pulcherrimo in tota superficie uniformiter diffuso. Sic
> etiam celorum machina nullo carens decore tali varietate componitur,
> ut corpora numero, singulumque eorum pondere, id est magnitudine,
> motusque mensura constent, que mensura si esset numeralis frustra
> videretur dictum numero et mensura.

It is clear that such an insistence upon the variety of nature will make
a scientific description of it much more difficult, and we might even
think that the admission of the "absurd" irrational ratios would make it
seem impossible for Oresme. But in fact he had himself in his *Algorismus
proportionum* and *De proportionibus proportionum* made considerable
advances in the numerical description of irrational ratios[45], and this may
have been in Oresme's mind when he made Geometria hint that irra-
tionality may lie in the eye of the beholder[46]:

> Solet si quidem sepe contingere ut homo subtilis in multa variatione
> pulchritudinem percipiat cuius diversitatis ordinem homo rudis non
> advertens totum estimat fore confusum, sicut irrationalem propor-
> tionem vocamus quam nostra ratio capere nequit, et ipsam tamen
> distincte cognoscit dei ratio infinita, et divino conspectui loco suo
> posita placet, celestesque circuitus efficit pulchriores.

But still a more varied world will prolong the scientific endeavour
indefinitely (a theme to which Oresme will return), while a world based
on simple numerical ratios should in principle be fathomable once and
for all.
In her speech Arithmetica quotes a mass of authorities in support of a

---

[43] Ibid.
[44] De comm. pp. 310—312.
[45] Cf. Molland: op. cit. (supra n. 13), pp. 117—119.
[46] De comm. p. 312.

commensurable arrangement of the world, and seems much concerned to defend the old order of things in which she held first rank[47]:

> Ego inter mathematicas primogenita sum teneoque primatum ita ut ob hoc Macrobius per argumenta multa concludit, "antiquiorem esse numerum superficie et lineis". Si ergo celestibus expellor sedibus, qua parte mundi fugiam, an extra mundi limites exulabor? O mi Jordane frustra me tam subtiliter exquisisti? Quis me dignabitur respicere si mei numeri ad celestes motus nequeant applicari?

To this claim of precedence Geometria gives short shrift, by remarking simply that all rational ratios may also be found among continuous quantities. "Habemus igitur quicquid habet et multo plus: que ergo est primogenitura sua?"[48] But still Arithmetica will have some numerical ratios in the heavens and so suffers no real loss.

Issue is also taken over the music of the spheres and the proper quantities to be used in determining such musical ratios[49], but of more concern to us is one of the consequences of assuming commensurability, for this entails the existence of the Great Year in which all the heavenly bodies return to the same places in which they now are. Arithmetica makes great play with this notion, and, by extending it to the effects of the heavenly bodies, produces a cyclic view of earthly happenings. Apollo had alluded to *Ecclesiastes* earlier when telling Oresme that he had taken on an impossible task, and now Arithmetica is able to use the book to back up her case[50]: "Quid est quod fuit? Ipsum quod futurum est. Quid est quod factum est? Ipsum quod faciendum est. Nihil sub sole novum nec valet quisquam dicere: Ecce hoc recens est; iam enim precessit in seculis, que fuerunt ante nos." According to Arithmetica the »Platonici" had also asserted the return of the very same men at the end of a Great Year. With this whole conception, based on various authorities, Arithmetica seems well pleased. But her sister will have nothing to do with it. Once again she draws on the idea of plenitude, and asserts the continual emergence of new configurations in the heavens, and with them ever new effects below, so that Pythagoras's golden chain of ages will proceed always directly forwards and not return upon itself[51]. The arguments from authority for the Great Year are valueless since the authorities disagree both amongst themselves and with astronomers.

Geometria also dismisses arguments asserting that incommensurability would entail human ignorance, for she says that knowledge of future

---

[47] De comm. pp. 294—296.
[48] De comm. p. 312.
[49] De comm. pp. 296—304, 314—316.
[50] De comm. p. 308. Ecclesiastes 1.9—10. Augustine had striven to liberate this passage from any suggestion of individual return: see De civitate Dei 12.14 (Corpus Christianorum Series Latina XLVIII. Turnhout 1955. Pp. 368—369).
[51] De comm. p. 316.

celestial happenings to an assigned degree of accuracy is sufficient, although she does not say for what it is sufficient. Further it is better that an exact knowledge of the heavenly motions should be impossible, for then men will be stimulated to ever more enquiry. If the motions were known exactly a perpetual almanach of all the effects of the world could be constructed by men. "Et sic forent similes diis immortalibus quorum et non hominum est prenoscere tempora et momenta futura que soli divine subiacent potestati."[52] The belief that future contingents can be known by men is a sign of pride, and indeed some of them are not in any way subject to celestial virtue.

Throughout her speech Geometria has given strong probable arguments for the incommensurability of some of the celestial motions, based largely on the idea of plenitude, and she encapsulates these arguments within the conception of a rectilinear time sequence[53], which will lead always to new events, and in which man will strive continually to know more and more about the universe. She concludes her speech with an allusion to a mathematical argument from Oresme's *De proportionibus proportionum* to the effect that given two unknown magnitudes it is more probable that they are incommensurable than commensurable[54]. But she had started her speech by a strong assertion that "nihil ... prohibet quedam falsa esse probabiliora quibusdam veris"[55]. Thus however heavily her arguments weighed with Oresme, nothing certain has been achieved. And at the end of the speeches he expresses his bewilderment at the sisters' not using arguments appropriate to their sciences[56]:

> Cum cuicumque vero consonet omne verum, cur sunt discordes iste veritatis parentes? Et quid est quod loquuntur rethoricis persuasionibus aut topicis probationibus que solent uti solum demonstrationibus omnem aliam argumentationem aspernantes? Cur incertioris scientie modum eis insolitum acceperunt?

Apollo assures him that there is no true disagreement between the sisters and that they were only in play mocking the procedures of an inferior science. He too will now join in the game and adopt the role of a judge, who after examining the cases will pronounce the truth in the form of a judgment. But at this point the dream vanishes, and Oresme is left without a resolution of his problem.

---

[52] De comm. p. 320.
[53] Cf. Zoubov: op. cit. (supra n. 25), pp. 105—107.
[54] De comm. p. 320. Oresme: De proportionibus proportionum (supra n. 7) pp. 246—262.
[55] De comm. p. 310.
[56] De comm. p. 322.

Conclusion

Our examination has revealed to us both Oresme's strong desire to make scientific progress and his scepticism about the possibility of attaining scientific knowledge. In both works it was the empirical element that was most troubling. In the *De configurationibus* no procedures were given for measuring the intensities of qualities, and in the *De commensurabilitate* sense experience was seen to be incapable of resolving a problem for which mathematics alone was incompetent. Admittedly Geometria stressed the sufficiency of knowledge to a given degree of approximation, but she did not say for what end such knowledge was sufficient, although the concept of sufficiency does imply an end. In his *Livre de divinacions* Oresme gave three ends for the study of astrology (a term which includes our "astronomy")[57]. The first is to have knowledge of the celestial bodies and so satisfy a natural human urge. The second and most important arises from the fact that such study leads to an increased knowledge of God the Creator. The third and least important end is to know certain present and future dispositions of corruptible nature. It would seem that knowledge to a given degree of approximation would only be strongly relevant to the third end, which Oresme ranks low. The lack of emphasis on the predictive power of knowledge of nature or on the possibility of its application to practice made it difficult for Oresme to envisage a satisfactory system of probable knowledge. He was thus caught between his desire for construction and his very clear-headed ability for criticism. By the time that he composed his last work on natural philosophy, the *Livre du ciel et du monde*, it seems that criticism had gained the upper hand.

---

[57] Coopland: op. cit. (supra n. 24) p. 112; cf. pp. 132—133.

XIII

MEDIEVAL IDEAS OF SCIENTIFIC PROGRESS

Edgar Zilsel's classic article[1] saw the genesis of the concept of scientific progress among the "superior artisans" of the sixteenth century. Subsequent studies supplemented this by accentuating the role of contemporary scholars in the formation of the notion.[2] But it is at first glance surprising that, given the great growth of interest in medieval science, little attempt has been made to push the idea back into earlier centuries.[3] A second more lingering glance reveals that the evidence is sparse; nevertheless it is not completely non-existent, although often ambiguous. The purpose of this paper is to sift some of the more noteworthy evidence and to enquire why it does not appear to mirror a full-blown concept of scientific progress.

Zilsel approached his task with three criteria to be sought:[4] "(1) the insight that scientific knowledge is brought about step by step through contributions of generations of explorers building upon and gradually amending the findings of their predecessors; (2) the belief that this process is never completed; (3) the conviction that contribution to this development, either for its own sake or for the public benefit, constitutes the very aim of the true scientist." These criteria were admirably adapted to his end, but for our purposes they are too harsh. We shall have to formulate and refine characterizations as we proceed, but we shall demand as a minimum something more than a mere consciousness of change. For that reason the numerous references to *antiqui* and *moderni* will not of and by themselves be relevant.[5] Similarly I shall not lay down any rigid definition of "science," but the main focus of

---

* Versions of this paper have been delivered to audiences in Oxford, Cambridge and Aberdeen. I have benefited from the comments and criticisms then received, as also from several discussions with Dr. A. W. Wear.

[1] E. Zilsel, "The Genesis of the Concept of Scientific Progress," *J.H.I.*, 6 (1945), 325-49.

[2] E.g., A. C. Keller, Zilsel, the Artisans and the Idea of Progress in the Renaissance," *J.H.I.*, 11(1950), 235-40; S. Lilley, "Robert Recorde and the Idea of Progress," *Renaissance and Modern Studies*, 2(1958), 3-37; P. Rossi, *Philosophy, Technology, and the Arts in the Early Modern Era*, trans. S. Attansio, (New York & London, 1970), Ch. 2, "The Idea of Scientific Progress."

[3] For a recent treatment of ideas of progress in different eras, with substantial bibliography, see A. C. Crombie, "Some Attitudes to Scientific Progress: Ancient, Medieval and Early Modern," *History of Science*, 13(1975), 213-30.

[4] Zilsel, *op. cit.*, 326.

[5] On the various senses in which these terms were used see M.-D. Chenu,

562

attention will be on systematized knowledge (or supposed knowledge) of the natural world.

History and cycles. Augustine and Hugh of St. Victor

Ideas of progress are closely linked with wider questions of how historical development is conceived. But that does not mean that we can latch onto any simple contrast between pagan cyclical time and Judeo-Christian directed time.[6] The sources are more ambiguous, and even the magisterial authority of Augustine did not rule out some notably cyclical conceptions among later writers. As we shall see, these were associated with the widespread view that in some sense the celestial bodies governed, though did not determine, the events of the sublunary world. In the *City of God* Augustine launched vigorous attacks upon both astrology and a cyclical conception of time,[7] but his rhetorical vehemence limited the coercive power of his arguments. He made good use of the argument from twins in his assault upon astrology, but, in common with many other writers, he did not distinguish clearly between the ontological or physical aspects of astrology and its epistemological ones. To assert celestial influence on sublunary events is not at all the same as to be able to predict sublunary events from the position of the stars. Augustine concentrated his main attack on the predictive powers of astrologers, and it was largely by extrapolation that he cast doubt upon the existence of celestial influence. And here his case could not be watertight, for it was difficult to deny the influence of the sun on the seasons and the moon on the tides.[8] He did not tangle with the commonplace that the stars only inclined and did not compel. If he had his argument would have been less clearcut. Likewise in his attack on cycles, he only considered the extreme form of the doctrine, in which the very same Plato would continually reappear to teach in the Academy. He did not close the way to milder beliefs in the revolutions of

"Notes de lexicographie philosophique médiévale. *Antiqui, moderni,*" *Revue des Sciences Philosophiques et Théologiques,* 17(1928), 82-94, and cf. M.-D. Chenu, *La Théologie au Douzième Siècle* (3rd ed., Paris, 1976), Ch. 18. "Tradition et Progrès," trans. in M.-D. Chenu, *Nature, Man and Society in the Twelfth Century* (Chicago & London, 1968), Ch. 9. *Miscellanea Mediaevalia 9. Antiqui und Moderni: Traditionsbewusstsein und Fortschrittsbewusstsein im späten Mittelalter,* ed. A. Zimmermann (Berlin & New York, 1974), has less on concepts of progress than the subtitle might suggest.

[6] On the dangers of such oversimplification see, e.g., A. Momigliano, "Time in Ancient Historiography," *History and the Concept of Time,* Beiheft 6 of *History and Theory,* 5(1966), 1-23.

[7] *De civitate Dei,* V.1-9, XII.10-21, in *Corpus Christianorum Series Latina* (Turnhout, 1953-), hereafter *CCSL*), XLVII, 128-40, XLVIII, 364-79; trans. H. Bettenson, *Concerning the City of God against the Pagans* (Harmondsworth, 1972), 179-94, 483-502.

[8] *De civitate Dei,* V.6, in CCSL, XLVII, 133-34; Bettenson, 186.

times in history. And he had to take on the famous cyclical passage from *Ecclesiastes:*[9] "What is it that has been? The same as what will be. What is it that has been done? The same as what will be done. There is nothing new under the sun. If anyone says: 'Look, here is something new,' it has already happened in the ages before us." Augustine gives this a minimalist interpretation in terms of the succession of generations and suchlike themes, but this could easily have been enriched by the idea that "history always repeats itself with a difference" without falling into the dire difficulties presented by the doctrine of individual return. Indeed we may even see a certain cyclical pattern in Augustine's likening of the epochs of history to the six days of Creation, although it is perhaps more appropriate to think of a cylindrical helix rather than a circle,[10] for despite the reservations that I have suggested, history for Augustine was still directed towards a very definite end. But this implied no simple progressivism, and certainly not for the earthly city.[11] Augustine did allude to the developments that had taken place in the arts, but this was to emphasize God's goodness to man even in the fallen state.[12] There was no focus on future progress.

The twelfth century has often been seen as giving rise to a new historical consciousness with greater emphasis on the directedness of history. But whereas F. Heer could entitle a chapter, "The Birth of History (Twelfth Century),"[13] R. W. Southern has written, "The intellectual climate of the twelfth century was not generally favorable to historical thought."[14] The apparent contradiction may arise from a difference of focus, with Heer looking mainly to Germany and Southern to France. Associated with this, but more relevant to our purpose, it may be that those with the historical attitude were not engaged in nor showed any particular enthusiasm for investigations into the philosophy of nature. A possible exception is Hugh of St. Victor who held a markedly developmental view of the history of man since the Fall, and who displayed more than an average interest in the liberal and mechani-

[9] *Ecclesiastes,* I.9-10. *De civitate Dei,* XII.14, in *CCSL,* XLVIII, 368-69; Bettenson, 488.

[10] *De civitate Dei,* XXII.30, in *CCSL,* XLVIII, 865-66; Bettenson, 1091, Cf. *De genesi contra Manichaeos,* I.23, ed. J.-P.Migne, *Patriologiae Cursus Completus. . . . Series Latina* (Paris, 1844-93) (hereafter *PL*), XXXIV, 190-93.

[11] On Augustine's conception of progress see T. E. Mommsen, "St. Augustine and the Christian Idea of Progress: The Background to *The City of God," J.H.I.,* 12(1951), 346-74, rpt. in T. E. Mommsen, *Medieval and Renaissance Studies* (Ithaca, N.Y., 1959), 265-98.

[12] *De civitate Dei,* XXII.24, in *CCSL,* XLVIII, 848-49; Bettenson, 1072-73.

[13] F. Heer, *The Intellectual History of Europe,* trans. J. Steinberg (London, 1966), 80.

[14] R. W. Southern, "Aspects of the European Tradition of Historical Writing: 2. Hugh of St. Victor and the Idea of Historical Development," *Transactions of the Royal Historical Society,* Fifth Series, XXI (1971), 159-79, at 163.

564

cal arts.[15] Both of these were creations of man after the Fall, and were made possible by there remaining in him some spark of the sempiternal fire of truth.[16] The arts were properly part of the process of restoring the integrity of human nature.[17] They did not come into being all at once, and in a sense they existed implicitly before being formalized.[18] "All sciences . . . were matters of use before they became matters of art. But when men subsequently considered that use can be transformed into art, and what was previously vague and subject to caprice can be brought into order by definite rules and precepts, they began, we are told, to reduce to art the habits which had arisen partly by chance, partly by nature—correcting what was bad in use, supplying what was missing, eliminating what was superfluous, and furthermore prescribing definite rules and precepts for each usage." But, once an art had been formed, Hugh gave little attention to its future development, and transmission was his main interest. In his account of the "authors of the arts"[19] the thousand years immediately before his own times were neglected. As Southern put it,[20] "In all essentials [the arts] had reached their final perfection when the third age of human history began with the birth of Christ. They were ready to play their part in the full unfolding of the truth in the third and last stage of history." Hugh's somewhat limited developmental view of the arts is not something that he extrapolated into the future. Nor have I found evidence that other historical writings of the period contain anything like a richer concept of scientific progress. This even applies to Joachim of Fiore, as regards himself rather than his possible influence on such later thinkers as Roger Bacon.[21]

Dwarfs and Giants

At first glance a more promising line of enquiry is presented by the image of dwarfs and giants, which seems to have originated with Bernard of Chartres, and was still used by Newton in a charitable moment in relation to Hooke and others.[22] But matters are not quite so simple.[23]

[15] On this and what follows see Southern, op. cit.

[16] Hugh of St. Victor, Epitome Dindimi in Philosophiam, 2, ed. R. Baron, Hugonis de Sancto Victore Opera Propadeutica (Notre Dame, Indiana, 1966), 193-94.

[17] Hugh of St. Victor, Didascalicon, I.5 (I.6 in PL), in PL, CLXXVI, 745, trans, J. Taylor, The Didascalicon of Hugh of St. Victor (New York & London, 1961), 51-52.

[18] Didascalicon, I.11 (I.12 in PL), ed. in PL, CLXXVI, 750, trans. Taylor, 59.

[19] Didascalicon, III.2, ed. in PL, CLXXVI, 765-67, trans. Taylor, 83-86.

[20] Southern, op. cit., 171.

[21] A case for strong Joachimite influence on Bacon is made out by S. C. Easton, Roger Bacon and his Search for a Universal Science (Oxford, 1952), 131-43, 188-96, and it may be that Joachim's ideas had an important role in shaping Bacon's view of history, and that this in turn conditioned his attitude to scientific progress.

The first extant use of the image seems to be in the first redaction of William of Conches's glosses on Priscian. Priscian in his introduction had said of grammatical authors that[24] "inasmuch as they are more recent so they are more perspicacious" (*quanto sunt iuniores tanto perspicaciores*), and William comments:[25] "He says well, because the moderns are more perspicacious than the ancients, but not wiser. The ancients only had the writings that they themselves composed, but we have all their writings, and moreover all those that were composed from the beginning up to our time. And so we perceive more, but do not know more. . . . Whence we are as a dwarf on the shoulder of a giant. He sees more not from his own size but from the size of his support. . . ." Later in the work William held that "we are reporters and expositors of the ancients, not the founders (*inventores*) of new things."[26] Nevertheless William was himself accused of novelties by William of St. Thierry.[27] John of Salisbury used the image in a discussion of Aristotle's *De interpretatione*. Isidore of Seville had epitomized the high genius of that work by saying that, "When he wrote the *De interpretatione* Aristotle dipped his pen into his mind,"[28] but on the other hand doctors of John's time could,[29] "except for the awe of the words, more concisely and lucidly provide everything that is taught in that book in the teaching primers that they call *Introductions*" with the addition of other things not less necessary for the attainment of knowledge of the art. The image is employed to explain the apparent contradiction:[30] "Bernard of Chartres used to say that we are as dwarfs perched on the shoulders of giants, so that we can see more numerous and more remote things, not, assuredly, by the sharpness of our sight or our bodily eminence, but because we are lifted up and exalted by their gigantic stature." John held that so far as possible the form of words of the ancient giants should be preserved, for they possess hidden as well as

[22] *The Correspondence of Isaac Newton*, ed. H. W. Turnbull *et al.* (Cambridge, 1959-), I, 418.

[23] In what follows I draw heavily on the important article by E. Jeauneau, " 'Nani gigantum humeris insidentes': Essai d'interprétation de Bernard de Chartres," *Vivarium*, 5 (1967), 79-99.

[24] Priscian, *Institutionum Grammaticarum Libri XVIII*, ed. M. Hertz (Leipzig, 1855) I,1; Vol. I-*Grammatici Latini*, ed. H. Keil, Vol. II.

[25] Translated from the quotation in Jeauneau, *op. cit.*, 84.

[26] *Ibid.*, 85.

[27] William of St. Thierry, *De erroribus Guillelmi de Conchis ad Sanctum Bernardum*, ed. in *PL*, CLXXX, 333.

[28] Isidore of Seville, *Etymologiarum sive Originum Libri XX*, ed. W. M. Lindsay (Oxford, 1911), II.xxvii, 1.

[29] John of Salisbury, *Metalogicon*, III.4, ed. C.C.I. Webb (Oxford, 1929), 135; translation modified from that by D. D. McGarry, *The Metalogicon of John of Salisbury* (rpt. Gloucester, Mass., 1971), 165-66.

[30] *Ibid.*, ed. Webb, 136.

apparent power, but he still had to admit some form of progress:[31] "I have not disdained to cite the opinions of the moderns, which in many matters I do not hesitate to prefer to those of the ancients."

Finally I cite the use of the image by Alexander Neckham, who, through associating it with a fable, implied that there was something dishonest in modern presumption.[32] "The birds agreed among themselves that the one who overcame all the others in lofty flight should be accorded the glory of regal dignity. The wren therefore by hiding under the wing of the eagle immediately seized the opportunity, for when the eagle, nearest the sanctuary of Jove, would have claimed the lordship for himself, the wren dared to sit on the head of the eagle and declare himself to be the victor. And thus he gained the name of prince (*regulus*). This fabulous tale applies to those who, entering upon the labors of others, presume to transfer to themselves the glory due to the others. 'And,' as the philosopher says, 'we are as dwarfs standing on the shoulders of giants.' And so we are bound to ascribe to our predecessors those things that we sometimes transfer to our own praise and glory (*in gloriam laudis nostrae*), like the wren who, by light labor, indeed by none, claimed to have beaten the eagle."

Thus the general force of the image in the twelfth century was to warn against pride, rather than to give even a modest affirmation of progress. But just as statutes can often give evidence of the existence of the abuses against which they were directed, so this image can suggest that there was a fairly widespread confidence that progress was being made. But progress in what fields? Where a definite context can be assigned to the image it was usually that of the trivium, although it occasionally crops up in medicine.[33] Can we speak of any similar consciousness of progress in natural philosophy? Here the definite evidence is fragmentary, and we need to depend largely on assessments of the attitudes of those interested in such studies. There is no doubt of the enthusiasm for a philosophic study of nature, but this was soon coupled with a feeling of inferiority. William of Conches's assertion in the passage quoted above[34] that "we have all [the ancients'] writings, and moreover all those that were composed from the beginning up to our time" could not apply, and moreover it was evident that the neighboring Muslim cultures had a far higher level of sophistication in these matters than the Christians. Much had to be learned before there could be talk of further advance. But there was still room for Adelard of Bath to affirm that,[35] "the generation (*generatio*) has the inborn vice that it thinks

[31]*Metalogicon*, Prologus, ed. Webb, 4.
[32] Neckham, *De naturis rerum*, I.78, ed. T. Wright (London, 1863), 122-23.
[33] Jeauneau, *op. cit.*, 88-90.   [34] See n. 25 above.
[35] *Die Quaestiones Naturales des Adelardus von Bath*, ed. M. Müller, *Beiträge zur Geschichte der Philosophie und Theologie des Mittlelalters*, 31, Heft 2 (Münster, 1934), 1.

that nothing found by the moderns should be received," and to assert vehemently the right of reason to judge authority, even if this was effectively a plea for a change of authorities rather than a rejection of authority itself.[36] But more importantly it was by the efforts of men like Adelard that a whole host of new learning was made available to the Latins and completely changed the state of natural philosophy among them.

Roger Bacon

Before carrying over our enquiry into the new state of affairs, it is advisable to make some distinctions. We may speak of three kinds of intellectual progress. First there is progress of the individual, which ties up closely with education. Secondly there is progress of a particular group, as, for instance, that of Western Christendom. And finally there is that kind of progress which demands absolute novelty, rather than being satisfied with the re-creation of something that had existed in the past. When we speak of progress in general we are usually thinking of only the last kind, and we easily neglect its close relation with the other forms. But in the Middle Ages the conceptual patterning was different, and we need to be sensitive to a range of differing emphases. This is particularly the case when we examine Roger Bacon.

Although Bacon may not be the most typical thinker of his time, we cannot maintain the old view of him as being temporally misplaced by three centuries, and hence completely unrepresentative of his age. And for our purposes he is particularly useful in that the form of his writings allows far more evidence to be culled as to his views on progress than can be done with most of the Schoolmen. In fact there is one striking passage, which Duhem adopted as an epigraph for his *Système du monde*,[37] in which Bacon appears unequivocally to affirm progress in our third and strongest sense. "Never in any age was any science discovered, but from the beginning of the world wisdom has increased gradually, and it has not yet been completed as regards this life." But there are complications. The context of the remark was educationalist, with Bacon attacking what he saw as the ignorant presumption of the teaching friars. The fuller quotation reads:[38] "But certainly the truth is that [the friars] know nothing useful when they come to the study of theology, nor moreover do they wish to learn from others. But they study by themselves in all things, and it is impossible that a man should acquire difficult sciences by himself. For never in any age was any science discovered, but from the beginning of

[36] *Ibid.*, 11-12. Cf. L. Thorndike, *A History of Magic and Experimental Science* (New York, 1923-58), II, 28-29.

[37] P. Duhem, *Le Système du Monde* (Paris, 1913-59), I, 1.

[38] Roger Bacon, Ch. 5, "Compendium studii philosophiae," in *Fr. Rogeri Bacon Opera Quaedam Hactenus Inedita [OQHI]*, ed. J. S. Brewer (London, 1859), I (only volume published), 429.

568

the world wisdom has increased gradually, and it has not yet been completed as regards this life. Therefore an infinite pride has invaded the orders, that they presume to teach before they learn." The main thrust of Bacon's argument here concerns progress in the first sense, that of the individual, and he only brings in his more general assertion as an argument for the impossibility of effective self-education. Given the general vehemence of this work, the *Compendium studii philosophiae,* we should be careful not to attach too much weight to a throwaway line. And indeed it is inconsistent with other more developed views, which led to Bacon putting much emphasis on progress of the second kind, that of the cultural group.

This was necessary for him because of his view that the plenitude of philosophy had been revealed to the patriarchs and prophets, "for it was impossible for man to reach the great things of the arts and sciences by himself, but it was necessary that he had revelation. . . . I say that the power of philosophy was given by God to the same people as was given the holy scriptures, namely the saints from the beginning, so that there should thus appear to be one complete wisdom necessary to men. For only the patriarchs and prophets were true philosophers who knew all things, that is not only the law of God, but all parts of philosophy."[39] From thence philosophy passed down through the ages by means of an elaborate genealogy of knowledge which Bacon constructs from the writings of Josephus, Augustine, and others. During this process the quality had deteriorated significantly, but Bacon was not a mere declinist and he saw means of ameliorating the situation.

Bacon frequently inveighed against the poor quality of Latin translations of ancient works, particularly those af Aristotle. "I am therefore certain that it would have been better that the wisdom of Aristotle had not been translated than that it had been delivered with such obscurity and perversity. . . . Whence the Lord Robert sometime Bishop of Lincoln disregarded altogether the books of Aristotle and their ways, and through his own experience and other authors and other sciences dealt with Aristotle's matters of wisdom. And he knew and wrote on those things of which the books of Aristotle speak a hundred thousand times better than could be gathered from the perverse translations."[40] Bacon's extravagance has gone beyond the bounds of consistency: neither he nor Grosseteste ignored the existing translations of Aristotle. But the other ways of advancing or recovering knowledge are characteristic of Bacon's programme, and for our purpose the most important is the way of experience.

[39] Bacon, *The "Opus maius" of Roger Bacon,* II, 9, ed. J. H. Bridges, (3 vols. Oxford, 1897-1900; rpt. Frankfurt, 1964), III, 53. Cf. Roger Bacon, Ch. 24, *Opus tertium,* ed. Brewer, *OQHI,* I, 79-81.

[40] *Compendium studii philosophiae,* Ch. 8, *op. cit.* 469.

Bacon's experimental science (*scientia experimentalis*) has come in for much attention,[41] although this has often been to confront Bacon's account with modern discussions of scientific method. Here I wish to take Bacon on his own terms with a particular view to seeing what sorts of progress he thought were possible through these means.[42] For Bacon, full knowledge of something reached through demonstration was not possible without experience. This even applied to mathematics. Experience was of two kinds, exterior and interior, and the latter included divine inspiration. Experimental science had three prerogatives with respect to other sciences. The first was to investigate by experience the conclusions deduced from the principles of the other sciences. His main examples were the rainbow and similar phenomena, and the central problem area was that of relating an established mathematical science to happenings in the natural world. Bacon clearly claims advance in at least the second sense in the application of experimental science. "The natural philosopher discourses of these things [*sc.* the rainbow etc.], and the *perspectivus* has many things to add that concern the mode of seeing, which is necessary in this regard. But neither Aristotle nor Avicenna in his *naturalia* give us knowledge (*notitia*) of things of this kind, nor Seneca, who composed a special book about them. But experimental science makes them known (*ista certificat*),"[43] But the emphasis on experience (which is an individual affair) means that there must also be emphasis on progress in the first sense, and on the question of haloes Bacon admitted that he himself had progress to make:[44] "I do not claim to have reached the full truth because I have not yet experienced (*nondum expertus sum*) all the things that are here necessary. . . ."

The second prerogative of experimental science was to produce truths which, although they were within the bounds of another science, were yet neither principles nor conclusions of that science. Here experience strictly preceded reason. Mathematics could construct a spherical astrolabe, but to make it rotate by celestial influence required experimental science. The allusion is clearly to the theory of magnetism, developed by Petrus Peregrinus,[45] who was Bacon's prime exemplar of an experimenter. Another, and for Bacon more important example of the second prerogative was the prolongation of human life, which fell

[41] For useful accounts see Thorndike, *op. cit.*, II, 649-59; A. C. Crombie, *Robert Grosseteste and the Origins of Experimental Science* (2nd imp., Oxford, 1961), 139-42, 155-62; N. W. Fisher & S. Unguru, "Experimental Science and Mathematics in Roger Bacon's Thought," *Traditio,* **27**(1971), 353-78.

[42] The principal account is in *The "Opus Maius" of Roger Bacon, op. cit.*, II, 167-222. Cf. *Part of the Opus Tertium of Roger Bacon*, ed. A. G. Little (Aberdeen, 1912), 43-54.

[43] *Opus maius*, VI.2, ed. Bridges, II, 173.

[44] *Ibid.*, VI.12, ed. Bridges, II, 201.

[45] Cf. *A Source Book in Medieval Science*, ed. E. Grant (Cambridge, Mass., 1974), 373.

within the bounds of medicine but could not be fully taught by the medical art. It was clear that the span of human life had badly deteriorated since the time of the patriarchs, but Bacon believed that the decline could be reversed by medical means. And this possibility of restoration tied up with Bacon's theory of knowledge, for long life gave time for experience.[46] "Josephus in the first book of Antiquities says that since the sons of Adam through Seth were religious men and made by God himself, God gave them six hundred years to live on account of the glorious parts of philosophy that they studied, so that through length of life they could experience what God revealed to them." We are here very much in the domain of progress in the second sense.

The third prerogative of experimental science was to investigate the secrets of nature that were outside the bounds of the other sciences. By these means we could have better knowledge of past, present and future events than could be given by judicial astrology. But Bacon put more emphasis on the practical possibilities of this prerogative, and cites, for example, the alteration of air to change character, and also Greek fire and explosives. Experimental science as a whole, and particularly its third prerogative, was Bacon's substitute for magic.[47] Bacon roundly condemned magic, particularly insofar as it involved the action of demons, but was fascinated by the power that seemed to be involved. Luckily most of the wonders that could be effected by magic Bacon believed could also be brought about by an understanding of the secrets of art and nature, and often magicians were in fact making use of natural means when they thought that they were employing demons. Experimental science could produce devices of the utmost value to Christendom, particularly for use in the Crusades.[48] Moreover, when Antichrist arrived, he would be particularly well versed in this science, and so there was a pressing need for defenses to be prepared by the same means.

Bacon clearly had a conception of progress in a certain sense, even if in his more considered moments he emphasized the restoration theme; but studies of the *prisca* tradition in later centuries have shown that he

[46] *Opus maius,* II.9, ed. Bridges, III, 54.

[47] On Bacon's relation to magic see A. G. Molland, "Roger Bacon as Magician," *Traditio,* 30(1974), 445-60, and its references.

[48] P. A. Throop, *Criticism of the Crusade* (Philadelphia, 1975), 132-33, portrays Bacon as a vehement opponent of the Crusades, Bacon certainly emphasized preaching over war, and criticized the Crusaders for not converting infidels and for not holding the lands that they had taken. But there were still the unconvertible, predestined to Hell, and they had to be driven out. Bacon was suspicious of the efficacy of laymen's wars, and recommended that they be supplemented if not replaced by "works of wisdom" (such as optical tricks). See *Opus maius,* III. 13-14, V.3.3.3., ed. Bridges, III, 120-25, II. 164; *Opus tertium,* 26, 36, ed. Brewer, 95-96, 116-17; *Comp. stud. phil.,* 1, ed. Brewer, 395-96. I am grateful to Mr. A. T. Hall for bringing Throop's book to my attention.

was by no means the last to do that.[49] The importance that he ascribed to experience meant that many of the advances he expected were in technics, but he did not have the clear luciferous-lucriferous distinction of his homonymous successor. It is perhaps significant that Petrus Peregrinus, his main hero in such matters, should almost certainly be ascribed to the class of "superior craftsmen" among whom Zilsel saw the genesis of the concept of scientific progress in the sixteenth century.[50] We can do little more than speculate whether there were not many more of his type who neither left a literary legacy nor had a Bacon to immortalize them. But apart from Bacon the extant sources reveal scant consciousness of technical progress.[51]

University Studies. New Sciences

A huge amount of the source material for medieval science had its origins in the universities, and the modes of instruction clearly had an overwhelming effect on how scholars conceived their aims. The commentary aimed at interpreting the text, and both commentaries and disputations examined an author's arguments and attempted to reconcile apparently conflicting passages. Sharply critical approaches led eventually to more skeptical tendencies, and this was probably abetted by a boredom factor which would forever seek new interpretations, but this usually produced a host of unordered novelties rather than a systematic development. Many previously outlandish doctrines were regarded as possible but rarely were they held actually to be the case. And even when they were, as with impetus theories, there was little sense of violently rocking the boat, for impetus can be seen as a rather inoffensive transfer of the moving power from the air to the projectile. The commentatorial spirit even invaded the special sciences, such as geometry, statics, and optics, where the dominant tendency was a desire to understand one's author and to analyze his arguments. There are occasional exceptions, such as Thomas Bradwardine's explicit assertion of novelty in his treatment of star polygons,[52] but these cannot

[49] See, e.g., C. B. Schmitt, "Perennial Philosophy: from Agostino Steuco to Leibniz," *J.H.I.*, 27(1966), 505-32, and J. E. McGuire & P. M. Rattansi, "Newton and the 'Pipes of Pan,'" *Notes and Records of the Royal Society of London*, 21(1966), 108-43.

[50] See the very careful study by E. Schlund, "Petrus Peregrinus von Maricourt," *Archivum Franciscanum Historicum*, 4(1911), 436-55, 633-43; 5(1912), 22-40.

[51] B. Gille, "Technological Developments in Europe: 1100-1400," *The Evolution of Science*, ed. G. S. Métraux & F. Crouzet (New York, 1963), 193, 205; but cf. L. White, "Cultural Climates and Technological Advance in the Middle Ages," *Viator*, 2(1971), 171-201.

[52] A. G. Molland, *The Geometria Speculativa of Thomas Bradwardine: Text with critical discussion* (Ph.D. thesis, Cambridge, 1967), 75.

572

add up to any general conscious aim to make progress in the special sciences by extending their frontiers.

A more promising area is where the lack of a special science was felt, as in the case of sublunary motion, for on this Antiquity had bequeathed little more than a few scattered remarks by Aristotle. I have argued elsewhere[53] that Bradwardine's *Tractatus de proportionibus* should be seen as at least a partial attempt to create a new mathematical science of motion rather than as the replacement of an Aristotelian law by a new law. In another work Bradwardine even gave hints of attempting to form a mathematical science of theology.[54] Bradwardine does not explicitly speak of trying to form new sciences, but Oresme reveals a clearer intent. At the beginning of his *De configurationibus* he says that the work is intended to be useful for *disciplina* as well as for *exercitatio*.[55] This, I believe, must be taken as asserting that Oresme means to contribute to the formation of a demonstrative science, and hinting that dialectical disputation was a road to the principles of that science. The central burden of the work was to provide a mathematical treatment of qualities in such a way that their science would be subalternate to geometry. Bradwardine and Oresme seem very clearly to have wished to effect progress by the production of new sciences, but the very attempts highlight the obstacles that were in the way. The most evident weakness in their schemes is the empirical basis. No practical procedures are laid down for measuring the required quantities, and moreover there are conceptual difficulties in quantification, as when Bradwardine wishes to compare powers that strictly speaking are indivisible.[56]

We should also note at this point that there was no universally standardized system of units for measuring. The Aristotelian theory of measure[57] was in terms of units, for instance of a particular length that was treated as if it were one and indivisible so that other lengths could be counted in terms of it. But the choice of unit was in most cases essentially arbitrary, and the image of lack of precision was rein-

[53] A. G. Molland, "Ancestors of Physics," *History of Science*, 14(1976), 60-61, 67-70.

[54] Bradwardine, *De causa Dei, contra Pelagium*, ed. H. Savile (London, 1618).

[55] *Nicole Oresme and the Medieval Geometry of Qualities and Motions. A Treatise on the Uniformity and Difformity of Intensities, known as Tractatus de configurationibus qualitatum et motuum*, ed. M. Clagett (Madison, 1968), 158. Cf. A. G. Molland, "Nicole Oresme and Scientific Progress," *Miscellanea Mediaevalia*, 9(1974), 208-09. To its references add G. E. L. Owen, Τιθέναι τὰ φαινόμενα" *Aristote et les problèmes de la méthode* (Louvain, 1961), 83-103, rpt. in *Aristotle*, ed. J. M. E. Moravcsik (London, 1968), 167-90, and Peter of Spain, *Tractatus*, ed. L. M. de Rijk (Assen, 1972), 1.

[56] Bradwardine, *Tractatus de proportionibus*, II.4, ed. H. L. Crosby (Madison, 1955), 104-10.

[57] See in particular *Metaphysics*, I.1, 1052a15-1053b9.

forced by the common habit of naming units of length after parts of the body. Thus John Buridan, in discussing Aristotle's theory of measure, spoke of the need to measure my ell against your ell, for my ell is better known to me, and yours to you.[58] Such impressions of subjectivity could suggest that a mathematical science would be built on logical sand, and Anneliese Maier has suggested that the *secundum institutionem* character of measure was a prime reason for the scholastics' not having developed an exact natural science.[59] While due weight must be ascribed to this argument, it is important not to exaggerate it, for on the formal theoretical side the language of ratios was adequate for the expression of most conceivable relationships.[60] It was at the time highly developed, and did not make direct appeal to units. Moreover it is by no means clear that the early development of classical physics depended heavily upon standardized units, although devices for measuring short periods of time were of major importance.

Celestial Governance

I now revert to consideration of how historical conceptions may have affected attitudes to scientific progress. In the *Meteorologica* and the *Metaphysica*,[61] Aristotle had spoken briefly of how the same opinions recurred infinitely often and how the arts and sciences had ever and again been found and lost. These strikingly non-progressive passages were sensibly but unexcitingly interpreted by Aquinas[62] as being a result of Aristotle's needing to operate with an infinite past time, while the beginnings of philosophy and the arts were taken to have occurred relatively recently. It would be inconvenient to suppose an infinite time in which nothing of this sort happened. Many other commentators simply neglected the passages, but in three closely related fourteenth-century sets of questions on the *Meteorologica* the sentiments are taken much more seriously. The works are by Nicole Oresme, Themo Judei and, putatively, Simon Tunsted.[63] The order of composi-

---

[58] Buridan, *In Metaph. X*, q.1, ed. J. Badius (1518, rpt. Frankfurt, 1964), f. 60v.

[59] A Maier, *Metaphysische Hintergründe der Spätscholastischen Naturphilosophie* (Rome, 1955), 398-402.

[60] See, e.g., J. E. Murdoch, "The Medieval Language of Proportions," *Scientific Change*, ed. A. C. Crombie (London, 1963), 237-71, and A. G. Molland, "The Geometrical Background to the 'Merton School,' " *British Journal for the History of Science*, 4 (1968-9), 108-25.

[61] *Meteorologica*, I.3, 339b28-29; *Metaphysica*, Λ.8, 1074b10-12.

[62] Thomas Aquinas, *In Meteor.* I, lect. 3, ed. in *Opera omnia iussa impensaque Leonis XIII P.M. edita* (Rome, 1882-), III, 332; *In Metaph. XII*, lect. 10, ed. in *Opera omnia* (Venice, 1594-93), IV, f.163r-v. Cf. Augustine, *De civitate Dei*, XII.10, ed. in *CCSL*, XLVIII, 365, trans. Bettenson, 483-84.

[63] Substantial extracts from all three writers' treatments of the question are given in H. Hugonnard-Roche, *L'Oeuvre Astronomique de Themon Juif* (Ge-

574

tion is in dispute,[64] but for our purposes this is not important, since the opinions in the relevant question are virtually identical. The question is, "Whether the same opinions are repeatedly infinitely often," and with qualifications the answer was in the affirmative. The word "infinitely" needed to be interpreted so as to exclude the eternity of the world, and certain self-evident truths had to be excepted from variation among sane men. These included the propositions that unimpeded fire was naturally warming, and that every father was to be honored; also the principles of mathematics. But among other propositions there was room for considerable variation, and this variation did in fact occur. The authors inquire into the causes of this. The universal efficient cause was the heavenly motions.[65] As Themo put it, "This kind of variation of opinion is brought about principally by the heavens as if generally by an efficient cause. This is proved from sayings in the preceding questions, because the whole inferior world is governed by the heavens, and therefore also inasmuch as relates to this variation of opinions." It has of course to be admitted that the stars incline and not compel, but further evidence can be gleaned from the astrological history of religions. "In the second place the conclusion is proved by the astrologers who posit some great conjunctions to be the causes of the beginning of sects and religions and the coming to be of prophets and heretics." The particular efficient causes included scarcity or destruction of men, and human desires for novelty. This had been characteristic of the Athenians of old, and putative-Tunsted suggests that it was then a habit of the English. The writers include for good measure the lack of honor accorded to speculative clerics, or even their persecution. Final causes are also given. Error can sometimes prevent evil, for if *per impossibile* heaven and hell did not exist, it would be necessary to invent them. Moreover, the variation serves to keep human ingenuity busy, and answers to the principle of plenitude, for the beauty of the whole is enhanced by an admixture of error.

The writers' treatment of this question makes it clear that the strictures of Augustine and others had not ruled out of court appeals to astrological influences in explaining the course of sublunary events. And Augustine himself may not have wanted to do so. It is significant that one of the authors was Nicole Oresme who is often portrayed as

---

neva & Paris, 1973), 40-44. Themo's question (I, q.4) is edited in *Questiones et decisiones physicales insignium virorum*, ed. G. Lokert (Paris, 1518), f.158r-v, and putative-Tunsted's (I, q.5) in John Duns Scotus, *Opera omnia* (Paris, 1891-95), IV, 22-26.

[64] Cf. Hugonnard-Roche, *op. cit.*, 39-53, and S. C. McCluskey, *Nicole Oresme on Light, Color, and the Rainbow* (Ph. D. thesis, Wisconsin, 1974), 28-48.

[65] On astrological interpretations of history in the Middle Ages see F. von Bezold, "Astrologische Geschichtesconstruction im Mittelalter," *Deutsche Zeitschrift für Geschichteswissenschaft*, 8(1892), 29-72.

a vehement opponent of astrology. But an examination of this and other writings of his makes clear that he by no means denied the reality of celestial governance. What he principally opposed was the presumption of judicial astrologers in supposing that their science could give exact knowledge of individual future events. But in a general way "we may know from the major conjunctions the great events of the world, as plagues, mortalities, famines, floods, great wars, the rise and fall of kingdoms, the appearance of prophets, new religions, and similar changes."[66]

In his study of such themes Oresme was especially interested in one question—whether all the celestial motions were mutually commensurable. This was the central concern in at least three works,[67] which can with little doubt be taken as subsequent to the questions on the *Meteorologica,* and Oresme's grappling with the problem rises to a peculiar poignancy. He shows to his own satisfaction that it is more probable that some of the motions are incommensurable with each other, but this is not a sufficiently strong conclusion on what for him was a fundamentally important question about the structure of the universe, for the answer should reveal the possibility or impossibility of the Great Year in which all the planets would return to their present positions. In his most mature work on the subject he employs the image of a vision of Apollo surrounded by the muses and sciences.[68] With allusion to *Ecclesiastes* Apollo discouragingly tells Oresme that his quest is an interminable labor and affliction of spirit. Arithmetic and geometry cannot answer the question, and the senses cannot rise to the required punctual exactitude. The depressed Oresme utters a cry of complaint:[69] "Immortal gods who know all things, why did you make it that men by nature desire to know and then cause this longing to be cheated or frustrated by concealing from us the best truths." The only thing possible seemed to be to request a revelation from Apollo. But the god was not so easily to be drawn. Instead he called for answers from Arithmetica and Geometria, who developed opposing views, Arithmetica for commensurability and Geometria for incommensurability. Arithmetica takes a traditionalist stance, and cites in support of her position numerous standard authorities. She is in favor of the possibility of exact knowledge entailed by commensurability, of

[66] Nicole Oresme, Ch. 1 "Livre de divinacions," *Nicole Oresme and the Astrologers,* ed. and trans. G. W. Coopland (Liverpool, 1952), 52-53.

[67] Oresme, *De proportionibus proportionum* and *Ad pauca respicientes,* ed. E. Grant (Madison, 1966); *Nicole Oresme and the Kinematics of Circular Motion. Tractatus de commensurabilitate vel incommensurabilitate motuum celi,* ed. E. Grant (Madison, 1971).

[68] *De commensurabilitate vel incommensurabilitate,* III, ed. Grant, 248-323. Cf. my "Nicole Oresme and Scientific Progress" (n. 55 above), 213-19.

[69] *De comm.,* III, ed. Grant, 286; I read *noscitis* for *noscis.*

the music of the spheres, of the Great Year, and perhaps even of individual return. Oresme clearly finds her sister's position more attractive, but I cannot maintain that Geometria was in any way a firm
partisan of scientific progress.[70] Her guiding idea was plenitude. A
richer mixture of ratios in the heavens that included some incommensurability would bring about a richer world here below. It would also
entail a rectilinear time sequence, with the continual emergence of
novelty "so that the extended succession of ages, which Pythagoras
understood as the golden chain, should not return in a circle, but proceed ever forward without end in a straight line, which could not happen without some incommensurability of the celestial motions."[71] The
continual occurrence of novelty must mean that there will always be
something new for men to investigate, and for Geometria incommensurability will mean that men can only obtain approximative knowledge
of the heavenly motions. This is all to the good. "If all the motions
were precisely known by men, there would be no need to go on making
observations nor to record the circuits of the heaven with watchful care.
It has therefore been best that concerning such excellent things something should be known and something should always remain unknown
and to be further investigated, which investigation with a previously
tasted sweetness would lead noble minds from earthly things and with
aroused desire continually keep them occupied in the admirable exercise
of such lofty endeavor."[72] Thus science can go on, but there is little
hint of anything like a progressive accumulation of knowledge. And
anyway Oresme was left after his vision with no firm assurance that
Geometria was right. Small wonder then that the latter years of his
life were far more occupied with criticism and making knowledge
available in French translation than with constructive endeavors of
his own.

Third World Knowledge

The above account has done little to disturb the traditional view
that saw few conceptions of scientific progress in the Middle Ages, although I hope that it has done something to enrich the picture and (if
this is not to be too progressivist about progress) to reveal embryonic
stirrings. When we seek underlying factors that may make more intelligible the difference between the Middle Ages and later times in this
regard, a clear candidate is the divorce between theory and practice
that characterized so much scholastic science. Oresme, for instance,
ranked very low the predictive value of natural knowledge. More important was the satisfaction of human curiosity, and most important an

[70] Not even to the limited extent that I did in my "Nicole Oresme and
Scientific Progress," 216-19.

[71] *De comm.*, III, ed. Grant, 316.

[72] *De comm.*, III, ed. Grant, 318-20.

increased knowledge of God the Creator.[73] Without some ideology of the usefulness of knowledge for practical needs, a concern with knowledge that was necessarily only approximative could seem rather pointless. Moreover, the divorce meant that the very definite technical progress that was made during the Middle Ages very rarely gave rise to any generalized conception of progress that could, among other things, be extrapolated into the future.

We may perhaps generalize this by suggesting a radical shift in the image of knowledge. Sir Karl Popper has recently propagandized for a third world of objective knowledge distinct from the worlds of physical objects and of mental states.[74] Whatever the philosophical difficulties of such a changing world of Platonic Forms, it does answer well to how scientific knowledge is often conceived: as something external, in a particular state at a given time, and hovering around if not located in libraries. (We may note how the locution "We know" does not entail "I know," although it may entail "I could learn.") In the Middle Ages the situation was different. *Scientia* was far more definitely a property of individuals, and, if externalized, was thought of as contained in a relatively small number of books by established *auctores*. The extreme example is the view sometimes found that all knowledge is contained in the Bible. Libraries were not very large, and one could rarely assume more than local access to modern writers. Thus the main aims were to increase individual knowledge by getting a richer and more thoroughly ingrained *habitus,* to draw knowledge out of the *auctores* by commentary and discussion, and in rare cases to become an *auctor* oneself by filling an apparent gap in the established scheme of knowledge. Galen indeed had shown something nearer a third world concept when, in commenting on the Hippocratic aphorism *vita brevis, ars longa* he preached the virtues of writing down what one knew, but this precept was little developed in the Middle Ages.[75] A crucial obstacle would have been the problem of widescale dissemination of large numbers of books. And so, besides being a standard example of the occurrence of modern progress, printing may also have had a more crucial role in the establishment of the idea.

University of Aberdeen.

[73] *Livre de divinacions,* 15, ed. Coopland, 112, cf. 132-33.
[74] K. R. Popper, *Objective Knowledge* (Oxford, 1972), Ch. 3, "Epistemology without a Knowing Subject."
[75] Galen, *Opera omnia,* ed. C. G. Kühn (Leipzig, 1821-33), XVII, Pt. 2, 352.

XIV

Mathematics in the Thought of Albertus Magnus

A. Introduction

In a letter to Marin Mersenne in 1638 René Descartes claimed that his physics was nothing but geometry.[1] The exact interpretation of this statement may be difficult, but similar sentiments abounded in the seventeenth century, and, with justice, are taken to reflect one of the most important characteristics of the science of the time. Thus for Galileo the book of the universe was written in the language of mathematics, and for Kepler geometry had provided God with the exemplars for the creation of the world. Newton produced the significant title *Mathematical Principles of Natural Philosophy*, and Leibniz saw infinitesimal analysis as linking geometry and physics. These writers had many differences, but they all shared a faith in the power of mathematics in natural philosophy.

There were many ancient precedents for this, particularly among Pythagoreans and Platonists. The complete tradition was not available to the Middle Ages, but there was quite sufficient evidence to show how much some ancient thinkers had valued mathematics. The part of Plato's *Timaeus* that appeared in Latin with Chalcidius'

---

[1] *Oeuvres de Descartes*, ed. Charles Adam and Paul Tannery (Paris, 1897-1913), 2: 268.

commentary[2] discussed the mathematical structure of the world and of the World Soul. Boethius regarded arithmetic as the exemplar for the creation, and dwelt on the harmonic structure of the world.[3] (We should remember that music in its theoretical aspect was regarded as a mathematical science.) And great authority had to be attached to the assertion to God in the *Wisdom of Solomon* that "Thou hast ordered all things in number, weight and measure."[4] Passages such as these received much attention in the twelfth century, but the situation became more complicated after the advent of the huge quantity of new learning in translation from Greek and Arabic. Not only was more knowledge of Greek mathematics available, but there was the massive achievement of Aristotle to be tangled with. And Aristotle was ambivalent towards mathematics.

This was largely a result of his historical situation. Mathematics was advancing rapidly in Aristotle's time, and he himself spent many years in Plato's Academy. In his *Posterior Analytics* geometry clearly provided the model for demonstrative science, and mathematical examples abound throughout the corpus. He regarded mathematics as providing one of the three branches of theoretical knowledge, along with physics and metaphysics, and he was also very conscious of what may be called separate branches of applied mathematics, such as optics, astronomy and musical theory. Nevertheless he was concerned to counter what he saw as an excessive exaltation of mathematics in the work of some of his predecessors, and in his writings there were many points of tension between what mathematics could seem to say the world was like and what he held it actually to be. These tensions were not adequately resolved, and so there was room for much divergence of opinion in the commentatorial tradition. As always this was abetted by the very laconic form of Aristotle's extant writings. In this paper my central aim will be to glean some understanding of Albertus Magnus' attitude towards mathematics mainly on the basis of what he says in the so-called Aristotelian paraphrases. I shall make little allusion to the commentary on Euclid ascribed to Albert, which is discussed by Paul Tummers in the next essay in this volume.

---

[2] Plato, *Timaeus a Calcidio translatus commentarioque instructus*, ed. J. H. Waszink (London and Leiden, 1962).

[3] Boethius, *De institutione arithmetica* 1.1, *De institutione musica* 1.2, ed. Gottfried Friedlein (Leipzig, 1867; repr. Frankfurt, 1966), pp. 10, 187-188.

[4] Wisd. 11: 21.

Albert is more renowned as a biologist than as a mathematician. This is just. His interests and abilities were far more in that direction, and he could be in danger of being classified by a mathematician as woolly minded. If we adopted Pierre Duhem's notorious contrast between the French and the English,[5] we should have to say that Albert's mind was ample and weak rather than deep and narrow. This incidentally means that the method of close textual analysis of particular passages can often lead us into a morass. To re-create effectively his vision of mathematics we need to adopt a more impressionistic approach and always search for the thought behind the words, for often this does not shine clearly through them. As we shall see, Albert did not think that mathematics was very important to natural philosophy, and at times it could be a snare and a delusion. Factors such as this have led to the comparative neglect of his mathematical thought. Nevertheless he had frequently to discuss mathematics, and it is important to assess his attitude towards the subject, both as part of his own intellectual make-up and as a foil to those scholastic writers who had a far higher opinion of the value of mathematics.

An important exception to the neglect of this aspect of Albert's thought is a valuable article by J. A. Weisheipl.[6] Weisheipl held that Albert was particularly concerned to attack "Plato's error" as it appeared in the work of Robert Grosseteste, Roger Bacon and Robert Kilwardby (particularly the last of these). These Weisheipl referred to as the "Oxford Platonists." This provides the important reminder that Albert was not operating in an intellectual vacuum, but I am not so confident as Weisheipl in identifying precise contemporary targets for Albert's attacks. In any case the onslaught must be regarded as oblique, for the explicit targets are almost always the views of ancient Pythagoreans and Platonists as presented by Aristotle and others. For this and other reasons I shall at this stage make little reference to Albert's contemporaries, although I shall occasionally bring in Grosseteste for purposes of comparison.

In Albert's time pure mathematics comprised arithmetic and geometry. Arithmetic was akin to what we should now call number theory. Its principal source was the work on the subject by Boethius,

---

[5] Pierre Duhem, *The Aim and Structure of Physical Theory*, tr. Philip P. Wiener (New York, 1962), pp. 55-104.

[6] James A. Weisheipl, "Albertus Magnus and the Oxford Platonists," *Proceedings of the American Catholic Philosophical Association*, 32 (1958), 124-139.

and its subject matter was number conceived as a collection of units, so that unity was in some sense the principle of number. Geometry derived mainly from Euclid's *Elements* and was concerned with continuous quantity. Albert made particular use of the commentary on this work by al-Nairīzī, the Anaritius of the Latins, and this encouraged him to regard the point as the principle of magnitude. By its motion the point generated a line, and from the motion of a line there arose a surface, and from that of a surface a body.[7] Important questions were the degree of independence of these disciplines and the ways in which they related to other branches of knowledge.

B. The Division of the Sciences

Albert followed Aristotle's division of theoretical science into metaphysics, mathematics and physics, although with some difference of nuance.

> The first in the real order (*secundum ordinem rei*) is that which is generally about being (*ens*) as being and not conceived with motion and sensible matter in itself or in its principles, neither according to being (*esse*) nor according to reason (*ratio*). And this is first philosophy, which is called metaphysics or theology. The second in the same real order is mathematics, which is conceived with motion and sensible matter according to being but not according to reason. The last is physics, which is totally conceived with motion and sensible matter, according to being and reason.[8]

Mathematics abstracts from motion and sensible qualities and considers quantity as pictured in the imagination, although its objects have real existence only in sensible bodies. A further act of abstraction removes quantity also, and we are in the realm of metaphysics.

This abstractive ascent can suggest that we are by steps approaching the real causes of things, and that we may reverse the process and see how all things proceed from their principles. And indeed in his *Physics* Albert hinted that this was the case.

---

[7] *Anaritii in decem libros priores Euclidis commentarii*, ed. Maximilian Curtze, in *Euclidis opera omnia*, ed. J. L. Heiberg and H. Menge, *Supplementum* (Leipzig, 1899), p. 1. On Albert's use of Anaritius see Paul M. J. E. Tummers, "The 'Commentary' of Albertus (Magnus?) on Euclid's 'Elements of Geometry'; Anaritius as his Source," xvth *International Congress of the History of Science. Abstracts of Scientific Section Papers* (Edinburgh, 1977), p. 51.

[8] Albert, *Physica* I, tr.1, c.1 (ed. Borgnet, 3: 2a). On Albert's classification of theoretical science, see Joseph Mariétan, *Problème de la classification des sciences d'Aristote à St-Thomas* (St. Maurice and Paris, 1901), pp. 166-171.

Since the quiddity which is unqualifiedly (*simpliciter*) first gives first being, from which flows the being of this [particular] quantity in what is measured by quantity, from which further flows forth the being of this sensible [thing], distinguished by quantity and distinguished by active and passive forms, the first will without a doubt be the cause of the second and third. Wherefore both mathematicals and naturals are caused by metaphysicals and take their principles from them.[9]

But in the later *Metaphysics* he made abundantly clear that he intended no such simple priority in the order of things.

Here there is need to beware of the error of Plato, who said that naturals were founded in mathematicals and mathematicals in divines, just as the third cause is founded in the second, and the second is founded in the primary, and therefore he said that mathematicals were principles of naturals, which is completely false.[10]

Sensible qualities do not inhere in bodies by reason of their spatial extension, but because the bodies have the aptitude of being extended.[11] Thus, as it were, quantity and sensible qualities arise simultaneously, and mathematics and physics are twin births from metaphysics.

C. MATHEMATICS AND THE UNDERSTANDING OF NATURE

This complex view of the interrelations of physics, mathematics, and metaphysics, with its distinction between what can be thought and what actually is the case, makes particularly difficult the question of how mathematics relates to physics. I have elsewhere spoken of realist and conceptualist poles in scholastic attitudes to this question.[12] The realist places his focus on the actual existence of mathematical objects in the outside world, and expects mathematics to tell him quite a lot about the world; he often hints at mathematical design in nature. The conceptualist on the other hand pays particular attention to the fact that the mathematician operates on objects pictured in the imagination, and he often seems to lose sight of their anchorage in external bodies. In this matter Albert veers very much towards the conceptualist pole.

---

[9] Albert, *Physica* I, tr.1, c.1 (ed. Borgnet 3: 3b).

[10] Albert, *Metaphysica* I, tr.1, c.1 (ed. Colon. 16/1: 2, vv. 31-35).

[11] Albert, *Metaph.* I, tr.1, c.1 and tr.4, c.1 (ed. Colon. 16/1: 2, vv. 62-67; 47, vv. 58-64).

[12] Andrew George Molland, "An Examination of Bradwardine's Geometry," *Archive for History of Exact Sciences*, 19 (1978): 113-175.

468

One passage where Aristotle seemed to assign a particularly important role to mathematics for the understanding of nature was in *Posterior Analytics* I, 13.

> The reason why [*propter quid* in medieval discussions] differs from the fact [*quia* in medieval discussions] in another fashion, when each is considered by means of a different science. And such are those which are related to each other in such a way that the one is under the other, e.g., optics to geometry, and mechanics to solid geometry, and harmonics to arithmetic, and star-gazing to astronomy.... For here it is for the empirical [scientist] to know the fact and for the mathematical [to know] the reason why; for the latter have the demonstrations of the explanations, and often they do not know the fact, just as those who consider the universal often do not know some of the particulars through lack of observation.[13]

Albert did not disagree, but he was careful to circumscribe the power of mathematics. Its proper concern was only with quantity as quantity.

> An example of this is a ray, which is a line. A line as line has [the property of] being straight or curved, and, by meeting another, of making an angle and the quantity of an angle, in that it meets it perpendicularly or obliquely. Because all these things are [properties] of quantity as such, the geometer considers them as to cause. But in as much as a ray has [the property of] being bent (*reflecti*)[14] at a clean and polished [surface], and in a concave mirror of being bent towards the middle, and in a round pervious [object] of being bent (*reflecti*) towards the opposite point, because these properties are not caused by a line in that it is quantity, therefore lines as such are not appropriate, nor can [the properties] be produced by the geometer from the proper principles of quantity, and so he cannot pronounce the *propter quid* in them. But they are properties of the visual line in that it is visual, and so the *propter quid* in such is pronounced by the *perspectivus*.[15]

For Albert mathematical properties were very much on the surface of things. Robert Grosseteste on the other hand had a vision which emphasised the penetration of mathematics into physics, and we may think of the basic mathematical structure being decked out by the addition of other qualities.

---

[13] Aristotle, *An. post.* I.13 (78b35-79a6). Translation from *Aristotle's Posterior Analytics*, trans., ann. Jonathan Barnes (Oxford, 1975), pp. 22-23.

[14] On the vagueness of Albert's terminology see Carl B. Boyer, *The Rainbow: From Myth to Mathematics* (New York and London, 1959), pp. 95-96.

[15] Albert, *Posteriora analytica* I, tr.3, c.7 (ed. Borgnet 2: 86a).

But one must know that an inferior science always adds a condition by which it appropriates to itself the subject and properties (*passiones*) of the superior science, and in the conclusion of the subordinated science they are like two natures, namely the nature which it receives from the superior and its own nature which it superadds of itself. And so the superior science does not pronounce the causes of what is superadded, and sometimes the inferior science pronounces these causes and sometimes not, but the superior science pronounces the causes of what the inferior science receives from the superior.[16]

With this type of view Grosseteste can well maintain the importance of mathematics. But Albert, although he agrees with Aristotle that there is no falsehood in abstraction,[17] gives a minimal assessment of what mathematics can say about the physical world. Significantly he does not attempt to reproduce the sophisticated mathematical account of the rainbow that Aristotle gave in *Meteorologica* III, 5.[18]

i. Geometrical Exactness

Albert may explicitly affirm that there is no falsehood in abstraction, but there are many passages in his writings where he seems strongly inclined to the opposite view. For instance, there is the problem of geometrical exactness, which provides a central difficulty for an abstractionist view of mathematics. How can the exact nature of geometrical objects arise from a mere stripping away of qualities in thought from the more chaotic sensible world? An example of the problem (as given by Albert) is the following: "A sensible circle, which has a bent line [as circumference] does not touch a ruler, which is a sensible straight line, in a point, while yet, as is demonstrated in the fifteenth and sixteenth [propositions] of the third [book] of our geometry, a line touching a circle only touches it in a point."[19] As a biologist too Albert was very conscious that the limited range of shapes with which the geometer operated did not fit well with the forms of living creatures. "Many of the geometers' figures are in no

---

[16] Robert Grosseteste, *In Aristotelis Posteriorum analyticorum libros* I.12 (78b35-79a16), ed. Pamphilus de monte Bononiensis (Venice, 1514; repr. Frankfurt, 1966), f. 14v. Cf. Alistair C. Crombie, *Robert Grosseteste and the Origins of Experimental Science*, 2nd imp. (Oxford, 1961), pp. 91-98, and William A. Wallace, *Causality and Scientific Explanation* (Ann Arbor, 1972-74), 1: 27-47.

[17] E.g., Albert, *Physica* II, tr.1, c.8 (ed. Borgnet 3: 108b).

[18] Aristotle, *Meteor.* III.5 (375b16-377a27). Albert, *Meteora* III, tr.4 (ed. Borgnet 4: 666-700).

[19] Albert, *Metaph.* III, tr.2, c.3 (ed. Colon. 16/1: 118, vv. 35-40).

way found in natural bodies, and many natural figures, and particularly those of animals and plants, are not determinable by the art of geometry."[20] Neither Aristotle nor Albert satisfactorily solved problems of this kind, but Albert's general strategy was to make more tenuous than had Aristotle the link between the geometer's mind and the outside world.

> All abstract and mathematical [objects] are received according to the understanding (*intellectus*), for, according to being (*esse*) in nature, this one or that one is not found, unless it be in light alone, as some say, although their view is not in accord with the philosophers. Although they are received according to the understanding, this understanding is caused by particular things, and refers to being, because it expresses the nature and being of the thing as it is what it is.[21]

Interestingly enough this passage may contain a reference to the "Oxford Platonists," for, when facing the problem of exactness, Roger Bacon had grounded geometry primarily in the multiplication of species and in celestial things.[22]

ii. Infinity

If the problem of exactness should seem rather pernickety, Albert could turn to questions of infinity for more dramatic instances of the power of mathematics to mislead, for the impulse of mathematics towards the infinite chafed at Aristotelian restrictions. Let us consider the question of infinite spatial extension. The Aristotelian world was finite. Moreover space did not exist apart from body, and so it was nonsensical to posit an infinite space beyond the outermost heaven. On the other hand geometry seemed to demand an infinite space for its constructions, and indeed Euclid's postulates asserted that a straight line could always be produced further, and that a circle could be described on any centre with radius of any length. Aristotle considered the apparent conflict between physics and geometry in a not altogether satisfactory passage of his *Physics*. He said that

---

[20] Albert, *Physica* III, tr.2, c.17 (ed. Borgnet 3: 235b).

[21] Albert, *De praedicamentis*, tr.3, c.3 (ed. Borgnet 1: 199b): "Omnia enim abstracta et mathematica sunt accepta secundum intellectum; secundum enim esse in natura hoc vel hoc, non invenitur nisi in sola luce, ut quidam dicunt, quamvis dictum eorum cum Philosophis non concordet. Quamvis ergo ista accepta sint secundum intellectum, iste tamen intellectus a specialibus rebus causatus est et ad esse refertur."

[22] Oxford, Bodleian Library, MS Digby 76, f. 78ra; Molland, "An Examination of Bradwardine's Geometry," *Archive for History of Exact Sciences*, 19 (1978), 113-175.

the geometers only postulated that a line be produced so far as was wished rather than to infinity, and he also suggested a scaling down argument. If a configuration was too large to allow the constructions necessary for proving a theorem, then the same theorem could be proved on a similar but smaller configuration. Albert refers to these points, but the main emphasis of his approach was to say that the geometer was dealing with imagined objects rather than real ones. "The mathematicians do not need in their science an infinite magnitude according to act, because they do not receive quantity according to being (*esse*), but according to imagination, and they proceed according to the power of the imagination to compose figures and angles, and not according to the power of the thing imagined."[23] In another part of his discussion of infinity Albert suggests an even more tenuous link between mathematics and the world when he accuses mathematicians of begging the question. "Because the mathematicians posit the principles, they prove something to be infinite from their positing it to be so (*ex illo probant aliquid esse infinitum hi qui ponunt ipsum esse*)."[24] This can suggest a purely formal view of mathematics in which the concern is not with the truth of categorical statements but only with validity of inference.

iii. The Nature of Space

The size of space was not its only feature that made for an uneasy relationship between Euclid and Aristotle; there was also the question of its structure. Alexandre Koyré proposed as one of the leading characteristics of the new science of the seventeenth century the following: "the geometrization of space — that is, the substitution of the homogeneous and abstract space of Euclidean geometry for the qualitatively differentiated and concrete world-space of the pre-Galilean physics."[25] Whatever terminology one uses, the Aristotelian world was certainly structured in a way different from that of the mechanical philosophy. Different properties followed from mere difference of position. Heavy bodies moved towards the centre of the world because it was the centre, and not because the earth was located there. If the whole earth were displaced it would naturally return to the centre. Moreover, Aristotle wished to ascribe an above

---

[23] Albert, *Physica* III, tr.2, c.17 (ed. Borgnet 3: 235b).
[24] Ibid., c.3 (p. 210a).
[25] Alexandre Koyré, *Metaphysics and Measurement* (London, 1968), pp. 19-20.

and a below, a right and a left, a front and a back to the world as a whole, just as a human being unambiguously possessed these features. Aristotle even hinted that these characteristics were also in geometrical objects: "Above is the principle of length, right of breadth, front of depth."[26] But elsewhere he modified this: "Though [the objects of mathematics] have no real place, they nevertheless, in respect of their position relatively to us, have a right and a left as attributes ascribed to them only in consequence of their relative position, not having by nature these various characteristics."[27] Albert developed Aristotle's references to animals and plants in this regard, but was concerned to emphasise that right and left, etc. were not intrinsic characteristics of mathematical objects.[28]

> Their difference of position is only in the intellect, just as they are received abstractly by the intellect alone, and they do not have by nature any difference among these six positions, because if they did have them by nature they would move to them by nature, and this is false since they are separated from motion.

Once again the burden is to maximise the gap between mathematics and the natural world.

iv. The Continuum

The term "mechanical philosophy" is applied to a varying cluster of ideas and images about the structure of the world, and how one is to give a scientific account of it. One image, by analogy with machines, is that one may understand the world by taking it to pieces — in thought if not in fact. In common with many biologists Albert has a far more holistic approach, and denies that enlightenment is to be gained by such metaphorical butchery. In this instance he could draw some support from mathematics, for even the continuum did not seem to be properly resolvable into parts, and continuous quantity was the subject-matter of geometry. In antiquity contradictions had appeared to arise within mathematics itself. This produced a divorce between arithmetic and geometry, and Albert

---

[26] Aristotle, *De coelo* II.2 (284b24-25). Cf. Leo Elders, *Aristotle's Cosmology: A Commentary on the De caelo* (Assen, 1966), p. 185, and Geoffrey E. R. Lloyd, "Right and Left in Greek Philosophy," *Journal of Hellenic Studies*, 82 (1962), 56-66.

[27] Aristotle, *Physica* IV.1 (208b22-24).

[28] Albert, *De caelo et mundo* II, tr.1, c.4 (ed. Colon. 5/1: 109, v. 47–113, v. 92). Quotation from Albert, *Physica* IV, tr.1, c.2 (ed. Borgnet 3: 243a).

was glad to welcome the weakening of the upper link in the "Platonic" hierarchy that descended from arithmetic to geometry to the world.

Let us see where some of the problems of continuity lay. It seemed quite innocuous, and indeed necessary to geometry, to hold that any straight line may be divided (at least mentally) into two equal parts, which are themselves straight lines. But this has the effect of asserting that a straight line may be divided into smaller and smaller parts without limit. There is then a temptation to take a leap, and ask what would be the result of an infinite process of division. Surely the line would have been decomposed into points or other indivisibles. But then how many points are necessary to form a line? If two suffice, the line they form is not divisible into divisible lines, contrary to our initial assumption, and the same difficulty applies to any finite number. But if an infinite number is necessary, we may ask, as Zeno did, whether or not the points have magnitude, and we seemed to be faced with the dilemma of having either a line of no length or one of infinite length.

By the time of Aristotle it was realised that one had to tread warily concerning such matters. Aristotle's basic strategy was to distinguish between potential infinite division and actual infinite division. Lines were potentially infinitely divisible, but this did not license one to speak of the state of affairs when they were actually infinitely divided. Lines were not made up of points, nor could one speak of one point of a line being immediately adjacent to another of its points. All this entailed a certain lack of correspondence between thought and its objects. Thought, or its verbal expressions, takes place in a finite number of discrete units, but the continuum seemed inextricably bound up with what F. Solmsen has called the "ocean of infinity,"[29] and as such could not be fully controlled. It was similar with the discovery of incommensurability. This meant, for example, that it was impossible to find any line, however small, that would exactly fit a whole number of times into both the side of a square and its diagonal. The Pythagorean dream of the dominance over geometry by number was severely shaken.

These matters were not simply the concern of mathematicians, for continuity emphatically entered into the physical world. Aristotle was firm in maintaining that physical bodies were essentially conti-

---

[29] Friedrich Solmsen, *Aristotle's System of the Physical World* (Ithaca, 1960), p. 201.

474

nuous, and not composed of indivisibles, and in this Albert enthusi-astically followed him. Albert was concerned to maintain the auton-omy of physics, but in this instance he was prepared to draw arguments from mathematics, for although his reasoning did not reach the sophistication of later writers, geometry seemed definitely to be on his side. "We shall first draw reasons from those things that are said in mathematics. The sayings of those sciences must either remain firmly supposed, or, if they are to be removed, they must be removed by stronger and more credible reasons than they are in themselves."[30] This is notably different from Albert's attitude in the case of infinite extension, but there still remained here differences between mathematics and physics. Two natural bodies could touch without being united into one, but this was not the case with mathe-matical objects. If two lines touched end to end, their end-points became one.[31] Moreover division in thought was not the same as actual physical division. In the division of a natural body "a mini-mum is received, and it is [the smallest part] that can perfect the operation of the natural body, because if it were divided it would be corrupted from operation and essence, because it could not resist alteration."[32] Nevertheless even mathematical quantity cannot be actually divided at every possible point, although at any stage it may be divided at any point.

Albert saw Plato (even more than Leucippus and Democritus) as the chief villain in the matter of composing continua from points. In this he may not have been altogether just, but the view could seem a plausible extension of the doctrine of the *Timaeus*, encouraged by Aristotle, who perhaps interpreted the "likely story" there presented in too literal a fashion. In the *Timaeus* the small particles of the four elements were assigned the shapes of four of the five regular solids, and in a somewhat obscure fashion these solids were said to be der-ived from triangles.[33] Like Aristotle, Albert regarded this sort of

---

[30] Albert, *De indivisibilibus lineis*, c.3 (ed. Borgnet 3: 469b). Pseudo-Aristotle expressed a similar sentiment in the corresponding place; *De lineis insecabilibus* 2 (969b29-970a17). See also Aristotle, *De coelo* III.1 (299a4-6).

[31] Albert, *Physica* v, tr.2, c.1, 3 (ed. Borgnet 3: 379a-b, 383a). Cf. John E. Murdoch, "Super-position, Congruence and Continuity in the Middle Ages," in *Mélanges Alexandre Koyré* (Par-is, 1964), 1: 416-441.

[32] Albert, *De generatione et corruptione* I, tr.1, c.14 (ed. Borgnet 4: 357a-b).

[33] Plato, *Timaeus* 53c-57d. Cf. Aristotle, *De coelo* III.1 (299a1-300a19); III.7-8 (305b29-307b24); *De gen. et corr.* I.2 (315b25-317a17); and A. T. Nicol, "Indivisible Lines," *Classical Quarterly*, 30 (1936), 120-126.

thing as undesirable mathematicism, taking eternal geometrical principles to be the principles of corruptible things.

> But the Platonists and some other ancients, on account of love of their teachers who exalted mathematicals too much on account of the incorruptibility and necessity that they found in them, and so said that they were the principles of natural things, did what those were wont to do who posit impossible sayings. For in the beginning and without much consideration they had used an impossible supposition, and since they posited impossibles as principles it was necessary that they take pains to justify and prove those things that they had said, which were often contrary to the truth, lest they seem to surrender, and lest the doctrines of their teachers with which they were imbued be annihilated.[34]

An objection to Plato's doctrine was that it involved constituting bodies from non-bodies (namely surfaces), and we see the affinity with the doctrine of the composition of lines from points. Elsewhere Aristotle had reported that Plato regarded indivisible lines (rather than points) as the principle of the line.[35]

In such questions Albert was usually a firm partisan of Aristotle, but there is one significant point of divergence which somewhat muddies the waters. This is Albert's frequent use of the idea of the generation of a line from the motion of a point, of a surface from that of a line, and of a body from that of a surface. At times he insists that the motion is merely imaginary, and indeed he agreed with Aristotle that it was impossible in the nature of things for an indivisible to move, except *per accidens*.[36] But on other occasions Albert seemed to slip into a rather more realist interpretation, and this allowed him to make an apparent concession to "Plato," while still preserving intact the mystery of the continuum.

> It is further to be noted that every quantity flows from an indivisible, as we have already remarked, for, if the essential flux of a point be taken, it will without doubt constitute a line, and the line a surface, and the surface a body. And so potentially there is a point everywhere in the line, and a line everywhere in the surface, and a surface everywhere in the body potentially. And so a point is in two ways related to a line. For if the line be considered as the essential flux of a point, the point is its material part or matter, and similarly the line of the surface, and the

---

[34] Albert, *De caelo* III, tr.2, c.7 (ed. Colon. 5/1: 236, vv. 27-39).

[35] Aristotle, *Metaph.* I.9 (992a20-23).

[36] Albert, *Physica* VI, tr.3, c.4 (ed. Borgnet 3: 456a-459a).

476

surface of the body. But if formal line be taken in the way said by
Euclid, namely as longitude terminated at two points, the two points
are formally in the line according to the act of the form, which is to ter-
minate and bound. And so the point is in some way the form of the
line.[37]

The concept of flow may seem an odd way to preserve the continuity
of body, but Albert's use of a flowing now to express the continuity
of time appears more natural.[38]

v. Measure and Number

After Albert's time several medieval writers disagreed with Aristotle, and held that the continuum was composed from indivisibles,
and earlier Grosseteste had at least veered towards this view. Grosseteste raised the question[39] of how, if there were only one line in the
universe, it was to be measured, when there was nothing else to compare it with. His answer was that it was properly measured by the
number of points that it contained. This was infinite, but for God an
infinite number was finite, and so he could know measure in this
way. This entailed there being different infinite numbers, and one
number could even have to another the irrational ratio of the diagonal of a square to its side. This position may be grounded in Grosseteste's cosmogony, in which extension derived from the infinite self-
multiplication of a point of light. Grossesteste showed an awareness
of the tradition. "This, as I believe, was the understanding of the philosophers who posited all things to be composed from atoms, and
said that bodies were composed from surfaces, and surfaces from
lines, and lines from points."[40] The overall effect of such a view was
to place a quasi-numerical structure at the very heart of physical
reality — something that Albert was vehemently opposed to.

Albert's own account of measure, like Aristotle's, was on a more
superficial level. Measurement was basically the expression of the
quantity of something in numerical terms. Numbers were collections

[37] Albert, *De gen. et corr.* I, tr.1, c.15 (ed. Borgnet 4: 358a). Cf. Wolfgang Breidert, *Das aris-totelische Kontinuum in der Scholastik,* in *Beiträge,* NF 1 (1970), 23-32.

[38] Albert, *Physica* VI, tr.1, c.7 (ed. Borgnet 3: 420a-421b); *Metaph.* V, tr.3, c.2 (ed. Colon. 16/1: 260, vv. 47-51).

[39] Robert Grosseteste, *Commentarius in VIII libros physicorum Aristotelis* IV (219b5-8), ed. R. C. Dales (Boulder, 1963), pp. 90-95.

[40] Robert Grosseteste, *De luce seu de inchoatione formarum,* in *Die Philosophischen Werke des Robert Grosseteste,* ed. Ludwig Baur, *Beiträge* 9 (1912), 53-54.

of units, and these units were indivisibles. Their indivisibility was ultimately rooted in the indivisibility of substantial form.[41] (What, for example, could be meant by half a substantial form?) Thus numbers seemed firmly anchored in the physical world. They were consequences of the existence of things, and not causes. As Albert frequently put it, they arose from the division or separation or discreteness that there was between things. In reality they were inseparable from the things numbered, but there were also abstract units in the soul from which were formed the numbers by which we number. Thus Albert often spoke of a twofold aspect of number: materially it was in the numbered or numerable things, while formally it was primarily located in the soul. By means of number quantity was known. For discrete collections this involved simple counting, but in the case of continuous objects there was no true minimum to be reached by division. Nevertheless certain quantities could be conventionally treated as atoms or units, as, for example, the foot in measuring length.[42] These units could then be counted, as was done in measuring discrete multitudes.

This conventional imposition of units could appear very arbitrary, and Anneliese Maier has suggested this as one of the main reasons why the Schoolmen did not develop an exact natural science.[43] In the next century the apparent arbitrariness was mitigated by the development of an elaborate language of ratios, which was also used to discuss intensive quantities in abundance. We do not know how Albert would have reacted to the new mathematicism, but we may suspect that it would have incurred his displeasure, if only because its empirical grounding was weak.

D. Conclusion

With hindsight it is tempting to say that Albert's influence was inimical to the growth of mathematical physics. But this is with hindsight, and is in any case too negative. More positively we may see Albert as warning against the dangers of fitting the variety of nature into an ill-fitting mathematical strait-jacket. Such warnings have

---

[41] See principally Albert, *Metaph.* v, tr.1, c.8, 10 (ed. Colon. 16/1: 227, v. 41 - 229, v. 26; 231 v. 61 - 233, v. 52).

[42] Albert, *Metaph.* x, tr.1, c.3 (ed. Colon. 16/2: 434, v. 22 - 435, v. 68).

[43] Anneliese Maier, *Metaphysische Hintergründe der spätscholastischen Naturphilosophie* (Rome, 1955), pp. 398-402.

478

continued in various contexts until the present. A. N. Whitehead remarked that, "It often happens. . . that in criticising a learned book of applied mathematics, or a memoir, one's whole trouble is with the first chapter, or even with the first page. For it is there, at the very outset, where the author will probably be found to slip in his assumptions."[44] Quantification may be applied with an inappropriate conceptual basis, although this may only be discoverable by trial and error. Moreover examples such as astrology and some modern social science show that mathematisation may be a smokescreen: it frightens off the uninitiated and conceals what may be shaky assumptions. Mathematics may be a very great aid to the natural and social sciences, but neither of them may be reduced to it.

Modern mathematics is very different from ancient and medieval mathematics. In particular the description of mathematics as the science of quantity has increasingly been seen to be too restrictive. Nevertheless there are numerous features which make them recognisably the same subject. Partly this is because of the perennial nature of the philosophical problems thrown up by mathematics. One such is the extent to which the objects of mathematics are simply given as opposed to being creations of the human intellect. In practice mathematicians talk of both existence and construction. Philosophers often try to interpret one in terms of the other, and the polar positions are sometimes dubbed platonism and constructivism. Aristotle rejected the existence of a separate realm of mathematicals, and instead grounded mathematical objects in physical objects. But he also spoke of constructions in terms of the geometer's thought bringing to actuality what had only been present potentially. Albert, as we have seen, emphasized the extent to which mathematics was a mental activity, and referred constantly to the generation of geometrical objects from imaginary motions. All this may be seen as a freeing of mathematics from the shackles of the physical world, and opening the way for a creative flowering of pure mathematics. But, for one reason or another, the times were not ripe for such a development. Perhaps the mathematician feels that it is solipsistic to talk of things that are only in his own mind.

---

[44] Alfred North Whitehead, *Science and the Modern World* (New York: Mentor Books, 1948), p. 29.

XV

THE ATOMISATION OF MOTION: A FACET OF THE SCIENTIFIC REVOLUTION

WHEN IN HIS highly metaphorical *Anatomie of the World* John Donne wrote that the world

> Is crumbled out again to his Atomies.
> 'Tis all in pieces, all coherence gone;
> All just supply, and all Relation,

he was expressing a sense of a growth of individualism and a revaluation of the relation of wholes to their parts which had manifestations in many fields, including natural science. It is evidently present in the various corpuscular philosophies of the seventeenth century, but also, I wish to maintain, lurks more reconditely in mathematical theories of motion. *Zeitgeister* are notoriously slippery creatures. In an effort at precision I shall concentrate in this pilot study on a comparison between Nicole Oresme and Galileo Galilei. The choice is not arbitrary. They are both men of acknowledged importance in the history of science, and, I believe, are in many ways paradigmatic of their respective ages. In order to present a relatively unencumbered story I defer consideration of many possible objections to my argument to a dialogue at the end of the article.

I. Aristotle

But first we must consider some background, which will largely be provided by Aristotle. Aristotle was emphatically not an atomist. He had no unique set of immutable and indivisible constituents of the universe, but a world in which all bodies were divisible, and for that reason did not form a constant set, for if a body is divided it becomes two bodies. In his system the concepts of continuity and divisibility played a key role, and were closely bound up with the individuation of bodies. Two things were said to be continuous, and hence really one thing, if they were contiguous and shared a single boundary.[1] Such a

---

[1] *Physica* V.3, 226b18 – 227b2.

Reprinted from *Stud. Hist. Phil. Sci.*, vol. 13, no. 1, pp. 31–54, 1982, with kind permission from Elsevier Science Ltd, The Boulevard, Langford Lane, Kidlington OX5 1GB, UK.

notion was foreign to atomism, for the touching of two Democritean atoms could not be accompanied by the merging of their boundaries. To the mathematician, Aristotelian continuity presented a converse problem, for it was difficult to see how two geometrical objects could touch without their boundaries becoming one where contact occurred. Averroes rather dismissively wrote that 'In mathematics we say things are continuous when one end is imagined to be common to them, such as a point, which is common to two lines, and a line to two surfaces. This continuity is not natural, and here we intend to describe natural continuity.'[2] But others did not allow such a gulf between mathematics and physics, and, as John Murdoch has shown, there were many medieval struggles with the notion of contiguity without continuity.[3]

On other issues Aristotle and mathematics could be in closer accord. Both, for instance, held that all continua were divisible into continua. The geometer by his constructions made many such divisions, and Aristotle accommodated this by saying that there could be mental division, in which the geometer's thinking brought potentially existing divisions into act.[4] In such a division the boundary was, so to speak, mentally doubled; for instance, in the division of a line the point of division was treated as two points, the end of one part and the beginning of the other.[5] Division of a continuum could proceed endlessly without any ultimate constituents being reached, such as might serve as natural units of measure. Instead, measure was a question of comparing divisible objects with one another, and the performing of divisions was essential to the reasoning. One might, for instance, divide a given line into three parts, and thus be able to show that it was three times as long as another given line. Or, by a more complex argument involving divisions and the establishment of congruences between figures, one might show that a given plane figure was equal in area to a certain square. This explains the large role played by ratios and quadratures in Greek geometry. Sophisticated techniques were available for obviating the problem of incommensurability and for dealing with curvilinear figures, but these did not involve the making of actually infinite divisions. The most one claimed was that a certain state of affairs obtained in all finite cases. Measurement in geometry thus depended on a sort of finite probing of the continuum, which, without reaching rock bottom, nevertheless produced an apparently firm structure. But, when the geometric model was applied in other areas, such probing could easily lose its promise of supplying unshakable knowledge. And this, I shall argue, is what happened in medieval

[2]*Physica* V, comm. 26, in *Aristotelis Opera cum Averrois Commentariis* (Venice, 1562–74; repr. Frankfurt: Minerva, 1962), IV, ff. 224v–225r.

[3]J. E. Murdoch, 'Superposition, Congruence and Continuity in the Middle Ages', *Mélanges Alexandre Koyré* (Paris: Hermann, 1964), I, pp. 416–444.

[4]*Metaphysica*Θ 9, 1051a21–34.

[5]*Physica* VIII.8, 263a23–263b2.

treatments of motion.

There are more analogies than is often realised between Aristotle's treatment of permanent objects, those whose parts all existed at the same time, and that which he accorded successive objects, such as motion. In particular this applied to their individuation, in which the focus was on the whole motion of the whole object, from its beginning to its end. In order to be continuous and unqualifiedly one, a motion had to be (1) of a single thing, (2) in a single species, (3) in a single time. Let us allow Aristotle to explicate these criteria somewhat.

(1) That which is in motion must be one – not in an accidental sense (*i.e.* it must be one as the white that blackens is one or Coriscus who walks is one, not in the accidental sense in which Coriscus and white may be one), nor merely in virtue of community of nature (for there might be a case of two men being restored to health at the same time in the same way, *e.g.* from inflammation of the eye, yet this motion is not really one, but only specifically one).[6]

(2) Motions that are not the same either specifically or generically may, it is true, be *contiguous* (*e.g.* a man may run and then at once fall ill of a fever), and again, in the torch-race we have contiguous but not continuous locomotion:[7] for according to our definition there can be continuity only when the ends of two things are one. Hence motions may be contiguous or successive in virtue of the time being continuous, but there can be continuity only in virtue of the motions themselves being continuous, that is when the end of each is one with the end of the other.[8]

(3) Unity is required in respect of time in order that there be no interval of immobility, for where there is intermission of motion there must be rest, and a motion that includes intervals of rest will not be one but many, so that a motion that is interrupted by stationariness is not one or continuous, and it is so interrupted if there is an interval of time.[9]

These passages remind us that in Aristotelian thought motion was by no means confined to local motion, even if this had a certain priority. They also make

[6]*Physica* V.4, 227b32 – 228a3 (Oxford translation).
[7]As W. D. Ross, *Aristotle's Physics: A Revised Text with Introduction and Commentary* (Oxford: Clarendon, 1936), p. 632, notes, the mention of the relay race seems a little out of place: it 'brings out a fresh point, that there are consecutive movements that *are* specifically like but not continuous (because they are not movements of the same subject)'. Averroes, *Physica* V, comm. 40, in *op.cit.* note 2, IV, f. 232r, holds likewise: 'In eis autem, quae conveniunt in specie, ut motus candelae de una manu in alteram, est seseus [*sc.* contiguous/consecutive], quia quies non interponitur, et privatur continuatione in rei veritate, quia motum non est unum.' But there is a puzzle here, for in a relay race it is surely the runners rather than the torch that change. Might it not be that, contrary to Averroes and Ross, Aristotle was saying that the motion of the torch was not continuous because the *movers* change? This would square well with his account of the lack of continuity of projectile motion; see below text referred to by note 66.
[8]*Physica* V.4, 228a26 – b1. I have changed the Oxford translation's 'consecutive' to 'contiguous' to emphasise that it is the case of the same Greek word.
[9]*Physica* V.4, 228b3 – 6.

34

clear that the individuation of motions was for various reasons a more complicated business than that of permanent objects, although the same basic strategy applied. A similar complication applies to the quantification of motions.

Aristotle did not develop this in any detail, but a quotation from his often obscure remarks on the divisibility of motion will reinforce the point that the primary focus was on the whole motion of the whole body.

> Motion is divisible in two senses. In the first place it is divisible in virtue of the time that it occupies. In the second place it is divisible according to the motions of the several parts of that which is in motion: e.g. if the whole $A\Gamma$ is in motion, there will be a motion of AB and a motion of $B\Gamma$. That being so let ΔE be the motion of the part AB and EZ the motion of the part $B\Gamma$. Then the whole ΔZ must be the motion of $A\Gamma$: for ΔZ must constitute the motion of $A\Gamma$ inasmuch as ΔE and BZ severally constitute the motion of each of its parts. But the motion of a thing can never be constituted by the motion of something else: consequently the whole motion is the motion of the whole magnitude.[10]

The task of developing such remarks into a theory of the measure of motion was left to the tradition. In the Middle Ages one of the clearest and most sophisticated accounts was provided by Nicole Oresme, who may therefore serve as a prime representative of the holist tradition in this regard.

II. Oresme

Oresme begins the second part of his fascinating *Tractatus de Configurationibus Qualitatum et Motuum* as follows:

> Every successive motion of a divisible subject has parts, and is divisible in one way according to the division and extension or continuity of the mobile, in another way according to the divisibility and duration or continuity of the time, and in a third way, at least imaginatively, according to the degrees and intensity of the speed. From the first continuity a motion is called great or small, from the second short or long, from the third swift or slow.[11]

The similarity to Aristotle is clear, but Oresme's crisp statement makes it apparent that we are, as it were, dealing with a five-dimensional object, with three spatial dimensions, one temporal dimension and one dimension of intensity of speed. The concept of speed is crucial to the problem of measure,

[10] *Physica* VI.4, 234b21 – 28.
[11] *'Nicole Oresme and the Medieval Geometry of Qualities and Motions. A Treatise on the Uniformity and Difformity of Intensities, known as Tractatus de Configurationibus Qualitatum et Motuum*, M. Clagett (ed.) (Madison: University of Wisconsin Press, 1968), p.270. Hereafter I shall cite this work as *De config*.

but it is essentially holistic, and should not be confused with instantaneous velocity. This role is more nearly played by intensity of speed,[12] which may vary with respect both to time and to the parts of the mobile. Both forms of variation were usually called difformity (as opposed to uniformity), although Oresme says that in the former case we should more properly speak of irregularity. 'And in this way it would be said the heaven's motion is difform and regular, while the downward motion of a heavy body can on the contrary be uniform and irregular, and can also be uniform and regular or difform and irregular.'[13] However, the similarity between intensity of speed and instantaneous velocity should not deceive us into thinking that we are on essentially modern ground. The medieval conceptions were far more fluid.

In considering the measure of speed there are, Oresme says, three closely related notions to be considered: (1) 'the quantity of the whole speed with both intensity and extension being taken into account (*pensatis intensione et extensione*)'; (2) 'the denomination by which a subject is said to be made thus more swiftly or more slowly'; (3) 'the graded (*gradualis*) intensity itself'.[14] Of these the third is tackled first.

> I say therefore that universally that degree of speed is unqualifiedly more intense or greater at which in an equal time there is gained or lost more of that perfection following (*secundum*) which the motion is made. For example, in local motion that degree of speed is greater and more intense at which there would be traversed more of space or of distance, and similarly in alteration that degree of speed is greater at which there would be gained or lost more of the quality's intensity, and so in augmentation at which there would be gained more of quantity, and in diminution at which there would be lost more of quantity or of extension. And so generally wherever motion would be found.[15]

Thus quantifying the intensity of speed depends upon quantifying what is being acquired or lost by the motion, and it is immediately made clear that this depends on how the situation is described, and so the second of the above notions is brought into play.

> It is not to be overlooked that the same motion or flux is called by many names connoting in different ways, and as a result of this (*secundum hoc*) the denominating speed is measured (*attenditur vel mensuratur*) in different ways, so that the quantity of graded intensity is assigned in many ways.[16]

Two examples help to make this clearer. In circular motion a body may be said

[12]On this concept see A. Maier, *Zwischen Philosophie und Mechanik* (Rome: Edizioni di Storia e Letteratura, 1958), chap. 3.
[13]*De config.*, p. 272.
[14]*De config.*, p. 276.
[15]*Ibid.*
[16]*Ibid.*

either to be moved or to circuit. 'The intensity of the speed of motion is measured (*attenditur*) by the linear space that would be traversed at that degree. But the intensity of the speed of circuiting is measured by the angles described about the centre.'[17] This may be easily translated into a modern distinction between linear and angular velocity, but the second example is less familiar. It concerns rectilinear motion of descent.

> The speed of motion is measured by the space traversed, but the speed of descent by nearness (*penes appropinquationem*) to the centre. Thus it is possible that *A* and *B* be moved equally swiftly but not descend equally swiftly, in that *A* is moved along a direct line to the centre and *B* along an oblique line, and so *A* descends more swiftly than *B*, and yet *B* is moved equally swiftly. Similarly, since descent is measured by the ratio of nearness (*penes proportionem approximationis*) to the centre, it happens that what is moved uniformly or regularly along a direct line from the centre descends difformly, because it nears the centre more swiftly when near than when far away, but with there always remaining an equal speed of motion.[18]

Oresme also provides examples from the motions of alteration and augmentation, but while remembering these additional complexities, let us stick to local motion.

In both the examples above the central strategy was to associate with a motion over a certain time something spatially extended to serve as its measure. This itself could then be measured in the way that geometric objects were measured. In the initial representation of the motion, which is a successive object, by a permanent spatially extended object, the verb *attendere* was regularly used. Thus in the circular motion the motion itself was said to be attended by (*attenditur penes*) the linear space traversed by the mobile, although for convenience I use the translation 'measured by' instead of the rather odd 'attended by'. If we are interested in speed of circuiting rather than speed of motion, the relevant 'measure' is the angle described by the radius vector from the centre. (It is intriguing to note that concentration on the area would in the case of a body obeying Kepler's second law result in a process — it needs a name — which was uniform.) In the second example speed of motion was again measured by a distance, but speed of descent by something less clearly visualisable, namely nearness. Oresme does not discuss in any detail the quantification of this, which indeed would be tricky for ordinary language discussion, but it clearly leans heavily on concepts such as 'twice as near'.[19]

[17]*De config.*, p. 278.
[18]*Ibid.*
[19]We may give a more formal treatment in something like the following way. Let the centre be *C*, and denote the nearness of *B* to *C* by $n(BC)$. For an arbitrary point A_0 let $n(A_0C) = 1$. In medieval fashion divide A_0C into proportional parts towards *C*, that is, let A_1 bisect A_0C, A_2 bisect A_1C, and so on. Intuitively A_1 is twice as near *C* as A_0, and so $n(A_1C) = 2$, and in general $n(A_iC) = 2^i$. Then, in traversing the first proportional part, the body gains one unit of nearness, in traversing the second two, in traversing the third four, and so on.

XV

When a body approaches the centre it doubles its nearness to it in ever shorter distances, and so, if the speed of motion is uniform, the speed of descent increases rapidly, and indeed paradoxically it will have reached an infinite value when the centre is attained.

This feature of the logic of nearness was well brought out by Richard Swineshead, who argued that if the intensity of a quality was to be measured by (*attendi penes*) its nearness to the top degree, then the top degree would be infinitely intense.

> For let some heat be intensified up to the top. Then that heat will be a certain amount (*aliqualiter*) more intense, and twice as intense, and four times as intense, and so on to infinity, because at some time it will be [thus much] near to the top degree, and [then] twice as near, and four times as near, and so on to infinity. And so proportionally as it is nearer to the top degree . . . so it is more intense. Therefore the heat will be infinitely intense before the end of the hour, and in the end it will be more intense than ever before the end. Therefore the top heat will be infinitely intense.[20]

Swineshead regarded this as a reason for rejecting the view that intensity should be so measured, and in general many of his arguments may be seen as attempts to establish 'correct' quantifications in various cases. Oresme on the other hand is more pluralistic, and seems to revel in the multifarious possibilities of measure. 'According to the multiple denominations, speed is multiply varied or denominated.'[21] The continuum may be hacked at in many different ways according to the language we use, and because a final analysis is inaccessible, there is a radical sense in which *we* rather than nature choose the language, for nature herself will tolerate many different ones.

So much for the determination of the intensity of speed. Now let us move to a consideration of how this relates to the quantification of the whole speed of the whole motion in the non-trivial cases where the intensity varies. Oresme's treatment of such difformity is closely bound up with his doctrine of configurations, in which a quality or a motion is 'graphically' represented by a figure whose altitude varies proportionally with the intensity of the quality or motion.

> There is a twofold difformity of speed, namely subjective and temporal, which, as regards the purpose in hand, differ in this, that subjective punctual speed, just like

[20]*Calculator. Subtilissimi Ricardi Suiseth Calculationes noviter emendate et revise* (Venice, 1520), f, 2r: 'Nam intendatur aliqua caliditas usque ad summum. Tunc ista caliditas erit intensior aliqualiter, et in duplo, et in quadruplo intensior, et sic in infinitum, quia aliquando erit propinqua gradui summo, et in duplo propinquior, et in quadruplo propinquior, et sic in infinitum. Et sic proportionaliter sicut propinquior erit gradui summo secundum illam positionem erit intensior. Ergo infinite intensa erit ista caliditas ante finem hore, et in fine erit intensior quam unquam ante finem. Ergo caliditas summa erit infinite intensa, quod fuit probandum.'
[21]*De config.*, p. 280.

> punctual quality is to be imagined by a straight line, and linear subjective speed is to be imagined by a surface or superficial figure, but the speed of a surface is to be imagined by a body, and similarly the speed of a body by a body, entirely in the same way as was said about the figuration of qualities. . . . But instantaneous punctual speed is imagined by a straight line, and temporal punctual speed is to be imagined by a surface, but the temporal speed of a line is imagined by a body, and similarly superficial and corporeal [speeds] are imagined by a body because there is not available (*non contingit dare*) a fourth dimension, as was said [above].[22]

Oresme may not be at his clearest in this passage, but we can see again an almost conscious thrust towards representing speed as a five-dimensional object in which its intensity is 'graphed' both against the three dimensions of body and against time. But Oresme quite naturally denies the existence of even a fourth spatial dimension, and so this representation is not available to him. Thus his quantification of speed is rather more piecemeal, and, in particular, subjective difformity is treated separately from temporal difformity.

Oresme lays it down as a principle of measure that, 'Universally the measure or ratio of any two qualities of lines or surfaces, and also that of speeds, is as that of the figures by which they are imagined in a mutually comparative way.'[23] This principle immediately allows for the equation of difform motions to uniform ones. For example, it is easy to demonstrate the so-called Merton Rule, which equates a uniformly difform motion (one whose intensity of speed increases or decreases uniformly) to a uniform motion over the same time with the intensity of speed that the uniformly difform motion has at the middle instant of time.[24] This is merely a matter of equating the triangle in the representation of uniformly difform motion with the rectangle in the representation of uniform motion. That the two motions are equal means that as much of the relevant perfection is acquired through one of them as through the other. For instance, if we are interested in the speed of motion in local motion, a body travels as far in the uniformly difform motion as it would in the uniform motion.

This conclusion is clear and well-known. But Oresme's principle has some fuzzier and less familiar consequences. 'I say first that the ratio of all uniform qualities of equal degrees is as that of their subjects, just as that of all rectangles (*quadrangulorum*) of equal altitude is that of their bases (*suarum longitudinum*).'[25] It does seem quite natural to think of the measure of a quality increasing when the volume of the subject is increased, intensity being maintained, but it is not so evident that this is appropriate in the case of speeds. Nevertheless Oresme pushes the analogy to a certain extent: 'A

[22]*De config.*, p. 292.
[23]*De config.*, p. 404.
[24]*De config.*, pp. 408 – 410.
[25]*De config.*, p. 404.

uniform speed that lasts for three days is equal (*est equalis*) to a speed three times as intense that lasts for one day.'[26] The word *velocitas* (speed) is very obviously related to *velox* (swift), but although the above two speeds are equal, one does not wish to say that the motions are equally swift, and indeed Oresme has already told us that it is by reason of the *intensity* of speed that a motion is called swift or slow. Linguistic strains are beginning to tell, and they can be even more apparent when we consider the speed as distributed over the subject, for we would surely not wish to say that something is moved more swiftly just because it is bulkier.

Such a point was made explicitly by Thomas Bradwardine and by Albert of Saxony when they considered motions that were difform with respect to the parts of the subject. Bradwardine remarked: 'To some it seems that the ratio of local motions in speed is as that of the corporeal positional spaces (*spatiorum situalium corporeorum*)[27] described in the same time. This is easily refuted, because then any moved body would be moved twice as swiftly as its half.'[28] Bradwardine also rejected the mathematically sophisticated position of Gerard of Brussels, and held instead that, 'The speed of local motion is measured by (*attenditur penes*) the speed of the most swiftly moved point in the locally moved body, because the speed of motion arises from the mobile traversing a large stationary space, be it true or imagined, in a short time. . . .'[29] The argument here seems to be linguistically orientated rather than concerned with what would be the appropriate measure of motion if we wished to consider it in relation to its causes. This feature is even more strongly accentuated in Albert of Saxony, who when discussing such difformity, continually appealed to proof from 'the common mode of speaking' (*ex communi modo loquendi*). Albert agreed with Bradwardine that the proper spatial representation for the speed of a body was linear, but had two thought experiments to confute the view that in rectilinear local motion the relevant line was that described by the most swiftly moved point. In the second of these Socrates and Plato are moving from one place to another in the same time, 'and towards the end of the motion Socrates extends his arm, but Plato does not. Then some point in Socrates describes a greater space than any point in Plato, and yet from the common way of speaking we should say that in such a case they were moved equally swiftly.'[30] Instead Albert held that what was relevant was the middle point of the body, or the equivalent. 'I say "or the equivalent" because if there were rarefaction or condensation of the mobile

[26]*De config.*, p. 406.

[27]Should this be read as an attempt to refer to a four-dimensional entity?

[28]Thomas Bradwardine, *Tractatus de Proportionibus*, H. L. Crosby (ed.) (Madison: University of Wisconsin Press, 1955), p. 128.

[29]Bradwardine, *op. cit.*, p. 130.

[30]H. H. L. Busard, 'Der "Tractatus Proportionum" von Albert von Sachsen', *Österreichische Akademie der Wissenschaften, Mathematisch-Naturwissenschaftliche Klasse, Denkschriften*, 116. Band 2, abhandlung (1971), 43 – 72, at p.68.

there would not remain the same middle point, except according to equivalence.'[31] At first glance this has greater physical plausibility and may even produce in us echoes of the concept of centre of gravity, but it only applies in the case of rectilinear motion. For circular motion Albert revived the previously rejected view that the speed was measured by the most swiftly moving point, 'for a mobile is moved as swiftly as some part of it, as is clear from the common way of speaking'.[32] Clearly we shall get no consistent general rule from this quarter.

Oresme, at least in the *De Configurationibus*, does not discuss this question, but from his general doctrines it would seem that he should proceed by equating areas or other bulks. In the case of a line rotating about its endpoint this would mean that for purposes of measure the line be considered as moving with a uniform intensity of speed equal to that of its midpoint. In similar vein John Buridan suggested that the total speed of a sphere should not be denominated from the speed of its most swiftly moved point; there should instead be recompensation among the parts.[33] But neither Buridan nor Oresme developed these suggestions in any detail, and we should note that if Oresme had tried to apply this type of analysis to *bodies* (which after all were the real mobiles in the natural world) he would have faced serious difficulties arising from the absence of a fourth dimension. But I would argue that it was not primarily a lack of mathematical techniques that produced an apparent lack of completeness in Oresme's discussion, but a basically 'unmodern' epistemic orientation. When presented with a complex situation Oresme and most other Schoolmen would characteristically produce, usually by dialectical disputation, an analysis that went so far as appeared necessary for the purpose in hand. (Oresme has, for instance, shown that equations can be made between difform and uniform motions.) There was no general urge to continue the analysis to the ultimate elements, from which there could proceed a uniquely appropriate synthesis. The Middle Ages had received the axiomatic method from the Greeks, but there are many signs that the Schoolmen were rather out of tune with its spirit. If the continuum was not ultimately fathomable, then neither, it would seem, were the rich and complicated states of affairs in which it was inextricably involved.

[31]*Ibid.*

[32]Busard, *op.cit.,* p. 70. *Cf.* M. Clagett, *The Science of Mechanics in the Middle Ages* (Madison: University of Wisconsin Press, 1959), pp. 228–229.

[33]John Buridan, *Questiones super Octo Phisicorum Libros Aristotelis* (Paris, 1509; repr. Frankfurt: Minerva, 1964), f. 15v (I, q.12); Clagett, *op.cit.,* pp. 216–217.

III. Galileo

Oresme's view of continuity was essentially Aristotelian, but Galileo was in this regard, as in many others, consciously anti-Aristotelian.[34] In the *Discorsi* he had Salviati ridicule the potentiality – actuality distinction: 'So that a line twenty spans long, for instance, is not said to contain twenty lines of one span each actually until after its division into twenty equal parts, but before that it is said to contain them only in potency. . . .'[35] As regarded the number of finite parts (*parti quante*) in a bounded continuum, it was neither finite nor infinite, for 'in speaking of discrete quantities it appears to me that between the finite and infinite there is a third, middle term, which is of answering to any designated (*segnato*) number.'[36] The number of finite parts in a continuum cannot be limited, but it cannot be said to be infinite, for an infinite number of *quanta* would make it of infinite size. 'So I concede to the philosophical gentlemen (*i Signori filosofi*) that the continuum contains as many parts as they please, and I grant them that it contains them in act or in potency, according to their taste and pleasure.'[37]

For all his sarcasm Galileo's account thus far does not deviate widely from Aristotelianism. But Salviati now hastens to take the argument into far murkier waters by asserting that in the same way as a line contains this or that number of equal parts it also contains an infinite number of points. And once again he quips that this may be said to be either in act or in potency according to Simplicio's wish. The latter very reasonably questions the analogy, and in particular asserts that dividing a line into an infinite number of points is a very different matter from dividing it into ten fathoms or forty braccia. 'In fact I hold it quite impossible to bring such a division to effect.'[38] Salviati of course has an answer for this, which, after various digressions, he produces. He first gets Simplicio to admit that bending a line into the form of a square or of a hexagon is sufficient for bringing its four or six equal potential parts to act. This is clearly generalisable to accommodate other regular polygons, but beyond this Salviati takes a leap into the infinite. 'When I form of this line a polygon of infinitely many sides, that is, when I bend it into the circumference of a circle, may I not with the same licence say that I have brought to act its

[34]On Galileo's account of continuity see also M. Clavelin, 'Le Problème du Continu et les Paradoxes de l'Infini chez Galilée', *Thalès* **10** (1959), 1 – 26, and A. M. Smith, 'Galileo's Theory of Indivisibles: Revolution or Compromise?' *J. Hist. Ideas* **37** (1976), 571 – 588. My emphases are different from those to be found in Smith's fine article.

[35]*Le Opere di Galileo Galilei. Edizione Nazionale*, A. Favaro (ed.) (Florence: G. Barbera, 1890 – 1937) [= EN], VIII, p. 80. I base my translations from the *Discorsi* on those given in Galileo Galilei, *Two New Sciences*, S. Drake (tr.) (Madison: University of Wisconsin Press, 1974), which has Favaro's page numbers in the margins.

[36]EN, VIII, p. 81.

[37]*Ibid.*

[38]EN, VIII, p. 82.

infinitely many parts, which you said were contained in it in potency earlier when it was straight.'[39] In this way Salviati claims to have resolved a whole infinity in *un tratto solo*, or as Drake translates it 'at one fell swoop'.[40] And so, Salviati continues, the composition of the continuum from absolutely indivisible atoms should be admitted, for the doctrine provides a fine road for getting us out of 'very intricate labyrinths'. At this onslaught Simplicio somewhat pusillanimously confesses himself baffled, although indicating a hope that abler Peripatetics may find an answer to Salviati's arguments. But no time is allowed for that at this point of the dialogue, for Salviati has already enthusiastically embarked on an application of his doctrine, that of explaining rarefaction and condensation.

Salviati's strategy is to show how a circle by its rotation may describe a line greater or less than its own circumference: this exemplifies how a line may, while retaining the same number of parts, be stretched without the creation of finite vacua or compressed without interpenetration of parts. To do this he employs 'Aristotle's wheel'.[41] Two concentric circles are conceived to be fixed together in the same plane, and one or other of them is imagined to roll along a straight line. Salviati again treats circles as polygons with infinite numbers of sides, and so makes a start from the corresponding finite cases, in which the circles are replaced by regular polygons with parallel sides. Suppose first that it is the larger polygon which is to 'roll' on a straight line. In this process its sides will successively lie flat on the line, and by this process of 'imprinting' it will cover the line without gaps. At the times at which a side of the larger polygon lies flat on its straight line, the corresponding side of the smaller polygon will lie flat on a parallel line, but there will be gaps (equal to the differences in length of the sides of the polygons) between successive imprints. Other things being equal, as the number of sides of the polygons increases, the gaps become less, and, when we take the leap to infinity and reach the circle, the gaps are of no magnitude, and we have as it were succeeded in stretching out the circumference of the circle into a line longer than itself, for 'by its touchings the circumference will have measured the whole of [the straight line] (*la circonferenza . . . averà con li suoi toccamenti misurata tutta la CE*)'.[42]

The representation of condensation is similar. This time the smaller polygon 'rolls' on a straight line, and we find that now the imprints of the larger polygon on its line overlap one another. As the number of sides of each polygon increases the length of overlap decreases, and when we reach infinity it has become of no size at all. By such means is achieved condensation without interpenetration of extended parts (*costipazione e condensazione senza veruna*

---

[39]EN, VIII, p. 92.
[40]EN, VIII, p. 93.
[41]EN, VIII, pp. 68 – 72, 93 – 96. *Cf.* I. E. Drabkin, 'Aristotle's Wheel: Notes on the History of a Paradox', *Osiris* **9** (1950), 162 – 198.
[42]EN, VIII, p. 70.

penetrazione di parti quante).[43]

From one point of view this playing around with infinity is alarming, for it suggests that lines are of variable length, and so hacks at any attempt at quantitative science. But Galileo did not see the matter thus. For him infinity was a splendid weapon for getting at the quantitative guts of things, and like many seventeenth-century writers he had small fear of the tricks that it could play if handled incautiously. He had the confidence that by taking a bold leap to the ultimate atoms he could then build up a reliable account of what happened in composite situations. This attitude is similar to that which led him to base his theory of motion on a consideration of what would happen in a few ideal situations. Unhindered horizontal motion is postulated (not of course arbitrarily) to be uniform, and unhindered vertical motion to be uniformly accelerated, and from these simple elements we can, for example, build up the parabolic path of projectiles.

But it was not only the theory of motion that was in this way atomised: motions themselves were. For Galileo speed was usually interpreted in the sense of *velocitas totalis*, the speed of the whole motion, but, contrary to the medieval tradition, he envisages this total speed as composed of a uniquely determined set of ultimate elements. In 1604 Galileo purported to demonstrate that if the speed of fall increased proportionally with the distance fallen, then the distance would be proportional to the square of the time.[44] He represented the path of fall by a straight line AB (containing points $C, D, etc.$) and the increasing degrees of speed by straight lines erected perpendicularly on AB. Since their lengths increase uniformly away from A, their endpoints (not those on AB) lie on a straight line AGH.

> Because the speed with which the mobile came from A to D is composed of all the degrees of speed gained in all the points of line AD, and the speed with which it traversed the line AC is composed of all the degrees of speed which it gained in all the points of line AC, therefore the speed with which it traversed the line AD to the speed with which it traversed the line AC has the ratio which all the parallel lines drawn up to AH from all the points of line AD have to all the parallels drawn up to AG from all the points of line AC; and this ratio is that which the triangle ADH has to the triangle ACG, that is the square of AD to the square of AC.

From this Galileo proceeds to his desired conclusion by means of a superficially plausible but erroneous proportional argument.[45] But another

[43]EN, VIII, p. 95.

[44]EN, VIII, pp. 373 – 374. *Cf.* 383 and X, pp. 115 – 116.

[45]*Cf.* W. L. Wisan, 'The New Science of Motion: A Study of Galileo's *De Motu Locali*', *Archs Hist. exact Sci.* **13** (1974), 103 – 306, at p. 208. For very different interpretations see S. Drake, 'Galileo's 1604 Fragment on Falling Bodies (Galileo Gleanings XVIII)', *Br. J. Hist. Sci.* **4** (1968 – 69), 340 – 358; *id.*, 'Galileo's Discovery of the Law of Free Fall, *Scient. Am.* **228** (5) (May 1973), 84 – 92; *id.*, 'Mathematics and Discovery in Galileo's Physics', *Historia Math.* **1** (1974), 129 – 150; *id.*, *Galileo at Work* (Chicago: University of Chicago Press, 1978), pp. 97 – 103.

44

error has crept in through Galileo's representation of the degrees of speed by an infinitude of parallel lines. No doubt the body would pass through all these degrees, but Galileo's summation leads to something that cannot properly be called total speed. Total speed should refer to the distance traversed in a given time, but here it does nothing of the kind: it is in fact proportional to the square of the distance, and time seems to have disappeared from the picture.[46] What has happened is that Galileo's expanding and contracting continuum has let him down. In order for their aggregate to be a proper measure of overall swiftness the parallels must, as it were, be spaced evenly with respect to time. But by arranging them evenly with respect to space, so that on the given assumption they constitute triangles, Galileo has produced too high a density in the swifter areas. If they were stretched and compressed to make them even with respect to time, their endpoints would produce a graph of speed against time that would not be rectilinear, and from which the proportionality of distances and squares of times could not legitimately be deduced.

Later, Galileo was to reject altogether the view that the speed of a body's fall was proportional to distance, but this does not mean that he had identified the sources of his former error. In the *Discorsi* Salviati reasons as follows:

When the speeds have the same ratio as the spaces traversed or to be traversed, those spaces come to be traversed in equal times; if therefore the speeds with which the falling body traversed the space of four braccia were the doubles of the speeds with which it traversed the first two braccia (as the space is double the space), then the times of passage are equal. But for the same mobile to traverse the four braccia and the two in the same time cannot happen except in instantaneous motion. But we see that the falling body makes its motion in time, and traverses the two braccia in less than the four. Therefore it is false that its speed increases as the space.[47]

In this argument the degrees of speed at the individual points of the first two braccia are being matched with their doubles over the first four braccia, in order to infer that the overall speed in the latter case is double that in the former. This ingenious sophism rests on the same error that we identified in the 1604 fragment: the individual speeds are distributed according to space rather than to time, and so are incorrectly bunched for giving total speeds. But although Galileo's reasons were wrong, his conclusion was right: on the assumption that it is possible, fall from rest with speed proportional to distance does entail instantaneous motion. Fermat pointed out that the result

[46]*Cf.* A. Koyré, *Études Galiléennes* (Paris: Hermann, 1939), p. 98.

[47]EN, VIII, 203 – 204. On this argument see I. B. Cohen, 'Galileo's Rejection of the Possibility of Velocity Changing Uniformly with Respect to Distance', *Isis* 47 (1956), 231 – 235; A. R. Hall, 'Galileo's Fallacy', *Isis* 49 (1958), 342 – 344; S. Drake, 'Uniform Acceleration, Space, and Time (Galileo Gleanings XIX), *Br. J. Hist. Sci.* 5 (1970 – 71), 21 – 43; *id.,* 'Galileo Gleanings — XXII: Velocity and Eudoxian Proportion Theory, *Physis* 15 (1973), 49 – 64.

was true but undemonstrated, and proceeded to give a rigorous demonstration *more Archimedeo* of Galileo's *illatio*.[48]

Fermat suggested that with his lynx-like eyes Galileo had seen, or thought he had seen, the demonstration through the cloudy skies. In this instant 'thought he had seen' is more appropriate, but in the much discussed first theorem on accelerated motion in his *De Motu Locali*[49] we may perhaps allow him to have seen indeed. The burden of the theorem is to show that a body uniformly accelerated from rest takes as much time to traverse a certain space as would a body moving at a uniform degree of speed half that of the final degree of speed of the accelerated motion. It is now the time that is represented by a straight line AB, which has perpendicular to it the parallels representing the degrees of speed. We need not analyse the argument in detail: a quotation from the proof will suffice to illustrate the type of atomising argument that is now becoming familiar to us:

Since to all the individual instants of the time AB there correspond all the individual points of the line AB, and the parallels made from these points contained in triangle AEB represent the increasing degrees of augmented speed, and the parallels contained inside the rectangle likewise represent as many degrees of a speed that is not augmented but equable, it [therefore] appears that just as many moments of speed (*velocitatis momenta*) are consumed in the accelerated motion represented by (*iuxta*) the increasing parallels of triangle AEB as in the equable motion represented by the parallels of rectangle GB. Also what there lacks to the moments in the first half of the accelerated motion [in comparison with the uniform motion] is restored by the moments represented by the parallels of the triangle IEF [*i.e.* those by which the degrees of speed of the accelerated motion exceed those of the uniform one in the second half].

It is significant of their different orientations towards problems of motion that this is one of the few places where we can make a direct comparison between Oresme and Galileo, and the comparison itself highlights their different interests. Oresme treats the so-called Merton Rule for speeds more or less as a corollary of its analogue for qualities.[50] His strategy is simply to show that the triangle representing the uniformly difform quality or speed is equal in area with the rectangle representing the uniform quality or speed, and then to assert the equality of the qualities or speeds. 'And so it is clear to which uniform quality or motion a uniformly difform quality or speed is equivalent (*adequatur*).'[51] Oresme's formulation of the proposition in terms of the

---

[48]*Oeuvres de Fermat*, P. Tannery, C. Henry and C. de Waard (eds.) (Paris: Gauthier-Villars, 1891 – 1922), II, pp. 267 – 276.
[49]EN, VIII, pp. 208 – 209. On this argument *cf.* S. Drake, 'The Uniform Motion Equivalent to a Uniformly Accelerated Motion from Rest (Galileo Gleanings XX)', *Isis* **63** (1972), 28 – 38.
[50]*De config.*, pp. 408 – 410.
[51]*De config.*, p. 410.

46

equation of speeds indicates his concern with the theory of measure, while Galileo's expression in terms of spaces and times is more appropriately adapted to experimentation. But the difference that may best symbolise the theme of this paper is that while Oresme compares speeds and the figures which represent them as wholes, Galileo is insistent on building up his picture from the lines representing degrees of speed at indivisible instants. It is this attitude of synthesising from ultimate elements, be they first principles or the final constituents of continua, that goes a long way towards justifying Galileo's claim to have advanced 'a very new science about a very old subject'.

IV. Doubts, Queries, Objections

(1) *Objicias:* Your argument appears to run directly counter to the views of Stillman Drake, who in an important series of papers[52] has characterised the medieval approach to problems of motion as essentially discrete, and that of Galileo as essentially continuous. In this and the two following doubts I shall draw heavily but not exclusively on Drake's arguments. (I shall not claim to be presenting them with complete fidelity.) Let us first consider John Buridan's explanation of the acceleration of falling bodies by means of impetus.

I suppose that the natural heaviness of the stone remains always the same and exactly similar (*consimilis*) before the motion, after the motion, and during the motion . . . . I also suppose that the resistance that arises from the medium remains the same and exactly similar . . . . Thirdly I suppose that, if the mobile is the same, and the total mover is the same, and the resistance is the same or exactly similar, the motion will remain equally swift, because the ratio of mover to mobile and resistance will remain [the same]. . . . It is necessary to imagine that from its principal mover, namely heaviness, the heavy body not only acquires to itself motion but also acquires to itself with that motion a certain impetus which has the virtue of moving the heavy body together with the persisting natural heaviness. And because the impetus is acquired jointly (*communiter*) with the motion, then as the motion is swifter, so the impetus is greater and stronger. So therefore from the beginning (*a principio*) the heavy body is moved by its natural heaviness alone, and hence is moved slowly. Afterwards (*postea*) it is moved jointly (*simul*) by the same heaviness and by the acquired impetus, and hence is moved more swiftly. And because the motion is made swifter therefore the impetus is also made greater and stronger, and so the heavy body is moved jointly by its natural heaviness and by that greater

[52]S. Drake, 'Impetus Theory and Quanta of Speed before and after Galileo', *Physics* **16** (1974), 47 – 65; *id.*, 'Impetus Theory Reappraised', *J. Hist. Ideas* **36** (1975), 27 – 46; *id.*, 'Free Fall from Albert of Saxony to Honoré Fabri', *Stud. Hist. Phil. Sci.* **5** (1974), 347 – 366; *id.*, 'A Further Reappraisal of Impetus Theory', *Stud. Hist. Phil. Sci.* **7** (1976), 319 – 336.

impetus, and so it is again moved more swiftly, and so it will always be continually (*continue*) accelerated until the end.[53]

It has been traditional to read this passage as describing a continuous acceleration brought about by a continuous increase of impetus. This appears natural, but in fact is incoherent. At the beginning the body is moved by its heaviness alone, which gives it a finite (albeit small) speed, and a proportionate impetus. But this means that the moving power is greater, and so it seems we should immediately have a swifter motion, which implies a greater impetus, which implies a yet swifter motion, and so on to infinity. It is fairly easy to show (assuming Bradwardine's law of motion) that this means an infinite speed, and unless we suppose intervals between infusions of impetus this should be reached immediately. This clearly does not happen in nature. If on the other hand we allow the impetus to increase by a series of quantum jumps, the process is slowed up, and we get the apparently continuous increase in speed that is actually observed. Buridan did not spell this out in precise detail, but it seems to be the only way to make sense of his intent, and receives confirmation from a later impetus theorist, Honoré Fabri, who made it quite clear that in natural acceleration impetus was acquired by a discrete series of finite increments.[54]

Respondeo:[55] Your argument is cogent, but not historically conclusive. It depends on giving particular weight to Buridan's assertion that 'from the beginning the heavy body is moved by its natural heaviness alone, and hence is moved slowly', which suggests that the body immediately acquires a finite speed. But other passages from the quotation suggest strongly that the natural heaviness produces impetus at precisely the same time as it does motion and that speed and impetus are strictly proportional. Concentration on these passages would mean ruling out the quantum interpretation. The basic point is that it is often possible to draw inferences from the writings of other people, which they themselves did not recognise: when I accuse someone of contradicting himself, I usually mean to inform him of something that beforehand he did not consciously know. If your argument had been put to Buridan, there would have been more than one strategy available to him for resolving the apparent contradiction. So far as we know the argument was not put, but Nicole Oresme later indicated a non-quantum way out of the dilemma.

[53]John Buridan, *Quaestiones super Libris Quattuor de Caelo et Mundo,* E. A. Moody (ed.) (Cambridge, Mass.: Mediaeval Academy of America, 1942), 179 – 180 (II, q. 12). *Cf.* Clagett, *op.cit.,* note 32, pp. 560 – 561, and Buridan, *op.cit.,* note 33, f. 120v (VIII, q. 12).
[54]H. Fabri, *Tractatus Physicus* (Lyons, 1646), pp. 87 – 88 *et passim.*
[55]*Cf.* A. Franklin, 'Stillman Drake's "Impetus Theory Reappraised"', *J. Hist. Ideas* **38** (1977), 307 – 315.

48

I say that every movement of a heavy or light thing, whatever it be, begins by working in such a way that whatever degree of speed is given or signified in it, it is fitting that it previously had less speed and less and less beyond all ratio, and this is what one is wont to call to begin *a non gradu*. And the cause in general is that the excess of the motive virtue over the resistance or the application of it to the resistance cannot be made suddenly, but it is fitting that such things be made one part after another, and each part in this way (*aussi*), and nothing of it can be made suddenly.[56]

We of course cannot be sure that Buridan would have adopted this interpretation, but *prima facie* Oresme would seem a more reliable guide than the much later Fabri. And in fact the latter is a very equivocal guide, for, in association with his jerky acceleration, he maintained that time was not continuous but that any finite interval was composed of a finite number of instants.[57] Buridan on the other hand was firmly with Aristotle in asserting the continuity of time.[58] I am in fact inclined to turn Fabri to my own use, and argue that his discrete approach arose not from his being an impetus theorist but from his being of the seventeenth century. Finally we should note that even if the discrete interpretation of Buridan were correct it is by no means clear that it would entail discontinuity in the Aristotelian sense in the motion of free fall, although it would suggest a compositionist view of motion of a type that I have been arguing was more characteristic of the seventeenth century.

(2) *Objicias:* It is important not to consider Buridan in isolation. He must be seen against the general medieval failure to grasp the theory of proportion for continuous quantities as developed in Book V of Euclid's *Elements* and usually ascribed to Eudoxus. In the version of this work by Campanus of Novara, which was standard in the later Middle Ages, the theory is completely garbled, and so recourse was made to an arithmetical theory of proportion of the type found in Euclid Book VII or in Boethius. Although ingenious developments were made in this, an irreducible aura of discreteness remained. The recovery of the Eudoxean theory in the sixteenth century was essential to Galileo's achievement.

Respondeo: This argument rests on several misconceptions. It is true that the so-called Eudoxean definition of being in the same ratio was misunderstood in the Middle Ages, and that Campanus's comments on the definitions of Book V are often obfuscating.[59] But this does not have all the implications that you suggest. In the first place we should note that a thorough examination of Book V reveals that, while he did not state it as a definition, Campanus had

[56]Nicole Oresme, *Le Livre du ciel et du monde,* A. D. Menut and A. J. Denomy (eds.) (Madison: University of Wisconsin Press, 1968), 414. *Cf.* A. Maier, *An der Grenze von Scholastik und Naturwissenschaft,* 2nd edn (Rome: Edizioni di Storia et Letteratura, 1952), 205 – 206.

[57]H. Fabri, *op.cit.,* note 54, pp. 87 – 88.

[58]Buridan, *op.cit.,* note 33, ff. 94v – 95v (VI, q. 2).

[59]See the classic account by J. E. Murdoch, 'The Medieval Language of Proportions', *Scientific Change,* A. C. Crombie (ed.) (London: Heinemann, 1963), pp. 237 – 271.

a perfectly good understanding of how the Eudoxean criterion actually operated.[60] This, however, is not crucial to my case. What is more important to realise is that one can have an intuitive awareness of continuity and the equality of continuous quantities (in geometry this fundamentally depended on the principle of superposition) independently of a universal criterion for the equality of ratios between continuous quantities. The Middle Ages did indeed rely heavily on numerical descriptions (*denominationes*) of ratios, and extended this language to accommodate many kinds of irrational ratio,[61] but to assert that this means replacing the continuous by the discrete is to confuse the *describens* with the *describendum*. Language, even mathematical language, consists of discrete units, and, if it could not be used for discussing continuity in the Middle Ages, then neither could it at any other time. To measure length in feet does not entail denying its continuity. So much for the medieval side of the case. On the seventeenth-century side we must note the curious fact that in his discussions of motion Galileo tends to restrict his use of Eudoxean procedures to the proof of 'rather obvious' theorems.[62] In crucial arguments about accelerated motion, of the type examined in the body of this article, the Eudoxean spirit is absent, although it could have been very useful for making the reasoning more rigorous. I therefore remain unconvinced by your claim that 'Eudoxus' was essential to Galileo's achievement.

(3) *Objicias:* You have omitted to point out that at the very end of the *Physics* Aristotle maintains that, 'The only continuous motion . . . is that which is caused by the unmoved movent.'[63] This means that sublunary motions at least will all be discontinuous. Aristotle pays particular attention to the case of projectile motion, in which the power of moving was transferred successively from one part of the air to the next, so that 'the motion is not continuous but only appears so'.[64] Moreover, this interpretation exerted an important influence in the Middle Ages when Roger Bacon adopted it as a model for his doctrine of the multiplication of species.[65] In this doctrine substances and qualities sent out likenesses of themselves, known as species, which were transmitted in a step-wise fashion through the medium. The

---

[60]I am preparing a short article on this. For the present *cf.* A. G. Molland, 'An Examination of Bradwardine's Geometry', *Archs Hist. exact Sci.* **19** (1978), 113 – 175, at p. 159.

[61]'On this see Murdoch, *op.cit.,* note 59; A. G. Molland, 'The Geometrical Background to the "Merton School"', *Br. J. Hist. Sci.* **4** (1968 – 69), 108 – 125; Molland, *op.cit.,* note 60; M. S. Mahoney, 'Mathematics', *Science in the Middle Ages,* D. C. Lindberg (ed.) (Chicago: University of Chicago Press, 1978), 145 – 178.

[62]*Cf.* EN, VIII, 192 – 193.

[63]*Physica* VIII. 10, 267b16.

[64]*Physica* VIII. 10, 267a13 – 14.

[65]In *The 'Opus Majus' of Roger Bacon,* J. H. Bridges (ed.) (Oxford, 1897 – 1900), II, 457, Bacon appeals in this connection to 'Aristoteles secundo de Somno et Vigilia' — *i.e. De Somniis* 2, 459a27sqq. — where Aristotle draws on the example of projectile motion. On Bacon's doctrine of multiplication of species, see A. G. Molland, 'Roger Bacon: Magic and the Multiplication of Species', *Paideia,* forthcoming.

50

species in the first small part of the medium drew out its likeness in the second (equal) part, which then acted on the third, and so on. We thus have a fundamental element of discontinuity introduced into Bacon's general science of apparent action at a distance.

Respondeo: We should first note that Aristotle's interest in Book VIII of the *Physics* was in an *eternal* continuous motion. The discussion in the body of this article will make it clear that he placed no ban on finite continuous motions. Discreteness had a role in that one motion was separate from another, but each single motion was continuous. (There is a certain linguistic difficulty in speaking of a motion being discontinuous, for strictly speaking it is then not 'a motion' but several motions.) The case of projectile motion is rather more to the point. Given Aristotle's general discussion of the continuity of motion we need not assume that he supposes this to be jerky, but only that the motion/motions is/are produced by a succession of movers (compare the torch race discussed above).[66] Nevertheless the motion is atomised in the sense we have been using in this article. We thus have in this instance a *prima facie* exception to our general thesis, but a historical thesis with no exceptions would be an alarming object indeed. Also Aristotle was not a medieval, and a medieval impetus theorist was not obliged to assert the discontinuity of projectile motion, for this was now caused by a persisting impetus (which could of course change in intensity). We are then left with Bacon, and here we must admit that he did adopt a significant atomisation in his account of the transmission of action, although it had little effect on his mathematical treatment of it, where he drew upon the traditions of optics. His atomisation may perhaps be associated with his having an attitude of mind that has led many to see him as more 'scientific' than most schoolmen.

(4) *Objicias:* But Bacon was not the only dissident in the Middle Ages. There were several people who explicitly argued for an anti-Aristotelian account of continuity, and wished to compose continua from either a finite or an infinite number of indivisibles.[67] This surely undermines further the monolithic view that you have been presenting.

Respondeo: I have no desire for a monolithic view, nor for a world without dissidents. But the use of the latter term points to the existence of an orthodoxy, which in matters of continuity in the Middle Ages was basically

[66]See note 7.

[67]See, for example, A Maier, *Die Vorläufer Galileis im 14. Jahrhundert*, 2nd edn (Rome: Edizioni di Storia e Letteratura, 1966); V. P. Zoubov, 'Walter Catton, Gerard d'Odon et Nicolas Bonet', *Physis* 1 (1959), 261 – 278; J. E. Murdoch, *'Rationes mathematice': un aspect du rapport des mathématiques et de la philosophie au moyen âge* (Paris: Palais de la Decouverte, 1962); *id., 'Mathesis in Philosophiam Scholasticam Introducta:* The Rise and Development of the Application of Mathematics in Fourteenth Century Philosophy and Theology', *Actes du Quatrième Congrès International de Philosophie Médiévale* (Montreal: Institut d'Études Médiévales and Paris: Vrin, 1969), 215 – 254, at pp. 216 – 221; J. E. Murdoch and E. A. Synan, 'Two Questions on the Continuum: Walter Chatton (?), O.F.M. and Adam Woodham, O.F.M.', *Franciscan Stud.* 26 (1966), 212 – 288.

Aristotelian. It would be of great interest to investigate whether the dissidents' positions on continuity can be linked with their views on other subjects. In general they appear to have been little concerned with mathematical accounts of motion, but it may well be possible to detect signs of their atomism in, for example, their political or theological views. Such an investigation could also reveal how deeply ingrained were their various versions of atomism — whether it was a case of established attitudes of mind or merely of a clever revival of positions that had been maintained in Antiquity. For our purposes attitudes of mind are more important than explicitly formulated positions. It therefore also follows that it is not crucial to my case to find a multitude of anti-Aristotelian accounts of continuity in the seventeenth century. All that is necessary is that there should be a general tendency at least among the 'more advanced' men of science to behave as if continua could be taken to pieces and then reassembled. Many seventeenth-century arguments using infinitesimals fit this bill admirably.

(5) *Objicias:* The differences that you posit between Oresme and Galileo are more apparent than real. This point was well made by Carl B. Boyer, who said of their demonstrations of the Merton Rule: 'Since neither one possessed the limit concept, each resorted, explicitly or implicitly, to infinitesimal considerations.'[68] And a little later: 'Galileo and Oresme patently employed the uncritical mathematical atomism which has appeared among mathematicians of all ages — in Democritus, Plato, Nicholas of Cusa, Kepler, and many others.'[69] This is backed up by a critical reading of the *De Configurationibus*, where for instance, we may find Oresme demanding that perpendiculars be erected along the whole of a line (*eriganturque super lineam AB per totum linee perpendiculares*) and speaking of all the instants of a time (*in omnibus instantibus temporis*).[70] This surely shows that at bottom he regards lines as composed of points and times of instants. Moreover, while on the subject of infinitesimals, we should note that they seem to have done Galileo precious little good, for the main thrust of your exposition was to show how they led him into error. If there existed the difference that you maintain between Oresme and Galileo, it was not that difference which made Galileo great.

Respondeo: I see no more reason for saying that Oresme appealed implicitly to 'infinitesimal considerations' than for saying that he appealed implicitly to the 'limit concept'. In fact he seems to have appealed to neither but to have rested on the intuition (unrigorous if you like) that speeds are properly measured by the areas of the configurations representing them. Equation of speeds of rectilinearly moving objects then becomes a simple matter of equation of areas. As for the phrases that made you think that Oresme was

[68]C. B. Boyer, *The Concepts of the Calculus*, 2nd printing (New York: Hafner, 1949), p. 114.
[69]*Op.cit.*, p. 115.
[70]*De config.*, p. 290.

really a compositionist at heart, these are merely careless talk, and harmless too, since they can easily be reformulated with the aid of the categorematic – syncategorematic distinction. In the very first chapter of the *De Configurationibus* Oresme explicitly denies the existence of points: 'Although indivisible points or lines are nothing (*nihil sunt*), yet it is necessary to feign them mathematically for understanding the measures of things and their ratios.'[71] Stronger atomistic tendencies appear in the *Liber de Motu* of Gerard of Brussels,[72] but this work shows signs of not being a legitimate offspring of the Latin Middle Ages,[73] and had very little influence on writers such as Oresme. Your contention that infinitesimals were not helpful to Galileo demands a twofold reply: on the one hand they gave him confidence in a mathematical structure of reality; on the other they quite often did work. Buccaneering may be dangerous, but it can also produce results.

(6) *Objicias:* Your attempt to make Galileo discrete is frustrated by his insistence on the continuous nature of the acceleration of falling bodies.[74] In the *Discorsi* Salviati takes great pains to convince his sceptical friends that a body that has fallen from rest and acquired a certain speed has also passed through all lesser degrees of speed. And even someone of the stature of Pierre Fermat could claim to demonstrate that Galileo's view was impossible.[75] Moreover, while denying the impossibility, Descartes held that this kind of continuous acceleration did not normally occur in nature.[76] This surely puts Galileo firmly on the side of continuity.

Respondeo: I have no wish to deny continuity to Galileo, only to maintain that his analysis of it makes it less alien from discreteness than it was for Aristotle. The example you adduce is important and puts Galileo and Oresme on the same side. It may also help us to get some insight into how the fourteenth century could have influenced the seventeenth. Both Galileo and Descartes wrote refutations of Fermat's demonstration (which he soon abandoned), and it is significant that both of them appeal to geometrical analogies. 'I do not believe that he would wish to deny that between the point A and the line BC [in triangle ABC] there are met all the widths less than BC' (Descartes).[77] 'Just as when departing from a point, which lacks length, one cannot enter upon a line without passing through all the infinite lines, less and less, that are comprehended between any signified line and the point, so the

[71]*De config.*, p. 164; *cf.* pp. 438 – 439.
[72]M. Clagett, 'The *Liber de Motu* of Gerard of Brussels and the Origin of Kinematics in the West', *Osiris* 12 (1956), 73 – 175.
[73]*Cf.* A. G. Molland, 'Ancestors of Physics', *Hist. Sci.* 13 (1975), 54 – 75, at pp. 64 – 67.
[74]EN, VIII, pp. 198 – 201.
[75]Fermat, *op.cit.*, note 48, supplément, pp. 36 – 37. *Cf.* pp. 68 – 70 where de Waard shows beyond reasonable doubt that the author is indeed Fermat and not Frenicle, as suggested in *Oeuvres de Descartes*, C. Adam and P. Tannery (eds.) (Nouvelle présentation, Paris: Vrin, 1964), II, p. 399 n.
[76]Descartes, *op.cit.* II, p. 399; Marin Mersenne, *Correspondance*, C. De Waard, R. Pintard and B. Rochet (eds.) (Paris, 1932), VIII, pp. 114 – 115.
[77]*Ibid.*

mobile that departs from rest, which does not have any speed, in order to acquire any degree of speed must pass through all the infinite degrees of slowness comprised between whatever be the speed and the greatest and infinite slowness' (Galileo).[78] One cannot conceive that Fermat would have advanced his rather Zenoesque argument if he had thought of the geometric analogy. It may seem trivially obvious to us to represent intensity of speed by a straight line, but the example of Fermat shows how hard the obvious can be to discover. May it not be that this apparently trivial idea constituted the most important medieval legacy in the field of motion, which when developed by the aggressive policy of mathematisation[79] of Galileo and others, grew into a new science very different from the one that it had been part of in the fourteenth century? If this be the case, it is hopeless to try to establish precise lines of influence. The simple little idea could have been found in so many places, and once assimilated would become 'obvious' to its receiver, and hence in no need of a source.[80]

(7) *Objicias:* You have more than once suggested that there is a linkage between a person's views on the continuum and his preferred mode of argument, but I fail to see that there is any necessary connection. Moreover your emphasis on Galileo's postulational approach is belied by his writing in dialogue form.

Respondeo: It is true that there is no logical relation of implication between views on the continuum and preferred modes of argument. The example of Euclid's *Elements*, which is axiomatic but does not rest on a compositionist view of the continuum, is sufficient to show that. But I maintain that there are sufficient analogies to make a linkage psychologically likely. This is indicated by the twofold usage of the terms 'analysis' and 'synthesis', which could either refer to taking things apart and putting them together, or to movements towards and away from first principles.[81] In the Middle Ages the continuum could not be analysed to its elements and there was rather little faith in reaching firmly established ultimate first principles by the way of analysis. The attitude was more tentative and probing. Galileo was far more confident, if not reckless, and in both areas believed that his analyses could achieve their proper ends, even if he did have to take infinite leaps. The fact that he wrote in

[78]Fermat, *op.cit.,* note 48, supplément, p. 60; EN, XVII, p. 92.

[79]On sixteenth-century 'Platonist' faith in the power of mathematics in natural philosophy and its possible influence on Galileo see the important article by P. Galluzzi, 'Il "Platonismo" del Tardo Cinquecento e la Filosofia di Galileo', *Ricerche sulla Cultura dell' Italia Moderna,* P. Zambelli (ed.) (Rome: Laterza, 1973), pp. 37 – 79.

[80]C. Lewis, *The Merton Tradition and Kinematics in Late Sixteenth and Early Seventeenth Century Italy* (Padua: Antenore, 1980), finds little detailed influence of the Mertonian tradition in the Italy of his period, but allows a general influence on Galileo as regards the concept of speed (see pp. 281 – 283).

[81]On analysis in Galileo, see N. Jardine, 'Galileo's Road to Truth and the Demonstrative Regress', *Stud. Hist. Phil. Sci.* 7 (1976), 277 – 318.

XV

54

dialogue form is a red herring. For him disputation was a means of vanquishing opponents: in the Middle Ages it was an essential source of knowledge.

Acknowledgements — Earlier versions of parts of this paper have been delivered to audiences in Leeds, Oberwolfach, New York and Pittsburgh, whereby I received much valuable comment and criticism; as also from the Editor, referees and Michael S. Mahoney. Membership of the Institute for Advanced Study, Princeton in the academic year 1980 – 1 provided a splendid environment for much of the work on the paper. The writings of Stillman Drake have been a particularly important stimulus, even though I have often come to conclusions different from those of the author.

XVI

CONTINUITY AND MEASURE IN MEDIEVAL NATURAL PHILOSOPHY

1. Introduction

Digital watches and digital thermometers tell times and temperatures by the display of a small number of numerals. In older fashioned instruments times and temperatures are represented by distances (either rectilinear or circular) on a scale, upon which numerals either appear or are understood. All this is a symbol of how ultimately measure is the expression of the size of something in terms of positive whole numbers, but also of how distances often enter into the measurement of other continuous quantities. Numbers and distances are paradigms of the discrete and the continuous, and the Middle Ages was more conscious of both the gulf and the connections between these than we usually are — especially after the so-called arithmetisation of the continuum. This is evidenced by discussions of the relation between Aristotle's definition of time as the number (or measure) of motion according to before and after, and his assertion that nevertheless time was continuous[1]. For reasons that I hope will become apparent I shall be presenting this paper as a somewhat casually ordered series of discrete units rather than as a narrative continuously developed from first principles.

2. Sources and context

The principal ancient sources are Aristotle, Euclid and Boethius: Aristotle for providing a radically non-atomistic natural philosophy in which objects and processes were essentially continuous, and Euclid and Boethius respectively for geometry and arithmetic, the mathematics of the continuous and of the discrete. This mixture is leavened by scholastic disputational procedures, which, I wish to maintain, robbed the discussions of much of the Greek axiomatic spirit, and instead gave them the character of a series of probes in which what was given but only vaguely perceived was made more precise, but in an open-ended way which did not preclude further analysis.

---

[1] Cf. A. Maier, Metaphysische Hintergründe der Spätscholastischen Naturphilosophie, Rome 1955, 65—91.

The focus of attention will be on the fourteenth century, and I shall make particular use of the Liber calculationum of Richard Swineshead[2] and the Tractatus de configurationibus qualitatum et motuum of Nicole Oresme[3]. I shall be as much concerned to identify tacit assumptions as to dwell on explicit solutions to particular problems.

3. Counting

The most basic form of measurement is the counting of a discrete collection of objects, and, if we neglect questions of the ontological status of number, it is relatively unproblematic. In it the members of the collection are paired with the units that were conceived as making up the relevant number. In such counting we have a good example of how a whole may be understood in terms of its parts, but a continuous object could seem in many ways to be prior to its parts, for *inter alia* it had in Aristotelian thought no set of ultimate parts.

4. Equality

Equality enters intimately into discussions of measure. It is not something absolute but is asserted of two or more objects in certain respects. Here we note that there are two different sorts of criteria for affirming equality: by identity of description and by comparison. If we count two flocks of sheep and find that there are twenty-nine in each, we assert equality in number on the basis of identity of description, but, if we pair off the members of the two flocks without actually counting them, we assert it on the basis of comparison. In geometry a simple example of equality by comparison was that of two straight lines which matched each other exactly when one was superposed on the other. Equality by identity of description was rather more problematic.

5. Artificial units

Aristotle's account of the measure of continuous objects was by analogy with counting discrete collections. Although lengths contained no natural

---

[2] Calculator. Subtilissimi Ricardi Suiseth Anglici Calculationes noviter emendate atque revise, Venice 1520. The best general account of this work is in J. E. Murdoch and E. D. Sylla, Swineshead (Swynesched, Suicet, etc.), Richard, in: Dictionary of Scientific Biography 13, 184–213.

[3] Nicole Oresme and the Medieval Geometry of Qualities and Motions. A Treatise on the Uniformity and Difformity of Intensities known as Tractatus de configurationibus qualitatum et motuum, ed. M. Clagett, Madison 1968. Cf. A. G. Molland, Oresme Redivivus, in: History of Science, 8 (1969) 106–119.

indivisible units, we could pretend that they did. "Even in lines we treat as indivisible the line a foot long"[4]. This may reflect what is done in practice, but it had the theoretical difficulty of not coping easily with incommensurability, and, to a lesser extent, that of needing the use of fractions. Moreover, the use of artificial units that were often named after parts of the body could easily produce a feeling of subjectivity, and John Buridan, for example, spoke of the necessity of correlating my ell with your ell[5]. It is thus not surprising that measurement of this kind found little place in mathematical works of natural philosophy.

6. Natural units

Robert Grosseteste held that the proper measure of a line was the number of points that it contained[6]. This was infinite, but Grosseteste maintained that there were all sorts of different infinite numbers, having between them both rational and irrational ratios. In orthodox Aristotelianism on the other hand it was not permissible to speak of the totality of points in a line, for in the interior of a line points had at most potential existence, to be actualised only by division. A line could not be simultaneously divided through and through, for then, as Aristotle asked[7], what would be left? The position of Grosseteste and his followers in this regard, such as Henry of Harclay, may be regarded as epistemologically optimistic, insofar as it posits a metrical structure at the very heart of things, and I have argued elsewhere that this was very much the case with similar positions in the seventeenth century[8]. But in the Middle Ages this optimism was tempered with it being a case of infinite numbers, which were only really comprehensible to God. Other Schoolmen adopted a more radical, and *prima facie* more optimistic position, by composing continua from finite numbers of indivisibles. This conception, even more than the infinitist one, ran foul of mathematical objections[9], but these could be obviated by attacking the relevance of geometry. For instance, one finitist author denied the unrestricted validity of Euclid's

---

[4] Metaph. I. 1, 1052 b 32—33.

[5] In Metaph. X, q. 1, ed. J. Badius, 1518, repr. Frankfurt 1964, f. 60 v.

[6] Commentarius in VIII Libros Physicorum Aristotelis, ed. R. C. Dales, Boulder 1963, 90—94. Cf. Die Philosophischen Werke des Robert Grosseteste, ed. L. Baur, Münster 1912, 52—54 (= BGPM 9).

[7] De gen. et corr. I. 2, 316 a 15—317 a 13.

[8] A. G. Molland, The Atomisation of Motion: A Facet of the Scientific Revolution, in: Studies in History and Philosophy of Science 13 (1982) 31—54.

[9] J. E. Murdoch, "Rationes Mathematice": Un Aspect du Rapport des Mathematiques et de la Philosophie au Moyen Age, Paris 1962, 22—36; id., Mathesis in Philosophiam Scholasticam Introducta: The Rise and Development of the Application of Mathematics in Fourteenth Century Philosophy and Theology, in: Actes du Quatrième Congrès International de Philosophie Médiévale, Montreal and Paris 1969, 215—254, espec. 216—221.

first postulate[10], and was in general concerned to distinguish what was true in reality (*in re*) from what merely held in the imagination of mathematicians (*in imaginatione mathematicorum*). This means that any optimism about the possibility of measure is counterbalanced by a denial of the proper applicability of the received mathematics to nature.

7. Rational ratios, and units for the occasion

By definition there exists for any two commensurable magnitudes a third magnitude that is an integral divisor of each. This serves as a unit for measuring each, and we achieve a pair of numbers whose ratio is the same as the ratio between the two magnitudes. This ratio may then be described in the rather elaborate language given by Boethius[11], in which ratios of great inequality (where the first term is greater than the second) were divided into five species: multiple (the first term is a multiple of the second); superparticular (the first is equal to the second and some aliquot part of it); superpartient (the first is equal to the second and more than one of its aliquot parts); multiple superparticular (the first is equal to a multiple of the second together with an aliquot part); multiple superpartient (the first is equal to a multiple of the second together with more than one aliquot part). These species were then subdivisible in order to give unique descriptions, in terms of which equality of ratios could be asserted on the basis of identity of description (cf. § 4 above). "Ratios are said to be similar one to another which receive the same denomination"[12]. In this way there is achieved an absolute determination of the relative measure of two quantities without the need to posit an arbitrary unit.

8. Equality of area

This is a case of equality in a certain respect (cf. § 4 above). The equality that is called congruence may be determined directly by superposition, but equality of areas usually demands something more. In the simpler cases it essentially involves dividing the figures into equal numbers of matching parts, such that each part of one is congruent with the corresponding part of

---

[10] J. E. Murdoch and E. A. Synan, Two Questions on the Continuum: Walter Chatton (?), O. F. M. and Adam Woodham, O. F. M., in: Franciscan Studies 26 (1966) 212–288, espec. 260.

[11] De institutione arithmetica I. 22–31, ed. G. Friedlein, Leipzig 1867, repr. Frankfurt 1966, 46–66.

[12] Jordanus de Nemore, Arithmetica, ed. Lefèvre d'Etaples, Paris 1514, sig. b. v r. Cf. J. E. Murdoch, The Medieval Language of Proportions, in: Scientific Change, ed. A. C. Crombie, London 1963, 237–271, espec. 257–258.

the other. (The further complications presented by curvilinear figures may be neglected here.) The usual strategy in measuring areas was to construct a square equal in area to the given figure, for, as Bradwardine[13] put it, "A square figure is of better known measure than any other figure, for when you have it that a given surface is of two square feet or of four or according to another number, you are then informed of its measure with the final assurance. On account of which geometers have been accustomed to reduce other figures to this, and not this to others".

9. Equality of whole and parts

Bradwardine laid it down as an axiom of geometry that, "Every whole is equal to all its parts taken together, and conversely"[14], but the exact meaning and the validity of this dictum vary with circumstances. For instance, a given plane figure remains equal in area with all its parts if these are moved around without overlapping each other, but it does not usually remain congruent with the new composite figure. In his Liber calculationum Swineshead[15] concluded that the desires to reach the centre of the parts of a falling body are not always additive, but that the desire of each individual part is subordinated to the desire of the whole.

10. Equality of whole and infinite parts

A continuum may not be composed of indivisibles (either finite or infinite in number), but there was still the possibility that it contained an infinite number of parts, even though these did not form a unique set of ultimate constituents. Consider the division of a line into proportional parts, in which the line is first bisected, and then the right hand part bisected, and then the furthest right part bisected, and so on. Clearly the process can continue indefinitely, and there is a temptation to see it completed, and the line divided into an infinite number of parts, each of which is half the size of its predecessor in order. We are here in Zenonian country, and Aristotle's solution of the relevant paradox was in terms of the parts being

---

[13] A.G. Molland, op. cit. (n. 14 infra), 146—147. Cf. id., An Examination of Bradwardine's Geometry, in: Archive for History of Exact Sciences 19 (1978) 113—175, espec. 160—162.

[14] A.G. Molland, The Geometria speculativa of Thomas Bradwardine, Ph. D. diss., University of Cambridge 1967, 64.

[15] M.A. Hoskin and A.G. Molland, Swineshead on Falling Bodies, in: British Journal for the History of Science 3 (1966—7) 150—182. Cf. A.G. Molland, The Geometrical Background to the "Merton School", in: British Journal for the History of Science 4 (1968—9) 108—125, expec. 121—123.

only potentially there, although he had earlier flirted with the possibility of allowing an infinite to be traversed in a finite time[16]. There were in any case tensions in applying Aristotle's essentially temporal concept of infinity to spatially extended objects, and to more than one medieval thinker there seemed to be something very odd in denying that the parts of the line were actually there. Thus Gregory of Rimini held that the parts were only potential in the sense that they did not form a discrete collection but a continuous whole. This did little to negate their presence, and indeed, "Every continuum has at the same time and actually infinite parts"[17]. In this way a continuum was equated with its infinite parts. A further step was to move the parts around, as we may see in an example from Nicole Oresme[18], in which he took two squares with bases AB and CD of one foot each. He then divided the second square into proportional parts by means of verticals, of which the first halved the square, the second halved its right-hand half, the third halved its right-hand quarter and so on. He then heaped these parts successively upon the first square, so that the right-edge of each part was vertically above B. The result was a staircase-like figure on AB, such that, if AB is imagined to be divided into proportional parts, the height above the first part is one foot, above the second two feet, above the third three feet, and so on to infinity, but the area of this infinitely high figure is nevertheless finite, namely two square feet. The example is from a work of natural philosophy, and the frequency with which infinity entered into such medieval discussions of measure may be taken as a sign of their scanty empirical reference.

11. Equality of ratios

As we have seen (§ 7 above) equality, similarity or identity of rational ratios was usually asserted on the basis of identity of description or denomination. Campanus[19] remarked that Euclid "could not define identity of ratios by identity of denominants, like an arithmetician, because . . . the denominations of many ratios are absolutely unknown". The reference is to irrational ratios, and Book V of Euclid's Elements contained a sophisticated

---

[16] Phys. VIII. 8, 263a10−b9; VI. 2, 233a21−31.

[17] Gregory of Rimini, Sent. I, dist. 42−44, q. 4, art. 1, Venice 1522, repr. St Bonaventure, NY 1955, I, f. 171v. In her fine account of the medieval continuum, A. Maier, Die Vorläufer Galileis im 14. Jahrhundert, 2nd edn, Rome 1966, 172−173, maintained that Gregory composed continua from infinitely small extended magnitudes. This is in error, for Gregory makes it clear that he is thinking of proportional parts, of which each one is of finite size. See especially Sent. II, dist. 2, q. 2, ed. A. D. Trapp, Berlin 1979−82, IV, 311−312 (II, f. 37v in the edition cited above).

[18] Op. cit. (n. 3 supra), 412−414.

[19] Euclidis Megarensis . . . opera a Campano interprete fidissimo translata . . . Lucas Paciolus . . . detersit emendavit . . ., Venice 1509, f. 37v.

definition, usually ascribed to Eudoxus, which accomodated these as well as rational ratios: "Magnitudes are said to be in the same ratio, the first to the second and the third to the fourth, when if any equimultiples whatever be taken of the first and third, and any equimultiples whatever of the second and fourth, the former equimultiples alike exceed, are alike equal to, or alike fall short of, the latter equimultiples respectively taken in corresponding order"[20]. This theory reached the Latin Middle Ages in corrupt form, but, contrary to what is often assumed, Campanus of Novara acquired a good understanding of how the criterion for equality actually operated[21]. Nevertheless this comparison-type criterion (cf. § 4 above) was little used in the Middle Ages, appeal being made instead to an extended technique of denomination (§ 12 below).

12. Measuring ratios

Ratios clearly have a quantitative aspect, and there was accordingly a temptation to treat them like continuous quantities by measuring them, but this depended upon the way in which ratios were divided into equal parts[22], for which there was more than one candidate. For instance, one strategy for halving a ratio was to halve its first member or double its second, and this view seems particularly natural when ratios are assimilated to fractions. Another strategy, equally natural in the Middle Ages, was to find the proportional means between the terms of the ratio: in this way $A:B$ (with A greater than B) will be divided into equal parts by C if $A:C$ equals $C:B$. These two approaches led to two different interpretations of the meaning of ratios of ratios (*proportiones proportionum*). For example, in the first the ratio of $8:1$ to $2:1$ is $4:1$, whereas in the second it is $3:1$. The second tradition had the more interesting consequences, for in it an irrational ratio could have a rational ratio to a rational ratio, and this allowed numerical descriptions or denominations to be applied to a host of irrational ratios. A simple example is that the ratio of the diagonal of a square to its side becomes half the double ratio. The theory was greatly extended by Nicole Oresme, who nevertheless admitted that many irrational ratios probably still escaped this more finely meshed net[23]. The mode of thought behind this treatment of ratios is similar to that behind the early treatment of logarithms, especially in Kepler's formulation.

---

[20] The Thirteen Books of Euclid's Elements, tr. T. L. Heath, 2nd edn, Cambridge 1926, repr. New York 1956, II, 114.

[21] A. G. Molland, Campanus and Eudoxus; or, Trouble with Texts and Quantifiers, in: Physis, forthcoming.

[22] Cf. Molland, op. cit. (n. 13 supra), 155–157.

[23] Nicole Oresme, De proportionibus proportionum and Ad pauca respicientes, ed. E. Grant, Madison 1966, 160–166.

13. Intensity of quality

Inevitably medieval discussions of the intension and remission of forms borrowed from the language of spatially extended quantity[24], and even in relatively non-mathematical writers we may find frequent references to latitudes, distances, etc.. The more mathematical were often very conscious that they were using the analogy. Swineshead[25], for example, speaks of a heat being "composed from qualitative parts, as a quantity is from its quantitative parts", and Oresme[26] explicitly demands the representation of intensities of qualities by straight lines, "for whatever ratio is found between intensity and intensity (among intensities of the same kind) a similar ratio is found between line and line, and conversely". But, despite the air of mathematical precision, the empirical basis was weak, as Oresme[27] himself admitted in a particularly meiotic throwaway line: "However, the ratio of intensities is not so properly or so easily attained by the senses as the ratio of extensions". Nevertheless this did little to dampen the enthusiasm with which theoretical problems of the measure of intensities were discussed.

14. The verb "attendere"

Attenditur is a word of frequent occurrence in medieval discussions of measure, and is usually translated as "is measured". This has good authority from scholastic writings where one can even meet the phrase "attenditur sive mensuratur"[28], but it still seems to miss a nuance. This may be brought out by noting that sometimes also *mensurare* and *numerare* are used synonymously, where the emphasis is on measure as providing a numerical description. So far as I am aware *attendere* is never used in this sense. Instead it refers to another stage in the process of measurement, in which a continuous object stands in for the one that is ultimately to be measured as the representative of its size in the relevant respect, but is still itself a candidate for measurement. This should become clearer by exemplification, but for the moment we may note a geometrical example where the use of the terminology seems appropriate, even if it did not actually occur. In quadrature (cf. § 8 above) a square is constructed equal in area to a given figure, and it could well be called the "attendant" of the area of that figure, for, while it is in one sense its measure, it also itself awaits numerical measure by comparison with a given square.

---

[24] For several examples of this see E. D. Sylla, Medieval Concepts of the Latitude of Forms: the Oxford Calculators, in: AHDLMA 40 (1973) 223–283.

[25] Op. cit. (n. 2 supra), f. 2v.

[26] Op. cit. (n. 3 supra), 166.

[27] Ibid., 404.

[28] Ibid., 276.

15. Attending the intensity of quality

We have seen (§ 13 above) how in the fourteenth century it was often assumed to be meaningful to speak of ratios between intensities of qualities, and to assimilate these intensities to extended qualities, but this did not exhaust the theoretical problems of measure, as may be seen from the first tractate of Swineshead's Liber calculationum, in which it was asked how intensity and remissness (*remissio*) of quality were to be attended. Swineshead[29] listed three possible positions: (1) Intensity is to be attended by nearness to the highest degree and remissness by distance from the highest degree; (2) intensity is to be attended by distance from no degree (*a non gradu*) and remissness by distance from the highest degree; (3) intensity is to be attended by distance from no degree and remissness by nearness to no degree. Much of the trouble arose from the presence of the correlative concepts of nearness and remissness, which also had to be quantified. No full theory for the measure of nearness was presented, but any discussion had to be compatible with the meaning of such phrases as "twice as near", "four times as near", etc., which could be directly explicated in terms of distance. This had some oddities. For instance, if point A approached point B until it reached it, its nearness to B increased to infinity, whereas it only traversed a finite distance. In turn this meant that under the first position the highest grade of heat would be infinitely intense, which combined oddly with the notion of there only being a finite "distance" between the highest degree and no degree. For suchlike reasons, and with arguments that were not always above suspicion, Swineshead rejected the first two positions and accepted the third, even though it did have the inconvenience that heat at the highest degree was still remiss. By contrast Oresme's scheme appears simpler and more natural. An intensity was simply represented by a line of the proportionate length, and the concept of remissness was otiose. Similarly nearness only appeared in rather special circumstances (cf. § 20 below).

16. Comparison across genera

According to Euclid, (in the Campanus version)[30], "A ratio is a relation one to the other of any two quantities whatever of the same genus." Campanus explains that, "It is necessary that they be of the same genus, such as two numbers or two lines or two surfaces or two bodies or two places or two times, for a line cannot be said to be greater nor less than a surface or a body, nor a time than a place . . ." By this token we may expect that different kinds of quality were not mutually comparable as regards intensity,

---

[29] Op. cit. (n. 2 supra), f. 2r.
[30] Op. cit. (n. 19 supra), f. 32r.

but this was not invariably the case. For instance, in Tractate 3 of the Liber calculationum Swineshead[31] enquires by what "the intensity of an element having two unequally intense primary qualities is to be attended." The intensities of the qualities (for example, heat and dryness) are regarded as directly comparable, as is made very clear by the three positions that Swineshead considers: (1) "the element corresponds to the mean degree of equal distance between the two qualities"; (2) "it is equally intense with its more remiss quality"; (3) "it is equally intense with the mean proportional degree between the two qualities". At first this seems to be empirically meaningless, but makes more sense when we remember that for qualities Swineshead usually assumed a finite distance between no degree and the highest degree. It was then quite natural to assume that this distance was the same for each quality. What is more difficult to rationalise is Swineshead's comparison of heat with motion[32]: "Let there be taken a motion which is as distant from no degree of motion as the highest degree of heat from no degree of heat . . . That this is possible is clear because the latitude of motion is infinite, since the latitude of ratio is infinite and the latitude of motion follows ratio or the latitude of ratio." Here it seems to be assumed that there is one point on the latitude of motion which corresponds, for no assignable reason, to the highest degree of heat, and in his Questiones super geometriam Euclidis, Oresme[33] reads similarly, for he asserts that, "If there is some linear difform quality that is to be imagined in the manner of a semi-circle, it is impossible for it to be imagined by a figure other than the semi-circle of which the subject would be the diameter." This posits direct comparability between the intensities of qualities and spatial distances, but in the De configurationibus Oresme took the opposite position and asserted that a quality that is representable by a semicircle is also representable by any other figure whose altitude is at every point proportional to the altitude of the semicircle[34]. This is well in accord with the subjectivising tendencies of this (presumably later) work, and also probably rules out direct comparability between intensities of different qualities or between intensities of qualities and those of motions.

17. Extended qualities

When a quality was uniformly intense over an extended subject, then the whole quality was of that intensity. More problems arose over non-uniform, or "difform", qualities and, here there were two principal strategies.

---

[31] Op. cit. (n. 2 supra), f. 9r.
[32] Ibid., f. 2v.
[33] Op. cit. (n. 3 supra), 540.
[34] Ibid., 198–200.

One was to say that a body thus qualified was as intense as some part of it. This is like measuring the height of the Empire State Building from its highest point. The other was to adopt some form of averaging procedure. The simplest example of this was to equate the intensity of a uniformly difformly qualified subject (where the intensity increased uniformly from one end of a linear, rectangular or cuboidal subject to the other) with that of a uniformly qualified subject having the intensity of the original one's middle degree. Swineshead[35] showed signs of wavering between the two approaches, but with his explicitly geometrical, or graphical representations, Oresme[36] came down naturally on the side of the second approach, in which the equalisation of intensities reduced to the equalisation of the sizes of geometric figures. To the modern eye arguments of this kind conspicuously lack any full discussion of the purpose for which the measures are being applied.

18. Motion[37]

In the Aristotelian tradition motion was of three kinds, namely, alteration, augmentation or diminution, and locomotion, which took place respectively in the categories of quality, quantity, and place. No one of these was reducible to either of the others. Moreover, the focus of attention was on the whole motion, conceived of as a continuous object, that is, on the motion of the whole object during the whole time, from the beginning of the motion to its end. As Oremse made clear this made motions rather like five dimensional objects, having three spatial dimensions, one temporal dimension and one dimension of intensity. "Every successive motion of a divisible subject has parts, and is divisible in one way according to the division and extension or continuity of the mobile, in another way according to the divisibility and duration or continuity of the time, and in a third way, at least imaginatively, according to the degrees and intensity of the speed"[38]. All this is very different from later conceptions in which composite motions were built up from the motions of individual mass points, and it meant that problems of measure were approached in a very different spirit.

19. Speed

There is a temptation to construe the medieval term *velocitas* as signifying instantaneous speed, and often the texts themselves do little to contradict

---

[35] Op. cit. (n. 2 supra), ff. 5r–9r.
[36] Op. cit. (n. 3 supra), 408–410.
[37] On §§ 18–20 cf. Molland, op. cit. (n. 8 supra).
[38] Op. cit. (n. 3 supra), 270.

this reading. Nevertheless it is almost always misleading. Certainly *velocitas* had connotations of swiftness, but it properly referred to the whole motion, not to an instantaneous state. One journey from Oxford to Cambridge would be swifter than another if accomplished in less time, regardless of the internal variations of speed in the two motions. The Schoolmen were of course alive to the possibility of such variations, and usually referred to them with the language of intension and remission. Oresme[39], for example, spoke explicitly of *intensio velocitatis*, and this concept was usually explicated subjunctively in terms of how a uniform speed at that degree of intensity would behave. In any motion speed could vary in intensity both with respect to time, and with respect to the parts of the mobile, and this added to the complications of measure.

20. Attending speed

The general assumption was that that degree of speed was more intense by which more of the relevant perfection would be acquired in a given time, and hence the amount of perfection, or its attendant, was the appropriate attendant of the speed. For instance, in uniform locomotion the appropriate attendant of the speed of motion was the distance traversed in a given time. But even in such apparently simple cases there could be complications, as Oresme made clear with two examples[40]. The first concerned circular motion, which could also be conceived as a "circuiting". The attendant of the intensity of speed of motion was the linear space traversed by the body, but that of the intensity of speed of circuiting was the angle subtended at the centre. The other concerned a motion of descent. Here the attendant of the speed of motion was again the space traversed, but that of the speed of descent was nearness to the centre. This meant that a body that was moved uniformly descended ever more swiftly. The case of locomotion that was difform with respect to time was relatively simple, for here the attendant of the speed of motion should clearly be the overall space traversed in a given time, and this led naturally to the so-called Merton Rule in which the speed of a uniformly difform motion was equated with that of a uniform motion with the degree of speed that the former had at the middle instant of time. Difformity with regard to the parts of the subject produced a difference of opinion similar to that concerning extended qualities (§ 17 above). One could either use the fastest moved point (or equivalent) to provide the attendant or one could adopt some form of averaging procedure. With respect to augmentation Swineshead[41] discussed two positions. In the first the speed

---

[39] E. g., ibid., 276.
[40] Ibid., 278.
[41] Op. cit. (n. 2 supra), ff. 22 r–25 v.

was attended by the "proportional acquisition of quantity". This meant that, if two unequal bodies were augmented equally swiftly, then when one was doubled so was the other. The other position holds that the appropriate attendant was simply the quantity acquired by the motion, and it was this position (when corrected to make clear that it was a question of nett acquisition) that Swineshead preferred. Oresme also alluded to these two positions, but regarded them not so much as rivals but as answering to different descriptions of the motions involved. "The speed of acquisition is attended by the quantity of what is acquired, but the speed of enlargement or of augmentation is attended by the ratio of the magnitude in the beginning of the motion to the magnitude in the end"[42]. This is an instance of Oresme's general position that, "According to the multiple denominations, speed is multiply varied or denominated"[43]. He has realised that many disputes about measure dissolve if the different positions are seen as being linguistically relative, but with this there may well have come a feeling that language provided a murky and possibly distorting barrier between us and the natural world.

21. Conclusion

The fourteenth century saw definite desires to mathematise the world, but the world's essentially continuous structure presented kaleidoscopic effects, and hindered the adoption of a single quantitative point of view. This was abetted by scholastic procedures, which insisted on seeing all sides of a case, rather than axiomatically pushing through a unique position. Such probing tactics were perhaps more sensitive, but they often left mathematically untidy loose ends. Moreover the tendency to accept the kernels of given opinions easily lays the Schoolmen open to charges of undue respect for authority. Nevertheless something of the spirit of their method is more appropriate to the intellectual historian than an attempt to impose a systematic axiomatic structure upon the texts. Hence this paper has proceeded in the form of a series of loosely connected forays upon the assumed theory rather than in that of a rigorously developed "rational reconstruction".

---

[42] Op. cit. (n. 3 supra), 278.
[43] Ibid., 280.

THE ORESMIAN STYLE:
SEMI-MATHEMATICAL, SEMI-HOLISTIC*

I. INTRODUCTION

In a letter to John Wallis in 1697 Leibniz said how pleased he was to see Wallis's reference to a description of a cycloid by Nicholas of Cusa. He then continued:

> In order to give something in return (for Cusanus was German by nationality), I shall point out that in the review of those who were once strong in calculus (*in calculo*) whom your *Algebra* enumerates, your countryman John Suisset, called par excellence the Calculator, has been omitted, who subjected the degrees of qualities or forms to calculus. I remember in my travels having seen some of his manuscripts, which on account of the time of the author seemed worthy of publication. You know that he was made much of by Julius Caesar Scaliger, and that other scholastics, following his example, put out certain *semi-mathematica*, which are extant[1].

The correspondence on this matter continued:

> [Wallis to Leibniz] Suicet's (or Suisset's) name was (unless I am mistaken) Roger (certainly not John), and I do not know whether he performed anything in algebra, but he was a man of subtle talent otherwise[2].
> [Leibniz to Wallis] Let me add just one thing more about your Suisset. It is true what you say that he did not treat of algebra, but, since in the beginning of your work on algebra, you also speak of the invention of arithmetical notation and of forms of calculating different from algebra, you could with perfect justice have made mention of your countryman Suisset, if he had come to mind[3].
> [Wallis to Leibniz] I could (as you rightly point out) have mentioned Suisset together with others (if it had then occurred to my mind), although he did not write directly on algebra. Indeed (if I am not mistaken) he first taught how to discuss physical matters in a mathematical way, and some others followed him, writing (as you aptly say) *semi-mathematica*. And those who in the present century (following Galileo) joined mathematics to natural philosophy have advanced physics to an enormous extent. This was also being attempted by Roger Bacon (a great man in a dark century) four [*sic*] hundred years ago (and more)[4].

For modern scholarship the Calculator is Richard Swineshead (or Suisset, etc.), although the contemporaneous existence of both a Roger and a John is also acknowledged[5]. Also an increased knowledge of Swineshead's intellectual ambience makes Thomas Bradwardine appear as a more appropriate fountainhead of the tradition, which may then be confidently said to include, besides the Mertonians, such Paris oriented writers as Nicole Oresme, Albert of Saxony and Themo Judei, as well as numerous later Italians and Spaniards. With all this said, Leibniz's description of the tradition as semi-mathematical remains both apt and richly suggestive, and in this paper I shall use it as a guiding thread in a re-examination of the work of Nicole Oresme, who is undisputedly one of the tradition's most interesting members.

II. DEMONSTRATION VERSUS DIALECTIC

Greek mathematics (at least of the high tradition) was characteristically anti-empirical and rigidly deductive from first principles. The Middle Ages received several examples of it in Latin translation, of which the most significant was Euclid's *Elements*. Also Aristotle's *Posterior Analytics* extolled this form of reasoning as being appropriate to a properly constituted science, and this work too was much studied in the Middle Ages. However, as has often been noted[6], Aristotle's scientific practice can seem to belie this ideal, and make far more use of dialectical reasoning of the type discussed in his *Topics*. This type of reasoning also fitted very naturally into medieval universities, where so much time was given over to disputation and examining a case from all sides. This was not very conducive to the formation of those «long chains of reasons»[7] which Descartes saw as being so characteristic of mathematics, and no more was the teaching practice of expounding and commenting upon an authoritative text. All this helps to explain why, although the Schoolmen were quite interested in mathematics and talked a lot about it, they produced very little new mathematics themselves, and even such an accomplished mathematician as Campanus of Novara was deeply imbued with this "commentatorial spirit"[8].

Was Oresme tarred with this brush? Or did he manage to escape the conventions of his time? The fact that he has recently been described as «probably the best mathematician of his own day»[9] suggests that he may have done. M.S. Mahoney, who gave this description, made particular reference to Oresme's work *De proportionibus proportionum*, which he saw as «by far the most abstract and venturesome piece of mathematical thinking in the period from Greek antiquity to the seventeenth century»[10]. This treatise was directed towards one of Oresme's perennial concerns, the question of whether or not all the celestial motions were mutually commensurable, but its first three parts are purely mathematical. These develop the consequences of treating the composition of ratios (whereby, if A is greater than B and B greater than C, the ratio of A to C is composed of the ratios of A to B and B to C) as addition. This idea had been latent in the musical tradition, and had been fruitfully applied by Thomas Bradwardine, but Oresme's treatment was much more developed and systematic, and in it he showed considerable concern for correct logical form. «In the first [chapter] I shall preface some preambles, as I presuppose some principles, without demonstration, for the sake of [having] a brief introduction. But in the other chapters nothing is supposed from the first that is not known in itself or, as is mentioned there, demonstrated elsewhere»[11]. For the less obvious *suppositiones* introduced both in the first chapter and later ones Oresme quite often appeals to Euclid, and throughout the extant part of the work he attaches much importance to rigour of demonstration. In general it can be said to approach sufficiently near to Euclidean form to make it ungracious in this respect to dub it semi-mathematical.

The situation is not so simple with what was the avowed end of this incomplete work, the question of the commensurability of the celestial motions. Oresme's work *Ad pauca respicientes*, which does address this question, is ostensibly highly Euclidean in form. A crucial proposition is the seventeenth of the second Part: «It is probable that in any instant the celestial bodies are mutually positioned in such a way as they never were in the past or ever will be in the future; nor was there, nor will there be a similar configuration or disposition for all eternity»[12]. This depends directly on the *suppositio* that, «Given several quantities whose ratio is unknown, it is possible, doubtful [*sc.* not known], and probable *(verisimile)* that some one of them is incommensurable to another»[13]. No justification is given for this, although, as Grant points out, it could have received some support from the later *De proportionibus proportionum*. More serious is the sleight of hand by which Oresme appears to move from probability to certainty in Proposition II.19, which asserts that even in a deterministic world correct astrological prediction would be impossible, «for a judgment about future matters is only made through observations of past ones, and, since it is probable that no future disposition is similar to any past one, as is evident from the seventeenth proposition, what is proposed also follows»[14].

In the more mature *De commensurabilitate vel incommensurabilitate motuum celi*, although Oresme's attitude to astrological prediction is much the same, the situation is thrown wider open, and Oresme is very conscious of the different forms of reasoning involved. The work falls into a prologue and three parts, and the general strategy is announced early in the first part. «Because it is necessary either that all the celestial motions are mutually commensurable or that some of them are mutually incommensurable, therefore in the first part of this work it will be seen what follows if they are commensurable, in the second what if they are incommensurable, and in the third the *suppositum* will be investigated, namely whether they are commensurable or not» [15]. The first two parts proceed deductively in an unexceptionable manner. It is in the third part that the trouble starts. Here Oresme portrays himself as receiving a vision of Apollo, surrounded by the Muses and Sciences, who assures him that he will not be able to attain the knowledge that he seeks, for the senses cannot reach such precision. «The ratio [of the celestial motions] is unknown, and you will be led to a knowledge of it neither by arithmetic nor by geometry, which, when they are applied to sensibles, rest upon sensible principles» [16]. As it happens arithmetic and geometry are in the company, in the personae of the sisters Arithmetica and Geometria, and when the despairing Oresme requests a revelation, Apollo draws them into the game by telling them to teach Oresme what he asks. They immediately contradict each other, with Arithmetica plumping for commensurability and Geometria for incommensurability. «With, as it were the legal contest entered (*factaque quasi litis contestatione)*, Apollo ordered each party to defend her case with reasons (*rationibus)*» [17]. The sisters then make long, but necessarily inconclusive speeches in favour of their respective positions, before the treatise concludes as follows:

> Geometria had not yet finished what she proposed when behold Apollo orders silence, and accounts himself adequately informed. But I, not unnaturally astonished and stunned by so much novelty of things, thought these thoughts within me. Since every truth is consonant with any truth, how is it that these parents of truth are discordant? And how is it that they speak with rhetorical persuasions and topical proofs (*probationibus*), these who are accustomed to use only demonstrations, spurning every other argumentation? How have they accepted the way foreign to them of less certain science? Seeing the thought of my heart, father Apollo says, «You should not seriously judge there to be true discord between these most illustrious mothers of evident truth, for they play and mock the style of inferior science. We also in talking with them shall assume the role of judge of a doubtful case; we shall review their proceedings and arguments (*processusque et causas earum visitabimus*), and then immediately pronounce the truth in the form of a judgment». While with the utmost desire I awaited the verdict, behold the dream vanishes: the conclusion remains in doubt, and I do not know what the judge Apollo decreed on the matter [18].

Thus, while rigorous demonstrative reasoning may be appropriate to pure mathematics, once one becomes deeply embroiled with the natural world, one is reduced to something far more like the language of the law courts. Can the resulting science be described as more than semi-mathematical?

III. WHOLES AND PARTS

In the treatise of his *Liber calculationum* usually knwon as *De loco elementi* [19] Richard Swineshead contemplated a heavy body falling through the centre of the world, and asked whether the part that had already passed the centre would resist the descent of the whole, since it would then be moving upwards and away from its natural place. Swineshead first supposes that it does resist, and then, by a very impressive series of mathematical arguments and the assumption of Bradwardine's "law of motion", succeeds in showing that this would entail that a naturally falling body would never actually reach the centre so that its centre coincided with the centre of the world, but would ever more slowly approach this position. This would mean that an altogether natural desire was incapable of fulfilment, which for Swineshead was an absurd position. He therefore rejected the view that the part past the centre was resisting and maintained instead that the body acted as a single whole with each part acting for the good of the whole.

We may contrast this with a famous thought experiment used by Galileo to combat the view that a heavier body would fall more rapidly than a lighter one of the same material. In the *Two New Sciences* Salviati asks Simplicio to consider two such bodies. «It is clear that, if we joined the slower to the swifter, the latter would be partly retarded by the slower, and the slower would be partly accelerated by the swifter» [20]. After obtaining Simplicio's ready agreement to this he continued:

> But if this is so, and at the same time it is true that a large stone is moved, for example, with eight degrees of speed and a smaller one with four, then with them both joined together, their composite will be moved with a speed less than eight degrees. But the two stones joined together make a stone greater than the first, which was moved with eight degrees of speed; therefore this greater is moved less swiftly than the lesser, which is contrary to your supposition. Thus you see how from supposing that the heavier mobile is moved more swiftly than the less heavy, I conclude to you that the heavier is moved less swiftly [21].

This argument, which was not original to Galileo [22], was sufficient to floor Simplicio, but he could with perfect justice have complained that it contains the implicit assumption that a body acts as the sum of its parts, and that two bodies when conjoined retain the same behavioural propensities that they had when separate [23]. Such a reply would have been natural to Swineshead, and also, I think, to Oresme.

Oresme uses the thought experiment of a body falling through the centre of the world [24], but to a different end from Swineshead, for Oresme has a theory of impetus, and holds that this would drive the body past the centre, whereupon it would be moving upwards, and so gradually come to rest, and then continue with an oscillatory motion about the centre. The question of the relation of whole and parts does not arise here, but elsewhere he explicitly asserts that if a body A has halves B and C, then «if B were separated it would have a different [natural] place from what it now has when conjoined» [25]. Moreover, in his famous speculation concerning the diurnal motion of the Earth, Oresme distinguished the natural circular motion of the whole Earth from the natural rectilinear motions of its displaced parts. «It is not improper that a simple body should have one simple motion according to its whole self in its own place, and another motion according to its parts in returning to their place» [26]. Once again the whole has properties which can in no simple way be regarded as the sum of those of its parts.

Like Galileo, Francis Bacon rejected the view that the speed of a body's fall was proportional to its weight, but he managed to draw a very different moral:

> Variation of experiment takes place thirdly in Quantity which must be treated with great care, as it is surrounded by many errors. For men believe that if the quantity be increased or multiplied, the power and virtue is increased or multiplied proportionately. And this they postulate and suppose as if it had a kind of mathematical certainty; which is utterly false. A leaden ball of a pound weight dropped from a tower reaches the ground in (say) ten seconds; will a ball of two pounds weight (in which the force of natural motion, as they call it, ought to be doubled) reach the ground in five seconds? No, but it will take almost the same time in falling, and will not be accelerated in proportion to the increase of quantity [27].

After another example, Bacon's holistic polemic on the dangers of quantification culminates with the delightful advice that «Men should therefore consider the story of the woman in Aesop, who expected that with a double measure of barley her hen would lay two eggs a day; whereas the hen grew fat and laid none» [28]. The same message, though less explicitly, comes through clearly in Swineshead's treatise discussed above. Whereas his treatment of the rejected position was highly mathematical, his account of the preferred holistic position had virtually no quantification, and instead biological analogies could seem more appropriate, as «in a generating, where something is produced by two, of which each helps the other to act, and one by itself would not be able to produce the same. At times the contrary occurs, as when a modicum of fire by itself in a subject would conserve health, whereas twice the fire of which that fire was the half would produce illness in the whole» [29].

IV. HOLISTIC HABITS OF THOUGHT

In fact, as has often been noted, holism can go quite naturally with biological ways of thought, and in all ages there have been biologists who have fiercely attacked reductionist tendencies, and argued that the whole organism is in some strong sense prior to its parts, and certainly more than their sum. Also the parts of an organism are variegated, and far from a uniform sameness. In the *De commensurabilitate* Geometria, with whom Oresme's sympathies clearly lie, makes an eloquent plea for a variegated universe on a similar model.

> Whether or not irrational ratio is nobler than rational, a harmonious mixture of both is more beautiful than a uniform sameness, for we see this in other cases. A mixture of elements is better than the best element, and the heavens are more distinguished than if the stars were everywhere through the whole. Indeed the universe is more perfect on account of corruptibles and even on account of monsters, and a song varied in its consonances is sweeter than if made continually from the best consonance, namely the octave, and a picture adorned with various colours is more handsome than the most beautiful colour uniformly diffused through the whole surface [30].

This insistence on a harmonious mixture of unequals also appears in Oresme's social thought:

> The husband is warmer, stronger and more active, and the wife colder, weaker and more passive. And this contrariety or difference has inclined them to different pursuits, which are profitable to them and suitable for their mutual concourse. And on this account, when the contrariety or dissimilarity exists naturally and is well proportioned in their habits, it is sweet and delectable. And accordingly the Sage says that when man and wife are agreeing and in concord together, that is a thing pleasing to his spirit, approved and praised by God and by men. And it seems to me that this is also like in music: the dissimilarity and inequality of the sounds makes a good accord and a good consonance, for it is sweetly proportioned. And perhaps to signify this, nature has ordained that the voice of man with respect to the voice of woman is commonly in that ratio which makes the best consonance, and it is called the octave (*dyapason*) in music [31]. Plutarch says to the emperor Trajan that "the state is a body that is animated as if by the help of divine authority, administered by the command of the highest equity, and ruled by a government of reason». Thus the state or kingdom is like a human body, and so Aristotle has it in the fifth book of the *Politics*. Therefore just as a body is badly disposed when the humours flow excessively to one of its members, so that that member is often by this inflamed and too much thickened, with the others being dried up and too much attenuated, and the due ratio is destroyed, and such a body cannot live long, so also is it for a community or kingdom when riches are attracted beyond measure by one of its parts. For a community or kingdom whose princes in comparison with their subjects increase immoderately as regards riches, power and position, is like a monster, like a man whose head is so big and gross that it cannot be supported by the remaining weak body. Therefore, just as such a man cannot have pleasure nor live long thus, so a kingdom cannot persist whose prince draws riches to himself in excess, as is done by alterations of the coinage... Again, just as in a mixture of voices equality does not please or delight, and too much or undue inequality destroys and disfigures the whole consonance, but a proportionate and commensurate inequality is required, by the continuance of which there mingle the charming melodies of a joyous choir, so also in general, as, by regards all parts of the community equality of possessions or power is not fitting or consonant, but too great a disparity dissipates and corrupts the harmony of the state, as is evident by Aristotle in the fifth book of the *Politics* [32].

Oresme should not be seen in these passages as strikingly original, but in many ways characteristically medieval, and, as the references to

Aristotle show, his views had ancient roots. In fact the transition from medieval to modern times has often been seen as crucially involving a change from holistic, organismic conceptions to individualistic, atomistic ones across a whole variety of fields [33]. Here I shall take no brief to defend such a general change of *Zeitgeist*, but merely draw attention to possible mathematical consequences of the holistic position. Oresme's references to music have strong mathematical overtones, for at his time music was emphatically a mathematical science. But it was a different sort of mathematics from that later to appear physics, and since the time of Kepler the search for aesthetically pleasing harmonies in nature and society has been a far less obvious part of the scientific quest. A telling example of how insistence on variegated mixtures could militate against quantification is given by medieval voting procedures, where the conception of "one man one vote" did not come naturally, but appeal was usually made to some quantitatively vaguer conceptions such as «the weightier part (*valentior pars*) of the citizens». This was vague because no obviously correct system of measure was available, for the more basic of such systems usually depend upon units or upon parts of a whole that can at least be treated as equal, and these were not easy to find unless there was some clear way of quantifying the worth of the unequal individual members of a community. An atomistic, democratic world would be far less resistant to simple quantification.

V. STRUCTURE OF THE CONTINUUM

But we do not need to go to biology or sociology to find important sources of holism. They also lay in the very heartland of mathematics, or, more precisely, in an area shared between mathematics and natural philosophy, namely in the question of the nature of continuity. This had been discussed theoretically by Aristotle [35], who linked it closely with that of individuation. If two bodies were contiguous and shared a common boundary, they were not really two bodies but one continuous whole. (Here there was some tension with mathematics, for it was not easily conceivable that two geometrical objects should be contiguous without sharing a common boundary). This meant that in a very real sense the whole body was prior to its parts, and each of these had only potential existence, which was not actualised until as a result of division, at least in thought, the whole had in a sense ceased to exist. Also it was impossible to specify a unique set of ultimate parts, for each part, however small, was divisible into yet smaller parts.

With the exception noted above, this holistic position was in general very compatible with mathematics, in particular with Euclidean geometry, and it in no way precluded a simple form of quantification [36]. The implicit theory of measure ultimately rested on a criterion of equality based on the principle of superposition. Two objects were equal (in the sense of congruence) if they fitted exactly on top of one another — however this was exactly to be interpreted. If two unequal objects could each be divided into a finite number of mutually equal parts (say, one straight line into five lines each a foot in length, and another into six), then an easy numerical comparison was at hand. Incommensurability, and curvilinear figures presented rather more difficulty, but by the time of Euclid a perfectly satisfactory strategy had evolved.

Interestingly enough it was in this instance the atomist position rather than the holistic one which presented obstacles to mathematisation. A variety of medieval thinkers tried to compose continua out of either a finite or an infinite number of indivisibles [38], but some of the strongest objections to such positions came from geometry. For instance, it was fairly easy to show that the circumferences of two unequal concentric circles should be composed from equal numbers of indivisibles, contrary to intuition. Perhaps the most highly developed attack on the indivisibilists was provided by Thomas Bradwardine in this *Tractatus de continuo* [39], but Bradwardine was very conscious that he might be accused of a *petitio principii* by assuming the truth of Euclid's geometry, and indeed one of his opponents denied the unrestricted validity of Euclid's first postulate, and was very concerned to distinguish what was true in reality (*in re*) from what merely held in the imagining of mathematicians (*in imaginatione mathematicorum*) [40]. But, as it was, no alternative system of geometry was available, and so, if one adopted an indivisibilist position, one was liable to be seriously impaired in trying to provide a mathematical account of the world. With an exception to be discussed later Oresme was an orthodox Aristotelian on the structure of the continuum, and so was not lumbered with this anti-mathematical disadvantage.

VI. ORESME AND HOLISTIC MOTION [41]

The holistic position on continuity may have adapted well to Euclidean geometry, which dealt with permanent objects (those whose parts all exist at the same time), but more trouble arose with successive objects, such as motion. In the Aristotelian tradition these were treated analogously with permanent objects, and that meant holistically. In later, so-called classical, mechanics the focus was to be on the instantaneous velocities of individual mass points, but in the Middle Ages it was on the motion of the whole object through the whole time, from the beginning of the motion to its end. This had interesting implications regarding the measure of motion. Aristotle expressed himself a little obscurely on the subject, but Oresme's development of his thought made it clear that motion was to be regarded as a five-dimensional object, with three spatial dimensions, one temporal dimension and one dimension of intensity of speed:

> Every successive motion of a divisible subject has parts and is divisible in one way according to the division and extension or continuity of the mobile, in another way according to the divisibility and duration or continuity of the time, and in a third way, at least imaginatively, according to the degrees and intensity of the speed. From the first continuity a motion is called great or small, from the second short or long, from the third swift or slow [42].

This conception makes for a rather unwieldy idea of speed, for there is a temptation to regard this as being in some way the size of the motion, but this would have the unacceptable consequence that a body would have twice the speed of its half. Nevertheless Oresme does accept that «a uniform speed that lasts for three days is equal *(est equalis)* to a speed three times as intense that lasts for one day» [43], even though the second motion seems obviously to be speedier.

One might expect that things would be simpler if one narrowed one's attention from total speed *(velocitas totalis)* to intensity of speed *(intensio velocitatis)*, which is more nearly equivalent to our concept of instantaneous velocity, but here too there were complications. Oresme introduced his discussion of its quantification thus:

> I say therefore that universally that degree of speed is unqualifiedly more intense or greater at which in an equal time there is gained or lost more of the perfection following *(secundum)* which the motion is made. For example, in local motion that degree of speed is greater and more intense at which there would be traversed more of space or of distance, and similarly in alteration that degree of speed is greater at which there would be gained or lost more of the quality's intensity, and so in augmentation at which there would be gained more of quantity, and in diminution at which there would be lost more of quantity or extension. And so generally wherever motions would be found [44].

But then he immediately opens the next chapter as follows:

> It is not to be overlooked that the same motion or flux is called by many names connoting differently, and consequently the denominating speed is measured *(attenditur vel mensuratur)* in different ways, so that the quantity of graded intensity is assigned in many ways [45].

For instance, in a circular motion, a body may either be said to be moved or to circuit. «The intensity of the speed of motion is measured *(attenditur)* by the linear space that would be traversed at that degree, but the intensity of the degree of the speed of circuiting is measured by the angles described about the centre» [46]. A second example concerns a rectilinear motion of descent, where a body may either be described as being moved or as descending. The speed of motion was measured by the distance travelled in a given time, but the speed of descent by nearness to the centre, and, since nearness was doubled as each time distance from the centre was halved, this meant that a uniformly moved body would increase its speed of descent infinitely in reaching the centre.

A third example allows us to draw a contrast with Richard Swineshead. In his *Liber calculationum* Swineshead argued at length as to what was the proper measure for motions of augmentation (increase of quantity or volume) [47]. Was it «proportional acquisition of quantity», whereby two unequal bodies would be being augmented equally swiftly when one was doubled in size in the same time as the other, or was it simply the quantity acquired by the motion. Oresme on the other hand refused to see these positions as rivals but merely as answering to different descriptions. «The speed of acquisition is measured by the quantity of what is acquired, but the speed of enlargement or of augmentation is measured by the ratio of the magnitude that is at the beginning of the motion to the magnitude that is at the end» [48]. Oresme is very conscious of his linguistically relativising tendencies, for in general «according to the multiple denominations, speed is multiply varied or denominated» [49]. But cognitively the outcome is that what is being quantified is not so much nature as our language for describing it, and this is not optimistic for mathematical science.

VII. OCCULT VIRTUES

The above discussion was based on the second part of Oresme's *Tractatus de configurationibus qualitatum et motuum*. The first part, which dealt with permanent objects, had some more optimistic features. Its leading idea was that of "graphing" the intensities of qualities across their subject's extension. Because of the lack of a fourth dimension this could not be done literally across a whole three dimensional subject, but it was easy to imagine a graph across a line in the subject, or a "relief map" across one of its surfaces. These representations, which Oresme called imaginations, were not imaginary in the sense of being idle exercises, but had definite explanatory value, for Oresme thought that the properties of the subject could be deduced from their shape, and explicitly compared his doctrine to ancient atomism.

It is manifest that bodies have different powers (*diversimode posse*) in their actions according to the difference of the figures of their bodies, on account of which the ancients who maintained that bodies were composed of atoms said that the atoms of fire were pyramidal on account of its vigorous activity. Wherefore according to the difference in the pyramids bodies can pierce more or less, and according to this or that sharpness it is certain that they can cut more or less strongly, and so for other actions and figures. And, since it is thus for the figures of bodies, it seems reasonable for it to be able to be spoken conformably about the aforesaid figurations of qualities, so that there is a quality whose particles are proportional in intensity to small pyramids, and on account of this it is more active, other things being equal, than an equal quality that was either simply uniform or proportional to another, not so penetrating, figure. Or, if there were two qualities of which the one's particles were proportional to sharper pyramids than the others particles, the quality that corresponded to the sharper particles would, other things being equal, be more active, and similarly for other figures [50].

In this way Oresme has achieved a quasi-mechanistic position, and one that is relevant to the question of occult virtues.

These were traditionally defined as properties of a body that did not appear to derive from its elemental composition. There were various views about their causation, some astrological, but perhaps the most common medieval opinion was that they arose irreducibly from the body's specific substantial form. This meant that there was a certain unintelligibility about them, so that they had to be known by experience rather than reason, a point that Henry Cornelius Agrippa was later to emphasise.

> They are called occult properties, because their causes are hidden, so that the human intellect cannot everywhere investigate them, wherefore philosophers arrived at the greatest part of them by long experience more than by the search of reason. For as in the stomach food is digested by heat, which we know, so it is transformed by a certain occult virtue, which we do not know, not indeed by heat, because then it would be more transformed in the hearth at the fire than in the stomach. Thus besides the elemental qualities, which we know, there are in things certain other innate virtues, and so created together by nature that we wonder at them, and are often amazed at them as unknown to us, or rarely or never descried [52].

Descartes on the other hand saw it as a major benefit of his mechanistic programme that it showed the way to find the causes of the «wonderful effects which are usually referred to occult qualities» [53], and he himself laboured at length to produce an ingenious if cumbersome corpuscular explanation of magnetism, which had been a paradigm example of an occult virtue.

Oresme is very similar though more tentative, for he suggests that by means of his doctrine «there could be briefly assigned a general rationale of certain occult virtues and marvellous effects or experiments whose causes are otherwise unknown, but nevertheless a specific and determinate cause most often lies hidden on account of this kind of imperceptible and occult figuration of qualities. Thus on account of the hiddeness of the cause some stupid nigromancers have said that the virtues were in [54] precious stones because of the presence of certain incorporeal spirits who settled (ceciderunt) in them» [55]. One of the main differences between Oresme's and Descartes's programmes of geometrisation lay in self-confidence. Descartes's schemes may often have had scanty empirical reference, but yet he persisted with his "fable". Oresme very quietly acknowledged that «the ratio of intensities is not so properly nor so easily attained by the senses as the ratio of extensions», but this was probably enough to make him wake out of his beautiful dream.

VIII "INFINITE SERIES"

I finally return to the question of continuity and infinity to show how in another instance Oresme may be seen as tentatively reaching out of Aristotelian holism to something more "mathematical". Aristotle's conception of infinity was essentially temporal: an infinite process was one which did not come to an end. But, when this conception was applied to permanent objects, tensions arose. Aristotle held that continuous objects were infinitely divisible, which meant that they could always be divided into more and more parts. A standard example was to consider a line being divided into proportional parts: for instance, it is first halved, and then its right-hand half halved, and then the right-hand half of that, halved and so on. But what of all these parts before the divisions were made? Aristotle held that they were only potentially there, but this could seem very odd, especially as one could, as it were, see them. Thus some fourteenth-century thinkers, such as William of Ockham and Gregory of Rimini, maintained that the parts were actually there, although not actually separated from one another [56]. But in escaping from the counter-intuitive denial of the actual existence of the parts, they had to admit that there was no last member of this set of actually existing parts, and to others this could seem equally counter-intuitive [57]. But such dilemmas have been perennial features of dealings with the infinite.

Once the actual existence of an infinity of proportional parts was admitted, a further step was to move them around, and this is what Oresme among others did. In one example [58] he contemplated two squares with bases AB and CD, each a foot in length. He divided the second square into proportional parts by means of vertical slices moving towards D. These parts were then successively heaped upon the first square in such a way that the right-hand edge of each slice was always vertically above B. The result was a new continuous figure whose first proportional part was one foot high, whose second two, whose third three, and so on until above B the figure was infinitely high. The total area was nevertheless two square feet. In modern terms one may wish to say that he has summed the infinite series:

$$\frac{1}{2} + 2\left(\frac{1}{2}\right)^2 + 3\left(\frac{1}{2}\right)^3 + 4\left(\frac{1}{2}\right)^4 + \ldots$$

Oresme's own main interest, however, was in showing how a finite object could nevertheless be infinite in a certain respect, and he worked from the whole to the parts rather than from the parts to the whole. But instead of arguing whether Oresme is properly described as summing infinite series, it is perhaps more profitable to emphasise how, by allowing the composition of the continuum from an infinite number of elements, even though these do not form a unique set of ultimate constituents, Oresme has somewhat loosened its holistic structure. In this way he holds out promise of its greater intelligibility.

Throughout the present century, Oresme, like the Mertonians, has occupied rather an uneasy position in the historiography of science. Some studies have assessed the degree to which he may be said to have anticipated such seventeenth-century figures as Galileo and Descartes, while others have rejected this approach and insisted on viewing Oresme in his own terms. While these latter have laudably reduced anachronism, they have been in danger of loosing sight of the diachronic dimension. My principal aim in this paper has been to provide some remedy for this by showing ways in which Oresme may be seen as occupying a halfway house between Aristotelian holism and seventeenth-century mathematical mechanism.

ABBREVIATIONS

* I use the following abbreviations for editions of Oresme's works:

Moneta = *The De Moneta of Nicholas Oresme and English Mint Documents*, ed. C. Johnson, London, 1956.

Ycon. = A.D. Menut, «Maistre Nicole Oresme: Le Livre de Yconomique d'Aristote», *Transactions of the American Philosophical Society,* N.S., XLVII (1957), 783-853.

Prop. prop. and *Pauc. resp.* = Nicole Oresme, *De proportionibus proportionum and Ad pauca respicientes,* ed. E. Grant, Madison, 1966.

Spera = *The Questiones de Spera of Nicole Oresme*, ed. G. Droppers (Ph. D. thesis), University of Wisconsin, 1966.

Ciel = Nicole Oresme, *Le Livre du ciel et du monde,* ed. A.D. Menut & A.J. Denomy, Madison, 1968.

Config. = *Nicole Oresme and the Medieval Geometry of Qualities and Motions: A Treatise on the Uniformity and Difformity of Intensities known as Tractatus de configurationibus qualitatum et motuum,* ed. M. Clagett, Madison, 1968.

Pol. = Nicole Oresme, *Le Livre de Politiques d'Aristote,* ed. A.D. Menut, Transactions of the American Philosophical Society, N.S., LX, Part 6, Philadelphia, 1970.

Commens. = *Nicole Oresme and the Kinematics of Circular Motion: Tractatus de commensurabilitate vel incommensurabilitate motuum celi*, ed E. Grant, Madison, 1971.

NOTES

1 *Leibnizens mathematische Schriften,* ed., C.I. Gerhardt (Halle, 1849-63), Erste Ab-theilung, iv, 13-14; J. Wallis, *Opera mathematica,* Oxford, 1693-99, iii, 673.

2 Leibniz, iv, 18; Wallis, iii, 675.

3 Leibniz, iv, 27; Wallis, iii, 680.

4 Leibniz, iv, 39; Wallis, iii, 685.

5 Cf. J.A. Weisheipl, «Roger Swyneshead, O.S.B., Logician, Natural Philosopher and Theologian», *Oxford Studies presented to Daniel Callus,* Oxford, 1964, 231-252.

6 Cf. G.E.L. Owen, "ΤΙΘΕΝΑΙ ΤΑ ΦΑΙΝΌΜΕΝΑ", *Aristote et les Problèmes de Méthode,* Louvain, 1961, 83-103, repr. *Aristotle: A Collection of Critical Essays,* ed. J.M.E. Moravcsik, London, 1968, 167-190.

7 R. Descartes, *Discours de la méthode* II, in *Oeuvres de Descartes,* ed. C. Adam & P. Tannery, Paris, 1897-1913, vi, 19.

8 A.G. Molland, «Campanus and Eudoxus; or, Trouble with Texts and Quantifiers», *Physis,* XXV (1983), 213-225.

9 M.S. Mahoney, "Mathematics", *Science in the Middle Ages,* ed. D.C. Lindberg, Chicago, 1978, 145-178, at 169.

10 *Ibid.,* 178.

11 *Prop. prop.,* 136.

12 *Pauc.resp.,* 422.

13 *Pauc.resp.,* 384-386.

14 *Pauc.resp.,* 424.

15 *Commens.,* 180. On what follows cf. my essay review of Grant's edition of the *De commensurabilitate* in *British Journal for the History of Science,* VI (1972-3), 311-313, and my «Nicole Oresme and Scientific Progress», *Miscellanea Mediaevalia,* IX (1974), 206-220.

16 *Commens.,* 286.

17 *Commens.,* 288.

18 *Commens.,* 320-322.

19 Edited in M.A. Hoskin & A.G. Molland, «Swineshead on Falling Bodies: An Example of Fourtheenth-Century Physics», *British Journal for the History of Science,* III (1966), 150-182.

20. *Le Opere di Galileo Galilei. Nuova Ristampa dell'Edizione Nazionale,* Florence, 1968, VII, 107-108; cf. I, 265.

21. *Ibid.,* 107-108.

22. Cf. S. Drake & I.E. Drabkin, *Mechanics in Sixteenth-Century Italy,* Madison, 1969, 206.

23. From a marginal note it appears that Galileo was conscious of this. See Galileo Galilei, *Two New Sciences,* tr. S. Drake, Madison, 1974, 67, n. 41.

24. *Ciel,* 144.

25. *Spera,* 98.

26. *Ciel,* 528.

27. Francis Bacon, *De augmentis scientiarum* V.2, in *The Works of Francis Bacon,* ed. J. Spedding, R.L. Ellis & D.D. Heath, London, 1857-62, IV, 414.

28. *Ibid.,* 415.

29. Hoskin & Molland, *op.cit.,* (n. 19 *supra*), 181.

30. *Commens.*, 310-312.

31. *Ycon.*, 815.

32. *Moneta,* 43-44. Cf. *Pol.,* 209.

33. Cf. recently C. Merchant, *The Death of Nature*, San Francisco, 1980, and M. Berman, *The Reenchantment of the World,* Ithaca, 1981.

34. W. Ullmann, *The Individual and Society in the Middle Ages,* London, 1967, 34-35, 138; *The Defensor Pacis of Marsilius of Padua*, ed. C.W. Previte-Orton, Cambridge, 1928, 49-50; Oresme, *Pol.,* 137.

35. See especially *Physica* V. 3, VI. 1-2.

36. Cf. A.G. Molland, *op.cit.,* (n. 37 *infra*) 32; J.E. Murdoch, «Superposition, Congruence and Continuity in the Middle Ages», *Mélanges Alexandre Koyré,* Paris, 1964, I, 416-441.

37. Cf. A.G. Molland, «Continuity and Measure in Medieval Natural Philosophy», *Miscellanea Mediaevalia,* XVI/I (1983), 132-144.

38. See, for instance, A. Maier, *Die Vorläufer Galileis im XIV. Jahrhundert,* 2nd edn, Rome, 1966, 155-179; V.P. Zoubov, «Walter Catton, Gerard d'Odon et Nicolas Bonet», *Physis,* I (1959), 261-278 L; J.E. Murdoch, *"Rationes Mathematice": Un Aspect du Rapport des Mathématiques et de la Philosophie au Moyen Âge,* Paris, 1962; *id.,* «*Mathesis in Philosophiam Scholasticam Introducta:* The Rise and Development of the Application of Mathematics in Fourteenth Century Philosophy and Theology», *Actes du Quatrième Congrès International de Philosophie Médiévale,* Montréal, 1969, 215-254, at 216-221.

39. Edited in J.E. Murdoch, *Geometry and the Continuum in the Fourteenth Century: A Philosophical Analysis of Thomas Bradwardine's Tractatus de Continuo* (Ph.D. thesis), University of Wisconsin, 1957.

40. J.E. Murdoch & E.A. Synan, «Two Questions on the Continuum: Walter Chatton (?), O.F.M. and Adam Woodham, O.F.M.», *Franciscan Studies,* xxvi (1966), 212-288, espec. 260.

41. On this section cf. A.G. Molland, «The Atomisation of Motion: A Facet of the Scientific Revolution», *Studies in History and Philosophy of Science,* XIII (1982), 31-54.

42. *Config.,* 270.

43. *Config.,* 406.

44. *Config.,* 276.

45. *Ibid.*

46. *Config.,* 278.

47. *Calculator. Subtilissimi Ricardi Suiseth Anglici Calculationes noviter emendate atque revise*, Venice 1520, ff. 22r-25v.

48. *Config.,* 278.

49. *Config.,* 280.

50. *Config.,* 226.

51. For a recent, not entirely unproblematic, account of these see K. Hutchison, «What happened to Occult Qualities in the Scientific Revolution?», *Isis,* lxxviii (1982), 233-253.

52. Henricus Cornelius Agrippa, *De occulta philosophia* I. 10, in his *Opera,* Lyon, n.d.; repr. Hildesheim, 1970, i, 21.

53. R. Descartes, *Principia philosophiae* IV, 187, in *ed.cit.* (n. 7 supra), viii-1, 314.

54. Reading *virtutes inesse* for *utes virtinesse.*

55. *Config.,* 236-238.

56. Guilhelmus de Ocham, *Super quatuor libros sententiarum annotationes,* lib. II, q. 8, Lyon 1495, sig. E.1 r-v; Gregorius Arimensis, *Lectura super primum et secundum sententiarum,* lib. I, dist. 42-44, 1.4, ed. A.D. Trapp, Berlin, 1979-84, iii, 441-442. Maier's account of Gregory in *loc.cit.* (n. 38 *supra*) is not quite accurate; cf. A.G. Molland, *op.cit.,* (n. 37 *supra*), 137, n. 17.

57. Cf. Gregorius, *op.cit.,* lib.II, dist. 2, q. 2, *ed.cit.,* iv, 294-313.

58. *De config.,* 412-414.

INDEX

Adelard of Bath: I 139, 165; II 214; XIII 566-7

Agrippa, Henricus Cornelius: VIII *passim*; X 56; XVII 24

Ahmad ibn Yūsuf (Ametus filius Josephi): IX 66

al-Battānî: XII 216

al-Kindî: IX 68; XI 445

Albert of Saxony; XV 39-40; XVII 14

Albertus Magnus: I 172; VII 2; VIII 218; X 56; XI 446, 450, 451 n.29; XIV *passim*

Alexander of Aphrodisias: VIII 218

Alhazen (Ibn al-Haytham): I 146-7; VII 2-4; X 50; XI 454-5

Allen, Thomas: XI 457 n.69

Amann, Fridericus: I 120-1; V 112

Anaritius (al-Nayrîzî): I 133, 142, 144, 145 nn.140-1, 171 n.255; XIV 466

Anselm, St: I 166 n.226

Apollonius of Perga: III 26, 32-3, 35, 38-9; IV 188, 193-4; VIII 210; X 46

Aquinas, Thomas: I 140; V 113, 123; VII 1; IX 63; XIII 573

Archimedes: I 122, 161-2, 171 n.255; III 25-6; IV 188-93; V 109; IX 60, 64; X 46, 61-2

Archytas: III 25; VIII 210

Aristaeus: III 33

Aristotle: I 119-21, 131-8, 140, 142, 146, 149-53, 161, 170-4; IV 183-4, 186-7, 190-1, 193; V 112-3, 119; VII 1-2, 4; IX 55, 59-60, 63, 68; X 46-9, 52-4, 56-8; XI 459; XII 207, 209, 211-2; XIII 565, 568-9, 572-3; XIV *passim*; XV 31-4, 41-2, 48-51; XVI 132-4, 136-7; XVII 14, 19-22, 25-6

Arnald of Villanova: IX 67-8; XI 446

Aubrey, John: III 42

Augustine, St: VIII 211; XII 218 n.50; XIII 562-3, 568, 574

Averroes: I 130, 133, 171-3; IV 191; V 113; VII 2-3; IX 68-9; XV 32, 33 n.7

Avicenna: VII 2; XIII 569

Bacon, Francis: XI 453; XVII 18

Bacon, Roger: I 120, 137-8, 168, 171-2; II 224-5; III 23; V 110, 116; VII 2; X 49-51, 57; XI *passim*; XIII 564, 567-71; XIV 465, 470; XV 49-50; XVII 13

Bale, John: XI 447

Barrow, Isaac: I 137, 157-8

Becket, Thomas: IX 65

Beeckman, Isaac: III 36; IV 195

Benedetti, Giovanni Battista: IV 192

Berkeley, George: XII 207

Bernard of Chartres: XIII 564-5

Biancani (Blancanus), Giuseppe: I 137

Billingsley, Henry: II 224 n.25